Statistical Power Analysis for Behavioral Sciences

This is the first book to demonstrate the application of power analysis to the newer more advanced statistical techniques that are increasingly used in the social and behavioral sciences. Both basic and advanced designs are covered. Readers are shown how to apply power analysis to techniques such as hierarchical linear modeling, meta-analysis, and structural equation modeling. Each chapter opens with a review of the statistical procedure and then proceeds to derive the power functions. This is followed by examples that demonstrate how to produce power tables and charts. The book clearly shows how to calculate power by providing open code for every design and procedure in R, SAS, and SPSS. Readers can verify the power computation using the computer programs on the book's website. Most chapters are self-standing and can be read in any order without much disruption. There is a growing requirement to include power analysis to justify sample sizes in grant proposals. This book will help readers do just that. Sample computer codes in R, SAS, and SPSS, available at www.routledge.com/9781848729810, are written to tabulate power values and produce power curves that can be included in a grant proposal.

Intended as a supplement for graduate courses on quantitative methods, multivariate statistics, hierarchical linear modeling (HLM) and/or multilevel modeling, and SEM taught in psychology, education, human development, nursing, and social and life sciences, this is the first text on statistical power for advanced procedures. Researchers and practitioners in these fields will also appreciate the book's unique coverage of the use of statistical power analysis to determine sample size in planning a study. A prerequisite of basic through multivariate statistics is assumed.

Xiaofeng Steven Liu is an Associate Professor at the University of South Carolina.

Statistical Power Analysis for the Social and Behavioral Sciences

Basic and Advanced Techniques

Xiaofeng Steven Liu

Routledge
Taylor & Francis Group

NEW YORK AND LONDON

First published 2014
by Routledge
711 Third Avenue, New York, NY 10017

and by Routledge
27 Church Road, Hove, East Sussex BN3 2FA

Routledge is an imprint of the Taylor & Francis Group, an informa business

© 2014 Taylor & Francis

Publisher's Note
This book has been prepared from camera-ready copy provided by the author.

Trademark notice: Product or corporate names may be trademarks or registered trademarks, and are used only for identification and explanation without intent to infringe.

Library of Congress Cataloging in Publication Data
Catalog record for this book has been requested

ISBN: 978-1-84872-980-3 (hbk)
ISBN: 978-1-84872-981-0 (pbk)
ISBN: 978-0-203-12769-8 (ebk)

Printed and bound by CPI Group (UK) Ltd, Croydon, CR0 4YY

Contents

vi

viii

List of Figures

x

List of Tables

Preface

Statistical power is a venerable subject for it is as old as statistical science itself. Almost a century ago Neyman and Pearson espoused the idea of not rejecting a false null hypothesis or an error of the second type. The probability of not making such an error is the statistical power, and it is crucial to hypothesis testing, which resembles a court trial. The rivalry between two competing theories can be adjudicated by hypothesis testing in a scientific study. In planning such a study, a researcher needs to calculate his or her chances of successfully confirming a new theory against the rival one, much as a district attorney would anticipate the odds of winning a conviction prior to starting the prosecution. In this regard, statistical power analysis serves as a litmus test of whether a scientific study is worthy of the time and effort. As the worthiness of a proposed study depends on statistical power, it is critical to grant application and is a revered topic in the statistical literature.

Cohen (1988) wrote a widely cited book on statistical power analysis, which is regarded by many as a classic. His book introduces the basic concept and describes its applications in many statistical procedures. His ground-breaking work in this area had a perennial impact on the behavioral sciences since the release of the book decades ago, although the past few decades have witnessed tremendous advances in new statistical procedures (i.e., hierarchical linear modeling, meta-analysis, and structural equation modeling). Yet few references address statistical power analysis for those procedures, which have been increasingly used in the social and behavioral sciences.

I write this book on statistical power to serve two purposes. First, I want to address recent developments in statistical analyses that involve hierarchical linear modeling, meta-analysis, and structural equation modeling. There is no book on statistical power that deals with these modern procedures. Second, I want to provide updated references on statistical power. Although Cohen's book is comprehensive, it uses approximation and tables for computing statistical power. The extensive tables in his book are quite a feat in view of the limited computing technology decades ago. With ubiquitous computers around us, these tables are now outdated. I therefore use exact methods rather than approximation in computing power for most procedures.

The book is organized according to various statistical procedures. The names of the statistical procedures are reflected in all the chapter titles except for the first three chapters.

The first three chapters introduce the basics of statistical power and sample size issues. Chapter 1 introduces the historical origin of statistical power and some preliminaries on distributions, expectation, and variance, which form the basis of statistical power analysis. Chapter 2 explains hypothesis testing and statistical power in t tests. Chapter 3 describes a fairly new perspective on sample size choice in planning confidence intervals instead of hypothesis testing. It acknowledges a current movement that emphasizes the use of confidence intervals in reporting effect sizes. It introduces power of confidence interval as its performance measure. Power of confidence interval is to confidence interval what statistical power is to hypothesis testing. There is a quantifiable relationship between statistical power and power of confidence interval. So the treatment of statistical power in the book has direct implications for planning sample sizes for confidence intervals.

Chapters 4, 5, and 6 cover common statistical procedures. Chapter 4 is on analysis of variance. Chapter 5 is on linear regression, which includes simple regression, correlation, multiple regression, and analysis of covariance. Chapter 6 is on multivariate analysis, and it covers the Hotelling T^2 test, multivariate analysis of variance, and multivariate analysis of covariance.

Chapters 7 through 11 are about new statistical procedures. Chapter 7 and 8 are on multi-level models. Chapter 9 is on meta-analysis, and Chapter 10 on structural equation modeling. Chapter 11 deals with longitudinal studies, which used to be analyzed as mixed ANOVA and MANOVA but are now analyzed as random coefficients models.

This book can be selected as supplementary reading material for a variety of relevant courses. The chapters parallel graduate courses on research methods, which are usually offered in the social and behavioral science departments at most universities. Most chapters are self-contained, and they can be selectively read without much disruption. For example, Chapters 1–5 can be used in a course on quantitative methods; Chapters 1–4 for a course on experimental design or ANOVA; Chapters 1, 2, 4, and 6 for a course on multivariate methods; Chapters 1, 2, 4, 7, and 8 for a course on HLM; Chapters 1, 2, 4, and 9 for a course on meta-analysis; and Chapters 1, 2, 4, 6, and 10 for a course on SEM. The book can also be used as a monograph for a seminar on statistical power and research design.

The mathematical contents of the book are on a par with standard textbooks on experimental design or multivariate methods. It is not a book for beginners who have little experience with quantitative methods. Readers who have covered two or three courses in quantitative methods should be able to comprehend Chapters 1, 2, 3, 4, and 5 on their own. The remaining chapters require solid algebra skills and some knowledge of multivariate statistics, HLM, meta-analysis, and SEM. Basic algebra is used to derive most of the statistical results, although some results may involve matrix notation (e.g., multivariate statistics). Detailed derivation provides a thorough treatment of statistical power in various procedures. Readers who are interested in these details will gain in-depth understanding of statistical power in the pertinent analyses, but these details can be skipped if preferred without disrupting one's reading.

The book also serves as a reference on statistical power for grant application. Readers who need to conduct power analysis in writing grant applications can use the book much like a recipe book without paying attention to the detailed derivation. They can go directly to the relevant chapter and locate the power functions for the statistical procedure of their choice. It is easy to navigate among those chapters because they follow the same pattern in developing power analysis for various statistical procedures. Each chapter opens with a brief review of the statistical procedure and then proceeds to derive the power functions, which are followed by illustrated examples with sample computer code in R, SAS, and SPSS. As long as readers have some familiarity with the parameters in the model, they can skim the chapter, use the example as a guide, and rerun power analysis with new parameter values, using the provided code in R, SAS, or SPSS. Sample codes are written to tabulate power values and produce power curves that can be included in a grant proposal.

The computer code is a unique feature of the book. The code is presented in three popular programming languages (R, SAS, and SPSS). There are several software packages for statistical power analysis. Some are commercial software; others are free without technical support. The different software packages do not necessarily have the same conceptual framework for the study design and analytic model (e.g., effect size or test statistic), and they may show discrepancies in power calculation. For instance, Cohen's power values for multiple regression are slightly different from those calculated in SAS. I try to show how the power in the book is calculated by providing open code for every design and procedure in three popular languages (R, SAS, and SPSS), at least one of which should be familiar to the readers. Readers who use the book for reference will most likely want to know exactly how power is computed in the statistical procedures. They can verify the power computation on their own, using the computer programs accessible at the publisher's website http://www.routledge.com/9781848729810.

Many people have helped me in writing the book. I am grateful to Professor Stephen Raudenbush, who taught me statistics and got me interested in power analysis. I have been working on this fascinating subject ever since. I thank the following reviewers for constructive comments on the book chapters: Geoff Cumming at the La Trobe University, Australia, Allen Huffcutt at the Bradley University, Russell Lenth at the University of Iowa, Jay Maddock at the University of Hawaii, and Warren W. Tryon at the Fordham University. I am thankful to Thomas Simpson, Brandon Loudermilk, Stan Haines, Phil Sherlock, and Jin Liu for reading and critiquing the manuscript. I also thank my parents for instilling in me an interest in academic excellence. Last but not least, the editorial and production team at Routledge/Taylor & Francis are wonderful. In particular, I am indebted to the senior editor Debra Riegert for being very supportive of the book project.

Xiaofeng Steven Liu
Columbia, SC
June 20, 2013

Chapter 1

Introduction

Statistical power analysis, often synonymous with sample size determination, is integral to study planning, which has great bearing on achieving the research goals of a scientific endeavor. Without proper planning, a study may fall short of making a full discovery or producing a definite answer to a research question. It needs little debate to convince people that planning is as important to a research study as to every life event. One can rarely accomplish something in life without giving some thought to planning, whether it is for education, career advancement, good retirement, or a business enterprise. It is especially true with a research study, which may consume many resources and affect public policies. The more research expenses and policy implications are involved, the more important it is to plan such a study so as to ensure its successful fruition. For instance, a health scientist may launch a study to evaluate the effects of limiting calories in pilot school lunch programs on reducing teenage obesity in public schools. As the study potentially incurs high expenses and impacts policy regulation, funding agencies will require sound justification and planning in a grant application to fund such research. One essential part of planning revolves around determining an adequate number of subjects to achieve efficient estimates of treatment effects in the ensuing statistical analysis, which permeates scientific research in the social and behavioral sciences.

The social and behavioral sciences intercept many disciplines ranging through education, psychology, sociology, psychiatry, public health, etc. In an era of rapid knowledge growth, the disciplinary boundaries are blurred by mutual dependence and interdisciplinary research. It is hard to imagine that research is solely based on any particular discipline without drawing ideas from new discoveries or findings in other related disciplines. For example, education science draws much influence from Skinner, who espouses behaviorism in predicting human responses to external stimuli, from Piaget in psychology, whose cognitive theory has shaped early childhood education, and from Vygosky, who believes knowledge is constructed by social interaction. The examples in the book, therefore, will come from a variety of research contexts in the social and behavioral sciences, although they all share a common theme of using empirical evidence to draw a causal inference about a treatment or intervention effect.

In this chapter, we will first review the basic ideas of empiricism and scientific research. Then, we will explain the historical origin of statistical power in modern statistics, which cuts across many disciplines. Finally, we will introduce some preliminary results on probability and distribution that form the foundation of statistical power analysis.

1.1 Scientific Research

Scientific research is greatly influenced by empiricism. The English word empiric originates from the Latin *experientia*, from which the words experience and experiment are derived. Notable philosophers in the school of empiricism include Aristotle, Francis Bacon, and John Locke.

Aristotle may be the first empiricist of ancient times. Unlike his teacher Plato, who was a rationalist and believed that knowledge was not something learned by looking but by thinking, Aristotle thought that knowledge could be based on sensory experience. In his book *De Anima* or *On the Soul*, Aristotle referred to the human mind as a "clear tablet" on which sensory experiences can be drawn just like letters. It took another thousand years for Western philosophers to fully embrace the notion of a "tabula rasa" or "blank slate" – in Locke's words, "white paper" – on which experiences through senses left impressions on a human mind born without innate ideas. Thus, human knowledge is a posteriori and comes from sensory experiences, which are central to empiricism and the birth of modern science.

Francis Bacon is considered by many the father of modern science. In his book *The Great Instauration*, he proposed the reformation of the process of advancing knowledge, human and divine. He advocated the use of experiments in processing information gained through senses. The sensory experience should not only be used to form ideas but also to corroborate hypotheses and theories. This philosophy has fundamentally changed modern science, which values data and experiments in advancing the relevant theories (Woolhouse, 1988).

In the social and behavioral sciences, empiricism has widely been accepted as the mainstream mode of inquiry. Theories must be framed in terms of working hypotheses, testable by observation and experiment. Some major theories have been based on controlled experiments and have continuously undergone refinement in ongoing empirical analysis. For example, the Tennessee class size study involved randomly assigning students to classes of different sizes. Students' achievements were later compared between classes of different sizes. It was found that students in small classes had outperformed those in large classes or the control. Further analysis indicated that students who originally moved from a regular-sized class to small classes during the study continued to outperform their counterparts who stayed in the regular-sized class when they returned to the regular-sized class in latter grades. The study provides strong empirical evidences that small class size is conducive to students' cognitive and academic development, and that such benefits in early grades can have a lasting impact on students' later achievement. The validity of the findings owes much to the fact that the Tennessee class size study is a randomized experiment, which strengthens the causal conclusion about the effect of class size (Finn and Achilles, 1990).

A randomized controlled experiment is the gold standard for drawing a causal inference about a possible treatment effect. A randomized controlled experiment or a true experiment is characterized by random assignment of subjects into treatment and control conditions. The treatment is then administered and subjects in the two groups are compared on their outcome performance. As subjects in the treatment and control condition only differ in treatments received, their later differential performance can be definitely attributed to the different treatments. There are no other factors that could have explained their differential performance on the outcome. The requirements of establishing a causal relationship between the treatment and the differential performance are fully met.

The three requirements for making a causal inference are temporal precedence, absence of intermediate factors between the cause and the effect, and association between the cause and the effect. The temporal precedence means that the treatment or cause must take place before the differential outcome performance or the effect. The absence of intermediate factors requires that the cause is a direct reason for the differential outcome performance or the effect. The association between the cause and the effect means that if the cause is present then the effect will occur. This is typically corroborated by statistics, which, if taken out of context, allow people to interpret results in different ways.

Statistics is surprisingly human even though the discipline as a science connotes objectivity rather than subjectivity. However, the thinking underlying statistical inference depends on one's philosophical outlook and orientation, which are subject to much debate and controversy even among the giants who founded statistical science. Fisher, Neyman, and Pearson are well known for developing the mathematical theories of modern statistics in the early twentieth century. However, the conflict on statistical power was never settled between Fisher on the one side and Neyman and Pearson on the other side during their lifetimes. There are documented polemic exchanges on the topic between Fisher and Pearson.

1.2   Origin of Statistical Power

The concept of statistical power is credited to Neyman and Pearson, who not only recognized the error of rejecting a true null hypothesis but also the error of not rejecting a false null hypothesis. Fisher, a giant figure in founding statistical science, however, opposed the idea of the Type-II error in published exchanges between him and Pearson. Fisher did not think that it was possible to calculate statistical power because of the unknown alternative hypothesis. So far as hypothesis was concerned, he argued that failing to reject the hypothesis did not certify its being true. By the same token, he thought it meaningless to claim the veracity of an alternative hypothesis. Fisher consistently used the term significance test for testing the hypothesis and did not seem to favor the term hypothesis testing under Neyman–Pearson formulation, which can imply the co-existence of the null hypothesis and the alternative hypothesis. In the Neyman–Pearson formulation, there exists the most powerful statistical test having a fixed Type-I error rate. Despite his opposition to quantifying statistical power, Fisher referred to the sensitiveness of statistical tests in his writing, which Lehmann (1993) interpreted as speaking of the existence of errors of the second type.

The difference between Fisher and Neyman and Pearson on statistical power is more philosophical than mathematical in nature. Neyman and Pearson acknowledged that they had largely benefited from Fisher's work on the level of significance, and that they had considered decision behavior in conjunction with the significance test. The concept of statistical power has long been accepted in current literature and practice. In fact, statistical power has become a revered topic in textbook treatment and grant application despite its controversial inception. There are books on running statistical power analysis (e.g., Cohen, 1969, 1988). Most funding agencies require grant applicants to conduct statistical power analysis to ensure adequate sample size in achieving efficient statistical estimates.

Statistical power analysis involves making assumptions about the statistics and their probabilistic behavior under different hypotheses. Statistical power indicates the chance of substantiating a research hypothesis by casting doubts about its rival hypothesis in hypothesis testing. The crux of hypothesis testing revolves around probability models under different competing hypotheses. Statisticians use probability models to calibrate the significance of the findings in hypothesis testing. In the following, we shall review some preliminaries on probability models, which are vital to statistical power analysis.

1.3 Some Preliminaries

Events can manifest systemic behavior even though they look fragmented or unpredictable individually. The simplest example is coin flipping. The outcome data are either heads or tails. If you flip a regular coin once, you cannot predict the outcome with absolute certainty. Either outcome can occur with a fifty percent chance in one coin flip. However, the outcome data taken together in many many coin flips are quite predictable. Fifty percent of the time, the coin turns up heads, and the other fifty percent of the time it turns up tails. The predictable part is the underlying probability model, which describes the data taken together. In the probability model, every distinctive outcome is associated with a probability.

A probability is the proportion of times that a certain outcome will occur in a long series of repeated trials. In the example of coin flipping, the probability of getting a head is the proportion of times that the coin comes up heads in many many flips. Such a probability in theory equals fifty percent. Likewise, the probability of obtaining a tail is fifty percent. The probabilities of all possible outcomes add up to one because at least one of all the possible outcomes will certainly occur with a one hundred percent chance. Every probability model must comply with this probability rule, which affects how we define the probability model for a continuous outcome that can take an infinite number of values on a continuous scale.

The probability model for a continuous outcome associates a probability to every interval of values on the continuous scale that the outcome takes. In other words, the continuous scale is truncated into individual intervals, which comprise a small segment of different values. Even though the outcome can assume any value on the continuous scale, the probability of obtaining a unique value cannot be defined. There are an infinite number of such values on a continuous scale. If every number has a positive probability of occurrence, the sum of the probabilities of all the possible values will exceed one or one hundred percent. The sum of infinite positive probabilities, however small they can be, does not converge to one. Therefore, we divide the continuous scale into distinctive intervals of different values and associate the probability to each such interval. The sum of the probabilities of all the intervals will add up to one hundred percent.

1.3.1   Distribution

One common probability model for a continuous outcome is the normal distribution, which appears in many natural phenomena (e.g., subjects' physical, psychological, and behavioral attributes). In a normal distribution the values of the outcome occur less often as they move away from the average value in the center, which forms the well-known bell shape. For example, men's heights follow a normal distribution. The great majority of height measures are concentrated around the average height with decreasing percentages of men being very short or very tall. The normal distribution is characterized by two numeric quantities, mean μ and standard deviation σ, which are called population parameters. The mean is simply the average, sometimes called the central tendency, of the distribution. The standard deviation portrays the spread or variation among the values of the outcome. The more varied the values are from each other, the larger the standard deviation becomes. Depending on the mean and standard deviation, there can be many possible normal distributions. However, if we standardize a normal outcome Y (i.e., $(Y - \mu)/\sigma$), the standardized outcome also follows a normal distribution with a zero mean and a unit standard deviation, which is called the standard normal distribution. We can use a capital Z to represent a standard normal variate.

Squaring a standard normal variate transforms it into a chi square variable with one degree of freedom ($Z^2 = \chi_1^2$). Independent chi square variables with one degree of freedom can be added to form another chi square variable with degrees of freedom equal to the number of independent chi squares,

$$\sum_{i=1}^{\nu} Z_i^2 = \chi_\nu^2. \tag{1.1}$$

The distribution of a chi square variable is right-skewed. It is often used to model the probabilistic behavior of a sum of squares, which appears in t and F tests.

The t statistic is a random variable comprising a standard normal variate and a chi square variate,

$$T = \frac{Z}{\sqrt{\chi_\nu^2/\nu}}. \tag{1.2}$$

The numerator of T contains a standard normal variate and the denominator a square root of a chi square over its degrees of freedom. A central t distribution is symmetrical around its mean zero. It resembles the standard normal distribution except with fatter tails on both ends (see Figure B.4 in Appendix B). As the degrees of freedom ν increase to infinity, the t distribution eventually converges to a standard normal distribution. The t distribution with a zero mean is called a central t distribution, in contrast with a non-central t distribution with a non-zero mean λ (see Figure 1.1).

A non-central t distribution can be easily derived from a normal variate with a non-zero mean λ and a unit variance, which is represented by $Z(\lambda)$. The non-zero mean is also called the non-centrality parameter, and it shows the departure of the shifted mean from zero in the standard normal distribution. The non-central t distribution is represented by T',

$$T' = \frac{Z(\lambda)}{\sqrt{\chi^2_\nu/\nu}}. \tag{1.3}$$

The non-central t distribution plays an important role in statistical power analysis, which assumes a non-zero mean for treatment effect in the research hypothesis, whether it is a two-group comparison in a t test or analysis of variance in an F test.

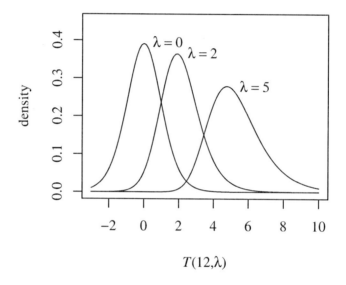

Figure 1.1: Central and non-central t distributions

An F random variable can be derived from two independent chi square variates with one in the numerator and the other in the denominator,

$$F = \frac{\chi^2_{\nu_1}/\nu_1}{\chi^2_{\nu_2}/\nu_2}. \tag{1.4}$$

The chi square in the numerator has ν_1 degrees of freedom, and that in the denominator ν_2 degrees of freedom. The F variate assumes a central F distribution when the chi square in the numerator (as shown) does not contain a non-centrality parameter. When the chi square in the numerator is a non-central one with a non-centrality parameter λ, the F variate has a non-central F distribution.

A non-central chi square $\chi^2_\nu(\lambda)$ can be similarly derived from normal variables with a shifted mean each,

$$\chi^2_\nu(\lambda) = \sum_{j=1}^{\nu} Z_i^2(\lambda_i), \qquad (1.5)$$

where the non-centrality parameter is

$$\lambda = \sum_{j=1}^{\nu} \lambda_i^2. \qquad (1.6)$$

Thus, a non-central chi square with ν degrees of freedom can be conceived of as comprising ν squared independent normal variables with a non-zero mean λ_i each. The non-centrality parameter λ for the non-central chi square is the sum of squared non-zero means λ_i^2. It should be noted that if all the means λ_i are zero the non-centrality parameter λ is zero. In this case, the non-central chi square reverts to a central chi square. In general a central distribution can be viewed as a special case of a non-central distribution with the non-centrality parameter λ equal to zero (see Figure 1.2).

A non-central F can be derived from a non-central chi square. If the chi square in the numerator of the F is a non-central chi square $\chi^2_{\nu_1}(\lambda)$ with a non-centrality parameter λ, then we have a non-central F, or F'.

$$F' = \frac{\chi^2_{\nu_1}(\lambda)/\nu_1}{\chi^2_{\nu_2}/\nu_2}. \qquad (1.7)$$

The non-central F plays an important role in statistical power analysis. For example, an F test can be used to check whether the treatment means differ between groups. The numerator of the F statistic measures the sum of squares of treatment means. If they differ from each other, then the between-group sum of squares has a non-central chi square. This is because, in calculating the between-group mean differences, the unequal treatment means change to the non-zero means of the normal variates. The sum of squares of those non-zero means contributes to the non-centrality parameter in the non-central chi square in the numerator of the F statistic.

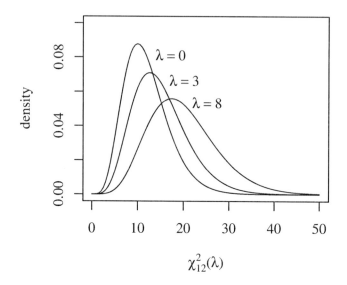

Figure 1.2: Central and non-central χ^2 distributions

The aforementioned probability distributions (i.e., Z, t, and F) can manifest themselves when data are combined in the relevant statistical procedures. For instance, a standardized score or Z score follows a standard normal distribution with a zero mean and unit variance $N(0, 1)$,

$$Z = \frac{Y - \mu}{\sigma} \sim N(0, 1), \tag{1.8}$$

where μ is the population mean of Y and σ is its standard deviation. The sample mean of n observations of Y can be standardized in a similar fashion, and it assumes a standard normal distribution according to the central limit theorem,

$$Z = \frac{\overline{Y} - \mu}{\sigma / \sqrt{n}} \sim N(0, 1). \tag{1.9}$$

The central limit theorem states that the population mean of the sample mean $\overline{Y}$ is the population mean of Y (i.e., μ), and that the standard error of $\overline{Y}$ is $\sigma / \sqrt{n}$. This forms the basis of a Z test, in which different hypotheses dictate that the population mean μ assume different values μ_0 or μ_a. Under the assumption of $\mu = \mu_a$, the Z based on μ_0 obviously has a non-zero mean or λ,

$$Z(\lambda) = \frac{\overline{Y} - \mu_0}{\sigma/\sqrt{n}} \sim N(\lambda, 1). \tag{1.10}$$

If μ is equal to μ_0, λ is zero, and $Z(\lambda)$ simplifies to a standard normal Z.

The chi square distribution can manifest in the sample variance of n independent observations of Y_i, which contains a sum of squares of the deviation scores $Y_i - \overline{Y}$. The sum of squares (SS) is related to a chi square distribution with degrees of freedom $n - 1$. In other words, the sum of squares comprises $n - 1$ independent squared normal variables (Z_i^2 $i : 1, 2, ..., n$), that is, SS $\sim \sigma^2 \chi_{n-1}^2$. Readers who are not interested in the derivation of this result may skip the next two paragraphs and move onto the next page.

We can derive the result from two obvious facts. First, the sum of squares of all the standardized scores of Y has a chi square distribution with degrees of freedom n,

$$\sum_{i=1}^{n} \left(\frac{Y_i - \mu}{\sigma} \right)^2 = \sum_{i=1}^{n} Z_i^2 \sim \chi_n^2. \tag{1.11}$$

Second, the squared standardized score of the sample mean $\overline{Y}$ is a chi square with one degree of freedom,

$$\left(\frac{\overline{Y} - \mu}{\sigma/\sqrt{n}} \right)^2 = Z^2 \sim \chi_1^2. \tag{1.12}$$

By the central limit theorem, the sample mean has a normal distribution with a mean μ and standard deviation $\sigma/\sqrt{n}$. Its standardized score $\sqrt{n}(\overline{Y} - \mu)/\sigma$ is a standard normal Z. Squaring a normal Z changes it to a chi square by definition.

Using Equations 1.11 and 1.12, we can prove that the sum of squares of Y is related to a chi square with degrees of freedom $n - 1$. Equation 1.11 minus Equation 1.12 is a chi square with degrees of freedom $n - 1$, that is,

$$\sum_{i=1}^{n} \left(\frac{Y_i - \mu}{\sigma} \right)^2 - \left(\frac{\overline{Y} - \mu}{\sigma/\sqrt{n}} \right)^2 = \chi_n^2 - \chi_1^2 = \chi_{n-1}^2. \tag{1.13}$$

We now expand the left side of Equation 1.13:

$$\sum_{i=1}^{n}\left(\frac{Y_i - \mu}{\sigma}\right)^2 - \left(\frac{\overline{Y} - \mu}{\sigma/\sqrt{n}}\right)^2$$

$$= \sum_{i=1}^{n}\left(\frac{Y_i - \overline{Y} + \overline{Y} - \mu}{\sigma}\right)^2 - \left(\frac{\overline{Y} - \mu}{\sigma/\sqrt{n}}\right)^2$$

$$= \sum_{i=1}^{n}\frac{(Y_i - \overline{Y})^2}{\sigma^2} + \sum_{i=1}^{n}\frac{2(Y_i - \overline{Y})(\overline{Y} - \mu)}{\sigma^2} + \sum_{i=1}^{n}\frac{(\overline{Y} - \mu)^2}{\sigma^2} - \left(\frac{\overline{Y} - \mu}{\sigma/\sqrt{n}}\right)^2.$$

There are four terms in the expanded equation. Only the first term after the equal sign will remain; it is the sum of squares divided by σ^2. The second term, $\sum_{i=1}^{n}(Y_i - \overline{Y})(\overline{Y} - \mu)$, is zero. The third and fourth terms cancel each other, that is,

$$\sum_{i=1}^{n}\frac{(\overline{Y} - \mu)^2}{\sigma^2} = \frac{n(\overline{Y} - \mu)^2}{\sigma^2} = \left(\frac{\overline{Y} - \mu}{\sigma/\sqrt{n}}\right)^2.$$

The left side of Equation 1.13 equals the sum of squares of Y_i divided by σ^2,

$$\sum_{i=1}^{n}\left(\frac{Y_i - \mu}{\sigma}\right)^2 - \left(\frac{\overline{Y} - \mu}{\sigma/\sqrt{n}}\right)^2 = \frac{\sum_{i=1}^{n}(Y_i - \overline{Y})^2}{\sigma^2}.$$

By Equation 1.13 we know that the left side of Equation 1.13 is a chi square with $n - 1$ degrees of freedom.

$$\sum_{i=1}^{n}\left(\frac{Y_i - \mu}{\sigma}\right)^2 - \left(\frac{\overline{Y} - \mu}{\sigma/\sqrt{n}}\right)^2 = \frac{\sum_{i=1}^{n}(Y_i - \overline{Y})^2}{\sigma^2} \sim \chi^2_{n-1}$$

The above equation shows that the sum of squares in the sample variance is the population variance times a chi square,

$$\sum_{i=1}^{n}(Y_i - \overline{Y})^2 \sim \sigma^2 \chi^2_{n-1}.$$

Thus, the sample variance contains a chi square variate with degrees of freedom $n - 1$,

$$\hat{\sigma}^2 = \sum_{i=1}^{n} \frac{(Y_i - \overline{Y})^2}{n - 1} \sim (n - 1)^{-1} \sigma^2 \chi_{n-1}^2. \tag{1.14}$$

A t distribution appears when the sample variance occupies the denominator of a t test. By definition, a t distribution contains a chi square in the denominator and a standard normal variable in the numerator. Equation 1.14 proves that the sample variance in a one sample t test contains a chi square. The numerator of the t test has the sample mean minus its hypothesized mean. Their difference can be related to a standard normal variable. A t distribution will manifest when the sample mean and sample variance are combined in a t test.

An F distribution occurs when two sums of squares become the numerator and denominator in an F test. As shown in Equation 1.14, the sums of squares are related to chi square distributions. This does not depend on whether the sums of squares are based on individual observations Y_i or group means $\overline{Y}_j$ (i for the ith observation within a group and j for the jth group). In the case of group means $\overline{Y}_j$, they can be viewed as a sample of independent observations on their own. Their sum of squares is also related to a chi square distribution. Thus, the ratio of two sums of squares in a one-way ANOVA contains two chi squares: one in the numerator and the other in the denominator. They form an F distribution (see Figure 1.3).

1.3.2 Expectation

A distribution can be characterized by its expectation, which describes its central tendency. The expectation of a discrete variable is the sum of the distinctive outcome values multiplied by their probabilities of occurrence. In the case of a coin toss, the expectation is $1 \times .5 + 0 \times .5 = .5$ if 1 stands for heads and 0 for tails. It is obvious that the expectation is the probability or proportion of heads in repeated coin flips. Similarly, the expectation of a Bernoulli outcome is the probability of getting whatever 1 stands for in a long-run series of events with a dichotomous outcome. So the expectation of a discrete variable is a weighted sum with distinctive values weighted by their respective probabilities.

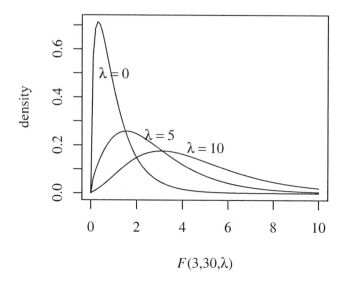

$$F(3,30,\lambda)$$

Figure 1.3: Central and non-central F distributions

The expectation of a continuous variable can be conceived of as coming from a weighted sum except that the distinctive values correspond to different small intervals evenly divided on a continuous scale. As the continuous scale of a standard normal Z can actually range from negative infinity to positive infinity, we can divide the entire scale into infinite small intervals. When the number of such small intervals reaches infinitely many, the weighted sum approaches the true expectation of a standard normal Z. The limit of the weighted sum is an integral,

$$E(Z) = \int_{-\infty}^{\infty} z f(z) dz, \tag{1.15}$$

where $f(z)$ is the density function of the standard normal distribution. Although the definition of the expectation for a continuous variable appears complicated, it simply means the average value of a distribution or the population mean μ. It is well known that the average of a normal distribution is the population mean, which is indeed the expectation of the normal distribution. The expectation indicates what is expected of the average value of a distribution. The sample estimate of the expectation is the sample mean or average. It is quite easy to prove that the expectation of the sample mean is the expectation:

$$E\left(\sum Y_i/n\right) = \frac{1}{n}\sum E(Y_i) = \frac{1}{n}nE(Y_i) = E(Y_i). \qquad (1.16)$$

The expectation determines the non-centrality parameter, which differs from the implied zero expectation under the null hypothesis. When the research hypothesis is true, test statistics will assume a non-zero expectation, which factors into the non-centrality parameter. In the case of a Z test, the test statistic has a non-zero expectation in the presence of a treatment effect.

1.3.3 Variance

The notion of expectation can be used to define variance, which is the expected value of the squared difference between the random variable and its expectation,

$$\sigma^2 = E(Y - \mu)^2, \qquad (1.17)$$

where μ is the expectation and σ^2 is the variance. In simple language, a variance is the average of the squared deviation scores. Its sample estimate is the sum of squared deviation scores divided by the sample size n, $\hat{\sigma}^2 = \sum(Y_i - \mu)^2/n$. When the expectation μ itself has to be estimated from a sample, a sample mean is substituted in lieu of μ. The estimation of the sample mean consumes one degree of freedom (see Equation 1.14). The estimated variance, therefore, becomes

$$\hat{\sigma}^2 = \frac{\sum(Y_i - \overline{Y})^2}{n - 1}. \qquad (1.18)$$

In a nutshell, the estimated variance is a sum of squares divided by the degrees of freedom. This formulation is not limited to individual observations. It can be extended to measure any variance due to different sources, whether the variance is based on original observations on individual subjects or mean observations on different groups of subjects. In analysis of variance, the sum of squares can use group means to measure the variance due to differential mean outcome between groups.

In short, the distribution, expectation, and variance form the basis of statistical tests that combine the individual data in a few summary statistics. Although it is mind boggling to make sense of individual data, the behavior of their summary statistics can be inferred easily from different hypothetical models or hypotheses. The different models or hypotheses determine the different expectations or variances that characterize the distributions of those summary statistics. The probability of observing the summary statistic can, therefore, be mathematically assessed under different models or hypotheses. It is the probabilities of observing the summary statistics under different hypotheses that become the cornerstone of statistical inference in hypothesis testing, where competing hypotheses or theories are rejected or provisionally accepted in view of the observed data and the summary statistics. Thus, hypothesis testing comprises two steps of logic thinking: induction and deduction. The inductive inference occurs while the individual data are compiled and summarized by statistics, which are used as a proxy of the otherwise unwieldy data. The deductive inference takes place when the distributions of the summary statistics are inferred from different models or hypotheses. Any discrepancy between the summary statistic and its expected value under the default theory or hypothesis is then checked to see whether the statistic (i.e., proxy of data) contradicts the theory. This culminates in a decision on whether the default hypothesis or theory is rejected or not.

Chapter 2

Statistical Power

In this chapter we will review hypothesis testing and statistical power. We will explain statistical power and its determinants in the z-test, one sample t test, two sample independent t test, and dependent t test.

2.1   Hypothesis Testing

Null hypothesis testing plays an important role in the social and behavioral sciences. It responds to important research questions by rendering a yes or no answer. For example, an educational researcher may want to know whether the after-school program can improve students' academic achievement. A clinical psychologist may want to learn whether a certain therapy helps lower anxiety. A health scientist may want to see whether a new drug can reduce patients' addiction to nicotine. These questions can all be formulated into two opposing hypotheses, which represent a yes and no answer to the research hypothesis. The decision on a yes or no answer is then negotiated through hypothesis testing with the help of empirical evidence.

The logic of hypothesis testing is based on falsification, which confirms our belief in one answer by diminishing the credibility of the other answer. Its close analogy is the legal trial in the criminal justice system, where a suspect is innocent until proven guilty beyond reasonable doubt (Kraemer and Thiemann, 1987). The default hypothesis states that the suspect is not guilty; and the opposing hypothesis says that he or she is guilty. The verdict of guilty or not guilty (i.e., yes or no answer) is rendered in light of the provided evidence. As evidence mounts against the suspect, his or her credibility diminishes and a guilty verdict follows. This inverted logic exemplifies a formal mechanism of how people make decisions about things that they do not know with absolute certainty. Although the logic of the criminal trial may sound foreign, people use the same reasoning one way or another in daily life. Imagine that you are talking to some stranger at a bar who claims that he is the best shooter in the area. When asked how to verify his claim, you would probably suggest that you take him to the shooting range and let him shoot. The suggestion is in essence a hypothesis test, which sets the original claim as the default hypothesis. The number of times the guy hits the bull's eye in the shooting range can be used as evidence to test the claim that he is a sharp shooter. If the number of hits is high, his claim will be accepted. If the observed evidence proves the contrary, then his claim will be rejected. So null hypothesis testing is akin to our common sense in spite of its mystic appearance.

On the surface, hypothesis testing starts with a default assumption about things, which is called the null hypothesis (H_0). Its complementary opposite is named the alternative hypothesis (H_a). The research hypothesis is usually set as the alternative hypothesis, while its plausibility is established through the rejection of its opposite, the null hypothesis. Rejecting the null hypothesis requires empirical evidence to contradict it. The empirical data are first combined into a numeric summary or a statistic, which is a function of the data. The probabilistic behavior of the statistic typically follows some known probability distribution when the null hypothesis is true. A computed statistic is expected to fall into the expected range under the probability distribution compatible with the null hypothesis. Any deviation of the statistic from its expected value is construed as contradicting the null hypothesis. If the computed statistic is highly discrepant from its most expected value, it means that the empirical data summarized by the statistic contradict the null hypothesis, which shall be rejected. In the example of the best shooter, a low number of hits will cast doubts about the original claim (the null hypothesis) because the observed data or statistic deviate from the expected value for the null hypothesis. How deviant the statistic must be before the null hypothesis can be rejected depends on a preset threshold called α.

The threshold α is a small probability that the statistic can deviate from the expected value. It is also called the significance level and is conventionally set at .05 or .01. If the probability of observing the discrepancy between the computed statistic and its expected value under the null is smaller than or equal to α, this suggests that the statistic or empirical data are highly incompatible with the null hypothesis, which shall be rejected. In other words, the chance of observing the actual data, though it exists, is very small when the null hypothesis is true. Such a low probability allows us to overturn the null hypothesis in favor of the alternative hypothesis. Thus, α represents a small amount of doubt that is allowed to overthrow the null hypothesis. In the example of the criminal trial, the significance level α parallels the reasonable doubt standard. This is the amount of risk that we can tolerate in convicting a person. In short, the α level sets a standard for rejecting the null in hypothesis testing. If the null hypothesis is indeed true, α presents the maximum probability of rejecting a true null hypothesis, which is a Type-I error.

The Type-I error is more serious than the Type-II error. The latter means failure to reject a false null hypothesis. Although we never know with absolute certainty whether the null hypothesis or alternative hypothesis is true, we can nevertheless play out both scenarios (Table 2.1). If the null hypothesis is true (the first column or scenario), we can either retain it or reject it. Rejecting a true null hypothesis commits an error of false positive – a Type-I error. In the other scenario of a false null hypothesis (the second column), failure to reject a false null hypothesis commits an error of false negative – a Type-II error. In a criminal trial, a Type-I error means convicting an innocent person; a Type-II error letting a criminal go free. The social consequences of the two types of error differ. Convicting an innocent person is more serious than letting loose a criminal. Similarly, in a new drug study the research hypothesis or alternative hypothesis asserts that the new drug works wonders; whereas the null hypothesis states that the new drug is not any better than placebo or no treatment. The Type-I error means declaring an ineffective drug effective; the Type-II error means labeling a wonder drug ineffective. The Type-I error (false claim about the effectiveness of a new drug) may bring expensive law suits; the Type-II error only forgoes the benefits of a wonder drug.

The asymmetry in the consequences of the two types of error affects how the null and alternative hypothesis are set up. Since the Type-I error is more serious, the null hypothesis should be chosen such that its rejection

Table 2.1: Types of error and statistical power in hypothesis testing

	H_0 is true	H_0 is false
reject H_0	Type-I error α	correct decision $1 - \beta$ = statistical power
do not reject H_0	correct decision	Type-II error β

is done with utmost care (Bickel and Doksum, 1977). In a criminal trial the null hypothesis always states that one is innocent until proven guilty, for convicting an innocent person carries enormous social, economic, and moral consequences. In social and behavioral science research the current practice or status quo should not be rejected in favor of some untested practice without serious negotiation or testing. The null hypothesis typically says that the new untested treatment or intervention does not work any better than business as usual or no intervention. The choice of null hypothesis reflects our innate aversion to the risk of untested ground. Any venture into new territory should be done with convincing evidence.

While the risk of Type-I error is deliberately controlled by the α level, the goal of a research investigation invariably seeks to find new ways or interventions that can help improve human life and move our society beyond the status quo. The credibility of the new intervention depends on our ability to reject the status quo represented by the null hypothesis with empirical evidence in hypothesis testing. Our ability to reject a false null hypothesis, therefore, holds the promise of betterment of life. The probability of rejecting a false null hypothesis is the statistical power of the hypothesis test, or power for short. A high statistical power reduces the chance of a false negative or Type-II error and improves the chance of making a new discovery. In conducting a scientific investigation, a researcher shall always be concerned about statistical power much as a district attorney is keen on the likelihood of a conviction in contemplating a criminal trial. Without adequate statistical power, the research endeavor is futile and lacks any prospect of a new discovery.

2.2   Statistical Power

2.2.1   Statistical Power of a z-test

Statistical power can be illustrated in a simple hypothesis test that employs a Z statistic to compare two population means with a known common variance σ^2. For example, an educator wants to examine the effect of a test preparatory program on improving students' test performance, where the population standard deviation of the test scores is published by the testing company. A sample of students is randomly assigned to the preparatory program or to the business-as-usual condition. The two means on test scores (i.e., μ_1 on test score for the preparatory program and μ_2 for business as usual) are compared in the ensuing hypothesis test. The research hypothesis postulates that the preparatory program works effectively to improve students' performance; the null hypothesis says that the program does not work any better than the business-as-usual condition.

The null hypothesis translates to two equal means $H_0 : \mu_1 = \mu_2$ or $\mu_1 - \mu_2 = 0$. This type of hypothesis is called a simple hypothesis because the hypothesized parameter $\mu_1 - \mu_2 = 0$ in the null hypothesis assumes a single value. The null hypothesis can also be set as $H_0 : \mu_1 - \mu_2 \leq 0$, which suggests that the preparatory program can have either a negative impact or no effect on students' test performance. Since the hypothesized parameter $\mu_1 - \mu_2$ in the null hypothesis assumes a range of values, the hypothesis is called a composite hypothesis. Both the null and the alternative hypotheses can be simple or composite. In social and behavioral science research, the null hypothesis is usually a simple hypothesis, and the alternative hypothesis is composite. In our example, we shall take a simple hypothesis $H_0 : \mu_1 - \mu_2 = 0$ for the null hypothesis unless the preparatory effort is believed to have a possibly negative effect on students. The alternative hypothesis states $H_a : \mu_1 \neq \mu_2$ or $\mu_1 - \mu_2 \neq 0$, which can mean either $\mu_1 > \mu_2$ or $\mu_1 < \mu_2$. The hypothesized value $\mu_1 - \mu_2$ in the alternative can be either on the negative or positive side, and it is therefore called a two-sided hypothesis. If we do not believe that the program can possibly lower students' performance, then we can set up a one-sided alternative hypothesis $H_a : \mu_1 > \mu_2$. The hypothesis test is then called a one-sided test. So hypothesis testing can be either two-sided or one-sided, depending on the sidedness of the alternative hypothesis. By default, the alternative hypothesis is two-sided.

Once the hypotheses are set up, the empirical data are combined into a test statistic. The statistic Z divides the sample mean difference with its standard error

$$Z = \frac{\overline{Y}_1 - \overline{Y}_2}{\sigma\sqrt{\frac{1}{n_1} + \frac{1}{n_2}}}, \tag{2.1}$$

where $\overline{Y}_1$ and $\overline{Y}_2$ are the sample means of the treatment and control groups, and n_1 and n_2 are the sample sizes of the two respective groups. We will use the upper case for a random variable and the lower case for the realized value of the random variable. Z means a normal random variable, and z a realized value of the Z random variable.

The test statistic follows a standard normal distribution Z when the null hypothesis is true. The most expected values of the test statistic are concentrated around zero or the mean of the standard normal distribution. It is intuitively easy to understand this, as the equal-means assumption in the null hypothesis implies that the sample mean difference $\overline{Y}_1 - \overline{Y}_2$ should not be far from zero in the numerator of the Z statistic. A large discrepancy between the realized value z of the Z statistic and its most expected value zero is construed as contradicting the null hypothesis. How incompatible the test statistic is with the null hypothesis is represented by the probability of obtaining a test statistic at least as contradictory as the realized z. In other words, it is the probability of obtaining z values as far from zero as the realized z value. We use a cumulative probability of obtaining a range of values to describe the relative standing of a z because the probability of getting an exact z is undefined. The continuous random variable Z can take an indefinite number of realized values. If each realized value occurs with a finite probability, the sum of the probabilities of all these values will not converge to one but exceed one, which violates the probability rule. It is analogous to gaging someone's relative height by checking the percentage of people taller than this person, for the probability of finding a person of exactly the same height cannot be defined. So we use the probability of obtaining a test statistic at least as contradictory as the realized z, which is called the p-value of the test statistic.

The p-value of the test statistic will consist of two probabilities on both sides of its distribution in a two-sided test because the values of the test statistic as far from zero as the realized z can occur on both sides. Thus, we need to multiply the probability tail on the one side by two in calculating the p-value for the two-sided test. If the test is one-sided, we do not have to multiply by two. The smaller the p-value is, the less likely we will observe such data if the null hypothesis is true. If the p-value is at least as small as the preset α level, say, .05, we will satisfy our "reasonable doubt" standard and reject the null hypothesis. In other words, we would rather believe that its opposite or the alternative hypothesis is true. The statistic whose p-value is exactly equal to α is called the critical value. In a two-sided test, the critical value at α can be the $(\alpha/2)$th or $(1 - \alpha/2)$th quantile of the standard normal distribution, which are denoted by $z_{\alpha/2}$ and $z_{1-\alpha/2}$, respectively (see Appendix A for the definition of quantile). In a one-sided test, the right-side critical value is $z_{1-\alpha}$, and the left-side one z_{α}. The critical value offers an alternative way to assess the p-value of the computed statistic. If the computed statistic lies any further from the most expected value than the critical value, the p-value of the computed statistic will be smaller than the significance level α – the p-value of the critical value. By that the null hypothesis will be rejected.

A researcher who tries to prove the existence of a treatment effect always wants to achieve a high chance of rejecting the null hypothesis or high statistical power. Failure to reject a false null hypothesis produces a Type-II error, the probability of which is β. In relation to the Type-II error rate β, the statistical power can be expressed as $1 - \beta$. When the alternative hypothesis is true (i.e., $H_a : \mu_1 > \mu_2$), $\mu_1 - \mu_2 = \Delta$ is non-zero. Under the assumption of the alternative hypothesis, the test statistic no longer follows a standard normal distribution with its mean equal to zero but a normal distribution with a shifted mean λ, called the non-centrality parameter.

The non-centrality parameter can be found by taking the expectation of the test statistic. Replacing the sample means by the population means in the test statistic yields its expectation,

$$\lambda = E\left(\frac{\bar{Y}_1 - \bar{Y}_2}{\sigma\sqrt{1/n_1 + 1/n_2}}\right) = \frac{\mu_1 - \mu_2}{\sigma\sqrt{\frac{n_1+n_2}{n_1 n_2}}} = \sqrt{\frac{n_1 n_2}{n_1 + n_2}}\frac{\Delta}{\sigma}. \qquad (2.2)$$

For simplicity of explanation, we will set the two sample sizes equal ($n_1 = $

$n_2 = n$). The non-centrality parameter simplifies to

$$\lambda = \sqrt{\frac{n}{2}} \frac{\Delta}{\sigma}. \tag{2.3}$$

In one sense the non-centrality parameter is the expected value of the test statistic for a specific non-zero Δ, which is called the simple effect size. Recall that any deviation of the test statistic from zero is conceived as challenging the null hypothesis. The non-centrality parameter simply portrays the expected departure of the statistic from zero when the alternative hypothesis is true. Such departure is magnified by the sample size n. The sample size does not affect the true mean difference Δ, rather it magnifies the perceived image of the mean difference so that the difference can be easily detected in hypothesis testing. When the alternative hypothesis holds true (i.e., $\Delta \neq 0$), we denote the test statistic Z', which is normally distributed with a unit variance and a non-centrality parameter λ.

Statistical power for the one-sided test can be expressed in terms of λ

$$1 - \beta = P\left[Z' \geq z_{1-\alpha}\right] = 1 - P\left[Z' < z_{1-\alpha}\right], \tag{2.4}$$

where $z_{1-\alpha}$ is the critical value for the one-sided test. Subtracting λ from both sides of $Z' < z_{1-\alpha}$ transforms Z' to a standard normal Z. Since $Z' - \lambda \sim Z$, the power then becomes

$$
\begin{aligned}
1 - \beta &= 1 - P\left[Z' - \lambda < z_{1-\alpha} - \lambda\right] \\
&= 1 - P\left[Z < z_{1-\alpha} - \lambda\right] \\
&= 1 - \Phi\left(z_{1-\alpha} - \lambda\right) \\
&= \Phi\left(\lambda - z_{1-\alpha}\right), \tag{2.5}
\end{aligned}
$$

where Φ is the cumulative distribution function of a standard normal variate. Note that the two areas represented by $1 - \Phi\left(z_{1-\alpha} - \lambda\right)$ and $\Phi\left(\lambda - z_{1-\alpha}\right)$ are symmetrical under the normal distribution curve. Therefore, the two areas are of equal size.

In a two-sided test, the power can be similarly derived;

$$1 - \beta = P\left[Z' \geq z_{1-\alpha/2} \cup Z' \leq z_{\alpha/2}\right]$$
$$= 1 - P\left[Z' < z_{1-\alpha/2}\right] + P\left[Z' \leq z_{\alpha/2}\right]$$
$$= 1 - P\left[Z' - \lambda < z_{1-\alpha/2} - \lambda\right] + P\left[Z' - \lambda \leq z_{\alpha/2} - \lambda\right]$$
$$= 1 - P\left[Z < z_{1-\alpha/2} - \lambda\right] + P\left[Z \leq z_{\alpha/2} - \lambda\right]$$
$$= 1 - \Phi\left(z_{1-\alpha/2} - \lambda\right) + \Phi\left(z_{\alpha/2} - \lambda\right)$$
$$= \Phi\left(\lambda - z_{1-\alpha/2}\right) + \Phi\left(z_{\alpha/2} - \lambda\right), \quad (2.6)$$

where $\Phi\left(\lambda - z_{1-\alpha/2}\right)$ represents the large shaded area on the right side of Figure 2.1, and $\Phi\left(z_{\alpha/2} - \lambda\right)$ the small shaded area on the far left.

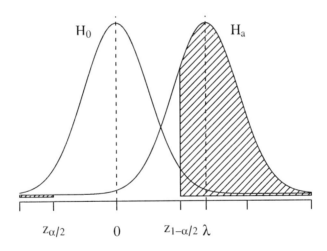

Figure 2.1: Statistical power $(1 - \beta)$ in a two-sided test

Other things being equal, a one-sided test produces a higher statistical power than does a two-sided test. The critical value in a one-sided test is closer to the most expected value zero than that in a two-sided test (i.e., $z_{\alpha/2} < z_\alpha$ on the negative side and $z_{1-\alpha/2} > z_{1-\alpha}$ on the positive side). It is easier to exceed the critical value for the one-sided test than the critical value for the two-sided test, as it requires a more deviant statistic to surpass the latter. So the one-sided test is less stringent in rejecting the null hypothesis than the two-sided test. The probability of rejecting the null hypothesis is therefore higher in a one-sided test than in a two-sided test. In short, the stringency of the rejection criterion affects statistical power. The more stringent the rejection criterion is, the lower the statistical power.

In a similar vein, the significance level α affects the stringency of the rejection criterion and, in turn, the statistical power. Reducing α to a smaller value makes the rejection criterion more stringent. Other things being equal, the statistical power will be lowered when α decreases in value, say, from .05 to .01. It is easy to verify the relationship between α, the sidedness of the test, and the power (Equations 2.5 and 2.6) by changing the parameter values in the following R code:

```
n=62
a=.05             # a stands for alpha
d=.5              # d=Delta/sigma
nc=d*sqrt(n/2)    # nc stands for non-centrality parameter
1-pnorm(qnorm(1-a)-nc) # power in a one-sided test
# power in a two-sided test
pnorm(nc-qnorm(1-a/2))+pnorm(qnorm(a/2)-nc)
```

The SAS code is:

```
data null;
n=62;
a=.05;
d=.5;
nc=d*sqrt(n/2);
p1=1-probnorm(probit(1-a)-nc);
p2=probnorm(nc-probit(1-a/2))+probnorm(probit(a/2)-nc);
put "power in a one-sided test is  " p1;
put "power in a two-sided test is  " p2;
run;
```

The corresponding SPSS code is:

```
DATA LIST LIST/N A D.
BEGIN DATA.
62 ,.05 ,.5
END DATA.
COMPUTE NC=D*SQRT(N/2).
COMPUTE P1=1-CDF.NORMAL(IDF.NORMAL(1-A,0,1)-NC,0,1).
COMPUTE P2=CDF.NORMAL(NC - IDF.NORMAL(1-A/2,0,1),0,1)
          +CDF.NORMAL(IDF.NORMAL(A/2,0,1)-NC,0,1).
EXECUTE.
```

Besides the sidedness of the test and significance level, effect size and sample size have a direct bearing on the non-centrality parameter and, in turn, statistical power. They both have a positive relationship with the non-centrality parameter and statistical power. The larger the effect size or sample size becomes, the higher the statistical power.

2.2.2   Effect Size

The population mean difference between treated and control groups is the simple effect size $\Delta = \mu_1 - \mu_2$. The term effect size is often synonymous with the term standardized effect size popularized by Cohen (1988). The standardized effect size divides the simple effect size Δ by the population standard deviation σ; $\delta = (\mu_1 - \mu_2)/\sigma$. Cohen defines rule-of-thumb effect sizes .2, .5, and .8 for small, medium, and large effects in the behavioral sciences. The standardized effect size expresses the mean difference between two contrasted populations as a percentage of the common standard deviation σ.

The standardized effect size can be viewed as the percentage of overlap between two contrasted normal populations. The overlap between two normal populations with a mean difference Δ and a common standard deviation σ is $2\Phi(-.5\Delta/\sigma)$. The small, medium, and large effect sizes .2, .5, and .8 correspond to .92, .80, and .69 overlaps between the two populations. For example, a medium effect size of .5 basically means that the two populations share 80% of their values (see Figure 2.2).

Alternatively, we may use a common language effect size that anyone can readily comprehend (McGraw and Wong, 1992). Like the standardized effect size, the common language effect size does not depend on the measurement scale or the standard deviation. The common language effect

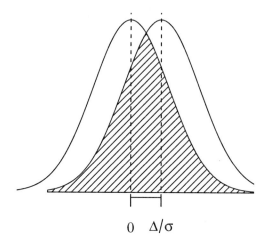

Figure 2.2: Percentage of population overlap $2\Phi(-.5\Delta/\sigma)$

size uses the probability of a randomly sampled observation from one population being larger than a randomly selected observation from the other population (i.e., probability of superiority) to gage the mean difference between the two populations. The larger the mean difference is, the more likely that a random observation from one population is superior to a random observation from the other population.

The common language effect size can easily be derived from the distribution of the difference between two normal populations. Let A and B stand for two random observations from two normal populations in a two-group comparison study. The common language effect size is the probability of superiority $P[A > B]$. It is equivalent to the probability of $A - B$ greater than 0,

$$P[A > B] = P[A - B > 0]. \tag{2.7}$$

The difference $A - B$ is also normally distributed because both A and B are normal. Suppose that A and B have population mean μ_A and μ_B with a common variance σ^2. The normal distribution of the difference $A - B$, therefore, has a mean $\mu_A - \mu_B$ and a variance $\sigma^2 + \sigma^2$.

$$A - B \sim N(\mu_A - \mu_B, 2\sigma^2). \tag{2.8}$$

The probability of superiority can be expressed in terms of a cumulative distribution function of a standard normal Z,

$$\begin{aligned}
P[A > B] &= P[A - B > 0] \\
&= P\left[\frac{A - B - (\mu_A - \mu_B)}{\sqrt{2}\sigma} > \frac{-(\mu_A - \mu_B)}{\sqrt{2}\sigma}\right] \\
&= P[Z > -\frac{\mu_A - \mu_B}{\sqrt{2}\sigma}] \\
&= 1 - \Phi(-\frac{\mu_A - \mu_B}{\sqrt{2}\sigma}) \\
&= 1 - \Phi(-\frac{\delta}{\sqrt{2}}), \tag{2.9}
\end{aligned}$$

where Φ is the cumulative distribution function of the standard normal Z. It is obvious that the common language effect size is a function of the standardized effect size $\delta = (\mu_A - \mu_B)/\sigma$. There exists a one-to-one correspondence between standardized effect size and common language effect size. Cohen's small, medium, and large effect sizes, namely, .2, .5, and .8, correspond to probabilities of superiority ($P[A > B]$) of .56, .64, and .71, respectively. Although the standardized effect size is mathematically equivalent to the common language effect size, the latter is more comprehensible to non-statisticians.

The standardized effect size depends on the simple effect size Δ and standard deviation σ. A large simple effect size increases the standardized effect size, whereas a large standard deviation decreases the standardized effect size. This complicates the interpretation of standardized effect size, as a large standardized effect size does not necessarily imply a big simple effect size. Rather, it can just mean a very small standard deviation or measurement error. For example, $\Delta = 10$ may mean a medium effect in a particular context. If the standard deviation σ is 20, the standardized effect size is $\delta = .5$. In this case, the standardized effect size has a similar interpretation to the simple effect size. Now suppose that the researcher can manage to reduce σ to 10 by using a better measuring instrument; the standardized effect size ($\delta = 1.0$) will look huge. The standardized effect no longer shares a similar interpretation with the simple effect size. It is mistaken to call it a large effect. Therefore, it is informative to specify Δ and σ separately in planning statistical power, as the simple effect size relates to the scale of the study in a more straightforward way than does the standardized effect size (Baguley, 2009), which can convolute the effect size.

The simple effect size affects the non-centrality parameter and statistical power. The larger the simple effect size is, the larger the non-centrality parameter and statistical power. This can be readily verified with Equation 2.5 or 2.6 because statistical power can be expressed as a function of the simple effect size Δ given the standard deviation σ, sample size n, and significance level α. In particular, statistical power is an increasing monotonic function of Δ. When planning a study, we can specify a minimum effect size Δ that is practically significant and choose sample size n to achieve a desired level of statistical power, say, .80. The power analysis can help determine an appropriate sample size and contain the sampling cost. A planned test with sufficient sample size will have adequate power to detect a practically important effect, but it will have less power if the magnitude of the effect size is smaller than the minimum effect size that is practically important.

Additionally, the standard deviation σ affects the non-centrality parameter and statistical power. A small σ is conducive to high statistical power because it increases the non-centrality parameter and, hence, statistical power. It does so by making the effect look prominent against the reduced background noise, if we compare the effect to a real signal and standard deviation to background noise. Unless a researcher can exercise some control over σ (e.g., reducing measurement error), the standard deviation has to be taken as it is in planning a study.

2.2.3 Sample Size

Sample size is normally under the control of a researcher, and it greatly affects statistical power. In a balanced design, power can be expressed as a function of the sample size n. Equation 2.5 suggests that the $(1 - \beta)$th quantile of the standard normal distribution is equal to $\lambda - z_{1-\alpha}$;

$$z_{1-\beta} = \lambda - z_{1-\alpha}$$
$$= \sqrt{\frac{n}{2}} \frac{\Delta}{\sigma} - z_{1-\alpha}. \tag{2.10}$$

Rearranging the elements in Equation 2.10 yields the sample size for achieving power $1 - \beta$ in the one-sided z-test;

$$n = 2\sigma^2 \left(\frac{z_{1-\beta} + z_{1-\alpha}}{\Delta} \right)^2. \tag{2.11}$$

For a two-sided test, we can approximate the sample size by replacing the critical value $z_{1-\alpha}$ with the two-sided critical value $z_{1-\alpha/2}$. The power in the two-sided test is approximately

$$1 - \beta = P\left[Z' \geq z_{1-\alpha/2} \cup Z' \leq z_{\alpha/2} \right]$$
$$= 1 - P\left[Z' < z_{1-\alpha/2} \right] + P\left[Z' \leq z_{\alpha/2} \right]$$
$$\approx 1 - P\left[Z' < z_{1-\alpha/2} \right]$$
$$\approx \Phi\left(\lambda - z_{1-\alpha/2} \right). \tag{2.12}$$

Note that the probability $P\left[Z' \leq z_{\alpha/2} \right]$ in the power function is usually small and can be omitted in the approximation (see Figure 2.1). Equation 2.12 is similar to Equation 2.5 except that the critical value now is $z_{1-\alpha/2}$. It follows from Equation 2.12 that

$$z_{1-\beta} = \lambda - z_{1-\alpha/2}$$
$$= \sqrt{\frac{n}{2}} \frac{\Delta}{\sigma} - z_{1-\alpha/2}. \tag{2.13}$$

The approximate sample size for achieving power $1 - \beta$ in a two-sided test (Cochran, 1983) is

$$n \approx 2\sigma^2 \left(\frac{z_{1-\beta} + z_{1-\alpha/2}}{\Delta} \right)^2. \tag{2.14}$$

We can rearrange this equation to express the minimum effect size Δ that the test can detect with power $1 - \beta$ for a given sample size n

$$\Delta \approx \sqrt{\frac{2}{n}} \sigma \left(z_{1-\beta} + z_{1-\alpha/2} \right). \qquad (2.15)$$

It is also referred to as the minimum detectable effect size at which a researcher can substantiate the effect's existence by rejecting the null hypothesis with a probability $1 - \beta$ (Bloom, 1995). As the sample size n increases, the minimum detectable effect size decreases. Holding sample size n constant, we can decrease the minimum detectable effect size Δ by lessening the power $1 - \beta$ (see Figure 2.3). The top curve in Figure 2.3 maintains power at .90. If power is lowered to .80, as the bottom curve, the minimum detectable effect size Δ will decrease for the sample size n.

The approach of minimum detectable effect size assumes that we are uncertain about the actual effect size but are interested in knowing how small the detectable effect size can be, given the sample size n and statistical power $1 - \beta$. It represents another way to explore the planned study, although it is mathematically equivalent to calculating statistical power for various sample sizes. Since researchers usually want to determine an appropriate sample size with respect to a minimum effect size, we will focus on power calculation instead of minimum detectable effect size.

2.3   Statistical Power and Sample Size for t Tests

A z-test is good for explaining statistical power and its determinants (e.g, significance level, sample size, effect size, and standard deviation). The effects of those determinants on statistical power can be generalized to other statistical tests. However, the z-test is not often used, as the population standard deviation σ is rarely known. When the population standard deviation needs to be estimated from the data, a sample standard deviation $\hat{\sigma}$ can be substituted for the population standard deviation in the z-test. The test statistic no longer follows a normal distribution but a t distribution. The t statistic differs from the standard normal Z in that the former has degrees of freedom ν. The sample standard deviation is the square root of the sample variance $\hat{\sigma}^2$ with degrees of freedom ν, which is related to a chi

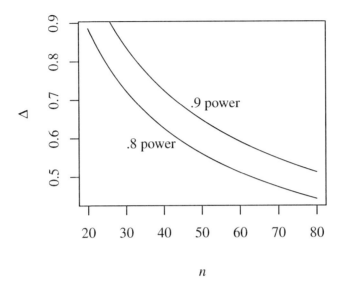

Figure 2.3: Minimum detectable effect size Δ and sample size n

square distribution (see Equation 1.14);

$$\frac{\hat{\sigma}}{\sigma} = \sqrt{\frac{\nu\hat{\sigma}^2}{\sigma^2}/\nu} \sim \sqrt{\chi_\nu^2/\nu}.$$

We can substitute $\hat{\sigma}$ for σ in the z-test by dividing Z with $\hat{\sigma}/\sigma$. Thus, we can obtain the t statistic

$$T = Z/\left(\frac{\hat{\sigma}}{\sigma}\right) \sim \frac{Z}{\sqrt{\chi_\nu^2/\nu}}. \tag{2.16}$$

In the following, we will derive statistical power in the one sample t test, the two sample independent t test, and the dependent t test.

2.3.1 One Sample *t* Test

The one sample t test is built on the z statistic that compares a sample mean $\overline{Y}$ with a hypothesized population mean μ_0 under the null hypothesis. For example, the office of student financial aid is interested in learning whether the bad economy has significantly changed the average income from summer jobs for college students who seek employment to offset the financial cost of attending college. The average summer income of college students who work in the summer was about \$3000 in the past (i.e., $H_0 : \mu_0 = 3000$). The office of student financial aid is concerned about whether the average summer income has lowered due to the bad economy. A group of the college students who reportedly have worked in the summer are randomly chosen to participate in a survey on summer income. If the standard deviation of the summer income σ is known, a z statistic can be used to test whether the average summer income has changed from the past,

$$Z = \frac{\overline{Y} - \mu_0}{\sigma/\sqrt{n}}. \tag{2.17}$$

Under the alternative hypothesis $H_a : \mu < \mu_0$ or $\mu = \mu_a$, the z statistic has a non-central normal distribution Z' with a unit variance and a non-zero mean or non-centrality parameter λ. The non-centrality parameter can be obtained by replacing the sample mean with the population mean under the alternative hypothesis,

$$\lambda = \frac{\mu_a - \mu_0}{\sigma/\sqrt{n}}. \tag{2.18}$$

The statistical power for the one-sided alternative hypothesis is, therefore,

$$\begin{aligned} 1 - \beta &= P[Z' \leq z_\alpha] \\ &= P[Z' - \lambda \leq z_\alpha - \lambda] \\ &= P[Z \leq z_\alpha - \lambda] \\ &= \Phi(z_\alpha - \lambda). \end{aligned} \tag{2.19}$$

Note that $\mu_a - \mu_0 < 0$ and the non-centrality parameter λ is actually negative. Had the non-centrality parameter been positive, then the power would have been $P[Z \geq z_{1-\alpha} - \lambda]$ or $1 - \Phi(z_{1-\alpha} - \lambda)$. It is obvious that the left-sided alternative requires the use of the left-side critical value z_α. So the statistical power function needs to be changed according to the sidedness of the alternative hypothesis. However, the statistical power function in the two-sided test does not change regardless of the sign of the non-centrality parameter. The power for the two sided hypothesis $H_a : \mu \neq \mu_0$ is

$$1 - \Phi(z_{1-\alpha/2} - \lambda) + \Phi(z_{\alpha/2} - \lambda).$$

When the population standard deviation σ is not available, a sample standard deviation $\hat{\sigma}$ can be substituted in the test. The sample standard deviation $\hat{\sigma}$ is the square root of the sample variance $\hat{\sigma}^2$,

$$\hat{\sigma}^2 = \frac{\sum\limits_{i=1}^{n}(Y_i - \overline{Y})^2}{n-1}.$$

The test statistic now assumes a t distribution,

$$T = \frac{\overline{Y} - \mu_0}{\hat{\sigma}/\sqrt{n}}. \tag{2.20}$$

The t statistic has degrees of freedom $n-1$ with the same non-centrality parameter as in the z-test. When the null hypothesis is true, the non-centrality parameter is zero. The t statistic follows a central t distribution. Under the alternative hypothesis, the t statistic assumes a non-central t distribution T' with degrees of freedom $n-1$ and a non-centrality parameter λ, as in Equation 2.18. We thereafter denote the non-central t distribution T'. The statistical power uses the cumulative distribution function of a non-central T'. In a two-sided test, power is

$$\begin{aligned}
1 - \beta &= P[|T'| \geq t_{1-\alpha/2,n-1}] \\
&= P[T' \geq t_{1-\alpha/2,n-1}] + P[T' \leq t_{\alpha/2,n-1}] \\
&= 1 - P[T' < t_{1-\alpha/2,n-1}] + P[T' \leq t_{\alpha/2,n-1}]. \tag{2.21}
\end{aligned}$$

The power in a one-sided test depends on the direction of the alternative hypothesis. In our example, the alternative hypothesis is left-sided. The left-side critical t value shall be used in the power function. The power for the left-sided alternative hypothesis is, therefore, $P[T' \leq t_{\alpha,n-1}]$. Had the one-sided test been a right-sided alternative hypothesis, the statistical power would have been $1 - P[T' < t_{1-\alpha,n-1}]$.

The following R code computes statistical power for the left-sided alternative hypothesis with the sample size ranging from 25 to 30.

```
#power for one-sample t
n=25:30              #n=25,26,27,28,29,30
v=n-1
```

```
a=.05
d=(2750-3000)/500   #sigma=500
nc=d*sqrt(n)
pt(qt(a,v),v,nc)
          #curve plots power vs n
curve(pt(qt(.05,x-1),x-1,-.5*sqrt(x))
,5,80,ylab="Power",xlab="n")
```

In SAS we can use the proc power procedure to compute statistical power in one sample *t* tests. The proc power procedure also has a graph option, which plots power over a range of sample sizes.

```
*one sample t test;
proc power;
onesamplemeans
mean = -250
sides= 1
ntotal = 30
stddev = 500
power = .;
plot x=n min=5 max=100;
run;
```

The sides option specifies a one-sided test. By default, a two-sided test is assumed, and the option sides can be left out for a two-sided test.

The SPSS syntax for computing power in a one-sided test is

```
*ONE SAMPLE T TEST.
DATA LIST LIST/N D.
BEGIN DATA
30 -.5
END DATA.
COMPUTE P=NCDF.T(IDF.T(.05,N-1),N-1,D*SQRT(N)).
EXECUTE.
```

2.3.2   Two Sample Independent *t* Test

We can use the example of the test preparatory program to explain the two sample independent *t* test. Test candidates are randomly assigned to take a preparatory program or not (control). The two groups of subjects are later compared in their performance on the high-stakes test. Suppose that the standard deviation of the test outcome is unknown this time. The standard deviation σ can be estimated from the pooled sample standard deviation $\hat{\sigma}$,

$$\hat{\sigma} = \sqrt{\frac{(n_1 - 1)s_1^2 + (n_2 - 1)s_2^2}{n_1 + n_2 - 2}}, \tag{2.22}$$

where s_1^2 and s_2^2 are the sample variance for the treatment and control group; n_1 and n_2 are their respective sample sizes. Replacing σ with its estimator $\hat{\sigma}$ in the Z statistic changes the test to a T statistic,

$$T = \frac{\overline{Y}_1 - \overline{Y}_2}{\hat{\sigma}\sqrt{\frac{1}{n_1} + \frac{1}{n_2}}}. \tag{2.23}$$

When the null hypothesis is true, the T statistic follows a central t distribution with degrees of freedom $v = n_1 + n_2 - 2$. The expectation of a central T statistic is equal to zero; and the deviation of the T statistic from the expected value zero follows a probabilistic pattern of the central t distribution. The p-value of the T statistic is the probability of obtaining a t statistic at least as far from zero as the realized t value of the T statistic (i.e., p-value $= P[T \geq |t|]$). Alternatively, we may use the critical values to decide on the rejection of the null hypothesis. The right- and left-side critical values are the $(1 - \alpha/2)$th and $(\alpha/2)$th quantile of the central t distribution (i.e., $t_{1-\alpha/2}$ and $t_{\alpha/2}$). A t value further away from zero than either critical value yields a p-value smaller than α and the rejection of the null hypothesis.

When the alternative hypothesis holds true, the two population means are not equal. Their difference is the simple effect size Δ. The test statistic under the alternative hypothesis no longer follows a central t distribution but a non-central t distribution T' with degrees of freedom v and a non-centrality parameter λ, as in Equation 2.2. Equation 2.2 shows the non-centrality parameter for the z-test in comparing a two mean difference. So the z-test and t test share the same non-centrality parameter.

Statistical power in a two-sided t test is the probability of rejecting the null hypothesis (i.e., having the test statistic T' exceed the critical value on either side),

$$1 - \beta = P[T' \geq t_{1-\alpha/2} \cup T' \leq t_{\alpha/2}]$$
$$= 1 - P[T' < t_{1-\alpha/2}] + P[T' \leq t_{\alpha/2}], \qquad (2.24)$$

where $P[T' \leq t_{1-\alpha/2}]$ and $P[T' \leq t_{\alpha/2}]$ are the cumulative distribution function of the non-central t distribution (see Appendix A). The non-central cumulative distribution function is readily accessible in statistical software. Equation 2.24 can be implemented in R:

```
n1=65
n2=65
v=n1+n2-2
a=.05                     # a stands for alpha
d=.5                      # d=Delta/sigma
# nc stands for non-centrality parameter
nc=d*sqrt(n1*n2/(n1+n2))
1-pt(qt(1-a/2,v),v,nc)+pt(qt(a/2,v),v,nc) #power.
```

The SAS program is:

```
data null;
n1=65;
n2=65;
v=n1+n2-2;
a=.05;
d=.5;
nc=d*sqrt(n1*n2/(n1+n2));
p=1-probt(tinv(1-a/2,v),v,nc)+probt(tinv(a/2,v),v,nc);
put "power in the independent t test is " p;
run;
```

The corresponding SPSS syntax is:

```
DATA LIST LIST/ N1 N2 A D.
BEGIN DATA
65,65,.05,.5
END DATA.
COMPUTE V=N1+N2-2.
```

```
COMPUTE NC=D*SQRT(N1*N2/(N1+N2)).
COMPUTE P=1-NCDF.T(IDF.T(1-A/2,V),V,NC)
           +NCDF.T(IDF.T(A/2,V),V,NC).
EXECUTE.
```

In the previous example, suppose that the test preparatory program is expected to improve students' test scores by at least 50 points ($\Delta = 50$). The students' scores can range from 100 to 500 95% of the time. Since four standard deviations comprise 95% of the cases, the standard deviation is estimated to be $\sigma = (500 - 100)/4 = 100$. The sample size $n = 65$ will produce a statistical power of .8076 at the five percent significance level ($\alpha = .05$).

The statistical power can be plotted over a range of sample sizes on a graph (Figure 2.4), which can be useful in exploring different choices of sample size when planning a study. The R code for producing such a graph is amazingly simple because it only involves a few lines of code. First, a function for calculating statistical power is defined. Second, the R built-in function curve() can be utilized to plot statistical power against sample size n.

```
pt1<-function(n,d=50/100){
v=2*n-2
a=.05     # a stands for alpha  d=Delta/sigma
nc=d*sqrt(n/2) # nc stands for non-centrality parameter
1-pt(qt(1-a/2,v),v,nc)+pt(qt(a/2,v),v,nc)
}

curve(pt1(x),5,300,xlab="sample size n", ylab="Power")
curve(pt1(x,.3),5,300,lty="dashed",add=TRUE)
```

To produce a similar graph in SAS, users can either use the proc power procedure or start from scratch. The SAS proc power routine can be used to tabulate and plot statistical power and sample size. The graph comes from the plot statement in the procedure. Alternatively, users can write a data step and compute statistical power for different sample sizes in loops (i.e., do; ...; end;). After the data step, users can write a SAS proc gplot procedure to produce the graph.

```
* use proc power to plot power curve for independent t ;
```

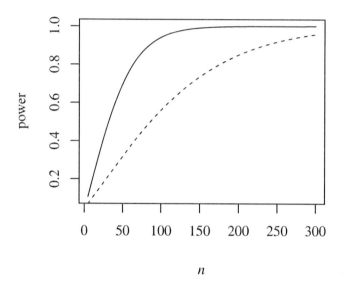

Figure 2.4: Statistical power vs. sample size *n* in the independent *t* test

```
proc power;
twosamplemeans test=diff
meandiff = 30 50
stddev = 100
npergroup = 20 to 300 by 5
power = .;
plot x=n min=20 max=300;
run;

*use data step and gplot to
produce power curve for independent t;
data it(keep=d n p);
a=.05; stddev=100;
do es=30, 50;
 do n=20 to 300 by 5;
   v=2*n-2;
   d=es/stddev;
   nc=d*sqrt(n/2);
```

```
  p=1-probt(tinv(1-a/2,v),v,nc)+probt(tinv(a/2,v),v,nc);
  output;
 end;
end;
label d='Effect size' p='Power';
run;

symbol1 c=b i=join l=3;
symbol2 c=bl i=join l=1;
proc gplot data=it;
 plot p*n=d;
 title h=2.5 j=c "Statistical power vs. sample size n
                   in independent t";
run;
```

In SPSS, users can first create a working data file through NEW FILE and then write INPUT PROGRAM. ... END INPUT PROGRAM. to calculate statistical power for various sample sizes. The SPSS program has a similar loop to the SAS program. The loop in SPSS starts with INPUT PROGRAM and ends with END INPUT PROGRAM. The LEAVE statement is necessary as it retains the old values of the variables until new values are supplied. The only quirky part of SPSS is that the variables need to be created separately in a series of COMPUTE statements. Once the data file is ready, users can easily obtain the graph either by using the Windows menus or running the GRAPH syntax.

```
* STATISTICAL POWER VS N IN INDEPENDENT T.
NEW FILE.
INPUT PROGRAM.
COMPUTE A=.05.
COMPUTE STDEV=100.
COMPUTE N=0.
COMPUTE V=0.
COMPUTE NC1=0.
COMPUTE NC2=0.
COMPUTE P1=0.
COMPUTE P2=0.
```

```
LEAVE A TO P2.
 LOOP N=20 TO 300 BY 5.
    COMPUTE V=2*N-2.
    COMPUTE NC1=30/STDEV*SQRT(N/2).
    COMPUTE NC2=50/STDEV*SQRT(N/2).
    COMPUTE P1=1- NCDF.T(IDF.T(1-A/2,V),V,NC1) +
     NCDF.T(IDF.T(A/2,V),V,NC1).
    COMPUTE P2=1- NCDF.T(IDF.T(1-A/2,V),V,NC2) +
     NCDF.T(IDF.T(A/2,V),V,NC2).
    END CASE.
 END LOOP.
END FILE.
END INPUT PROGRAM.
EXECUTE.

DELETE VARIABLES A STDEV V NC1 NC2.
VARIABLE LABELS P1 'Power for ES .3' P2  'Power for ES .5'.
*LIST.

GRAPH
  /LINE(MULTIPLE)=VALUE(P1 P2) BY N
  /TITLE='Statistical power vs sample size in'+
         'independent t test'.
```

The example assumes a balanced design with equal sample size in both groups (i.e., $n_1 = n_2 = n$). A balanced design is preferred if the costs for sampling the subject are equal between the "treatment" and "control" conditions. Sometimes, the cost of adding a subject to the treatment group can be much more expensive than that for the control group because the expense in treating a subject is higher than that of using a "control" subject. Equal sample sizes mean a smaller total sample size for the study. An unbalanced design can produce a larger total sample size (i.e., $N = n_1 + n_2$) for the study, since it recruits more inexpensive subjects in the control group than expensive subjects in the treatment group. A larger total sample size can produce a higher statistical power. Suppose that the cost ratio per subject between the treatment and control conditions is $c_1 : c_2$, where c_1 is the cost of using one subject in the treatment group and c_2 the cost of one subject in the control group. The optimal sample allocation ratio is inversely related to the cost ratio (Hsu, 1994),

$$\frac{n_1}{n_2} = \sqrt{\frac{c_2}{c_1}}. \tag{2.25}$$

The more expensive a treatment is, the fewer subjects should be allocated to the treatment group and the more subjects should be added to the control group. The optimal sample ratio produces the maximum total sample size and statistical power for a fixed total budget; the optimal ratio can also minimize the total budget of the study for a fixed level of statistical power. Hence, power can be optimized for study designs; this is especially relevant in complex designs involving multiple sample sizes discussed in later chapters.

2.3.3 Dependent t Test

Unlike the independent t test, the dependent t statistic involves a single group of subjects or a group of paired subjects, say, twins. The two samples of data are obtained from the same group of subjects before and after treatment (e.g., Y_1 as pretest and Y_2 as posttest) or from the group of paired subjects (e.g., one of the pair randomly placed in each group). The outcome of interest is the difference ($d = Y_1 - Y_2$) in observed performance before and after the treatment or the difference in performance within pairs. The average difference before and after treatment is estimated as $\bar{d} = \overline{Y}_1 - \overline{Y}_2$. This is the same as that in the independent t test, but the standard error of the mean difference is different. The standard deviation of the difference score d is

$$\sigma_d = \sqrt{\sigma_{Y_1}^2 + \sigma_{Y_2}^2 - 2\rho\sigma_{Y_1}\sigma_{Y_2}}$$
$$= \sigma\sqrt{2(1-\rho)}, \tag{2.26}$$

where ρ is the correlation between Y_1 and Y_2, and Y_1 and Y_2 have equal variance, namely, $\sigma_{Y_1}^2 = \sigma_{Y_2}^2 = \sigma^2$. According to the central limit theorem, the standard error of the average difference score $\bar{d}$ is

$$\sigma_{\bar{d}} = \frac{\sigma_d}{\sqrt{n}}, \tag{2.27}$$

where n is the number of subjects or pairs in the group. Thus, the dependent t test can be modeled after a one sample t test if we treat the difference score between pretest and posttest or between matched pairs as the outcome variable.

The null hypothesis states that the population means before and after the treatment are the same or the population mean of the difference score is zero $H_0 : \mu_1 = \mu_2$ or $\mu_d = 0$. When the null hypothesis is true, the mean of the difference score $\bar{d}$ follows a standard normal distribution $\bar{d} \sim N(0, \sigma_{\bar{d}})$. If the standard deviation σ and correlation ρ are known, a z-test can be formed to test the null hypothesis;

$$Z = \frac{\bar{d}}{\sigma_{\bar{d}}} = \frac{\bar{d}}{\sigma_d/\sqrt{n}} = \frac{\bar{d}}{\sigma\sqrt{1-\rho}\sqrt{\frac{2}{n}}}. \tag{2.28}$$

When the standard deviation $\sigma_{\bar{d}}$ is not known, the sample standard deviation of difference scores can be used, that is,

$$\hat{\sigma}_d = \sqrt{\frac{\sum_{i=1}^{n}(d_i - \bar{d})^2}{n-1}}, \tag{2.29}$$

where d_i represents the difference score for the ith subject or pair. Substituting Equation 2.29 for σ_d in Equation 2.28 changes the z-test to a t test,

$$T = \frac{\bar{d}}{\hat{\sigma}_d/\sqrt{n}}. \tag{2.30}$$

The T statistic follows a central t distribution with a degrees of freedom $n-1$ when the null hypothesis is true.

When the population mean of the difference score differs from zero, there exists a treatment effect. The alternative hypothesis therefore states $H_a : \mu_d \neq 0$ (i.e., $\mu_d = \Delta$). The T statistic under the alternative hypothesis no longer assumes a central t distribution and is denoted by T'. It follows a non-central t distribution with degrees of freedom $n-1$ and a non-centrality parameter,

$$\lambda = \frac{\Delta}{\sigma_d/\sqrt{n}} = \frac{\Delta}{\sigma\sqrt{2(1-\rho)}/\sqrt{n}} = \frac{\Delta}{\sigma\sqrt{1-\rho}}\sqrt{\frac{n}{2}}. \tag{2.31}$$

The statistical power is the probability of having a T' at least as large as the right critical value $t_{1-\alpha/2}$ or at least as small as the left critical value $t_{\alpha/2}$ in the two-sided test. The power function in the dependent t test can be expressed as

$$1 - \beta = P[T' \geq t_{1-\alpha/2} \cup T' \leq t_{\alpha/2}]$$
$$= 1 - P[T' < t_{1-\alpha/2}] + P[T' \leq t_{\alpha/2}], \qquad (2.32)$$

where $P[T' \leq t_{1-\alpha/2}]$ and $P[T' \leq t_{\alpha/2}]$ are the cumulative distribution functions of the non-central T' with degrees of freedom $n - 1$ and non-centrality parameter λ, as in Equation 2.31. The R code for implementing Equation 2.32 is as follows:

```
n=34
a=.05   # alpha
r=.5    #correlation
d=.5    # d=Delta/sigma
nc=sqrt(n/2)*d/sqrt(1-r)
1 pt(qt(1 a/2,n 1),n-1,nc)+pt(qt(a/2,n-1),n-1,nc).
```

The SAS program is:

```
data null;
n=34;
a=.05;
r=.5;
d=.5;
nc=sqrt(n/2)*d/sqrt(1-r);
p=1-probt(tinv(1-a/2,n-1),n-1,nc)
    +probt(tinv(a/2,n-1),n-1,nc);
put "power in the dependent t test is " p;
run;
```

The corresponding SPSS syntax is:

```
DATA LIST LIST/ N A R D.
BEGIN DATA
34,.05,.5,.5
END DATA.
```

```
COMPUTE NC=SQRT(N/2)*D/SQRT(1-R).
COMPUTE P=1-NCDF.T(IDF.T(1-A/2,N-1),N-1,NC)
          +NCDF.T(IDF.T(A/2,N-1),N-1,NC).
EXECUTE.
```

The non-centrality parameter for the dependent t resembles the non-centrality parameter for the independent t except that the standard deviation σ is now multiplied by an adjustment factor $\sqrt{1-\rho}$. As the correlation ρ between the pretest and posttest is typically larger than zero, the standard deviation σ is adjusted downward. Other things being equal, the non-centrality parameter is increased in the dependent t test. A large non-centrality parameter is conducive to high statistical power because the statistical power function is an increasing monotonic function of the non-centrality parameter. The larger the non-centrality parameter is, the higher the statistical power becomes. Unless the correlation ρ is zero, the dependent t test requires a smaller sample size than does an independent t test to achieve the same level of statistical power. Nevertheless, the dependent t test design is not always appropriate if the practice effect of the pretest affects the performance on the posttest and, in turn, confounds the treatment effect. In the example of the test preparatory program, the same group of students cannot take the exam and then take it again after going through the preparatory program. Test practice can confound the potential effect of the preparatory program, as the prior exposure to the test may improve the students' later performance on the same exam even without the help of the preparatory efforts. In this case, the one-group dependent design has to give way to a two-group design and an independent t test. However, if the practice effect of the pretest does not pose a validity threat to the causal inference about the treatment effect, a dependent group design with a dependent t test is preferred because of its efficient estimate and high power.

For example, a clinical psychologist may be interested in using some behavioral psychotherapy to lower blood pressure among patients whose hypertension is induced by chronic stress. He or she may work with a random sample of such patients in a dependent group design, where each patient's average blood pressure is measured before and after the psychotherapy. Suppose that the minimum effect size of some clinical importance is 5 mmHg ($\Delta = 5$), and the clinical psychologist learns from his or her experience that the patients' systolic blood pressures fall into the range of 140 and 180 mmHg 95% of the time. Since four standard deviations comprise 95% of the cases, the estimated standard deviation is one-quarter of that range ($\sigma = (180 - 140)/4 = 10$). The correlation between pretest and posttest of blood pressure is estimated to be around .50 ($\rho = .50$). After running the R code for Equation 2.32, the clinical psychologist finds that a sample size n of 34 is needed to attain a statistical power of .8078. The required sample size is much smaller than that of an independent *t* test.

As in the independent *t* test, a researcher can plot statistical power against sample size (Figure 2.5), using R, SAS, or SPSS. The computer code is similar to that of the independent *t* test. The R code is as follows:

```
#correlation btw pretest and posttest r=.5
#standardized effect size d=Delta/sigma d=.5

pt2=function(n=34,r=.5,d=.5){
a=.05   # alpha
nc=sqrt(n/2)*d/sqrt(1-r)

1-pt(qt(1-a/2,n-1),n-1,nc)+pt(qt(a/2,n-1),n-1,nc)
}

curve(pt2(x),5,100,xlab="sample size n", ylab="Power")
curve(pt2(x,r=.3),5,100,lty="dashed",add=TRUE)
```

While using SAS, the user can choose either proc power or proc gplot. The former requires simple coding, although the latter affords more options in conditioning the graph (e.g., tick spacing).

```
*power curve for dependent t ;
proc power;
pairedmeans test=diff
meandiff =3 5
corr = 0.5
stddev = 10
npairs = 5 to 100 by 5
power = .;
plot x=n min=5 max=100;
```

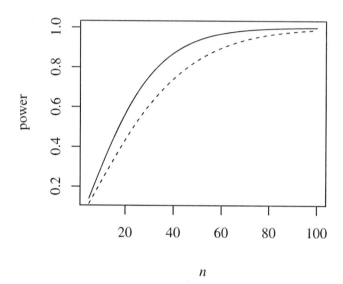

Figure 2.5: Statistical power vs. sample size *n* in the dependent *t* test

```
run;

*use data step and gplot to
produce power curve for dependent t;
data dt(keep=d n p);
a=.05; stddev=10; r=0.5;
do es=3, 5;
 do n=5 to 100 by 5;
  v=n-1;
  d=es/stddev;
  nc=sqrt(n/2)*d/sqrt(1-r);
  p=1-probt(tinv(1-a/2,v),v,nc)+probt(tinv(a/2,v),v,nc);
  output;
 end;
end;
label d='Effect size' p='Power';
run;
```

```
symbol1 c=b i=join l=3;
symbol2 c=bl i=join l=1;
proc gplot data=dt;
 plot p*n=d;
 title h=2.5 j=c "Statistical power vs. sample size n
                  in dependent t";
run;
```

The SPSS syntax is essentially the same as that in the independent *t* test. The user needs to change the statistical power function in the loops. Other parts of the syntax remain unchanged.

```
* STATISTICAL POWER VS N IN DEPENDENT T.
NEW FILE.
INPUT PROGRAM.
COMPUTE A=.05.
COMPUTE STDEV=10.
COMPUTE R=.5.
COMPUTE N=0.
COMPUTE V=0.
COMPUTE NC1=0.
COMPUTE NC2=0.
COMPUTE P1=0.
COMPUTE P2=0.

LEAVE A TO P2.
 LOOP N=5 TO 100 BY 5.
   COMPUTE V=N-1.
   COMPUTE NC1=3/STDEV*SQRT(N/2)/SQRT(1-R).
   COMPUTE NC2=5/STDEV*SQRT(N/2)/SQRT(1-R).
   COMPUTE P1=1- NCDF.T(IDF.T(1-A/2,V),V,NC1) +
    NCDF.T(IDF.T(A/2,V),V,NC1).
   COMPUTE P2=1- NCDF.T(IDF.T(1-A/2,V),V,NC2) +
    NCDF.T(IDF.T(A/2,V),V,NC2).
   END CASE.
 END LOOP.
END FILE.
END INPUT PROGRAM.
```

```
EXECUTE.

DELETE VARIABLES A STDEV V NC1 NC2.
VARIABLE LABELS P1 'Power for ES .3' P2  'Power for ES .5'.
*LIST.

GRAPH
  /LINE(MULTIPLE)=VALUE(P1 P2) BY N
  /TITLE='Statistical power vs sample size'+
         'in dependent t test'.
```

2.3.4   Uncertainty in Power Analysis

When running statistical power analysis, a researcher needs to specify a minimum treatment effect for which the statistical test will have a high chance of rejecting the null hypothesis. The researcher also needs to conjecture the population variance based on a prior study of similar nature. With the minimum treatment effect and the estimated variance, he or she can search for an appropriate sample size to achieve the desired power, say, .80. Although a standardized effect size can be used to circumvent the task of estimating the population variance, it is not in compliance with recommended good practice. Lenth (2001) advises against using "small", "medium", and "large" standardized effect sizes (i.e., .2, .5, and .8) in power analysis because the rule-of-thumb numbers do not fit all the studies in different disciplines. A large standardized effect size of .80 may mean different things depending on the context. It can mean either a large unstandardized effect or a small variance. The former can imply a large treatment effect; the latter a precise measuring instrument, which significantly reduces the measurement variance. Unless standardized effect size has an established meaning in the field, researchers should avoid using it in computing statistical power. Instead, researchers should use a simple effect size that is meaningful in the context and estimate the population variance in completing the power analysis.

    A single-value estimate of statistical power based on a sample variance is usually reported in planning a study. We will call the power based on a sample variance the nominal power and the power based on the population variance the actual power. The nominal power uses a sample variance instead of the population variance; it is not the same as the actual power. There is always some inaccuracy involved in using the nominal power to estimate the actual power. Reporting only the nominal power does not incorporate the uncertainty in anticipating the actual power, which can be lower than the nominal power (Browne, 1995).

The chance of the nominal power being larger than the actual power is slightly more than fifty percent. It is the probability by which the sample variance may underestimate the population variance. As statistical power is a decreasing function of the variance, an underestimated variance will produce a higher statistical power than the true population variance. Specifically, we can define the power function in terms of the variance. The actual power is

$$1 - \beta = f(\sigma^2).$$

If the sample variance $\hat{\sigma}^2$ is used instead, the nominal power is

$$1 - \hat{\beta} = f(\hat{\sigma}^2).$$

It is well known that $\hat{\sigma}^2$ is an unbiased estimate (i.e., $E(\hat{\sigma}^2) = \sigma^2$). The distribution of $\hat{\sigma}^2$ is related to a chi square distribution with degrees of freedom ν (see Equation 1.14),

$$\nu \frac{\hat{\sigma}^2}{\sigma^2} \sim \chi_\nu^2.$$

Using the chi square distribution, we can find the probability that the sample variance $\hat{\sigma}^2$ underestimates the population variance σ^2,

$$P[\hat{\sigma}^2 < \sigma^2] = P[\nu \frac{\hat{\sigma}^2}{\sigma^2} < \nu]$$
$$= P[\chi_\nu^2 < E(\chi_\nu^2)] > 50\%. \tag{2.33}$$

The expectation of the chi square distribution is its degrees of freedom $(E(\chi_\nu^2) = \nu)$ (Johnson, Kotz, and Balakrishnan, 1995). Since the chi square distribution is right skewed, the chi square variate falls behind its expectation more than fifty percent of the time. The inequality $\hat{\sigma}^2 < \sigma^2$ is equivalent to $f(\hat{\sigma}^2) > f(\sigma^2)$ because statistical power is a decreasing function of the variance. It follows that the nominal power $1 - \hat{\beta}$ more likely exceeds the actual power $1 - \beta$;

$$
\begin{aligned}
P[\hat{\sigma}^2 < \sigma^2] &= P[f(\hat{\sigma}^2) > f(\sigma^2)] \\
&= P[1 - \hat{\beta} > 1 - \beta] \\
&= P[\chi_v^2 < E(\chi_v^2)] > 50\%.
\end{aligned}
\tag{2.34}
$$

The probability $P[1 - \hat{\beta} > 1 - \beta]$ is slightly more than 50%, depending on the degrees of freedom v. The number of degrees of freedom, in turn, depends on the sample size. As the sample size increases, the sample variance differs little from the population variance by chance. The probability $P[\chi_v^2 < E(\chi_v^2)]$ approaches 50%. For instance, $P[\chi_{v=30}^2 < E(\chi_{v=30}^2)]$ evaluates to .5343. When v is 200, the probability $P[\chi_{v=200}^2 < E(\chi_{v=200}^2)]$ becomes .5133. Note that the probability $P[\chi_v^2 < E(\chi_v^2)]$ is in essence the chance of having a nominal power larger than the actual power ($P[1 - \hat{\beta} > 1 - \beta]$). Thus, $P[1 - \hat{\beta} > 1 - \beta]$ is a little more likely than a coin flip when the sample size is large. When the sample variance uses a small sample size, the chance of the nominal power being higher than the actual power is more than 50% by a few percentage points. In short, the sample variance tends to produce an optimistic estimate of power, and this is more pronounced with small sample sizes than with large sample sizes.

A confidence interval for statistical power can be constructed to account for uncertainty in using the sample variance. The computed statistical power depends on the minimum effect size and the variance. A researcher usually knows from experience what minimum effect size is practically important in the context, but the variance always requires some guess or estimation from prior experience or studies. A confidence interval can overcome the limitation of the nominal power estimate and realistically portray what actual power may be achieved.

The confidence interval for statistical power can be derived from the confidence limits of the variance σ^2. It is known in the literature that if the confidence interval for σ^2 is $L \le \sigma^2 \le U$ (L is the lower confidence limit and U the upper confidence limit), then the confidence interval for power is $f(U) \le f(\sigma^2) \le f(L)$ (Tarasińska, 2005). The confidence level is the same between the two confidence intervals,

$$
L \le \sigma^2 \le U \Rightarrow f(L) \ge f(\sigma^2) \ge f(U) \Leftrightarrow f(L) \ge 1 - \beta \ge f(U), \tag{2.35}
$$

where $f()$ is the statistical power function with the variance as its argument. As statistical power is a decreasing monotonic function of the variance, the upper and lower bound for statistical power are the power functions evaluated at the lower limit (L) and upper limit (U) of σ^2. The $100(1-\alpha)\%$ confidence interval for σ^2 can be computed by using the sample variance;

$$\text{CI for } \sigma^2 : \quad \frac{v\hat{\sigma}^2}{\chi^2_{1-\alpha/2,v}} \leq \sigma^2 \leq \frac{v\hat{\sigma}^2}{\chi^2_{\alpha/2,v}}, \tag{2.36}$$

where $\chi^2_{1-\alpha/2,v}$ and $\chi^2_{\alpha/2,v}$ are the $100(1-\alpha/2)$ and $100\alpha/2$ quantile of a chi square distribution with degrees of freedom v. The lower and upper limits are, therefore, $L = v\hat{\sigma}^2/\chi^2_{1-\alpha/2,v}$ and $U = v\hat{\sigma}^2/\chi^2_{\alpha/2,v}$. Alternatively, the confidence interval for the standard deviation σ can be used instead. The results will be the same;

$$\text{CI for } \sigma : \quad \hat{\sigma}\sqrt{\frac{v}{\chi^2_{1-\alpha/2,v}}} \leq \sigma \leq \hat{\sigma}\sqrt{\frac{v}{\chi^2_{\alpha/2,v}}}. \tag{2.37}$$

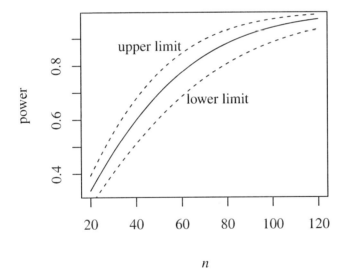

Figure 2.6: Confidence interval for statistical power

For example, we can use the study on the test preparatory program to illustrate the computation of a confidence interval for power in a two sample independent t test. The parameters for power analysis remain the same. The minimum effect size is 50 points between the treatment group that takes the preparatory program and the control group ($\Delta = 50$). The estimated standard deviation is the same $\hat{\sigma} = 100$, but it is based on a sample of 86 subjects from previous records. Using the sample estimate $\hat{\sigma} = 100$, we have previously calculated the statistical power .8076 for the sample size $n = 65$. Now we will account for the uncertainty in using the sample estimate by computing an 80% confidence interval for power in the two sample t test. The 80% confidence interval for σ is $91.2518 \leq \sigma \leq 111.1699$, according to Equation 2.37. The 80% confidence interval for the power is between .7207 and .8729. In particular, the power function (Equation 2.24) evaluates to .8729 at $\sigma = 91.2518$ (the lower bound of σ) and to .7207 at $\sigma = 111.1699$ (the upper bound) for $n = 65$ and $\Delta = 50$. The values .8729 and .7207 are the upper and lower limits of the confidence interval for power at $n = 65$. Similar confidence intervals can be computed for other sample sizes, and a confidence band can be constructed around the power over a range of sample sizes for $\Delta = 50$. In Figure 2.6, the upper and lower limits of the confidence interval for power are shown by the dashed lines. The solid line represents the nominal power, which substitutes the sample standard deviation for the population standard deviation in power analysis.

The nominal power sits approximately in the middle, between the upper and lower limits. It can be viewed as an average of the estimated power, although the actual power can range anywhere between the upper and lower limits. The band width between the upper and lower limits depends on the sample size from which the sample variance or standard deviation is calculated. A sample variance based on a larger sample produces a narrower band of the power estimate than does a sample variance based on a smaller sample, even though the computed nominal power is the same in both cases. This suggests that nominal power is not accurate if the estimated variance or standard deviation from the previous study uses a small sample. Thus, a confidence interval for power can be computed to show the range of the actual power realistically.

Chapter 3

Power of Confidence Interval

There has been a recent movement to shift the emphasis from hypothesis testing to confidence interval (Cumming and Finch, 2001). The critics of hypothesis testing argue that a p-value does not suggest the size of the treatment effect and that non-statisticians confuse statistical significance with practical importance. Some journal editorials (International Committee of Medical Journal Editors, 1988; Wilkinson, 1999) have called directly for the use of confidence intervals in lieu of hypothesis tests. Although misconceptions about hypothesis testing are common, it will remain the main vehicle of research inquiry in the social sciences. Nevertheless, a confidence interval accompanying a hypothesis test is encouraged in research practice.

The wide use of confidence intervals will not automatically improve statistical practice unless people pay attention to sample size and the precision of the confidence interval. A wide confidence interval is not informative about the true size of the parameter because such a confidence interval shows a wide range of plausible values that the parameter can take. For example, a confidence interval for the mean age on a university campus may indicate that the mean age is between 10 and 40 years old. Although the confidence interval is very likely correct, it does not offer useful information about the actual ages on the campus. The width of a confidence interval needs to be sufficiently narrow to be useful. Sample size plays an important role in achieving a narrow interval width. In the following, we will first describe the formation of a confidence interval and then explain the relationship between its width and sample size.

3.1 Sample Size and Confidence Interval in a z-test

A confidence interval can be formed by extending a certain number of standard errors around a point estimate of the parameter. In the example of the test preparatory program, the confidence interval for the mean difference $\mu_1 - \mu_2$ anchors its middle point at the point estimate $\overline{Y}_1 - \overline{Y}_2$, and the upper and lower limits of the confidence interval are the point estimate $\overline{Y}_1 - \overline{Y}_2$ plus or minus the critical value $z_{1-\alpha/2}$ multiplied by standard error $\sigma\sqrt{1/n_1 + 1/n_2}$. Thus, the confidence interval for $\mu_1 - \mu_2$ is

$$\overline{Y}_1 - \overline{Y}_2 \pm z_{1-\alpha/2}\sigma\sqrt{\frac{1}{n_1} + \frac{1}{n_2}}. \tag{3.1}$$

The confidence level for the confidence interval is $1 - \alpha$. It indicates the percentage of the time that the confidence intervals thus generated would contain the population parameter had the same study been replicated many times. It is easy to see this because

$$P\left[\overline{Y}_1 - \overline{Y}_2 - z_{1-\alpha/2}\sigma\sqrt{\frac{1}{n_1} + \frac{1}{n_2}} \leq \mu_1 - \mu_2 \leq \overline{Y}_1 - \overline{Y}_2 + z_{1-\alpha/2}\sigma\sqrt{\frac{1}{n_1} + \frac{1}{n_2}}\right]$$

$$= P\left[-z_{1-\alpha/2} \leq \frac{(\overline{Y}_1 - \overline{Y}_2) - (\mu_1 - \mu_2)}{\sigma\sqrt{\frac{1}{n_1} + \frac{1}{n_2}}} \leq z_{1-\alpha/2}\right]$$

$$= P[-z_{1-\alpha/2} \leq Z \leq z_{1-\alpha/2}]$$

$$= 1 - \alpha. \tag{3.2}$$

The confidence level $1 - \alpha$ and the critical z value are predetermined, and the confidence level is conventionally set at 95%.

The half width of the confidence interval w is often called the margin of error, namely, $w = z_{1-\alpha/2}\sigma\sqrt{1/n_1 + 1/n_2}$. To obtain a narrow width of the confidence interval, we can impose an upper bound U on w (i.e, $w \leq U$). For simplicity of illustration, we make the two sample sizes equal $n_1 = n_2 = n$. The half width now becomes

$$w = z_{1-\alpha/2}\sigma\sqrt{\frac{2}{n}}. \tag{3.3}$$

The standard deviation σ has a positive relationship with the half width w. The larger the standard deviation is, the wider the half interval width. Increasing the sample size n, however, reduces the half interval width. Substituting Equation 3.3 into $w \leq U$ and expressing n in terms of U, we obtain the sample size necessary to achieve the upper bound U,

$$n \geq 2 \left(\frac{z_{1-\alpha/2}\sigma}{U} \right)^2.$$
(3.4)

3.2 Sample Size and Confidence Interval in a t Test

When the standard deviation needs to be estimated from the data, the confidence interval based on the t distribution should be used. The $100(1 - \alpha)\%$ confidence interval is

$$\overline{Y}_1 - \overline{Y}_2 \pm t_{1-\alpha/2}\hat{\sigma}\sqrt{\frac{1}{n_1} + \frac{1}{n_2}},$$
(3.5)

where $t_{1-\alpha/2}$ is the critical value, and $\hat{\sigma}$ is the pooled sample standard deviation, as in Equation 2.22. The half width of the confidence interval is

$$w = t_{1-\alpha/2}\hat{\sigma}\sqrt{\frac{1}{n_1} + \frac{1}{n_2}}.$$
(3.6)

When the sample sizes are equal ($n_1 = n_2 = n$), the half width is simplified to $w = t_{1-\alpha/2}\hat{\sigma}\sqrt{2/n}$.

The half width w of the confidence interval based on t is inherently a random variable. Ignoring its stochastic nature may result in serious underestimation of the required sample size to achieve a short interval width. A common mistake is applying the sample size formulas in Equation 3.4 based on the z to the confidence interval based on the t. Had this miscalculation occurred, the chances of achieving the upper bound U for the confidence interval based on the t would be no better than getting a head in a coin toss (Liu, 2009). The explanation for this is intuitive because the unbiased estimate $\hat{\sigma}^2$, though equal to σ^2 on average, may overestimate σ^2 about half of the time. Had σ^2 been overestimated, the width of the confidence interval w would exceed the upper bound U. Thus, Equation

3.4 cannot be used as a good approximation of the required sample size for the confidence interval based on the t distribution.

One way to account for the stochastic nature of w is to calculate its expectation. The expectation shows the average size of the margin of error w in the planned confidence interval but does not provide any idea of how likely a short width may occur in an actual confidence interval. When researchers are faced with gaging an existing confidence interval with some realized margin of error, they are interested in knowing how likely the realized margin of error may occur again in a repeated study. Comparing the realized margin of error with its expectation may not immediately clarify how likely a margin of error at least as narrow as the observed one will occur again in another similarly generated sample. This likelihood is important for evaluating the usefulness of a confidence interval. If the observed margin of error, although small, is unlikely to occur in another repeated sample, the result will be less trustworthy than the same margin of error with a high probability of recurrence. Thus, it becomes informative to gage a confidence interval by the probability of achieving a certain width or margin of error. In other words, the margin of error in a computed confidence interval is viewed as the realized value of a random variable following some distribution. The probability of obtaining a margin of error as narrow as that observed indicates the reproducibility of the result. Thus, we will focus on the desired probability of achieving a certain width in determining sample size for confidence intervals (Beal, 1989; Graybill, 1958; Grieve, 1991; Jiroutek et al, 2003; Kelley, Maxwell, and Rausch, 2003; Pan and Kupper, 1999).

The probability of obtaining a certain width $P[w \leq U]$ can be calculated by using the cumulative distribution function of a chi square distribution,

$$w \leq U$$

$$t_{1-\alpha/2}\hat{\sigma}\sqrt{\frac{2}{n}} \leq U. \tag{3.7}$$

Squaring this inequality and multiplying both sides by ν/σ^2 produces

$$\nu\frac{\hat{\sigma}^2}{\sigma^2} \leq \frac{n\nu}{2t_{1-\alpha/2}^2}\frac{U^2}{\sigma^2}.$$

Since $v\hat{\sigma}^2/\sigma^2 \sim \chi_v^2$ (Equation 1.14), we have

$$\pi = P[w \leq U] = P\left[\chi_v^2 \leq \frac{nv}{2t_{1-\alpha/2}^2}\frac{U^2}{\sigma^2}\right].\qquad(3.8)$$

We can use π to represent the probability $P[w \leq U]$. The probability π can be computed based on the cumulative distribution function of a chi square χ_v^2 with degrees of freedom v.

The probability π is the unconditional probability, regardless of whether the confidence interval includes the parameter or not. In theory, it is desirable to obtain a narrow confidence interval when it actually includes the parameter, and not otherwise (Lehmann, 1959). Beal (1989) distinguishes two probabilities of the half width w being shorter than an upper bound U. One is the unconditional probability, and the other the conditional probability, which is conditional on whether the confidence interval includes the parameter or not. The unconditional probability π is related to two conditional probabilities π_1 and π_2

$$\begin{aligned}\pi &= P[w \leq U|I]P[I] + P[w \leq U|\bar{I}]P[\bar{I}]\\&= \pi_1(1-\alpha) + \pi_2\alpha,\end{aligned}\qquad(3.9)$$

where $1-\alpha$ is the confidence level or the percentage of the time the confidence interval contains the parameter $P[I]$, and α is the percentage of the time the confidence interval does not contain the parameter $P[\bar{I}]$. The term π_1 is the conditional probability of $w \leq U$ when the confidence interval captures the parameter of interest (i.e., event I). The term π_2 is the conditional probability of $w \leq U$ when the confidence interval excludes the parameter (event $\bar{I}$). The conditional probability π_1 is named the power of confidence interval, and it is currently implemented as the default option in the SAS proc power procedure for two means comparisons,

$$\begin{aligned}\pi_1 &= P[w \leq U|I]\\&= P[w \leq U \cap I]/(1-\alpha)\\&= \frac{\gamma}{1-\alpha},\end{aligned}\qquad(3.10)$$

where the joint probability $P[w \leq U \cap I]$ is denoted by γ.

The conditional probability π_1 and unconditional probability π often do not differ much, although the former is philosophically appealing and mathematically elegant. In the past, π_1 was more difficult to calculate than π. Grieve (1991) found that the difference between π and π_1 was too small to be of practical importance, and that π should be used for computational simplicity. In view of today's computer technology, the computational effort is trivial, and probabilities can be readily calculated without any difficulty. The choice between π and π_1 is a subjective preference. The SAS proc power procedure currently calculates both π and π_1. Either probability can be used to choose sample size as the answers do not differ by much most of the time. It is easy to verify this with Equation 3.9, which implies $\pi_1 = (\pi - \pi_2\alpha)/(1 - \alpha)$. Since $\pi_2 < 1.0$, we can replace π_2 by 1.0 in the numerator and obtain the lower bound of π_1 (Liu, 2009);

$$\pi_1 > \frac{\pi - \alpha}{1 - \alpha}. \tag{3.11}$$

The lower bound $(\pi - \alpha)/(1 - \alpha)$ approximately equals $\pi - .01$ for $\pi_1 \geq .7$. For simplicity, we can first choose a sample size to compute π and then use $\pi - .01$ for π_1.

For example, a researcher may study test accommodation for special education students and compare the students' average reading time with and without accommodation. The researcher wants to have the confidence interval for the mean difference of reading time accurate to ± 1 minute ($U = 1$). Suppose that all the students in the control population finish reading all the test questions in 3 to 15 minutes. Using the fact that six standard deviations almost comprise the entire range of the score distribution, the researcher can infer that the standard deviation of reading time is 2 ($\sigma = 2$). If the researcher recruited 74 participants ($n = 37$), the probability of achieving the desired margin of error 1 minute in a 95% confidence interval is at least above .80 ($\pi = .839$ and $\pi_1 = .834$). According to Equation 3.8,

$$\pi = P\left[\chi^2_{v=2\times 37-2} \leq \frac{37(2\times 37 - 2)}{2t^2_{.975;v=72}}\frac{1^2}{2^2}\right] = .839.$$

The R code for calculating π and π_1 is as follows:

```
pi<-function(n=30,U=1,s=2){a=.05
    t0=qt(1-a/2,2*n-2)
    pchisq(.5*n*(2*n-2)*U^2/(t0*s)^2,2*n-2) }
pi(37)
```

```
pi1<-function(n=30,U=1,s=2){ a=.05
  t0=qt(1-a/2,2*n-2)
  integrate(function(x){(2*pnorm(t0*sqrt(x/(2*n-2)))-1)*
  dchisq(x,2*n-2)}, 0,.5*n*(2*n-2)*U^2/(t0*s)^2
  )$val/(1-a)}
pi1(37).
```

The SAS program is:

```
*sample size and power of confidence interval;
proc power;
twosamplemeans ci=diff
halfwidth=1
stddev=2
/*probtype=unconditional*/
probwidth=.
ntotal=74;
run;
*probtype=unconditional yields pi instead of the default pi1;
```

3.3 Statistical Power and Confidence Interval [1]

Sample size determination for confidence intervals has largely used an approach different from that for hypothesis testing. Current study planning follows a splintered vision when it comes to the choice of sample size. Sample size can be chosen to achieve either power or precision but not necessarily both, even though a confidence interval may well accompany a hypothesis test. Most of the time, sample size is determined to attain a desired power in a proposal because funding agencies routinely require applicants to use statistical power analysis to justify the expense of resources for the proposed study. However, little is known about how the sample size based on statistical power affects the precision of the accompanying confidence interval. In this section, we will show that sample size for statistical power has great implication for the width of the corresponding confidence interval.

---

[1] Adapted from Liu, X. (2012). *British Journal of Mathematical and Statistical Psychology,* 65, 427–437.

We will use statistical power to gage the performance of null hypothesis testing, and we will utilize the interval width to assess the precision of confidence interval estimation. The term precision is sometimes associated with measurement error and test reliability in other contexts. Here it refers to the width of a confidence interval. The narrower the interval width is, the more precise the confidence interval becomes. We will first see the relationship between statistical power and interval width in the simple case of a z-test, and then we will derive the formulas for achieving a short confidence interval given a certain level of statistical power in the independent t test.

3.3.1 Statistical Power and Confidence Interval Width in a z-test

When the population standard deviation is known (e.g., a published standard deviation of a well-known norm-referenced test), a z-test can be used to compare the means of test scores between two populations. We will use a two-group comparison for illustration, although the results can be easily generalized to the one-group situation. Suppose that a Z statistic is used to compare two population means (i.e., $H_0 : \mu_1 = \mu_2$) with a known standard deviation σ. The test statistic is

$$Z = \frac{\overline{Y}_1 - \overline{Y}_2}{\sigma \sqrt{2/n}},$$

where $\overline{Y}_1$ and $\overline{Y}_2$ are the sample means of the two groups, and n is the group sample size.

In a z-test the width of the confidence interval is a function of statistical power. First, we will find the required sample size n to obtain statistical power $1 - \beta$ for a minimum effect size Δ that is practically important to detect. Second, we will use the sample size n for power $1 - \beta$ to calculate the realized width of the confidence interval for the two-mean difference. The sample size n for achieving power $1 - \beta$ (see Equation 2.14) is

$$n \approx 2\sigma^2 \left(\frac{z_{1-\beta} + z_{1-\alpha/2}}{\Delta} \right)^2. \tag{3.12}$$

The confidence interval for the two-mean difference (Equation 3.1) is

$$\overline{Y}_1 - \overline{Y}_2 \pm z_{1-\alpha/2}\sigma\sqrt{\frac{2}{n}}.$$

It should be noted that there is a direct correspondence between the two-sided hypothesis test and the confidence interval. If the confidence interval contains zero, then the two means in the null hypothesis are possibly equal. The null hypothesis will not be rejected. On the contrary, a confidence interval that excludes zero suggests that the two means are not possibly equal, and the null hypothesis shall be rejected. Therefore, the statistical power of rejecting the null hypothesis can be expressed in terms of the upper and lower limits of the confidence interval. The power is equal to the probability of having the upper limit smaller than zero or having the lower limit larger than zero,

$$
\begin{aligned}
1 - \beta &= P\left[\overline{Y}_1 - \overline{Y}_2 - z_{1-\alpha/2}\sigma\sqrt{\frac{2}{n}} \geq 0 \cup \overline{Y}_1 - \overline{Y}_2 + z_{1-\alpha/2}\sigma\sqrt{\frac{2}{n}} \leq 0\right] \\
&= P\left[Z' \geq z_{1-\alpha/2}\right] + P\left[Z' \leq -z_{1-\alpha/2}\right] \\
&= P\left[Z' \geq z_{1-\alpha/2}\right] + P\left[Z' \leq z_{\alpha/2}\right],
\end{aligned}
\tag{3.13}
$$

where Z' is the non-central normal variate with a unit variance and a non-zero mean equal to the non-centrality parameter $\lambda = \Delta/\sigma\sqrt{n/2}$ (see Chapter 2). It is obvious that the power function is the same as the previously mentioned one. In parallel with the hypothesis test and confidence interval, there is also a correspondence between statistical power and interval width.

We now examine the width of the confidence interval that is evaluated at the sample size that produces statistical power $1 - \beta$ in the hypothesis test. The half width of the confidence interval is $w = z_{1-\alpha/2}\sigma\sqrt{2/n}$. Substituting the sample size n for power $1 - \beta$ in Equation 3.12 into the formula for w produces

$$
w = \frac{z_{1-\alpha/2}}{z_{1-\beta} + z_{1-\alpha/2}}\Delta = \phi\Delta,
$$

where

$$
\phi = \frac{z_{1-\alpha/2}}{z_{1-\beta} + z_{1-\alpha/2}}.
\tag{3.14}
$$

The ratio ϕ is a function of statistical power $1 - \beta$ (i.e., $\phi = f(\beta)$). Alternatively, ϕ can be viewed as the ratio between the half interval width w and the minimum effect size Δ;

$$w = \phi \Delta \;\Rightarrow\; \phi = \frac{w}{\Delta}. \tag{3.15}$$

We can call ϕ the precision-to-effect ratio. As the minimum effect size Δ is given or constant, a small ϕ indicates a narrow interval width.

There is a one-to-one correspondence between statistical power $1 - \beta$ and the precision-to-effect ratio ϕ. Assume that the significance level is set at five percent ($\alpha = .05$). When statistical power is .5, the ratio ϕ is 1.0, which means that the half width of the confidence interval equals the minimum effect size Δ. The ratio ϕ reduces to .70 when the statistical power $1 - \beta$ reaches .80. If the statistical power is very high, say, $> .975$, w is less than half the minimum effect size Δ. In this case, the confidence interval will exclude zero as a plausible value for the effect size (i.e., rejecting the null hypothesis) as long as the sample mean difference exceeds the half minimum effect size $.5\Delta$ (see Table 3.1). The precision-to-effect ratio ϕ can be plotted against statistical power $1 - \beta$ (see Figure 3.1). As the statistical power increases, the ratio ϕ and the half width w decreases for a given value of the minimum effect size Δ.

Table 3.1: Statistical power $1 - \beta$ and precision-to-effect ratio ϕ

$1 - \beta$	ϕ
0.500	1.000
0.600	0.886
0.700	0.789
0.800	0.700
0.950	0.544
0.975	0.500
0.990	0.457

3.3.2   Statistical Power and Confidence Interval Width in a t Test

When the population standard deviation is unknown, a t test can be used to compare two population means. Replacing the population standard

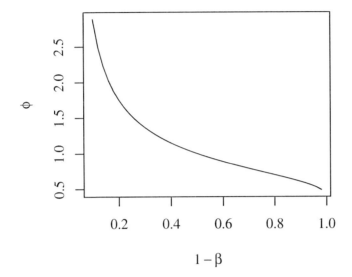

Figure 3.1: ϕ vs. statistical power $1 - \beta$

deviation in the z-test by its sample estimate yields the independent t test,

$$T = \frac{\overline{Y}_1 - \overline{Y}_2}{\hat{\sigma}\sqrt{2/n}},$$

where $\hat{\sigma}$ is the pooled sample standard deviation with degrees of freedom $v = 2n - 2$. Under the alternative hypothesis, the t statistic follows a non-central t distribution T' with the same non-centrality parameter λ as in the z-test. The statistical power $(1 - \beta)$ is the probability of rejecting the null hypothesis (event R),

$$1 - \beta = P[R] = [T' \geq t_0 \cup T' \leq -t_0],$$

where t_0 is the $100(1 - \alpha/2)$th quantile of the central t distribution or the right-side critical value for the t test, and $-t_0$ is the left-side critical t value. A sample size can be found to achieve the desired statistical power for a minimum effect size Δ. Conditioning on the sample size and the level of statistical power, we can assess the width of the confidence interval in the independent t test. We can show that the sample size based on statistical power affects the probability of attaining a certain interval width.

The width of the confidence interval in a t test depends both on the sample size n and the sample standard deviation $\hat{\sigma}$. Assume for simplicity of illustration that the two groups have equal sample size n. The confidence interval for the two-mean difference is

$$\overline{Y}_1 - \overline{Y}_2 \pm t_0 \hat{\sigma} \sqrt{2/n}.$$

The half width of the confidence interval is $w = t_0 \hat{\sigma} \sqrt{2/n}$. The sample standard deviation $\hat{\sigma}$ is a random variable; as is the half width w. The current approach to assessing the width w uses the probability of obtaining a short width (π) or the probability of obtaining a short width conditional that the confidence interval includes the parameter (π_1). Since there is only a slight difference between π and π_1 most of the time, we will use π to simplify the computation.

In examining w given power $1 - \beta$, we are interested in the conditional probability of having a width shorter than an upper bound conditional on rejecting the null (event R),

$$\omega = P[w \le U | R]. \tag{3.16}$$

The probability ω has practical relevance in a randomized experiment, through which a researcher may want not only to confirm the existence of a treatment effect but also to measure its magnitude following the rejection of the null hypothesis. The researcher may follow up the rejection of the null hypothesis by constructing a post-hoc confidence interval for the treatment effect. In theory, it is more interesting to obtain a short confidence interval in the presence of statistical significance than in its absence. We can easily see the reasoning by examining two conditional probabilities of achieving a certain width, conditioning on whether the hypothesis test has rejected the null hypothesis or not, that is,

$$P[w \le U] = P[w \le U | R]P[R] + P[w \le U | \overline{R}]P[\overline{R}], \tag{3.17}$$

where $\overline{R}$ stands for failure to reject the null hypothesis or the complement of the event R. After the hypothesis test has been conducted, the conditional probability $P[w \le U | R]$ is of more interest than the conditional probability $P[w \le U | \overline{R}]$. If the hypothesis test fails to rule out chance as a plausible explanation of the observed effect, the precision in measuring such as an effect becomes a moot issue. In other words, it is premature, if not unjustified, to be overly concerned about the precision in measuring an effect when the empirical evidence does not even substantiate its existence. Thus, it is desirable to achieve high precision only when the effect of interest likely exists (i.e., the rejection of the null hypothesis or event R). The probability ω echoes the importance of estimate precision following a statistically significant result.

To calculate ω, we need to find the the joint probability of width attainment and null rejection $P[w \leq U \cap R]$. We can then compute the probability ω using Bayes' theorem,

$$\omega = \frac{P[w \leq U \cap R]}{P[R]}. \tag{3.18}$$

The denominator $P[R]$ is the probability of rejecting the null hypothesis or statistical power, that is, $P[R] = 1 - \beta$. We are most interested in ω given statistical power $P[R] \geq .8$.

The R code for calculating ω is

```
# d=Delta/sigma
# ud=U/sigma

omega<-function(n,d=.5,ud=.35){
    v=2*n-2
    lambda=sqrt(n/2)*d
    a=.05
    t0=qt(1-a/2,v)

    upper=(ud*sqrt(n*v/2)/t0)^2
    pwr1=integrate(function(x1){(1-pnorm(t0*sqrt(x1/v)
     -lambda))*dchisq(x1,v)}, 0, upper )$val
    pwr2=integrate(function(x2){ pnorm(-t0*sqrt(x2/v)
     -lambda)*dchisq(x2,v)
                   }, 0, upper )$val
    pwr=pwr1+pwr2

 power=pt(-t0,v,lambda)+1-pt(t0,v,lambda)
```

Table 3.2: Sample size, power, and omega

n	$1-\beta$	ω	n	$1-\beta$	ω
51	0.7056	0.0713	66	0.8135	0.6347
52	0.7141	0.0882	67	0.8193	0.6812
53	0.7224	0.1082	68	0.8250	0.7253
54	0.7306	0.1314	69	0.8305	0.7663
55	0.7385	0.1581	70	0.8358	0.8039
56	0.7462	0.1884	71	0.8410	0.8376
57	0.7538	0.2222	72	0.8461	0.8675
58	0.7611	0.2596	73	0.8510	0.8935
59	0.7683	0.3002	74	0.8557	0.9156
60	0.7753	0.3439	75	0.8604	0.9342
61	0.7821	0.3900	76	0.8649	0.9495
62	0.7887	0.4380	77	0.8692	0.9618
63	0.7952	0.4872	78	0.8735	0.9716
64	0.8015	0.5369	79	0.8776	0.9793
65	0.8076	0.5864	80	0.8816	0.9851

The table assumes $\Delta = 5$, $\sigma = 10$, and $U = 3.5$ (i.e., $\phi_{max} = U/\Delta = .7$).

```
return(pwr/power)
}

>omega(70)
>[1] 0.8038647
```

As with the z-test, achieving a short width can be expressed in terms of the precision-to-effect ratio ϕ. We can express the interval width as $w = \phi\Delta$ and the upper bound as $U = \phi_{max}\Delta$, where ϕ_{max} is the maximum tolerable precision-to-effect ratio. The probability $P[w \leq U]$ is equivalent to $P[\phi \leq \phi_{max}]$. In planning a study we can first specify Δ, σ, and ϕ_{max} and then find an appropriate sample size to achieve the desired power $(1 - \beta)$ and the conditional probability of obtaining ϕ_{max} conditional on the rejection of the null (i.e., ω).

For example, a researcher may be interested in examining the effect of daily exercise on lowering blood pressure. In a proposed study a sample of patients will be randomly assigned either to undergo daily exercise for six months or to no intervention. The researcher wants to determine the appropriate sample size for the significance test and the accompanying confidence interval in the case of a statistically significant result. The researcher learns from experience that 95% of the patients' blood pressures fall in the range of 140 to 180 mmHg. Using four standard deviations for 95% of the population range, the researcher infers that the population standard deviation is 10 mmHg ($\sigma = 10$). Suppose that a 5 mmHg difference in blood pressure is the minimum effect size of some clinical significance ($\Delta = 5$), and that the confidence interval is expected to be accurate to ± 3.5 mmHg (i.e., $U = 3.5$ or $\phi_{max} = \Delta/\sigma = .7$). It should be noted that the standardized effect size ($\delta = \Delta/\sigma$) and the maximum tolerable ϕ_{max} are sufficient to compute $1 - \beta$ and w, but it is advisable to estimate the simple effect size Δ and standard deviation σ separately. The unstandardized effect size Δ relates to the measurement scale of the study in a more straightforward way than does the standardized effect size δ. It is recommended that unstandardized effect size be used in reporting an effect (Baguley, 2009), and this is also true when planning a study. Table 3.2 lists sample size, statistical power, and the probability of achieving the desired interval width conditional on rejection of the null hypothesis. The researcher needs to choose the sample size $n = 70$ to keep both the statistical power and the probability w above .80.

Choosing the sample size for adequate statistical power in a t test may not necessarily produce a good chance of achieving the desired precision in the post-hoc confidence interval. As shown in Table 3.2, the probability of achieving a short width given the rejection of the null hypothesis can be low even when the statistical power is sufficiently high. For instance, at $n = 64$ the hypothesis test should have adequate statistical power ($1 - \beta = .8015$), but the precision of the following confidence interval would be poor ($w = .5369$). In other words, the chance of achieving the desired width after rejecting the null hypothesis is only a little better than the odds of getting a head in a coin flip. Thus, additional sampling is required to ratchet up the probability w. Unlike the z-test, a high statistical power of a t test does not deterministically translate to a fixed narrow width in the follow-up confidence interval. The minimum sample size for power above .80 yields about a 50% chance of obtaining $\phi \leq .7$ in the accompanying confidence interval when the minimum effect size is half

Table 3.3: Effect size, power, and omega

δ	n	$1-\beta$	ω
0.2	393	0.7996	0.5097
0.2	394	0.8006	0.5297
0.5	63	0.7952	0.4872
0.5	64	0.8015	0.5369
0.8	25	0.7915	0.4962
0.8	26	0.8075	0.5742

The probability ω assumes a maximum precision-to-effect ratio $\phi_{max} = .7$ (i.e., $\omega = P[\phi \leq \phi_{max}|R]$).

the standard deviation. It is easy to explain this intuitively because the estimated variance $\hat{\sigma}^2$ for the standard error can exceed the population variance σ^2 about half the time even though the unbiased estimator equals the population variance on average.

In short, sample size planning is very important in both null hypothesis testing and confidence interval estimation. A sufficient sample size is necessary to ensure a reasonable chance of rejecting the null hypothesis and confirming the research hypothesis in a significance test. Following a statistically significant result, a post-hoc confidence interval can be constructed to measure the magnitude of the treatment effect. Sample size also has great bearing on the width of the confidence interval. An inadequate sample size will likely return a large interval width, which is not informative about the size of the treatment effect. As high statistical power and estimate precision are essential to good statistical practice, sample size determination should become an integral part of any study planning.

The conditional probability ω offers a simple and coherent way to determine sample size for statistical power and estimate precision in a randomized experiment, the goal of which is to confirm the existence of the treatment effect in a hypothesis test and then to measure the size of the treatment effect in a confidence interval. The primary goal of the randomized experiment can be linked to statistical power, and the secondary goal can be tied to the probability of obtaining a short interval width conditional on the rejection of the null hypothesis. The interval width relative to the minimum effect size can be defined in a precision-to-effect ratio, $\phi = w/\Delta$.

As a rule of thumb, statistical power .80 for the t test yields about a 50% chance of obtaining a confidence interval accurate to $\pm.7\Delta$ (i.e., $\phi_{max} = .7$). Table 3.3 lists the standardized effect size δ, statistical power $1 - \beta$, and the conditional probability ω. The standardized effect size δ assumes Cohen's small, medium, and large effect sizes for simplicity of illustration (Cohen, 1988). It is obvious from Table 3.3 that the conditional probability ω is in the vicinity of .50 as the statistical power $1 - \beta$ approaches .80. In the remaining chapters, we will focus on statistical power in significance tests, although its implications for confidence intervals can be readily deduced from the rule-of-thumb numbers in Table 3.3.

3.4 Derivation of π_1 and ω

This section contains the technical details on mathematical derivation and computation, and it is included only for further reference. Readers who are not interested in technical details can skip the derivation without any disruption in reading the text.

If the confidence interval contains the parameter (event I), then we have

$$\overline{Y}_1 - \overline{Y}_2 - t_0\hat{\sigma}\sqrt{\frac{2}{n}} \leq \mu_1 - \mu_2 \leq \overline{Y}_1 - \overline{Y}_2 + t_0\hat{\sigma}\sqrt{\frac{2}{n}}$$

$$-t_0 \leq \frac{(\overline{Y}_1 - \overline{Y}_2) - (\mu_1 - \mu_2)}{\hat{\sigma}\sqrt{\frac{2}{n}}} \leq t_0$$

$$-t_0 \leq T \leq t_0$$

$$|T| \leq t_0, \qquad (3.19)$$

where t_0 is the critical value $t_{1-\alpha/2}$. The joint probability γ is the probability of width attainment $w \leq U$ and parameter inclusion I (i.e., $|T| \leq t_0$),

$$\gamma = P[w \leq U \cap I]$$

$$= P[w \leq U \cap |T| \leq t_0]$$

$$= P\left[\chi_\nu^2 \leq \frac{n\nu}{2t_0^2}\frac{U^2}{\sigma^2} \cap \left|T\frac{\hat{\sigma}}{\sigma}\right| \leq t_0\frac{\hat{\sigma}}{\sigma}\right]$$

$$= P\left[x \leq c \cap |Z| \leq t_0\sqrt{\frac{x}{\nu}}\right], \qquad (3.20)$$

where $v\hat{\sigma}^2/\sigma^2 \sim \chi_v^2$, $x = \chi_v^2$, and

$$c = \frac{nv}{2t_0^2}\frac{U^2}{\sigma^2}.$$

The joint probability γ can be computed by conditioning the probability on x and marginalizing the conditional probability $\gamma|x$,

$$\gamma = \int \gamma|x f(x)dx$$

$$= \int P[x \le c \cap |Z| \le t_0\sqrt{\frac{x}{v}}|x]f(x)dx$$

$$= \int_0^c \left[2\Phi\left(t_0\sqrt{\frac{x}{v}}\right) - 1\right]f(x)dx, \qquad (3.21)$$

where $f(x)$ is the density function of x. The power of confidence interval π_1 is $\gamma/(1-\alpha)$ by Bayes' theorem (Beal, 1989).

In calculating the probability $P[w \le U|R]$, we will first find the probability of obtaining a certain width $P[w \le U]$ and the probability of rejecting the null $P[R]$, and then we will combine the two probabilities. The probability of attaining a certain width can be transformed to a cumulative distribution for a chi square with degrees of freedom v

$$P[w \le U] = P\left[t_0\hat{\sigma}\sqrt{\frac{2}{n}} \le U\right]$$

$$= P\left[t_0\frac{\hat{\sigma}}{\sigma}\sqrt{\frac{2}{n}} \le \frac{U}{\sigma}\right]$$

$$= P\left[v\frac{\hat{\sigma}^2}{\sigma^2} \le \frac{nv}{2t_0^2}\frac{U^2}{\sigma^2}\right]$$

$$= P\left[x \le \frac{nv}{2t_0^2}\frac{U^2}{\sigma^2}\right]$$

$$= P[x \le c], \qquad (3.22)$$

where $v\hat{\sigma}^2/\sigma^2 \sim \chi_v^2$ (see Equation 1.14), and x is a chi square variate with v degrees of freedom.

The statistical power can be changed to

$$
P[R] = P\left[T' \geq t_0 \cup T' \leq -t_0\right]
$$

$$
= P\left[\frac{\overline{Y}_1 - \overline{Y}_2}{\hat{\sigma}\sqrt{2/n}} \geq t_0\right] + P\left[\frac{\overline{Y}_1 - \overline{Y}_2}{\hat{\sigma}\sqrt{2/n}} \leq -t_0\right]
$$

$$
= P\left[\frac{\overline{Y}_1 - \overline{Y}_2}{\sigma\sqrt{2/n}} \geq t_0\frac{\hat{\sigma}}{\sigma}\right] + P\left[\frac{\overline{Y}_1 - \overline{Y}_2}{\sigma\sqrt{2/n}} \leq -t_0\frac{\hat{\sigma}}{\sigma}\right]
$$

$$
= P\left[\frac{\overline{Y}_1 - \overline{Y}_2}{\sigma\sqrt{2/n}} - \frac{\Delta}{\sigma\sqrt{2/n}} \geq t_0\frac{\hat{\sigma}}{\sigma} - \frac{\Delta}{\sigma\sqrt{2/n}}\right] +
$$

$$
P\left[\frac{\overline{Y}_1 - \overline{Y}_2}{\sigma\sqrt{2/n}} - \frac{\Delta}{\sigma\sqrt{2/n}} \leq -t_0\frac{\hat{\sigma}}{\sigma} - \frac{\Delta}{\sigma\sqrt{2/n}}\right]
$$

$$
= P\left[Z \geq t_0\frac{\hat{\sigma}}{\sigma} - \lambda\right] + P\left[Z \leq -t_0\frac{\hat{\sigma}}{\sigma} - \lambda\right]
$$

$$
= P\left[Z \geq t_0\sqrt{\frac{x}{\nu}} - \lambda\right] + P\left[Z \leq -t_0\sqrt{\frac{x}{\nu}} - \lambda\right], \tag{3.23}
$$

where Z is the standard normal variate, λ is the non-centrality parameter, and x is a chi square with ν degrees of freedom.

Using the common variable x in these two probabilities, we can derive the joint probability of achieving a short width and rejecting the null hypothesis:

$$
P[w \leq U \cap R]
$$

$$
= P\left[x \leq c \cap \left(Z \geq t_0\sqrt{\frac{x}{\nu}} - \lambda \cup Z \leq -t_0\sqrt{\frac{x}{\nu}} - \lambda\right)\right]
$$

$$
= P\left[\left(x \leq c \cap Z \geq t_0\sqrt{\frac{x}{\nu}} - \lambda\right) \cup \left(x \leq c \cap Z \leq -t_0\sqrt{\frac{x}{\nu}} - \lambda\right)\right]
$$

$$
= P\left[x \leq c \cap Z \geq t_0\sqrt{\frac{x}{\nu}} - \lambda\right] + P\left[x \leq c \cap Z \leq -t_0\sqrt{\frac{x}{\nu}} - \lambda\right]
$$

$$
= \int_{x=0}^{c}\left[1 - \Phi\left(t_0\sqrt{\frac{x}{\nu}} - \lambda\right)\right]f(x)dx + \int_{x=0}^{c}\Phi\left(-t_0\sqrt{\frac{x}{\nu}} - \lambda\right)f(x)dx, \tag{3.24}
$$

where c is the upper limit of the integral, and $f(x)$ is the density function of a chi square with ν degrees of freedom. The conditional probability w can be computed as $P[w \leq U \cap R]/P[R]$ using Bayes' theorem (Liu, 2012).

Chapter 4

Analysis of Variance

Analysis of variance (ANOVA) is a collection of statistical methods used to compare more than two means. It extends the capability of a two sample independent t test, which is a special case of ANOVA. As ANOVA is computationally elegant and relatively robust against assumption violations, it has been widely used to analyze data from a variety of experimental designs. Even though ANOVA may involve multiple factors, the analytical approach remains the same. We will focus on one-way and two-way ANOVA without loss of generality. We will start with one-way ANOVA and then proceed to two-way ANOVA and random-effects ANOVA.

4.1 One-way Analysis of Variance

The null hypothesis in a one-way ANOVA states that all the means are equal;

$$H_0 : \mu_1 = \mu_2 = \dots = \mu_J.$$

Under the null hypothesis, the test statistic F follows a central F distribution.

$$F = \frac{\sum_{j=1}^{J} n_j (\bar{Y}_{.j} - \bar{Y}_{..})^2 / (J - 1)}{\sum_{j=1}^{J} \sum_{i=1}^{n_j} (Y_{ij} - \bar{Y}_{.j})^2 / (N - J)}, \tag{4.1}$$

where n_j is the sample size for the jth group, N is the total sample size $(\sum_{j=1}^{J} n_j)$, Y_{ij} is the outcome on the ith subject in the jth group, $\overline{Y}_{.j}$ is the jth group mean, and $\overline{Y}_{..}$ is the grand mean. The numerator of the F statistic divides the between-group sum of squares by its degrees of freedom $J - 1$. The numerator is called the between-group mean square (MST). The denominator of the F averages the within-group sum of squares over its degrees of freedom $N - J$. The denominator is, therefore, called the within-group mean square (MSE).

The between-group mean square measures the variance of the group means, which under the null hypothesis would not exist had it not been haphazard chance. The within-group mean square taps into the random variance that is not induced by the different treatments received but occurs naturally among individual subjects. The F statistic compares the variation in average group performance with the random variation in individual performance. If the null hypothesis is true, the group variation as measured by the between-group mean square will appear less prominent than the individual variation in the denominator. If the within-group mean square in the denominator of the F ratio prevails over the between-group mean square in the numerator, it will result in a small test statistic and a large p-value. The large p-value suggests that the empirical data do not contradict the null hypothesis; the null hypothesis will be retained. However, if the variation of the group means looks overwhelmingly large over the random variation due to individual random error, this suggests that the different treatments may have substantially differentiated the average group performance. In this case the large numerator of the F ratio can push the test statistic over its critical value, leading to statistical significance and rejection of the null hypothesis. The rejection of the null hypothesis makes the alternative hypothesis plausible.

The alternative hypothesis suggests that not all means are equal;

$$H_a : \mu_1 \neq \mu_2 \neq ... \neq \mu_J.$$

In other words, as long as any pair among the J number of means differs, the alternative hypothesis holds true. It opens up a variety of ways in which the J means can differ among themselves. The way they differ from each other determines the magnitude of effect size under the alternative hypothesis. The effect size influences the non-centrality parameter of the F

statistic, which assumes a non-central F distribution under the alternative hypothesis. To differentiate from the central F, we use F' to stand for the non-central F distribution. The non-centrality parameter of the F' statistic often baffles people, but there is an easy way to derive the non-centrality parameter λ.

4.1.1 Non-centrality Parameter in ANOVA

The non-centrality parameter λ is defined in terms of the population parameters in the ANOVA model:

$$Y_{ij} = \mu + \alpha_j + e_{ij}, \tag{4.2}$$

where μ is the population grand mean, α_j is the treatment effect due to the jth condition, and e_{ij} is the individual random error. The random error term is normally distributed with a variance σ^2 ($e_{ij} \sim N(0, \sigma^2)$). The treatment effect α_j is the difference between the population mean of the jth treatment (μ_j) and the population grand mean (μ), that is,

$$\alpha_j = \mu_j - \mu. \tag{4.3}$$

The non-centrality parameter λ can be obtained by replacing the elements of the F ratio in Equation 4.1 with their population counterparts. First, the within-group mean squares, which assesses the variance of the random error, equals its population counterpart σ^2 on average. In other words, the expected value of MSE is the variance of the random error σ^2. It is quite simple to derive this based on a well-known fact that a sample variance is an unbiased estimate of the population variance. Within the jth treatment group the sample variance is

$$\frac{\sum\limits_{i=1}^{n_j} (Y_{ij} - \overline{Y}_{.j})^2}{n_j - 1}. \tag{4.4}$$

Its expectation is equal to the variance σ^2,

$$E\left(\frac{\sum\limits_{i=1}^{n_j} (Y_{ij} - \overline{Y}_{.j})^2}{n_j - 1} \right) = \sigma^2. \tag{4.5}$$

Multiplying both sides by the group degrees of freedom $n_j - 1$ yields

$$E\left(\sum_{i=1}^{n_j}(Y_{ij} - \overline{Y}_{.j})^2\right) = (n_j - 1)\sigma^2. \tag{4.6}$$

Summing both sides of Equation 4.6 over all of the groups produces the expected value of the within-group sum of squares. Dividing the within-group sum of squares by its degrees of freedom $N - J$ produces the expected value of MSE;

$$E\left(\sum_{j=1}^{J}\sum_{i=1}^{n_j}(Y_{ij} - \overline{Y}_{.j})^2\right) = \sum_{j=1}^{J}(n_j - 1)\sigma^2$$

$$E\left(\sum_{j=1}^{J}\sum_{i=1}^{n_j}(Y_{ij} - \overline{Y}_{.j})^2\right) = (N - J)\sigma^2$$

$$E\left(\sum_{j=1}^{J}\sum_{i=1}^{n_j}(Y_{ij} - \overline{Y}_{.j})^2/(N - J)\right) = \sigma^2$$

$$E\left(MSE\right) = \sigma^2. \tag{4.7}$$

Replacing MSE in the F ratio by its expected value σ^2 gives

$$\frac{\sum_{j=1}^{J}n_j(\overline{Y}_{.j} - \overline{Y}_{..})^2/(J - 1)}{\sigma^2} = \sum_{j=1}^{J}\left(\frac{\overline{Y}_{.j} - \overline{Y}_{..}}{\sigma/\sqrt{n_j}}\right)^2/(J - 1). \tag{4.8}$$

Next replacing $\overline{Y}_{..}$ with its population counterpart μ in this equation produces

$$\sum_{j=1}^{J}\left(\frac{\overline{Y}_{.j} - \overline{Y}_{..}}{\sigma/\sqrt{n_j}}\right)^2/(J - 1) \Rightarrow \sum_{j=1}^{J}\left(\frac{\overline{Y}_{.j} - \mu}{\sigma/\sqrt{n_j}}\right)^2/(J - 1) = \sum_{j=1}^{J}Z_j^2/(J - 1), \tag{4.9}$$

where Z_j^2 is the squared normal variate. In effect, Equation 4.8 becomes a sum of squared normal variates over the degrees of freedom $J - 1$, which befits the definition of the numerator of the F distribution. The numerator of the F is a chi square over degrees of freedom $J - 1$. The sum of squared normal variates $\sum_{j=1}^{J}Z_j^2$ is a chi square by definition. As the estimation of the grand mean μ consumes one degree of freedom, the number of degrees of freedom for the chi square becomes J less one (i.e., $J - 1$). Under the null hypothesis, the group mean $\overline{Y}_{.j}$ equals the grand mean μ, which means $Z_j^2 \sim N(0, 1)$. Under the alternative hypothesis, $Z_j \sim N(\lambda_j, 1)$. Each Z_j deviates from the standard normal distribution with a non-zero mean λ_j,

$$\lambda_j = \frac{\mu_j - \mu}{\sigma / \sqrt{n_j}}. \tag{4.10}$$

The sum of squared λ_j becomes the non-centrality parameter for the chi square in the numerator of the F statistic, and that is also the non-centrality parameter for the non-central F', namely,

$$\begin{aligned}
\lambda &= \sum_{j=1}^{J} \lambda_j^2 \\
&= \sum_{j=1}^{J} \left(\frac{\mu_j - \mu}{\sigma / \sqrt{n_j}} \right)^2 \\
&= \sum_{j=1}^{J} n_j (\mu_j - \mu)^2 / \sigma^2 \\
&= \sum_{j=1}^{J} n_j \alpha_j^2 / \sigma^2,
\end{aligned} \tag{4.11}$$

where $\alpha_j = \mu_j - \mu$.

The non-centrality parameter can also be viewed as the weighted sum of squares of treatment means μ_j (Liu and Raudenbush, 2004). The weights are calculated from the reciprocal of the variance of the treatment mean estimate $\hat{\mu}_j$ or the precision of the treatment mean estimate;

$$w_j = \frac{1}{var(\hat{\mu}_j)} = \frac{1}{\frac{\sigma^2}{n_j}}. \tag{4.12}$$

The non-centrality parameter can be expressed in terms of those weights;

$$\lambda = \sum_{j=1}^{J} w_j (\mu_j - \mu)^2, \tag{4.13}$$

where the grand mean μ is a weighted mean;

$$\mu = \frac{\sum\limits_{j=1}^{J} n_j \mu_j}{\sum\limits_{j=1}^{J} n_j} = \frac{\sum\limits_{j=1}^{J} w_j \mu_j}{\sum\limits_{j=1}^{J} w_j}. \tag{4.14}$$

Thus, the non-centrality parameter measures the variation in treatment means just as the sum of squares in the sample variance assesses the variability in the sample data. The more varied the treatment means are, the larger the non-centrality parameter. In this way, the non-centrality parameter shows how the alternative hypothesis is deviated from the null hypothesis.

It is worth noting two special cases of the non-centrality parameter. First, when the groups have equal sample sizes, the non-centrality parameter can be simplified to

$$\lambda = \sum_{j=1}^{J} n\alpha_j^2 / \sigma^2.$$

Second, if there are only two groups involved, the non-centrality parameter becomes

$$\lambda = \frac{n}{\sigma^2}\left[(\mu_1 - \mu)^2 + (\mu_2 - \mu)^2\right]$$
$$= \frac{n}{\sigma^2}\left[\left(\mu_1 - \frac{\mu_1 + \mu_2}{2}\right)^2 + \left(\mu_2 - \frac{\mu_1 + \mu_2}{2}\right)^2\right]$$
$$= \frac{n}{2}\frac{(\mu_1 - \mu_2)^2}{\sigma^2}. \tag{4.15}$$

This is simply the squared non-centrality parameter for the non-central T' in the two sample independent t test because the t test is a special case of ANOVA. Squaring the t test produces an F statistic.

Previously, we derived the non-centrality parameter by replacing the sample estimates with their population counterparts. If we reverse the process, we can replace the population parameters in the non-centrality parameter with their sample estimates. We can easily see that the test statistic F is an estimate of the non-centrality parameter λ. Substituting $\overline{Y}_{.j}$

for μ_j, $\overline{Y}_{..}$ for μ, and MSE for σ^2 in Equation 4.11 produces an estimated non-centrality parameter,

$$\hat{\lambda} = \frac{\sum\limits_{j=1}^{J} n_j (\overline{Y}_{.j} - \overline{Y}_{..})^2}{MSE} = (J-1)F. \qquad (4.16)$$

So the F statistic is an estimate of the non-centrality parameter, albeit averaged by the number of groups less one; $F = \hat{\lambda}/(J-1)$. It is worth noting that the non-centrality parameter measures the overall variation among treatment means by using the sum of squares, whereas the F statistic adjusts such a measure by the number of groups present in the study. In one sense, the F statistic assesses the average squared distance between the group mean and the grand mean, much like a sample variance.

4.1.2   Statistical Power for the F Test

The statistical power of the F test is the probability of having an F statistic exceeding its critical value F_0. The critical value F_0 is the $100(1-\alpha)$ quantile of a central F distribution ($F_0 = F_{1-\alpha;\nu_1;\nu_2}$). There are two degrees of freedom: one in the numerator, $\nu_1 = J-1$, and the other in the denominator, $\nu_2 = N-J$. Since we seek to obtain a significant statistic in the presence of mean differences, we are most interested in the non-central F statistic F', which under the alternative hypothesis has two degrees of freedom ν_1 and ν_2, with a non-centrality parameter $\lambda = \sum n_j \alpha_j^2 / \sigma^2$ as in Equation 4.11. We can denote the non-central F as $F'(\nu_1, \nu_2, \lambda)$. The power function $1-\beta$ is therefore

$$\begin{aligned} 1 - \beta &= P[F'(\nu_1, \nu_2, \lambda) \geq F_0] \\ &= 1 - P[F'(\nu_1, \nu_2, \lambda) < F_0]. \qquad (4.17) \end{aligned}$$

The probability $P[F'(\nu_1, \nu_2, \lambda) < F_0]$ is the cumulative distribution function for the non-central F distribution.

For example, a researcher may be interested in the effect of exercise intensity and diet control on weight loss. In the study, a sample of obese children are randomly assigned to three groups of equal numbers. The first group of children are expected to undergo exercise twice a week; the second group of children will exercise five times per week; and the third

Table 4.1: Statistical power for the F test

n	$1 - \beta$
5	0.5820
6	0.6899
7	0.7753
8	0.8404
9	0.8886
10	0.9235
11	0.9482
12	0.9653

group will exercise five times every week and limit their daily sugar intake. The intervention will last for three months before the participants' weight loss is measured. ANOVA will be used to test the mean differences in weight loss. In running power analysis for the ANOVA, the researcher gleans from similar studies that the standard deviation in weight loss is 4 kg among children who undergo a weight loss regimen with potential average weight losses of 8 kg for the first group, 11 kg for the second group, and 15 kg for the third group. The statistical power for the F test can be calculated based on Equation 4.17. The non-centrality parameter assumes $\sigma = 4$, $\mu_1 = 8$, $\mu_2 = 11$, and $\mu_3 = 15$,

$$\lambda = n \frac{(8 - \frac{8+11+15}{3})^2 + (11 - \frac{8+11+15}{3})^2 + (15 - \frac{8+11+15}{3})^2}{4^2}$$

$$= 1.541666667n$$

The power function (see Table 4.1) is

$$1 - \beta = 1 - P[F'(2, 3n - 3, \lambda) < F_{1-\alpha,2,3n-3}].$$

The researcher may plot the power function over n in searching for an appropriate sample size (see Figure 4.1).

The R code is:

```
mu<-c(8,11,15)
s<-4
```

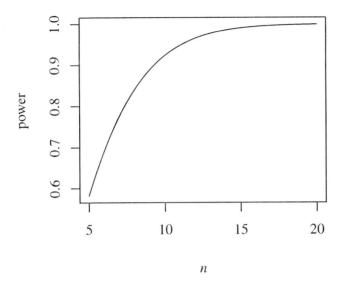

Figure 4.1: Statistical power vs. sample size n

```
p4f=function(n,mu,s,a=.05){
  nu1=length(mu)-1
  nu2=length(mu)*(n-1)
  f0=qf(1-a,nu1,nu2)
  lambda=n*sum( (mu -mean(mu))^2 )/s^2

  return(1-pf(f0,nu1,nu2,lambda))
}

#table 4.1
for(n in 5:12){cat("n=", n, "\t", "power=",
      p4f(n,mu,s), "\n")}

#figure 4.1
curve(p4f(x,mu,s),5,20, ylab="Power", xlab="n").
```

The following SAS program computes the power for the overall F test and plots the power against sample size n:

```
proc power;
* proc power plotonly; /*plotonly produces only the plot */
  onewayanova test=overall
    groupmeans = 8 | 11 | 15
    stddev = 4
    npergroup = 5 to 12
    power = .;
  plot x=n min=5 max=20;
run;
```

The relevant SPSS syntax is as follows:

```
*STATISTICAL POWER IN ONE-WAY ANOVA.
NEW FILE.
INPUT PROGRAM.
COMPUTE A=.05.
COMPUTE STDEV=4.
COMPUTE N=0.
COMPUTE J=3.
COMPUTE V=0.
COMPUTE NC=0.
COMPUTE P=0.

LEAVE A TO P.
 LOOP N=5 TO 12.
   COMPUTE V=J*(N-1).
   COMPUTE NC=N*(J-1)*VARIANCE(8,11,15)/STDEV**2.
   COMPUTE P=1- NCDF.F(IDF.F(1-A,J-1,V),J-1,V,NC).
   END CASE.
 END LOOP.
END FILE.
END INPUT PROGRAM.
EXECUTE.

DELETE VARIABLES A STDEV J V NC.
VARIABLE LABELS P 'Power'.
LIST.
```

```
GRAPH
  /LINE(SIMPLE)=VALUE(P) BY N
  /TITLE='Statistical power vs sample size in one-way ANOVA'.
```

4.1.3   Statistical Power for Contrast Tests

The F test checks whether there is any difference among means. It does not show which pairs of means differ. After a significant overall F test, one may follow up with simultaneous pair-wise comparison tests to locate the mean differences among treatment conditions.

To compare the mean for the jth group and the j'th group ($H_0 : \mu_j = \mu_{j'}$), we can apply the t test;

$$T = \frac{\overline{Y}_j - \overline{Y}_{j'}}{\hat{\sigma}\sqrt{\frac{1}{n_j} + \frac{1}{n_{j'}}}}, \qquad (4.18)$$

where $\overline{Y}_j$ and $\overline{Y}_{j'}$ are the group means, and n_j and $n_{j'}$ are the group sizes. The estimated standard deviation is $\hat{\sigma} = \sqrt{MSE}$ because the expectation of MSE is σ^2 (see Equation 4.7) and its square root is an unbiased estimate of σ. As MSE is used to estimate $\hat{\sigma}$, its degrees of freedom $N - J$ become the degrees of freedom for the t statistic.

The statistical power for the two-sided t test is

$$1 - \beta = 1 - P[T'(N - J, \lambda) < t_{1-\frac{\alpha}{2m}, N-J}] + P[T'(N - J, \lambda) \le t_{\frac{\alpha}{2m}, N-J}], \qquad (4.19)$$

where m is the number of simultaneous comparison tests. The Bonferroni adjustment divides the significance level α by m to control for the family-wise Type-I error rate in the m simultaneous tests. When the alternative hypothesis is true, the two means differ (i.e., $\mu_j - \mu_{j'} \ne 0$). The t statistic follows a non-central t distribution T' with a non-centrality parameter λ similar to that in the regular two sample independent t test;

$$\lambda = \sqrt{\frac{n_j n_{j'}}{n_j + n_{j'}}} \frac{\mu_j - \mu_{j'}}{\sigma}. \qquad (4.20)$$

The power computation is basically the same as that in the regular t test, except that the significance level and the degrees of freedom are α/m and $N - J$.

The contrast tests may occasionally involve a complex comparison of treatment means, which can be expressed as a weighted sum of all the treatment means in the null hypothesis,

$$H_0 : \phi = c_1\mu_1 + c_2\mu_2 + \dots + c_J\mu_J \neq 0, \qquad (4.21)$$

where the weights c must sum to zero ($\sum_{j=1}^{J} c_j = 0$). For instance, the complex comparison may compare the average mean of the two treatment conditions with the control condition,

$$\phi = \frac{1}{2}\mu_1 + \frac{1}{2}\mu_2 - \mu_3.$$

To test the complex comparison in the null hypothesis, we can still use a t statistic. The sample estimate of the complex comparison simply involves substituting the sample means for the population means in ϕ,

$$\hat{\phi} = \frac{1}{2}\overline{Y}_1 + \frac{1}{2}\overline{Y}_2 - \overline{Y}_3.$$

The variance of the estimate is the weighted sum of the respective variances of the sample means. Since $Var(\overline{Y}_j) = \sigma^2/n_j$, we can obtain

$$Var(c_j\overline{Y}_j) = c_j^2\sigma^2/n_j.$$

For instance, when the average mean of the first two treatment conditions is compared with the mean of the third condition, the variance of the contrast is

$$Var(\hat{\phi}) = \left(\frac{1}{2}\right)^2 \frac{\sigma^2}{n_1} + \left(\frac{1}{2}\right)^2 \frac{\sigma^2}{n_2} + (-1)^2\frac{\sigma^2}{n_3}. \qquad (4.22)$$

If we use MSE to replace σ^2, we obtain the estimated variance

$$\widehat{Var}(\hat{\phi}) = MSE \left(\left(\frac{1}{2}\right)^2 \frac{1}{n_1} + \left(\frac{1}{2}\right)^2 \frac{1}{n_2} + (-1)^2\frac{1}{n_3} \right).$$

Taking the square root of the estimated variance produces the standard error of the contrast estimate. The estimate $\hat{\phi}$ divided by its standard error forms a t statistic. In general, we can express the t test for the complex comparison as

$$T = \frac{\hat{\phi}}{\widehat{Var}(\hat{\phi})}$$
$$= \frac{c_1 \overline{Y}_1 + c_2 \overline{Y}_2 + \dots + c_J \overline{Y}_J}{\sqrt{MSE \left(\frac{c_1^2}{n_1} + \frac{c_2^2}{n_2} + \dots + \frac{c_J^2}{n_J} \right)}}. \tag{4.23}$$

If the null hypothesis is true, the complex comparison of means on average evaluates to zero. The test statistic T follows a central t distribution with degrees of freedom $N - J$.

When the alternative hypothesis is true, the complex comparison of the means does not average zero (i.e., $H_a : \phi = c_1 \mu_1 + c_2 \mu_2 + \dots + c_J \mu_J \neq 0$). The statistical power for testing the non-zero ϕ is

$$1 - \beta = 1 - P[T'(N - J, \lambda) < t_{1-\frac{\alpha}{2}, N-J)}] + P[T'(N - J, \lambda) \leq t_{\frac{\alpha}{2}, N-J)}]. \tag{4.24}$$

The expression of the power function bears the same elements as that in the simple contrast except that there is no Bonferroni adjustment. One may forgo the necessity of the overall F test if the key interest lies in the complex comparisons.

The non-centrality parameter λ takes a different form for the complex contrast test;

$$\lambda = \frac{c_1 \mu_1 + c_2 \mu_2 + \dots + c_J \mu_J}{\sqrt{\sigma^2 \left(\frac{c_1^2}{n_1} + \frac{c_2^2}{n_2} + \dots + \frac{c_J^2}{n_J} \right)}}. \tag{4.25}$$

It is interesting to note the correspondence between the test statistic T and its non-centrality parameter λ. Replacing the sample estimates with their population counterparts in T produces the non-centrality parameter λ. In other words, the test statistic T is a sample estimate of the non-centrality parameter, which shows by how much the alternative hypothesis deviates from the null hypothesis.

A set of complex comparisons can be made a priori without the overall F test. By convention, a-priori orthogonal contrast tests do not require Bonferroni adjustment, which boosts the statistical power because the significance level is inversely related to statistical power. In practice, researchers can choose to use a set of orthogonal contrasts. The set of weights in each contrast still sum to zero, but the cross products of the weights between any two contrasts add up to zero, that is, the sets of weights among different contrasts are orthogonal to each other. Such a set of contrasts are called orthogonal contrasts. There can be no more than $J - 1$ contrasts in a set of orthogonal contrasts, although many more such sets exist. For instance, the previous contrast,

$$\phi_1 = \frac{1}{2}\mu_1 + \frac{1}{2}\mu_2 - \mu_3,$$

is orthogonal to the contrast

$$\phi_2 = 1 \times \mu_1 - 1 \times \mu_2 + 0 \times \mu_3.$$

The first contrast has weight coefficients $1/2, 1/2, -1$ for the three treatment means, and the second contrast uses weights $1, -1$, and 0. The cross products of the weights add to zero;

$$\frac{1}{2} \times 1 + \frac{1}{2} \times -1 + (-1) \times 0 = 0.$$

Since there are three treatment conditions ($J = 3$), there are only two orthogonal contrasts at a time.

The statistical power for orthogonal contrasts uses the same power function as Equation 4.24. Each orthogonal contrast test yields a non-centrality parameter λ_m ($m = 1, 2, ... J - 1$). The sum of squared λ_m is equal to the non-centrality parameter of the overall F test in Equation 4.11 (Liu, 2010),

$$\sum_{m=1}^{J-1} \lambda_m^2 = \sum_{j=1}^{J} n(\mu_j - \mu)^2/\sigma^2. \tag{4.26}$$

For illustration, we can continue to use the previous example of weight loss. The first group of children exercise twice a week; the second group five times a week; and the third group five times per week with limited sugar intake. It is assumed that after three months the weight loss for the first group is 8 kg, 11 kg for the second group, and 15 kg for the third (i.e., $\mu_1 = 8$, $\mu_2 = 11$, and $\mu_3 = 15$). The standard deviation σ is still set to 4 kg. First, we are interested in comparing the average weight loss of the second and third groups with the weight loss of the first group. This corresponds to the contrast $\frac{\mu_2 + \mu_3}{2} - \mu_1$. Second, we want to compare the weight loss between the second and third groups or $\mu_3 - \mu_2$. It is obvious that the two contrasts are orthogonal to each other, and both contrast tests can use a t statistic with degrees of freedom $N - J$. According to Equation 4.25, the non-centrality parameter for the first contrast λ_1 is

$$\lambda_1 = \frac{\frac{11+15}{2} - 8}{4\sqrt{\left(\left(\frac{1}{2}\right)^2 + \left(\frac{1}{2}\right)^2 + (-1)^2\right)/n}}.$$

The second contrast has a non-centrality parameter λ_2;

$$\lambda_2 = \frac{15 - 11}{4\sqrt{(1^2 + (-1)^2)/n}}.$$

It is easy to verify that the squared non-centrality parameters for the two orthogonal contrast tests add up to the non-centrality parameter of the omnibus F test, namely, $\lambda_1^2 + \lambda_2^2 = 1.541666667n$.

The following R code computes statistical power for the two orthogonal contrast tests. Suppose that the contrast tests are expected to be done on an a-priori basis without Bonferroni adjustment. Figure 4.2 portrays the statistical power for the two orthogonal contrast tests. The solid line represents the first contrast test; the dashed line the second contrast test. As the first contrast has a larger effect size than the second one, there is some noticeable difference in power between the two contrast tests.

```
#contrast tests
c1=c(.5,.5,-1)
c2=c(1,-1,0)
phi1=(15+11)/2-8
phi2=15-11

p=function(n=5,J=3,phi=phi1,c=c1,s=4){
   a=.05
   t0=qt(1-a/2,J*(n-1))
   nc=phi/(s*sqrt(sum(c^2)/n))
   1-pt(t0,J*(n-1),nc)+pt(-t0,J*(n-1),nc)
}
```

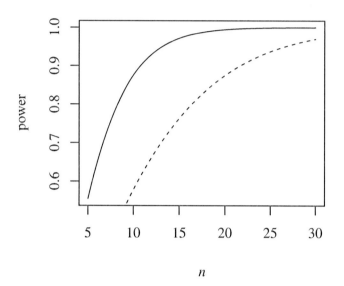

Figure 4.2: Statistical power in post-hoc contrast tests

```
for(n in 5:30) cat('n=',n,'\t','power=',p(n),'\n')
for(n in 5:30) cat('n=',n,'\t','power=',p(n,c=c2,phi=phi2),'\n')

curve(p(x),5,30,ylab="power",xlab="n")
curve(p(x,c=c2,phi=phi2),5,30,add=TRUE,lty=2)
```

In SAS, the onewayanova statement in the proc power procedure calculates statistical power in a contrast test. It can be used to produce Figure
4.2.

```
* power for contrast test;
proc power plotonly;
  onewayanova test=contrast
    contrast = (-1 .5 .5) (0 -1 1)
    groupmeans = 8 | 11 | 15
    stddev = 4
    npergroup = 5 to 30
    power = .;
```

```
  plot x=n min=5 max=30;
run;
```

If the option `plotonly` is left out, the SAS program will produce the plot as well as the power values for the specified range of sample size (i.e., npergroup = 5 to 30).

The SPSS syntax uses INPUT PROGRAMS ... END INPUT PROGRAM to run the LOOP. In each iteration of the loop, statistical power is computed for the two contrast tests. The power values can be plotted on a graph through the command GRAPH.

```
*STATISTICAL POWER IN CONTRAST TESTS.
NEW FILE.
INPUT PROGRAM.
COMPUTE A=.05.
COMPUTE STDEV=4.
COMPUTE N=0.
COMPUTE J=3.
COMPUTE V=0.
COMPUTE NC1=0.
COMPUTE NC2=0.
COMPUTE P1=0.
COMPUTE P2=0.

LEAVE A TO P2.
 LOOP N=5 TO 30.
   COMPUTE V=J*(N-1).
   COMPUTE NC1=(15*.5+11*.5-8)/STDEV*SQRT(N)/
   SQRT((J-1)*VARIANCE(.5,.5,-1)).
   COMPUTE NC2=(15*1+11*-1)/STDEV*SQRT(N)/
   SQRT((J-1)*VARIANCE(1,-1,0)).
   COMPUTE P1=1- NCDF.T(IDF.T(1-A/2,V),V,NC1) +
              NCDF.T(IDF.T(A/2,V),V,NC1).
   COMPUTE P2=1- NCDF.T(IDF.T(1-A/2,V),V,NC2) +
              NCDF.T(IDF.T(A/2,V),V,NC2).
   END CASE.
 END LOOP.
END FILE.
```

```
END INPUT PROGRAM.
EXECUTE.

DELETE VARIABLES A STDEV V NC1 NC2.
VARIABLE LABELS P1 'Power for contrast (.5,.5,-1)'
               P2 'Power for contrast (1,-1,0)' .
LIST.
GRAPH
  /LINE(MULTIPLE)=VALUE(P1 P2) BY N
  /TITLE='Statistical power for contrast'+
        '(.5,.5,-1) and (1,-1,0)'.
```

4.2   Two-way Analysis of Variance

The two-way ANOVA relates the outcome measure to two factors. It is an extension of the one-way ANOVA except that the model now includes two main effects and one interaction effect. The interaction effect suggests that the treatment mean is uniquely determined based on the specific levels of both factors. In the presence of an interaction effect, the main effect loses its importance. The main effect of either factor is no longer consistent across different levels of the other factor. We will discuss the statistical power first for the main effects and then for an interaction effect.

4.2.1   Statistical Power for Testing Main Effects

The statistical model for a two-way ANOVA is

$$Y_{ijk} = \mu + \alpha_j + \beta_k + \alpha\beta_{ij} + e_{ijk}, \ (i:1,...,n; j=1,...,J; k=1,...,K) \quad (4.27)$$

where Y_{ijk} is the outcome for the ith subject in the jth condition (level) of factor A within the kth condition (level) of factor B, μ is the grand mean, α_j is the effect due to the jth level of factor A, β_k is the effect due to the kth level of factor B, $\alpha\beta_{ij}$ is the interaction associated with the combination of the jth level of factor A and the kth level of factor B, and e_{ij} is the individual random error ($e_{ijk} \sim N(0, \sigma^2)$).

The statistical test for either main effect (A or B) is similar to that in testing a single factor in one-way ANOVA. The test is still an F ratio with the between-group mean square (MST) in the numerator and the within-group mean square (MSE) in the denominator. For simplicity of illustration, we assume a balanced design with equal sample size n in each combination of both factors or each cell. The within-group mean square is the sum of all the within-cell sum of squares divided by the sum of the cell degrees of freedom $JK(n-1)$.

$$MSE = \frac{\sum\limits_{k=1}^{K}\sum\limits_{j=1}^{J}\sum\limits_{i=1}^{n} Y_{ijk} - \overline{Y}_{.jk}}{JK(n-1)}, \tag{4.28}$$

where $\overline{Y}_{.jk}$ is the cell mean, and $n-1$ is the degrees of freedom for each cell. There are JK cells in the two-way factorial ANOVA. To find the between-group mean square for factor A, we may ignore the existence of factor B and aggregate data over all the levels of factor B. This leaves us with J means $\overline{Y}_{.j.}$, which are aggregated over all the levels of factor B. The between-group mean square for factor A (MSA) is

$$MSA = \frac{\sum\limits_{j=1}^{J} nK(\overline{Y}_{.j.} - \overline{Y}_{...})^2}{J-1}, \tag{4.29}$$

where $\overline{Y}_{...}$ is the grand average of all the observations of the outcome.

$$F = \frac{MSA}{MSE}.$$

Under the null hypothesis, the F ratio follows a central F distribution with degrees of freedom $J-1$ in the numerator and $JK(n-1)$ in the denominator. The F test for factor A bears great resemblance to its counterpart in one-way ANOVA, and so does its power function.

The statistical power for testing the main effect of factor A uses the same formula as that in one-way ANOVA except that the degrees of freedom and the non-centrality parameter have changed,

$$1 - \beta = 1 - P[F'(\nu_1, \nu_2, \lambda_A) < F_0], \tag{4.30}$$

where ν_1 and ν_2 are $J-1$ and $JK(n-1)$, respectively. The non-centrality parameter is slightly different because the jth level aggregated over all the levels of factor B now contains Kn subjects. So changing the sample size n_j to Kn in the non-centrality for the one-way ANOVA (Equation 4.11) yields the non-central parameter for the test of factor A in the two-way ANOVA,

$$\lambda_A = \sum_{j=1}^{J} Kn\alpha_j^2/\sigma^2. \qquad (4.31)$$

Similarly, we can construct an F ratio to test factor B. In testing factor B, we aggregate the data over the levels of factor A and obtain the between-group mean square for factor B (MSB),

$$MSB = \frac{\sum_{k=1}^{K} nJ(\overline{Y}_{..k} - \overline{Y}_{...})^2}{K-1}. \qquad (4.32)$$

The F ratio uses MSB as the numerator and MSE (Equation 4.28) as the denominator;

$$F = \frac{MSB}{MSE}.$$

When the null hypothesis is true, the F ratio has a central F distribution with degrees of freedom $K-1$ in the numerator and $JK(n-1)$ in the denominator. Under the alternative hypothesis, the power function is similar to Equation 4.30, except that the degrees of freedom and the non-centrality parameter are different.

$$1 - \beta = 1 - P[F'(\nu_1, \nu_2, \lambda_B) < F_0], \qquad (4.33)$$

where $\nu_1 = K - 1$ and $\nu_2 = JK(n-1)$. The non-centrality parameter becomes

$$\lambda_B = \sum_{k=1}^{K} Jn\beta_k^2/\sigma^2. \qquad (4.34)$$

The effect β_k is the difference between the aggregated mean μ_k for the kth level of factor B and the grand mean μ, similar to the definition for α_j;

$$\beta_k = \mu_k - \mu. \qquad (4.35)$$

To illustrate power analysis for main effects, we can use an experimental study on sleep deprivation and reaction time in a two-way factorial design without interaction. Sleep deprivation can impair one's perceptual and motor skills, which can lead to accidents while driving (Philip et al, 2005). An experimental psychologist wants to study how sleep deprivation may affect young adults' reaction times under different driving conditions. Their sleep times (factor A) will be restricted to 3 hours, 4 hours, and 5 hours on the day before a simulated driving test. The driving condition (factor B) takes two levels: complex and simple. Each driving condition includes a few similar scenarios that call for visual perception, mental reasoning, and muscle coordination. The average reaction time will be recorded in milliseconds for each participating subject. A group of college students in good health will be recruited to participate in a randomized experiment. They will be randomly assigned to the six combination conditions of factors A and B. They will undergo the required sleep restriction and take the test on the driving simulator the next morning. The psychologist estimates that the mean reaction time in milliseconds (ms) is 650 ms for 5 hours' sleep, 670 ms for 4 hours' sleep, and 720 ms for 3 hours' sleep (i.e., $\mu_{1.} = 650$, $\mu_{2.} = 670$, $\mu_{3.} = 720$). The average reaction time for the simple driving condition is 660 ms and 700 ms for the complex driving condition (i.e., $\mu_{.1} = 660$, $\mu_{.2} = 700$). The hypothesized means are really the marginal means in Table 4.2. In addition, any interaction effect between factors A and B is ruled out.

Table 4.2: Marginal means in a 3×2 ANOVA

	simple driving	complex driving	
5 hours			650
4 hours			670
3 hours			720
	660	700	680

The grand mean of the reaction time is 680 ms ($\mu = 680$). The standard deviation of the reaction time is assumed to be 110 ms (i.e., $\sigma = 110$). If forty subjects are used in each of the six combination conditions ($n = 40$), the statistical power will be .97 for testing factor A and .80 for testing factor B (see the R code, next, and Figure 4.3).

```
pa=function(n=25,J=3,K=2,s=110,mua=c(650,670,720)){
```

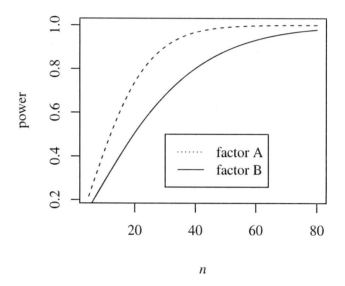

Figure 4.3: Statistical power for testing factors A and B

```
a=.05
v1=length(mua)-1
v2=J*K*(n-1)
ss=var(mua)*v1
nc=n*K*ss/s^2
f0=qf(1-a,v1,v2)
1-pf(f0,v1,v2,nc)
}

pb=function(n=25,J=3,K=2,s=110,mub=c(660,700)){
a=.05
v1=length(mub)-1
v2=J*K*(n-1)
ss=var(mub)*v1
nc=n*J*ss/s^2
f0=qf(1-a,v1,v2)
1-pf(f0,v1,v2,nc)
}
```

```
pa(40)
pb(40)

curve(pa(x),5,80,ylab="Power",xlab="n",lty=2)
curve(pb(x),5,80,add=TRUE)
legend(30,.5,legend=c("factor A","factor B"),
lty=c("dotted","solid"))
```

4.2.2 Statistical Power for Testing Interaction

The example of sleep deprivation does not assume any interaction effect between factors A and B. The effect of one factor is constant across the different levels of the other factor. In the absence of any interaction effect, the cell means in Table 4.2 can be filled out easily. Table 4.3 shows the cell means without any interaction effect. Any deviation from the listed cell means in Table 4.3 indicates an interaction effect.

Table 4.3: Cell means in absence of interaction effect

	simple driving	complex driving	
5 hours	630	670	650
4 hours	650	690	670
3 hours	700	740	720
	660	700	680

The interaction effect can be expressed in terms of the main effects α_j and β_k. We first relate the outcome observation to the cell mean,

$$Y_{ijk} = \mu_{jk} + e_{ijk},\tag{4.36}$$

where Y_{ijk} is the outcome observation, μ_{jk} is the cell mean, and e_{ijk} is an individual random error. Comparing this equation with

$$Y_{ijk} = \mu + \alpha_j + \beta_k + \alpha\beta_{ij} + e_{ijk},$$

we then have the cell mean μ_{ij} as a linear function of the main effects and the interaction between factors A and B,

$$\mu_{ij} = \mu + \alpha_j + \beta_k + \alpha\beta_{ij}.\tag{4.37}$$

Rearranging the elements in Equation 4.37, we can express the interaction in terms of α_j and β_k;

$$\alpha\beta_{jk} = \mu_{jk} - \mu - \alpha_j - \beta_k. \tag{4.38}$$

The estimated interaction effect can be obtained by replacing the population parameters with their sample estimates,

$$\widehat{\alpha\beta}_{jk} = \overline{Y}_{.jk} - \overline{Y}_{...} - (\overline{Y}_{.j.} - \overline{Y}_{...}) - (\overline{Y}_{..k} - \overline{Y}_{...})$$
$$= \overline{Y}_{.jk} - \overline{Y}_{.j.} - \overline{Y}_{..k} + \overline{Y}_{...}, \tag{4.39}$$

where $\overline{Y}_{.j.} - \overline{Y}_{...}$ and $\overline{Y}_{..k} - \overline{Y}_{...}$ are the sample estimates of α_j and β_k, respectively.

The test for the interaction effect uses an F ratio with the same within-group mean squares MSE in the denominator and the interaction mean square $MSAB$ in the numerator.

$$F = \frac{MSAB}{MSE}, \tag{4.40}$$

where

$$MSAB = \frac{\sum\limits_{k=1}^{K} \sum\limits_{j=1}^{J} n(\overline{Y}_{.jk} - \overline{Y}_{.j.} - \overline{Y}_{..k} + \overline{Y}_{...})^2}{(J-1)(K-1)}. \tag{4.41}$$

In the absence of any interaction under $H_0 : \alpha\beta_{jk} = 0$, the F ratio has a central distribution with degrees of freedom $(J-1)(K-1)$ in the numerator and $JK(n-1)$ in the denominator.

We can use the function $1 - P[F'(\nu_1, \nu_2, \lambda_{AB}) < F_0]$ to compute the statistical power for testing the interaction effect under the alternative hypothesis $(H_a : \alpha\beta_{jk} \neq 0)$. The two degrees of freedom are $\nu_1 = (J-1)(K-1)$ and $\nu_2 = JK(n-1)$. The non-centrality parameter λ_{AB} can be derived from the sum of squares for the interaction $SSAB$, which is the numerator of $MSAB$ in Equation 4.41,

$$SSAB = \sum\limits_{k=1}^{K} \sum\limits_{j=1}^{J} n(\overline{Y}_{.jk} - \overline{Y}_{.j.} - \overline{Y}_{..k} + \overline{Y}_{...})^2. \tag{4.42}$$

Replacing the sample means by their population means and dividing the sum of squares by σ^2 produces the non-centrality parameter in the F test for the interaction effect,

$$\lambda = \sum_{k=1}^{K} \sum_{j=1}^{J} n(\mu_{jk} - \mu_j - \mu_k + \mu)^2 / \sigma^2. \qquad (4.43)$$

The non-centrality parameter for the interaction test comprises sample size n, variance σ^2, and the effect size for the interaction

$$\sum_{k=1}^{K} \sum_{j=1}^{J} (\mu_{jk} - \mu_j - \mu_k + \mu)^2.$$

To calculate the effect size for an interaction, one needs to know the population means for all the unique combinations of the two factors. It is often tedious to spell out all the population means in the two-way table. If the study uses a three-by-two factorial design, there are six cell means. A researcher may not easily figure out all the population means for the six cells at one time. However, there is a much easy way to estimate the effect size for the interaction.

The effect size for the interaction is basically a sum of squares, which can be decomposed to distinctive parts associated with orthogonal contrasts. The ANOVA model can be rewritten in a regression equation with orthogonal coding for the main effects and the interaction effects. For simplicity of illustration, we use the cell means model in a three-by-two factorial design,

$$\mu_{jk} = \beta_0 + \beta_1 X_{1jk} + \beta_2 X_{2jk} + \beta_3 X_{3jk} + \beta_4 X_{4jk} + \beta_5 X_{5jk},$$
$$j = 1, 2, 3 \text{ and } k = 1, 2,$$

where the Xs are the predictors based on orthogonal coding. The first two predictors, X_{1jk} and X_{2jk}, use Helmert coding (see Appendix B) to represent the main effect due to factor A indexed by the subscript j, and the third predictor X_{3jk} is for factor B indexed by the subscript k. The predictors X_{4jk} and X_{5jk} are associated with the interaction effect. They are the cross products of the previous predictors between the two factors, that is, $X_{4jk} = X_{1jk} * X_{3jk}$ and $X_{5jk} = X_{2jk} * X_{3jk}$. In matrix formation, the cell mean μ_{jk} is regressed on the five X predictors using orthogonal coding;

$$
\begin{array}{ccccccc}
\mu_{jk} = & \beta_0 & +\beta_1 X_{1jk} & +\beta_2 X_{2jk} & +\beta_3 X_{3jk} & +\beta_4 X_{4jk} & +\beta_5 X_{5jk} \\
\mu_{11} & & 1/3 & 1/2 & 1/2 & 1/6 & 1/4 \\
\mu_{12} & & 1/3 & 1/2 & -1/2 & -1/6 & -1/4 \\
\mu_{21} & & 1/3 & -1/2 & 1/2 & 1/6 & -1/4 \\
\mu_{22} & & 1/3 & -1/2 & -1/2 & -1/6 & 1/4 \\
\mu_{31} & & -2/3 & 0 & 1/2 & -1/3 & 0 \\
\mu_{32} & & -2/3 & 0 & -1/2 & 1/3 & 0
\end{array}
$$

The orthogonal coding for the factor A implies two Helmert contrasts β_1 and β_2,

$$
\beta_1 = \sum_{j=1}^{3} c_{1j}\mu_j \text{ and } \beta_2 = \sum_{j=1}^{3} c_{2j}\mu_j, \tag{4.44}
$$

where the μ_j is the marginal mean for the jth level of factor A. The contrast coefficients c_{1j} and c_{2j} are

$$
c_{1j} : c_{11} = \frac{1}{2}, c_{12} = \frac{1}{2}, c_{13} = -1;
$$
$$
c_{2j} : c_{21} = 1, c_{22} = -1, c_{23} = 0. \tag{4.45}
$$

The coded values on X_{1jk} are derived from those contrast coefficients c_{1j} such that $X_{1jk} = c_{1j} / \sum_{j=1}^{J} c_{1j}^2$. Similarly, we can obtain $X_{2jk} = c_{2j} / \sum_{j=1}^{J} c_{2j}^2$.

For the predictor X_{3ij}, the regression coefficient β_3 represents the mean contrast between the two levels of factor B,

$$
\beta_3 = \sum_{k=1}^{2} c_{3k}\mu_k = \mu_{k=1} - \mu_{k=2}, \tag{4.46}
$$

where μ_k is the marginal mean for the kth level of factor B. The contrast coefficient c_{3k} takes 1 for $k = 1$ and -1 for $k = 2$. The values on X_{3ij} are derived from c_{3k} ($X_{3ij} = c_{3k} / \sum_{k=1}^{2} c_{3k}^2$).

The regression coefficients β_4 and β_5 are related to the interaction effects. In particular, β_4 compares the difference in the first Helmert contrast between the two levels of factor B,

$$
\beta_4 = \left(\frac{1}{2}\mu_{11} + \frac{1}{2}\mu_{21} - \mu_{31} \right) - \left(\frac{1}{2}\mu_{12} + \frac{1}{2}\mu_{22} - \mu_{32} \right). \tag{4.47}
$$

The regression coefficient β_5 measures the difference in the second Helmert contrast between the two levels of factor B,

$$\beta_5 = (\mu_{11} - \mu_{21}) - (\mu_{12} - \mu_{22}). \qquad (4.48)$$

The effect size for the interaction $\sum_{k=1}^{K} \sum_{j=1}^{J} (\mu_{jk} - \mu_j - \mu_k + \mu)^2$ can be decomposed into two regression sums of squares due to the predictors X_{4jk} and X_{5jk}. As the orthogonal coding is used, the regression sum of squares is the squared regression coefficient multiplied by the sum of squared values of the predictor. The regression sums of squares due to X_{4jk} and X_{5jk} are $\beta_4^2 \sum_{j=1} \sum_{k=1} X_{4jk}^2$ and $\beta_5^2 \sum_{j=1} \sum_{k=1} X_{5jk}^2$, respectively. The effect size for the interaction (Liu, in press) is

$$\sum_{k=1}^{K} \sum_{j=1}^{J} (\mu_{jk} - \mu_j - \mu_k + \mu)^2 = \beta_4^2 \sum_{j=1} \sum_{k=1} X_{4jk}^2 + \beta_5^2 \sum_{j=1} \sum_{k=1} X_{5jk}^2. \qquad (4.49)$$

It becomes a little easier to conjecture the effect size for interaction in this way because the researcher only needs to guess the values of β_4 and β_5. These two regression coefficients represent contrast differences, which read more intuitively than the sums of squares of six means in a two-way table.

For example, a social scientist may want to compare political views among the Republicans, Moderate Independents, and Democrats in a Midwest state. A representative random sample of state residents will be recruited, and the subjects will self-rate their political view on a 1-to-7 point scale with 1 being extremely liberal and 7 being extremely conservative (Agresti and Finlay, 2009). The data will be analyzed in a two-way ANOVA with party as factor A and sex as factor B. The social scientist is particularly interested in examining the interaction between party affiliation and sex. In planning for the potential study, he or she needs to conduct a statistical power analysis to test the interaction effect between party and sex.

The social scientist knows from past experience that the Republicans and Independents often cross over and vote for the other party. So the Republicans and Independents as an aggregated group are compared with the Democrats, which rarely cross the party line in state voting, that is,

$$\frac{1}{2}\mu_{1.} + \frac{1}{2}\mu_{2.} - \mu_{3.}, \ j = 1(\text{Republican}), 2(\text{Independent}), 3(\text{Democrat}).$$

This corresponds to the first Helmert contrast. The social scientist is also interested in comparing the Republicans' and Independents' political ideologies, which gives rise to the second Helmert contrast,

$$\mu_{1\cdot} - \mu_{2\cdot}.$$

The interaction effect occurs when the two Helmert contrast differs between the two sexes. For the first Helmert contrast, it is estimated that there is a difference of .75 on the scale of the self-rated political view (i.e., $\beta_4 = .75$).

$$\left(\frac{1}{2}\mu_{11} + \frac{1}{2}\mu_{21} - \mu_{31}\right) - \left(\frac{1}{2}\mu_{12} + \frac{1}{2}\mu_{22} - \mu_{32}\right) = .75,$$
$$k = 1(\text{female}),\ 2(\text{male}).$$

Likewise, the expected difference is -2.5 for the second Helmert contrast, as Republicans are generally more conservative than Independents and this is more pronounced among male voters than among female voters.

$$(\mu_{11} - \mu_{21}) - (\mu_{12} - \mu_{22}) = -2.5.$$

So the regression coefficient β_5 is -2.5.

Using Equation 4.49, the social scientist then calculates the effect size for the interaction,

$$\sum_{k=1}^{K}\sum_{j=1}^{J}(\mu_{jk} - \mu_j - \mu_k + \mu)^2$$
$$= \beta_4^2 \sum_{j=1}^{}\sum_{k=1}^{} X_{4jk}^2 + \beta_5^2 \sum_{j=1}^{}\sum_{k=1}^{} X_{5jk}^2$$
$$= (.75)^2 \times ((1/6)^2 + (-1/6)^2 + (1/6)^2 + (-1/6)^2 + (-1/3)^2 + (1/3)^2)$$
$$+ (-2.5)^2 \times ((1/4)^2 + (-1/4)^2 + (-1/4)^2 + (1/4)^2 + 0^2 + 0^2)$$
$$= 1.75.$$

The effect size for the interaction is the same as that computed from the six cell means in Table 4.4. The following R code can be used to compute the effect size for the interaction based on the six cell means:

```
mu=c(1.5,3,4.5,2.5,2.0,6.0)
pa=rep(c("d","i","r"),2)
```

```
ge=c(rep("f",3),rep("m",3))
ch4t2=data.frame(mu,pa,ge)
aov(mu~pa+ge+pa*ge,data=ch4t2)

#output
#Terms:
#                      pa      ge   pa:ge
#Sum of Squares   12.250   0.375   1.750
#Deg. of Freedom       2       1       2
#effect size for interaction is the sum squares under pa:ge
```

Table 4.4: Cell means in a two-way ANOVA

μ_{jk}	female	male	μ_j
Republic	4.5	6.0	5.25
Independent	3.0	2.0	2.50
Democrat	1.5	2.5	2.00
μ_k	3.0	3.5	3.25

To calculate statistical power for testing the interaction effect, we assume that the standard deviation of people's political view is one ($\sigma = 1$). If seven subjects are used in each combination of the political party and sex ($n = 7$), the statistical power will be .86:

```
#power for testing interaction
n=7
s=1
a=.05
beta4=.75
beta5=-2.5

x1=c(rep(1/3,2), rep(1/3,2), rep(-2/3,2))
x2=c(rep(1/2,2), rep(-1/2,2), rep(0,2))
x3=rep(c(1/2,-1/2),3)
x4=x1*x3
x5=x2*x3
```

```
x4x4=sum(x4^2)
x5x5=sum(x5^2)

esab=beta4^2*x4x4+beta5^2*x5x5
ncab=n*esab/s^2
f0=qf(1-a,(3-1)*(2-1), 3*2*(n-1))
1-pf(f0,(3-1)*(2-1), 3*2*(n-1),ncab)
# power 0.8610103
```

4.3 Random-effects ANOVA

The random-effects one-way ANOVA treats the group means as a random sample from the population. The actual deviation of the group mean from the grand mean is less a concern than the overall variability among the group means. The variability of group means is of great interest in random-effects ANOVA. For example, in school-based research, school variability is an important measurement. The schools are treated as a random sample of all the schools in the population. The students' achievement can be modeled in a random-effects model:

$$Y_{ij} = \mu + \alpha_j + e_{ij}, \tag{4.50}$$

where two random effects are the school effect ($\alpha_j \sim N(0, \tau)$) and random error ($e_{ij} \sim N(0, \sigma^2)$). The individual school effect α_j is of less interest than the variance of the school effect τ because the school effects are conceived of as a random sample in the random-effects ANOVA.

The null hypothesis states that there is no variability among group means ($H_0 : \tau = 0$). To test the null hypothesis, we can still use the same F statistic as in the fixed-effects ANOVA (Equation 4.1), which has a central F distribution with $J - 1$ degrees of freedom in the numerator and $N - J$ in the denominator, that is,

$$F = \frac{MST}{MSE}.$$

When the alternative hypothesis is true, the F ratio does not exactly have a central distribution. We will denote it as F_a. However, the statistic F_a

multiplied by a multiplier $\sigma^2/(n\tau + \sigma^2)$ follows a central F distribution,

$$F_a \frac{\sigma^2}{n\tau + \sigma^2} \sim F(J - 1, N - J). \tag{4.51}$$

The multiplicative factor $\sigma^2/(n\tau + \sigma^2)$ is the ratio between the expected within-group mean squares and the expected between-group mean squares,

$$\frac{\sigma^2}{n\tau + \sigma^2} = \frac{E(MSE)}{E(MST)}.$$

The expectation of the within-group mean squares is always the error variance or $E(MSE) = \sigma^2$. The expectation of the between-group mean squares is also σ^2 when the null hypothesis is true (i.e., $H_0 : \tau = 0$). If the variance $\tau = 0$ is not null ($H_a : \tau \neq 0$), it pops in the expectation of the between-group mean squares. Its expectation can be found by using the fact that the between-group mean squares is just n multiplied by the sample variance of the group means. As the sample variance is an unbiased estimate, it equals the population variance. The population variance of the group mean is

$$Var(\overline{Y}_j) = \tau + \frac{\sigma^2}{n}. \tag{4.52}$$

As $\overline{Y}_j$'s are independent identically distributed random variables with a common variance $\tau + \sigma^2/n$, the unbiased estimate of $Var(\overline{Y}_j)$ is the sample variance of the group mean,

$$\widehat{Var}(\overline{Y}_j) = \frac{\sum\limits_{j=1}^{J} (\overline{Y}_{.j} - \overline{Y}_{..})^2}{(J - 1)}. \tag{4.53}$$

Since the estimate $\widehat{Var}(\overline{Y}_j)$ is unbiased, its expectation equals the population variance $E(\widehat{Var}(\overline{Y}_j)) = \tau + \sigma^2/n$. Note that $n\widehat{Var}(\overline{Y}_j)$ is indeed the between-group mean squares MST. Thus, the expectation of the between-group mean squares MST is

$$E(MST) = E\left(\frac{\sum\limits_{j=1}^{J} n(\overline{Y}_{.j} - \overline{Y}_{..})^2}{(J-1)}\right)$$

$$= E\left(n\widehat{Var}(\overline{Y}_j)\right)$$

$$= nE\left(\widehat{Var}(\overline{Y}_j)\right)$$

$$= n(\tau + \frac{\sigma^2}{n})$$

$$= n\tau + \sigma^2. \tag{4.54}$$

Since $E(MSE) = \sigma^2$ (Equation 4.7), the ratio of the expected between-group mean squares and within-group mean squares is

$$\frac{E(MST)}{E(MSE)} = \frac{n\tau + \sigma^2}{\sigma^2}. \tag{4.55}$$

Its reciprocal $\sigma^2/(n\tau + \sigma^2)$ becomes the multiplicative factor, which transforms the F_a statistic under the alternative hypothesis into a central F statistic.

In other words, the numerator of the F ratio on average exceeds the denominator by $n\tau$ when the variance τ is not null under the alternative hypothesis. Therefore, F ratio does not conform to the central F distribution. However, the multiplicative factor can reverse the discrepancy between the numerator and denominator of the F ratio and convert it to a central F,

$$F_a \sim \frac{n\tau + \sigma^2}{\sigma^2} F_{J-1,N-J}$$

$$F_a \frac{\sigma^2}{n\tau + \sigma^2} \sim F_{J-1,N-J}.$$

The statistical power function for testing the variance component τ

uses the central F distribution under the alternative hypothesis,

$$
\begin{aligned}
1 - \beta &= P[F_a \geq F_0] \\
&= 1 - P[F_a < F_0] \\
&= 1 - P\left[F_a \frac{\sigma^2}{n\tau + \sigma^2} < F_0 \frac{\sigma^2}{n\tau + \sigma^2}\right] \\
&= 1 - P\left[F < F_0 \frac{\sigma^2}{n\tau + \sigma^2}\right],
\end{aligned}
\tag{4.56}
$$

where F is a central F distribution with degrees of freedom $\nu_1 = J - 1$ and $\nu_2 = N - J$. The probability $P[F < F_0\sigma^2/(n\tau + \sigma^2)]$ is a cumulative distribution function of a central F.

The variance of the random effect τ can be represented by its proportion over the total variance $\tau + \sigma^2$. The ratio of τ and $\tau + \sigma^2$ is called the intraclass correlation ρ,

$$
\rho = \frac{\tau}{\tau + \sigma^2}.
\tag{4.57}
$$

The intraclass correlation is frequently cited in school-based research. It shows how correlated the observations in the same group (e.g., school) are. For instance, we can find the correlation between two students' achievement scores Y_{ij} and $Y_{i'j}$ within the jth school:

$$
\begin{aligned}
corr(Y_{ij}, Y_{i'j}) &= \frac{cov(Y_{ij}, Y_{i'j})}{\sigma_{Y_{ij}} \sigma_{Y_{i'j}}} \\
&= \frac{E(Y_{ij} - E(Y_{ij}))(Y_{i'j} - E(Y_{i'j}))}{\sqrt{\sigma^2 + \tau}\sqrt{\sigma^2 + \tau}} \\
&= \frac{E(\alpha_j + e_{ij})(\alpha_j + e_{i'j})}{\sigma^2 + \tau} \\
&= \frac{E(\alpha_j^2)}{\sigma^2 + \tau} \\
&= \frac{\tau}{\sigma^2 + \tau}.
\end{aligned}
\tag{4.58}
$$

Note that $Y_{ij} - E(Y_{ij}) = \mu + \alpha_j + e_{ij} - \mu = \alpha_j + e_{ij}$, and that e_{ij} and $e_{i'j}$ are independent of each other and of α_j. The latter suggests that $E(\alpha_j + e_{ij})(\alpha_j + e_{i'j}) = E(\alpha_j^2)$. Since the random effect α_j has a normal distribution with a variance τ and a zero mean $E(\alpha_j) = 0$, we have $\tau = E(\alpha_j - E(\alpha_j))^2 = E(\alpha_j^2)$. So the intraclass correlation portrays how similar or correlated the observations within the same group or school are. The more similar the students are within the schools, the more variability lies between the schools. This indicates that there is a wide variation in student achievement among schools, which calls for further analysis to explain why some schools perform better than others.

The null hypothesis about τ can be expressed in terms of ρ ($H_0 : \rho = 0$) because a null variance of τ means zero intraclass correlation. The test statistic remains the same. The multiplicative factor can be written in terms of ρ instead,

$$\frac{\sigma^2}{n\tau + \sigma^2} = \frac{1 - \rho}{n\rho + (1 - \rho)}. \tag{4.59}$$

The statistical power for testing $H_0 : \rho = 0$ or $\tau = 0$ is

$$1 - P[F < F_{1-\alpha, J-1, J(n-1)} \frac{1 - \rho}{n\rho + (1 - \rho)}]. \tag{4.60}$$

For example, an educational researcher may be interested in testing the intraclass correlation among schools in a large school district. Past experience indicates that the variability among schools is about thirty percent ($\rho = .30$) in students' test scores on the state mandatory math assessment. Thirty percent suggests that schools vary widely in producing educational outcomes, and that some district-wide measures need to be taken to reduce school variation in the district. The researcher plans to sample twenty tenth graders from each school ($n = 20$) and run a statistical test on the intraclass correlation. The question is how many schools need to be recruited to achieve a statistical power of .80. If an insufficient number of schools are used, the researcher may not statistically substantiate his or her research hypothesis about school inequality in the district. On the contrary, if too many schools are involved, it might unnecessarily waste resources and time. To choose an appropriate number of schools, the researcher will conduct statistical power analysis. The power analysis shows that four randomly selected schools from the district will attain power .84 in hypothesis testing (see R code).

```
p=function(J=4,n=20,rho=.3){
  a=.05
```

```
 f0=qf(1-a,J-1,J*(n-1))
 m=(1-rho)/(n*rho+(1-rho))
 1-pf(f0*m,J-1,J*(n-1))
}
```

```
p(J=3:6) # 3:6 supplies J with the values 3,4,5,6
```

The SAS `proc power` procedure does not compute statistical power in a random-effects ANOVA analysis. Nevertheless, we can use the SAS built-in distribution function for the F random variable to calculate power in a data step. The power values can then be tabulated through the `proc print` procedure.

```
*power for random-effects ANOVA;
data raov(keep=n J power);
 a=.05;
 n=20;
 rho=.30;
 m=(1-rho)/(n*rho+(1-rho));

 do J=3 to 10;
  f0=finv(1-a,J-1,J*(n-1));
  power=1-probf(f0*m,J-1,J*(n-1));
  output;
 end;
run;
```

```
proc print data=raov;run;
```

The relevant SPSS syntax uses the cumulative distribution function for the central F (i.e., `CDF.F( )`) to compute power in a random-effects ANOVA. The command `LIST` prints out the number of schools J and statistical power.

```
*STATISTICAL POWER IN RANDOM-EFFECTS ANOVA.
NEW FILE.
INPUT PROGRAM.
COMPUTE A=.05.
COMPUTE RHO=.30.
```

```
COMPUTE N=20.
COMPUTE M=(1-RHO)/(N*RHO+(1-RHO)).
COMPUTE V=0.
COMPUTE J=0.
COMPUTE P=0.

LEAVE A TO P.
 LOOP J=3 TO 6.
   COMPUTE V=J*(N-1).
   COMPUTE P=1- CDF.F(IDF.F(1-A,J-1,V)*M,J-1,V).
   END CASE.
 END LOOP.
END FILE.
END INPUT PROGRAM.
EXECUTE.

DELETE VARIABLES A RHO N M V.
VARIABLE LABELS P 'Power'.
LIST.
```

Chapter 5

Linear Regression

Linear regression relates an outcome variable or dependent variable to a number of explanatory variables or independent variables in a linear function. The outcome is expressed as a weighted sum of the explanatory variables. The weights are called the regression coefficients. The relationship between the outcome and explanatory variables are regulated by those regression coefficients, which weight the explanatory variables in their contributions to the outcome variable.

The linear regression model is flexible in taking either categorical variables or continuous variables as independent variables. Linear regression can be employed to analyze data either from randomized experiments or from observational studies. Depending on the nature of the study, linear regression can be used to predict the outcome or explain it. In an exploratory study, one typically wants to know whether some independent variables substantially account for the variation in the subjects' outcome. In an experiment, the key interest lies in testing the regression coefficient for the independent variable of the treatment assignment. A statistically significant regression coefficient means that the different treatments received differentiate the subjects' performance. In other words, there is a treatment effect. If the goal is to make a prediction of the outcome variable (e.g., job performance), linear regression offers a straightforward application. One can observe the data of the outcome and explanatory variables and then establish the relationship between the response and explanatory variables by estimating the regression coefficients for the observed data. The estimated regression coefficients in the linear regression equation are then used to evaluate the predicted value on the outcome, given the values of the explanatory variables.

We will first describe statistical power analysis for simple regression with one dependent variable and one independent variable. We will then move on to multiple linear regression with several independent variables. We conclude the chapter with a discussion of the case that includes both categorical and continuous independent variables in analysis of covariance.

5.1   Simple Regression

Simple regression uses one explanatory variable to explain the variation in the outcome. For example, we may regress students' scores in a statistics course Y on their prior aptitude X. The regression model is

$$Y_i = \beta_0 + \beta_1 X_i + e_i, \ i = 1, 2, ..., n. \tag{5.1}$$

The statistics score Y_i is conceived of as comprising an intercept β_0, the explained part due to the aptitude score $\beta_1 X_i$, and a residual error e_i. Every student's residual error is assumed to have an independent and identical normal distribution ($e_i \sim i.i.d. \ N(0, \sigma^2)$). If we take the expectation of Equation 5.1 on both sides, we can see that the expected value of the outcome is a linear function of the regression coefficients and the explanatory variable,

$$E(Y_i) = \beta_0 + \beta_1 X_i$$
$$E(Y_i) = \mu_{Y_i}. \tag{5.2}$$

So the outcome Y_i has an independent and identical distribution (i.i.d.), $Y_i \sim N(\beta_0 + \beta_1 X, \sigma^2)$.

If we apply the estimated regression coefficients β_0 and β_1 to a value of X and make a prediction of Y, the predicted value $\hat{Y} = \hat{\beta}_0 + \hat{\beta}_1 X$ is simply an estimate of the expected value of the outcome for the given value of X, that is,

$$\hat{\mu}_{Y_i} = \hat{\beta}_0 + \hat{\beta}_1 X_i. \tag{5.3}$$

We can use the observed data and obtain the least squares estimates (LSE) of the regression coefficients $\hat{\beta}_0$ and $\hat{\beta}_1$, which minimize the sum of squares of the observed Y_i and its prediction $\hat{Y}_i$ (i.e., $\sum_{i=1}^{n}(Y_i - \hat{Y}_i)^2$). The LSE estimate for the slope β_1 is

$$\hat{\beta}_1 = \frac{\sum\limits_{i=1}^{n}(X_i - \overline{X})Y_i}{\sum\limits_{i=1}^{n}(X_i - \overline{X})^2}, \tag{5.4}$$

where $\overline{X}$ is the sample mean of the explanatory variable. The LSE estimate for the intercept β_0 can be obtained from $\hat{\beta}_1$,

$$\hat{\beta}_0 = \overline{Y} - \hat{\beta}_1 \overline{X}. \tag{5.5}$$

Using the LSE estimates in the regression model, we can calculate the predicted value of the statistics score $\hat{Y}_i$ for the ith subject based on the aptitude score X_i.

Through the predicted value $\hat{Y}_i$, we can divide the variation of the outcome Y_i into two portions: the explained variation due to regression and the unexplained variation due to residual error. First, we start from

$$Y_i - \overline{Y} = \hat{Y}_i - \overline{Y} + Y_i - \hat{Y}_i. \tag{5.6}$$

This equality always holds true. The left side is the deviation score $Y_i - \overline{Y}$, which measures the variation of the outcome for the ith subject. On the right side, the residual error is the discrepancy between the observed outcome and its predicted value $(Y_i - \hat{Y}_i)$. The variation of the predicted value for the ith subject is the deviation score of the predicted value from its mean $(\hat{Y}_i - \overline{Y})$. Note that the predicted value $\hat{Y}_i$ has the same sample mean as the observed outcome Y_i. Taking the sum of squares on both sides of Equation 5.6, we have the total sum of squares (TSS) on the left side of the equal sign and the regression sum of squares (SSR) and residual sum of squares (SSE) on the right side,

$$\sum_{i=1}^{n}(Y_i - \overline{Y})^2 = \sum_{i=1}^{n}(\hat{Y}_i - \overline{Y})^2 + \sum_{i=1}^{n}(Y_i - \hat{Y}_i)^2$$
$$TSS = SSR + SSE. \tag{5.7}$$

The degrees of freedom for the three sums of squares are $n - 1$ for TSS, 1 for SSR, and $n - 2$ for SSE. The sum of squares divided by its degrees of freedom becomes the mean square.

The ratio of regression mean square and the residual mean square can be used to test whether the regression explains any significant amount of the variation in the outcome relative to the variation of the residual error. This is equivalent to testing whether the regression slope is zero ($H_0 : \beta_1 = 0$). When the regression slope is indeed zero, as in the null hypothesis, the regression model can be simplified to $Y_i = \beta_0 + e_i$. The predicted outcome is its sample mean (i.e., $\hat{Y}_i = \overline{Y}$). The regression sum of squares reduces to zero. To test the null hypothesis, we use the ratio of the two mean squares to form an F statistic,

$$F = \frac{SSR/1}{SSE/(n-2)}$$

$$= \frac{\sum_{i=1}^{n}(\hat{Y}_i - \overline{Y})^2}{\sum_{i=1}^{n}(Y_i - \hat{Y}_i)^2/(n-2)}. \tag{5.8}$$

The F statistic has degrees of freedom 1 in the numerator and $n-2$ in the denominator.

When the alternative hypothesis is true ($H_a : \beta_1 \neq 0$), the F test has a non-central F distribution. We therefore denote the F statistic under the alternative hypothesis as F'. The non-central F' has a non-centrality parameter λ,

$$\lambda = \frac{\beta_1^2 \sum_{i=1}^{n}(X_i - \overline{X})^2}{\sigma^2}. \tag{5.9}$$

The non-centrality parameter can be easily derived from the expected values of the numerator and denominator of the F ratio. We will first expand the expression in the F statistic. Substituting $\hat{\beta}_0 + \hat{\beta}_1 X_i$ to $\hat{Y}_i$ in the F ratio (Equation 5.8), we have

$$F = \frac{\sum_{i=1}^{n}(\hat{\beta}_0 + \hat{\beta}_1 X_i - \overline{Y})^2}{\sum_{i=1}^{n}(Y_i - \hat{\beta}_0 - \hat{\beta}_1 X_i)^2/(n-2)}.$$

Substituting Equation 5.5 for $\hat{\beta}_0$ into the numerator, we obtain

$$F = \frac{\sum_{i=1}^{n}(\overline{Y} - \hat{\beta}_1\overline{X} + \hat{\beta}_1 X_i - \overline{Y})^2}{\sum_{i=1}^{n}(Y_i - \hat{\beta}_0 - \hat{\beta}_1 X_i)^2/(n-2)}$$

$$= \frac{\sum_{i=1}^{n}\hat{\beta}_1^2(X_i - \overline{X})^2}{\sum_{i=1}^{n}(Y_i - \hat{\beta}_0 - \hat{\beta}_1 X_i)^2/(n-2)}. \qquad (5.10)$$

Having expanded the F ratio, we now try to figure out the expected values for the numerator and denominator. Replacing the coefficient estimate $\hat{\beta}_1$ with its population counterpart β_1 yields the expected value of the numerator because $\hat{\beta}_1$ is a LSE estimate, which is an unbiased estimate ($E(\hat{\beta}_1) = \beta_1$). Specifically, we have the expected value of the numerator;

$$E\left(\sum_{i=1}^{n}\hat{\beta}_1^2(X_i - \overline{X})^2\right) = \sum_{i=1}^{n}\beta_1^2(X_i - \overline{X})^2. \qquad (5.11)$$

The denominator of the F ratio can be changed to

$$\sum_{i=1}^{n}(Y_i - \hat{\beta}_0 - \hat{\beta}_1 X_i)^2/(n-2) = \frac{\sum_{i=1}^{n}(Y_i - \hat{\mu}_{Y_i})^2}{n-2},$$

because Equation 5.3 suggests $\hat{\mu}_{Y_i} = \hat{\beta}_0 + \hat{\beta}_1 X$. The denominator is essentially a sample variance, and it is an unbiased estimate of the residual variance of Y, that is,

$$E\left(\frac{\sum_{i=1}^{n}(Y_i - \hat{\mu}_Y)^2}{n-2}\right) = \sigma^2. \qquad (5.12)$$

In short, the non-centrality parameter of the F test can be obtained by replacing the numerator and denominator of the F ratio with their respective expectations,

$$\lambda = \frac{E(SSR/1)}{E(SSE/(n-2))}$$

$$= \frac{\beta_1^2 \sum\limits_{i=1}^{n} (X_i - \overline{X})^2}{\sigma^2}. \tag{5.13}$$

The statistical power for testing the regression slope is therefore

$$1 - \beta = P[F'(1, n-2, \lambda) \geq F_{1-\alpha,1,n-2}]$$

$$= 1 - P[F'(1, n-2, \lambda) < F_{1-\alpha,1,n-2}]. \tag{5.14}$$

For example, the researcher may expect to see a 6 point increase in the score on the statistics course for every 10 point increase in the aptitude score ($\beta_1 = .6$). The standard deviation of the residual is set at 12 points ($\sigma = 12$). Since the explanatory variable X_i is presumably treated as constant, its values will not be known until the study is completed. There is always some difficulty in conjecturing the value of the sum of squares $\sum_{i=1}^{n}(X_i - \overline{X})^2$. If the sample size is large, the sum of squares will be approximately close to the population variance of X_i multiplied by the sample size n. We can therefore estimate the sum of squares, using $\sum_{i=1}^{n}(X_i - \overline{X})^2 \approx n\sigma_X^2$. In our case, the researcher can nevertheless learn from experience about the standard deviation of the explanatory variable σ_X. In particular, he or she knows that the aptitude scores almost always fall between 10 and 100. As six standard deviations around the mean comprises 99.7 % of all the possible aptitude scores, he or she reasons that the standard deviation of X_i is

$$\sqrt{\sum_{i=1}^{n} (X_i - \overline{X})^2/n} = (100 - 10)/6 = 15.$$

So the observed sum of squares is $\sum_{i=1}^{n}(X_i - \overline{X})^2 \approx 225n$. If we choose a sample size twenty ($n = 20$), the statistical power is expected to be .887 (see R code).

```
# statistical power for simple regression

p4sr=function(n=20,b1=.6,sigma=12,sigmax=15){
```

```
  f0=qf(.95,1,n-2)
  lambda=b1^2*sigmax^2*n/sigma^2
  1-pf(f0,1,n-2,lambda)
}

p4sr()
#>[1] 0.8869702
```

The SAS proc power procedure does not take the slope for an input in computing the statistical power for regression analysis. We can define and compute the power for simple regression in a data step (i.e., data sr). The following SAS program shows the same results as the aforementioned R code. The data step computes the power for the sample size that ranges from 10 to 50. The proc print procedure tabulates sample sizes and power values. The proc gplot procedure plots power against sample size.

```
*power in simple regression;
data sr(keep=n power);
 a=.05;
 b1=.6;
 sigma=12;
 sigmax=15;
 do n=10 to 50;
  f0=finv(1-a,1,n-2);
  lambda=b1**2*sigmax**2*n/sigma**2;
  power=1-probf(f0,1,n-2,lambda);
  output;
 end;
run;

proc print data=sr; run;

proc gplot data=sr;
 plot power*n;
 title "Statistical power in simple regression";
run;
```

The relevant SPSS syntax is as follows:

```
* POWER IN SIMPLE REGRESSION.
DATA LIST LIST/N B1 SIGMA SIGMAX.
BEGIN DATA
20 .6 12 15
END DATA.
COMPUTE LAMBDA=B1**2*SIGMAX**2*N/SIGMA**2.
COMPUTE P=1-NCDF.F(IDF.F(.95,1,N-2),1,N-2,LAMBDA).
EXECUTE.
```

There is a special case when the sum of squares $\sum_{i=1}^{n}(X_i - \overline{X})^2$ can be known in advance. If the explanatory variable indicates the subjects' assignment to treatment and control groups, then X_i can take .5 for the treatment group and $-.5$ for the control group. Assume that the treatment and control group are of equal sample size ($n/2$) with half the subjects in the treatment group and the other half in the control group. The sum of squares then becomes

$$\sum_{i=1}^{n}(X_i - \overline{X})^2 = \frac{n}{4}. \tag{5.15}$$

The non-centrality parameter simplifies to

$$\lambda = \beta_1^2 \frac{n}{4}.$$

It can also be shown that the regression slope is actually the simple effect size or the average mean difference in outcome between the treatment and control groups. For the treatment condition, the simple regression model is

$$Y_{ei} = \beta_0 + \beta_1.5 + e_i. \tag{5.16}$$

Averaging the above equation on both sides over i yields $\mu_{Y_e} = \beta_0 + .5\beta_1$. Similarly, we can obtain $\mu_{Y_c} = \beta_0 - .5\beta_1$ for the control condition. The average difference in outcome between the treatment and control groups is therefore $\mu_{Y_e} - \mu_{Y_c} = \beta_1$. So β_1 is the same as the simple effect size Δ in a regular two sample independent t test. In fact, simple regression can be applied to a two sample independent t test. The F test works the same as a regular t test except that λ for the non-central F' is the squared non-centrality of the t test.

5.2 Testing Correlation r

We are often interested in testing the model fit by using the correlation between the observed outcome Y and its predicted values $\hat{Y}$. In general, such a correlation is called the multiple correlation coefficient R because the linear regression can take more than one explanatory variable. In estimating the population multiple correlation coefficient, we use $\hat{R}^2$ to estimate R^2.

$$\hat{R}^2 = \frac{SSR}{TSS}. \tag{5.17}$$

In simple regression with one explanatory variable, the multiple correlation coefficient $\hat{R}$ is just the correlation coefficient between the outcome Y and its predictor X (i.e., $\hat{R} = r_{XY}$).

We can still use the F statistic to test whether the population correlation ρ_{XY} between Y and X is zero ($H_0 : \rho_{XY} = 0$). This null hypothesis is the same as the null hypothesis about the regression slope, that is, $H_0 : \rho_{XY} = 0 \Leftrightarrow H_0 : \beta_1 = 0$. We can actually express the F statistic in terms of the sample correlation coefficient r_{XY},

$$
\begin{aligned}
F &= \frac{SSR/1}{SSE/(n-2)} \\
&= \frac{r_{XY}^2 SST}{(1 - r_{XY}^2) SST/(n-2)} \\
&= \frac{r_{XY}^2}{(1 - r_{XY}^2)/(n-2)}.
\end{aligned} \tag{5.18}
$$

So the F statistic is a function of the sample correlation between Y and X. Since the F statistic has one degree of freedom in the numerator, taking the square root of the F ratio yields a t statistic,

$$T = \frac{r_{XY}\sqrt{n-2}}{\sqrt{1 - r_{XY}^2}}, \tag{5.19}$$

where t has $n - 2$ degrees of freedom. When the null hypothesis is true, the t statistic has a central t distribution.

When the alternative hypothesis ($H_a : \rho_{XY} \neq 0$) holds true, the t statistic follows a non-central t distribution (T') with a non-centrality parameter

λ. We can obtain the non-centrality parameter for T' by taking the square root of the non-centrality parameter in the F test (Equation 5.9) and then expressing the regression slope β_1 in ρ_{XY},

$$
\begin{aligned}
\lambda &= \sqrt{\frac{\beta_1^2 \sum_{i=1}^n (X_i - \overline{X})^2}{\sigma^2}} \\
&= \frac{\rho_{XY} \frac{\sigma_Y}{\sigma_X} \sqrt{\sum_{i=1}^n (X_i - \overline{X})^2}}{\sigma} \\
&= \frac{\rho_{XY}}{\sqrt{1 - \rho_{XY}^2}} \sqrt{\frac{\sum_{i=1}^n (X_i - \overline{X})^2}{\sigma_X^2}},
\end{aligned}
\tag{5.20}
$$

where we replace σ with $\sigma_Y \sqrt{1 - \rho_{XY}^2}$. The variance σ^2 is the residual variance after the total variance σ_Y^2 has been explained or reduced by ρ_{XY}^2 percent through the regression (i.e., $\sigma^2 = \sigma_Y^2 (1 - \rho_{XY}^2)$). Note that σ_X^2 is the variance of the predictor X,

$$
\sigma_X^2 = \frac{\sum_{i=1}^n (X_i - \overline{X})^2}{n}.
\tag{5.21}
$$

As the values of the predictor X are treated as constants in the linear regression, there is no loss of degrees of freedom in computing $\overline{X}$. So the variance σ_X^2 uses n instead of its usual $n - 1$ degrees of freedom in the denominator (Diggle, Heagerty, Liang, and Zeger, 2002, p.28). Substituting the variance σ_X^2 into λ, we obtain

$$
\lambda = \frac{\rho_{XY} \sqrt{n}}{\sqrt{1 - \rho_{XY}^2}}.
\tag{5.22}
$$

Statistical power for testing correlation coefficient ρ_{XY} uses the cumulative distribution function for the non-central t distribution T' with the degrees of freedom $n - 2$ and the non-centrality parameter λ,

$$
1 - \beta = 1 - P[T' < t_{1-\alpha/2, n-2}] + P[T' < t_{\alpha/2, n-2}].
\tag{5.23}
$$

The correlation coefficient ρ_{XY} does not assume that the observations of X and Y are measured with errors. If X and Y contain measurement errors, the formulas need to be modified to include reliability coefficients for each variable. The reliability coefficient shows the proportion of the variance of the true score over the variance of the observed score, that is,

$$\rho_{XT}^2 = \frac{\sigma_{TX}^2}{\sigma_X^2} \text{ and } \rho_{YT}^2 = \frac{\sigma_{TY}^2}{\sigma_Y^2}, \tag{5.24}$$

where ρ_{XT}^2 and ρ_{YT}^2 are the reliability coefficients for X and Y, respectively. The true variance of X is σ_{TX}^2; the true variance of Y is σ_{TY}^2. The symbol σ_Y^2 represents the variance of the observed Y. Taking the reliability coefficients into account, we can calculate the correlation between the true scores of X and Y. We will use TX and TY to denote the true scores of X and Y. The correlation between the two true scores ρ_{TXTY} (Spearman, 1904) is

$$\rho_{TXTY} = \frac{\rho_{XY}}{\sqrt{\rho_{XT}^2 \rho_{YT}^2}}. \tag{5.25}$$

Unless the reliability coefficients ρ_{XT}^2 and ρ_{YT}^2 are both one, the correlation of the true scores ρ_{TXTY} is always larger than the correlation of the observed scores. The attenuation of the correlation of the observed scores is due to the measurement errors in the observed X and Y.

We can change the non-centrality parameter for testing the correlation of the true scores. The modified non-centrality parameter becomes

$$\lambda = \frac{\rho_{XY}\sqrt{n}}{\sqrt{(1-\rho_{XY}^2)}}$$

$$= \frac{\rho_{TXTY}\rho_{XT}\rho_{YT}\sqrt{n}}{\sqrt{1-\rho_{TXTY}^2\rho_{XT}^2\rho_{YT}^2}}. \tag{5.26}$$

It is obvious that the non-centrality parameter for testing the correlation of the true scores can be obtained by simply replacing ρ_{XY} with $\rho_{TXTY}\rho_{XT}\rho_{YT}$ in the non-centrality parameter for testing the correlation of the observed scores.

We can use the following R code to compute statistical power in testing a correlation of observed X and Y (e.g., $\rho_{XY} = .40$). When the sample size is set to forty-four ($n = 44$), power starts to exceed .80 in value.

```
#power for testing a correlation

p4r=function(n=20,r=.40){
 a=.05
 t0=qt(1-a/2,n-2)
 nc=r*sqrt(n)/sqrt(1-r^2)
 1-pt(t0,n-2,nc)+pt(-t0,n-2,nc)
}


for(n in 10:50) cat(n, '\t', p4r(n),'\n')
```

There are two ways to calculate power for testing the same correlation coefficient in SAS: the onecorr statement and the multreg statement in the proc power procedure.

```
* power for testing a correlation;

*use onecorr statement in proc power;
proc power;
 onecorr
   dist=t
   model=fixed    /*by default model=random        */
   corr=.40       /*It treats both x and y as random */
   ntotal=10 to 50
   power= .;
 plot x=n min=10 max=50;
run;


*use multreg statement;
   *R square= r^2=.4^2=.16;
   *R square w/o 1 predictor is 0. So R square diff is .16;
proc power;
 multreg
   model = fixed
   nfullpredictors = 1
   ntestpredictors = 1
   rsquarefull = 0.16
   rsquarediff = 0.16
```

```
    ntotal = 10 to 50
    power = .;
run;
```

The power computation here assumes that one variable Y is random but the other one X is `fixed` in the `model`. Had the variable X been treated as `random` too, the power value would be slightly lower. The difference in power between the fixed and random X is typically small when the sample size is large. Hence, the distinction is more a theoretical one than a practical necessity.

The SPSS syntax can be created to produce power in testing a correlation coefficient:

```
* POWER FOR TESTING A CORRELATION.
DATA LIST LIST/N R.
BEGIN DATA
44 .40
END DATA.
COMPUTE TO=IDF.T(.975,N-2).
COMPUTE NC=R*SQRT(N)/SQRT(1-R**2).
COMPUTE P=1-NCDF.T(TO,N-2,NC)+NCDF.T(-TO,N-2,NC).
EXECUTE.
```

5.3 Multiple Regression

Linear regression analysis may involve more than one explanatory variable in accounting for the variation in the outcome. It naturally gives rise to multiple regression where all the relevant variables can be utilized to explain or predict the outcome. For example, a management consulting company may use a variety of variables to make decisions on personnel selection in a sales department. The outcome variable can measure annual sales volume, and the explanatory variables can be aptitude test, prior annual sales, and experience in years. The regression of the outcome on the three predictors becomes multiple regression analysis. The regression model is a natural extension of simple regression with additional explanatory variables and regression coefficients,

$$Y_i = \beta_0 + \beta_1 X_{1i} + \beta_2 X_{2i} + \beta_3 X_{3i} + e_i, i = 1, 2, ..., n. \qquad (5.27)$$

The test of the model fit or regression coefficients still uses the F statistic. In general, the F ratio compares the mean squares of the explained variation due to the regression with the mean squares of the residual error.

$$F = \frac{SSR/df_1}{SSE/df_2},$$ (5.28)

where the number of degrees of freedom in the numerator df_1 is the number of explanatory or independent variables, and the number of degrees of freedom in the denominator is df_2. As the regression sum of squares over the total sum of squares forms the multiple correlation coefficient $\hat{R}^2 = SSR/TSS$, the residual sum of squares is $SSE = (1 - \hat{R}^2)TSS$. We can, therefore, express the F ratio in terms of $\hat{R}^2$,

$$F = \frac{\hat{R}^2}{1 - \hat{R}^2}\frac{df_2}{df_1}.$$ (5.29)

Aside from the degrees of freedom, $\hat{R}^2/(1 - \hat{R}^2)$ estimates the effect size in multiple regression. Cohen (1988) uses $f^2 = \hat{R}^2/(1 - \hat{R}^2)$ as the effect size measure for multiple regression. The effect size compares the proportion of the explained variation against the proportion of the unexplained variation or residual variation. A large effect size suggests that the multiple regression has accounted for a substantial amount of variance in the outcome compared with the unexplained remaining variance. The estimated effect size adjusted by the degrees of freedom becomes the F test,

$$F = \hat{f}^2\frac{df_2}{df_1}.$$ (5.30)

The F ratio is versatile in checking the statistical significance of the explained variation due to different sources. It can be used to test the model fit or the statistical significance of a single explanatory variable or a set of explanatory variables. Depending on which source of explained variation the F statistic tests, the multiple correlation çoefficient $\hat{R}^2$ will change accordingly.

To test model fit, we want to see whether all the explanatory or independent variables in the regression have accounted for a substantial amount of the variation when compared with that in a null model without any explanatory variable. The $\hat{R}$ is the multiple correlation coefficient between

Y and all the predictors X_1, X_2, and X_3 in the example of sales personnel selection. We hereby denote it as $\hat{R}^2_{YX_1X_2X_3}$. The F statistic is

$$F = \frac{\hat{R}^2_{YX_1X_2X_3}}{1 - \hat{R}^2_{YX_1X_2X_3}} \frac{df_2}{df_1},$$ (5.31)

where df_1 is 3, and df_2 is $n - 4$ in our example. The effect size is

$$f^2 = \frac{R^2_{YX_1X_2X_3}}{1 - R^2_{YX_1X_2X_3}}.$$

To test a single predictor, say X_3, the F ratio becomes

$$F = \frac{\hat{R}^2_{Y(X_3.X_1X_2)}}{1 - \hat{R}^2_{YX_1X_2X_3}} \frac{df_2}{df_1},$$ (5.32)

where $\hat{R}_{Y(X_3.X_1X_2)}$ is the semi-partial correlation between X_3 and Y with X_1 and X_2 being partialled out. The squared semi-partial correlation $\hat{R}^2_{Y(X_3.X_1X_2)}$ measures the unique explained variation in outcome due to the addition of X_3 in the model,

$$\hat{R}^2_{Y(X_3.X_1X_2)} = \hat{R}^2_{YX_1X_2X_3} - \hat{R}^2_{YX_1X_2},$$ (5.33)

where $\hat{R}^2_{YX_1X_2}$ is the squared multiple correlation between the outcome Y and explanatory variables X_1 and X_2 in the reduced model without X_3. Now df_1 is 1 because the explained variation in the numerator is the difference in accounted variation between the model with three explanatory variables and the reduced model with two explanatory variables, and such a difference is due to one variable X_3. The df_2 is the same as that in the full model with all the explanatory variables X_1, X_2, and X_3 ($df_2 = n - 4$), as the denominator of the F ratio is still the same (i.e., $1 - \hat{R}^2_{YX_1X_2X_3}$). The population effect size is

$$f^2 = \frac{R^2_{Y(X_3.X_1X_2)}}{1 - R^2_{YX_1X_2X_3}}.$$

To test a set of explanatory variables, the F ratio uses the semi-partial multiple correlation between Y and those variables in the set. For instance, we may want to test whether predictors X_2 and X_3 together account for a significant amount of variation in the outcome. The numerator in the F ratio is now $\hat{R}^2_{Y(X_2X_3.X_1)}$. The F statistic therefore becomes

$$F = \frac{\hat{R}^2_{Y(X_2X_3.X_1)}}{1 - \hat{R}^2_{YX_1X_2X_3}} \frac{df_2}{df_1}, \tag{5.34}$$

where df_1 is 2, and df_2 is still $n - 4$. The population effect size is

$$f^2 = \frac{R^2_{Y(X_2X_3.X_1)}}{1 - R^2_{YX_1X_2X_3}}.$$

When the null hypothesis is true in both scenarios (i.e., a single variable or a set of variables), the effect size f^2 is assumed to be zero. The F statistic follows a central F distribution. When the alternative hypothesis holds true, the effect size f^2 is non-zero ($H_a : f^2 \neq 0$). Under the alternative hypothesis, the F statistic assumes a non-central F distribution or $F' = F(df_1, df_2, \lambda)$. The statistical power of the F test is

$$1 - \beta = 1 - P[F(df_1, df_2, \lambda) < F_{1-\alpha, df_1, df_2}], \tag{5.35}$$

where the non-centrality parameter can be expressed in terms of the effect size and degrees of freedom (Cohen, 1988),

$$\lambda_r = f^2(df_1 + df_2 + 1). \tag{5.36}$$

Cohen's non-centrality parameter uses $df_1 + df_2 + 1$ instead of the total sample size n. It differs from the SAS proc power procedure, which uses the total sample size n in the `multreg` statement. The SAS proc power uses f^2n as the non-centrality parameter in power analysis for multiple regression with fixed independent variables. In a fixed model, the observed values on the independent variables are treated as fixed or constant. This is an implied assumption in regular multiple regression analysis, although it is seldom made conspicuous, as the other four assumptions are (i.e., linearity, normality, independence, and homoscedasticity). Gatsonis and Sampson (1989) distinguish two types of multiple regression. One assumes fixed independent variables, the other random independent variables. In the random model, the independent variables themselves are random variables.

They can form a multivariate normal distribution. Gatsonis and Sampson (1989) find that Cohen's non-centrality parameter $f^2(df_1 + df_2 + 1)$ serendipitously provides a good approximation of the power in the random multiple regression, although Cohen (1988) does not explain the adjustment of the non-centrality parameter. The SAS proc power procedure currently calculates power values in both models. The exact power computation in the random model is rather complicated, and the power differs by a negligible percentage (e.g., 1 or 2 percent) from the power in the fixed multiple regression. We will employ Cohen's non-centrality parameter λ_r for calculating power in the random multiple regression. In a fixed model, we will use

$$\lambda_f = f^2 n. \tag{5.37}$$

We can use the example in Cohen (1988, pp. 431–432) to show the difference between Cohen and SAS. The example concerns the regression of attitude toward socialized medicine on age, age squared, age cubed, years of education, and squared years of education. The number of independent variables is five ($p = 5$). In calculating the power for testing two independent variables on years of education, Cohen estimates that the full model with the five independent variables yields $R^2 = .25$. The reduced model contains three age-related independent variables without the polynomial terms of years of education. The difference in R^2 between the full model and the reduced model is set to .12. The effect size is, therefore, $f^2 = .12/(1 - .25) = .16$. The following R code uses Cohen's non-centrality parameter under the random model (i.e., m='random'). Cohen's non-centrality parameter is $\lambda_r = .16 \times (2 + 84 + 1)$. When the sample size is 90 ($n = 90$), the power is .77 (Cohen, 1988, p. 432, line 5).

```
# power in multiple regression

#parameter values are from Cohen p.432
p4mr=function(n=90, a=.01,p=5,df1=2,r2s=.12,
r2e=1-.25,m='fixed'){
  df2=n-p-1
  f2=r2s/r2e
  if (m=='fixed') nc=f2*n else nc=f2*(df1+df2+1)
# nc=f2*(df1+df2+1)
# Cohen 1988 p.414, Gatsonis and Sampson 1989
```

```
f0=qf(1-a,df1,df2)
p=1-pf(f0,df1,df2,nc)
cat('f0=',f0,'\t','nc=',nc,'\t','power=',p)
}

p4mr(m='random')
#>0.7725136  Cohen p432
```

Had the fixed model been assumed, the non-centrality parameter would have been $\lambda_f = .16 * 90$. In the fixed model, the power would be .79. We can obtain a power of .79 by using the power function in the R code (i.e., p4mr()). Alternatively, we can use SAS proc power to get the same power value:

```
* power in multiple regression;
  *parameter values from Cohen p 432;
proc power;
 multreg
   model = fixed
   alpha=.01
   nfullpredictors = 5
   ntestpredictors = 2
   rsquarefull = 0.25
   rsquarediff = 0.12
   ntotal = 90
   power = .;
run;
```

The SPSS syntax can be created to duplicate the power values under the two models:

```
* POWER IN MULTIPLE REGRESSION.
DATA LIST LIST/N A P DF1 R2S R2F.
BEGIN DATA
90 .01 5  2  .12 .25
END DATA.
COMPUTE F2=R2S/(1-R2F).
COMPUTE DF2=N-P-1.
```

```
COMPUTE NCF=F2*N.
COMPUTE NCR=F2*(DF1+DF2+1).
COMPUTE PF=1-NCDF.F(IDF.F(1-A,DF1,DF2),DF1,DF2,NCF).
COMPUTE PR=1-NCDF.F(IDF.F(1-A,DF1,DF2),DF1,DF2,NCR).
EXECUTE.
VARIABLE LABELS PF 'Power-fixed model'
                PR 'Power-random model'.
DELETE VARIABLES A TO R2F.
```

5.4   Analysis of Covariance

5.4.1   Statistical Power with Covariate Adjustment

Analysis of covariance (ANCOVA) combines analysis of variance with linear regression. It extends the regular analysis of variance by including a continuous covariate or concomitant variable. The covariate is linearly related to the outcome variable, and it is observed along with the outcome variable. Including the covariate allows one to remove otherwise unaccounted variance from the residual error, so as to produce a smaller standard error in estimating the treatment effect.

The estimate of the treatment effect is adjusted by using the covariate mean differences between the treatment conditions. The adjusted effect estimates usually have a smaller standard error than the unadjusted estimates. A smaller standard error is conducive to producing a higher statistical power. Because of this, ANCOVA is liberally used in data analysis. The procedure is subject to misuse and abuse if caution is not exercised over violation of the underlying assumptions (Porter and Raudenbush, 1987).

There are four basic assumptions for ANCOVA analysis. The first assumption states that residual errors are normally distributed; the second assumption requires that individual observations are independent of each other; the third assumption is that the outcome is linearly related to the covariates; and the fourth one assumes that the regression of the outcome on the covariate remains the same among the different treatment conditions. Sometimes an additional assumption is made about the absence of measurement errors in the covariate.

Although ANCOVA analysis does not require random assignment, it can be used in non-randomized studies to remove potential bias. It is in non-randomized studies that ANCOVA causes great misinterpretation about the treatment effect. The lack of random assignment introduces many validity threats to the causal inference about the possible treatment effect. The covariate-adjusted analysis can correct the bias due to the observed confounders, but it cannot eliminate the confounding effect due to the unobserved ones. For instance, if the subjects are not randomly assigned to the treatments, the received treatment may be correlated with the subjects' prior attributes that influence the outcome. The treatment group may have more subjects whose prior attributes favor better performance on the outcome than does the control group. Any observed difference in the outcome between the treatment and control groups can then be ascribed to the different treatments received or to the difference in the prior attributes that exist between the treatment and control groups before the intervention. Thus, the subjects' prior attributes can confound the interpretation of the treatment effect and discredit the causal link between the treatment and its effect. In non-randomized studies, it is always problematic to use ANCOVA analysis and draw a clear inference about the treatment effect. We will therefore focus on covariate adjusted analyses in randomized experiments.

The ANCOVA model can be written as

$$Y_{ij} = \mu + \alpha_j + \beta(X_{ij} - \overline{X}) + e_{ij}, i = 1, 2, \cdots, n, \ j = 1, 2, \cdots, J, \quad (5.38)$$

where β is the regression coefficient for the covariate X, $\overline{X}$ is the covariate mean, and e_{ij} is the residual error. It has a normal distribution $e_{ij} \sim N(0, \sigma^2)$. The covariate is centered around its mean (i.e., $X_{ij} - \overline{X}$), which makes it easy to interpret the meaning of the parameter μ. The parameter μ is now the overall mean. If the covariate is not centered around its mean, the overall mean will be $\mu + \beta\overline{X}$. So centering is preferred in formulating the ANCOVA model.

The ANCOVA model can be rearranged so that it becomes a special case of the ANOVA model. Statistical power analysis in ANOVA can be readily adapted to accommodate ANCOVA. The covariate on the right side of the equation can be moved to the left side. The outcome now becomes the covariate-adjusted outcome on the left side, and right side of the equation is a regular ANOVA model;

$$Y_{ij} - \beta(X_{ij} - \overline{X}) = \mu + \alpha_j + e_{ij}$$
$$Y'_{ij} = \mu + \alpha_j + e_{ij}, \tag{5.39}$$

where Y'_{ij} is the covariate-adjusted outcome. It has a smaller error variance than the original variance of Y_{ij}. The reduction in error variance depends on the correlation between the original outcome Y_{ij} and the covariate X_{ij}. Suppose that the correlation between Y_{ij} and X_{ij} is r and the variance of Y_{ij} is σ_Y^2. It is generally known that

$$\sigma^2 = (1 - r^2)\sigma_Y^2. \tag{5.40}$$

The error variance σ^2 in the ANCOVA model is reduced by a fraction of r^2 over the error variance σ_Y^2 in the model that does not include a covariate. The higher the correlation r is, the smaller the error variance σ^2 becomes. The reduced error variance tends to produce higher statistical power in ANCOVA than in ANOVA without using the covariate.

The term α_j in Equation 5.39 represents the adjusted treatment effect for the jth group. It is different from the same term in ANOVA. The latter is estimated by the sample mean of the jth group without covariate adjustment. In ANCOVA, the adjusted treatment effect α_j is estimated as the sample mean of the jth group minus the estimated regression coefficient $\hat{\beta}$ multiplied by the difference between the group mean on the covariate and the grand mean of the covariate $\overline{X}_j - \overline{X}$,

$$\hat{\alpha}_j = \overline{Y}_j - \overline{Y} - \hat{\beta}(\overline{X}_j - \overline{X}), \tag{5.41}$$

where $\overline{Y}$ is the grand sample mean, and $\hat{\beta}$ can be a least squares estimate (Kirk, 1995).

The statistical analysis in ANCOVA basically uses the adjusted means to test the null hypothesis that there is no mean difference among the groups ($H_0 : \alpha_j = 0$). The test still uses an F statistic with numerator degrees of freedom $\nu_1 = J - 1$ and denominator degrees of freedom $\nu_2 = J(n-1) - 1$. The denominator has one less degree of freedom than its counterpart in ANOVA because the estimate $\hat{\beta}$ consumes one degree of freedom. Under the alternative hypothesis, the F statistic has a non-central F distribution F'

with a non-centrality parameter λ,

$$\lambda = \sum_{j=1}^{J} n\alpha_j^2 / \sigma^2 \qquad (5.42)$$

$$= \sum_{j=1}^{J} n\alpha_j^2 / ((1 - r^2)\sigma_Y^2). \qquad (5.43)$$

In the presence of multiple covariates, the residual variance σ^2 is reduced by R^2 percent. The symbol R is the multiple correlation coefficient between the outcome Y and p number of covariates,

$$\sigma^2 = (1 - R^2)\sigma_Y^2. \qquad (5.44)$$

In general, we have

$$\lambda = \sum_{j=1}^{J} n\alpha_j^2 / ((1 - R^2)\sigma_Y^2), \qquad (5.45)$$

The statistical power function is

$$1 - \beta = 1 - P[F^{'}(\nu_1, \nu_2, \lambda) \geq F_{1-\alpha, \nu_1, \nu_2}], \qquad (5.46)$$

where $\nu_1 = J - 1$, $\nu_2 = N - J - p$, and p is the number of covariates.

The non-centrality parameter in Equation 5.42 looks the same as that in ANOVA, but there are noteworthy differences. First, the error σ^2 is smaller than its counterpart in ANOVA. The non-centrality parameter in ANCOVA is, therefore, larger than its counterpart in ANOVA, other things being equal. By that, ANCOVA yields a higher statistical power than does ANOVA. Second, the treatment effect α_j is based on the adjusted mean, that is,

$$\alpha_j = \mu_j - \mu - \beta(\overline{X}_j - \overline{X}), \qquad (5.47)$$

where $\mu_j = E(\overline{Y}_j)$. When the sample size is relatively large and random assignment is used, the covariate mean difference $\overline{X}_j - \overline{X}$ is small or negligible. The sum of squares of the adjusted effects is then approximately equal to the sum of squares of the unadjusted effects or the effect size for ANOVA,

$$\sum_{j=1}^{J} \alpha_j^2 \approx \sum_{j=1}^{J} (\mu_j - \mu)^2. \qquad (5.48)$$

This effect size for ANOVA can be approximately applied to statistical power analysis in ANCOVA. The statistical power analysis is similar between ANOVA and ANCOVA except that the error variance is reduced in the latter case. With the same effect size and a reduced error variance, ANCOVA typically produces a higher statistical power estimate than does ANOVA.

It should be noted that this power analysis assumes that there is a sufficient sample size in ANCOVA. When the sample size is small, it is difficult to conjecture the true effect size based on the adjusted means. The groups may differ substantially in the covariate profile even under random assignment. The term $\overline{X}_j - \overline{X}$ is then no longer negligible. If the effect size for ANOVA is used in the power analysis for ANCOVA, it may produce spuriously high power values. Although it is complicated to assess power in covariate-adjusted analysis with small sample sizes, we can nevertheless examine the performance of the standard error of the treatment effect estimate to infer its consequence on statistical power. The standard error is intimately related to the statistical power because the test statistic is typically a ratio of the effect estimate and its standard error. A small standard error increases the absolute value of the test statistic and helps obtain statistical significance, which is conducive to a higher statistical power. On the contrary, if covariate adjustment does not reduce the standard error of the treatment effect estimate, including covariates will unlikely improve the statistical power in testing the treatment effect.

5.4.2 Small Sample Size and Standard Error with Covariate Adjustment

ANCOVA does not necessarily help gain precision in estimating the treatment effect when the sample size is relatively small. Liu (2011) shows that for small sample sizes the covariate-adjusted treatment effect estimate can have a larger standard error than the unadjusted treatment effect estimate.

We can compare the standard errors of the treatment effect estimate with and without covariate adjustment by calculating their ratio. For simplicity of explanation, we can examine the treatment effect estimate between the jth and j'th condition. The standard error of the treatment effect estimate without covariate adjustment is

$$\sigma_{\overline{Y}_j - \overline{Y}_{j'}} = \sigma_Y \sqrt{\frac{2}{n}}.$$

The standard error with covariate adjustment is

$$\sigma_{\overline{Y}'_j - \overline{Y}'_{j'}} = \sigma \sqrt{\frac{2}{n} + \frac{(\overline{X}_j - \overline{X}_{j'})^2}{\sum_j^J \sum_i^n (X_{ij} - \overline{X}_j)^2}},$$

where $\overline{X}_j - \overline{X}_{j'}$ is the covariate mean difference between the jth and j'th condition, and $\sum_j^J \sum_i^n (X_{ij} - \overline{X}_j)^2$ is the within-group sum of squares for the covariate. The covariate mean difference and within-group sum of squares are normally treated as constant in the linear regression model. It is difficult to fill in actual values for the covariate mean difference and within-group sum of squares when assessing the standard error with covariate adjustment. However, if the covariate is conceived of as a normal random variable, it becomes quite simple to model the probabilistic behavior of the covariate mean difference and within-group sum of squares;

$$t = \frac{\overline{X}_j - \overline{X}_{j'}}{\sqrt{\frac{2}{n}} \sqrt{\frac{\sum_j^J \sum_i^n (X_{ij} - \overline{X}_j)^2}{J(n-1)}}},$$

where

$$\frac{\sum_j^J \sum_i^n (X_{ij} - \overline{X}_j)^2}{J(n-1)}$$

is a sample estimate of the variance of the covariate. So the covariate mean difference and within-group sum of squares are related to a t statistic with degrees of freedom $v = J(n-1)$. The standard error with covariate adjustment can be expressed in terms of the t statistic;

$$\sigma_{\overline{Y}'_j - \overline{Y}'_{j'}} = \sigma \sqrt{\frac{2}{n}\left(1 + \frac{t^2}{v}\right)}.$$

Table 5.1: Sample size n and $P[\theta < 1]$

n	$P[\theta < 1]$
4	0.4496
5	0.5140
6	0.5668
7	0.6113
8	0.6496
9	0.6829
10	0.7122
11	0.7382
12	0.7613
13	0.7820
14	0.8005
15	0.8173

The ratio of the standard errors with and without covariate adjustment is

$$\theta = \frac{\sigma_{\bar{Y}'_j - \bar{Y}'_{j'}}}{\sigma_{\bar{Y}_j - \bar{Y}_{j'}}}$$
$$= \frac{\sigma \sqrt{1 + t^2/v}}{\sigma_Y}$$
$$= \sqrt{(1 - r^2)(1 + t^2/v)}. \tag{5.49}$$

When the ratio θ is smaller than one, covariate adjustment reduces the standard error. Otherwise, covariate adjustment may not gain any precision in estimating the treatment effect. For instance, suppose that there are only one treatment and one control condition with five subjects in each ($J = 2$ and $n = 5$). The correlation between the covariate and the outcome is .3, and the chance covariate mean difference produces a t statistic equal to one ($r = .25$ and $t = 1$). The ratio θ is, therefore, 1.027, which means that the standard error is larger with covariate adjustment than without covariate adjustment. In this case, including a covariate will not help improve precision in estimating the treatment effect. Other things being equal, the more the groups differ in the covariate profile, the larger the t statistic and the ratio θ.

We do not need to focus on the realized t value because it randomly varies from study to study. Instead, we can check the probability of obtaining θ less than one;

$$P[\theta < 1] = P\left[t^2 < \frac{vr^2}{1 - r^2}\right]$$
$$= P\left[F(1, v) < \frac{vr^2}{1 - r^2}\right]. \tag{5.50}$$

So the probability $P[\theta < 1]$ is a cumulative distribution function of a central F with one degree of freedom in the numerator and v degrees of freedom in the denominator. Table 5.1 lists the sample size n and the probability $P[\theta < 1]$. The chance of gaining precision is not superior when covariate-adjusted analysis uses limited sample size.

Chapter 6

Multivariate Analysis

Research studies in the social and behavioral sciences may involve multiple outcomes. The multivariate measures can portray different but correlated characteristics that are integral to a full description of the subjects. For example, students' academic achievements can be calibrated on verbal and quantitative skills. Their scores on verbal and quantitative test sections of a Graduate Record Examination (GRE) form a natural set of outcomes that are indispensable in characterizing the students' academic aptitude. The multiple outcomes give rise to multivariate analysis, which can be extended from the corresponding univariate procedures (e.g., two sample t and univariate ANOVA). In the following, we will first deal with the Hotelling T^2 test in a two-group comparison and then with multivariate analysis of variance that involves more than two groups.

6.1   Hotelling T^2 for Two-group Comparison

The Hotelling T^2 statistic is closely related to its univariate counterpart, the two sample t. The t test is

$$T = \frac{\bar{y}_1 - \bar{y}_2}{\hat{\sigma}\sqrt{\frac{1}{n_1} + \frac{1}{n_2}}},$$

where $\bar{y}_1$ and $\bar{y}_2$ are the group sample means, and n_1 and n_2 are the group sizes. After we square the t statistic, we have

$$T^2 = \left(\frac{n_1 n_2}{n_1 + n_2}\right)(\bar{y}_1 - \bar{y}_2)(\hat{\sigma}^2)^{-1}(\bar{y}_1 - \bar{y}_2).$$

If we replace the sample mean by a vector of means on multiple outcomes ($\bar{y}_1$ and $\bar{y}_2$) and the estimated variance $\hat{\sigma}^2$ by the estimated variance covariance matrix of the multiple outcomes ($\hat{\Sigma}$), we can obtain the multivariate Hotelling T^2 statistic,

$$T^2 = \left(\frac{n_1 n_2}{n_1 + n_2}\right)(\bar{y}_1 - \bar{y}_2)'\hat{\Sigma}^{-1}(\bar{y}_1 - \bar{y}_2). \tag{6.1}$$

The mean vector $\bar{y}_1$ contains the sample means on the multiple outcomes for the treatment group, and the mean vector $\bar{y}_2$ holds the sample means for the control group. For simplicity of illustration, we assume that there are two outcome variables. The mean vectors are

$$\bar{y}_1 = \begin{bmatrix} \bar{y}_{11} \\ \bar{y}_{21} \end{bmatrix}, \ \bar{y}_2 = \begin{bmatrix} \bar{y}_{12} \\ \bar{y}_{22} \end{bmatrix}.$$

The first subscript of $\bar{y}$ indicates which outcome it is; the second subscript shows to which group the sample mean belongs. For instance, $\bar{y}_{21}$ is the sample mean on the second outcome for the treatment group.

The estimated variance covariance matrix is

$$\hat{\Sigma} = \frac{1}{n_1 + n_2 - 2}\left(\begin{bmatrix} \sum(y_{i11} - \bar{y}_{11})^2 & \sum(y_{i11} - \bar{y}_{11})(y_{i21} - \bar{y}_{21}) \\ \sum(y_{i21} - \bar{y}_{21})(y_{i11} - \bar{y}_{11}) & \sum(y_{i21} - \bar{y}_{21})^2 \end{bmatrix}\right.$$
$$\left. + \begin{bmatrix} \sum(y_{i12} - \bar{y}_{12})^2 & \sum(y_{i12} - \bar{y}_{12})(y_{i22} - \bar{y}_{22}) \\ \sum(y_{i22} - \bar{y}_{22})(y_{i12} - \bar{y}_{12}) & \sum(y_{i22} - \bar{y}_{22})^2 \end{bmatrix}\right), \tag{6.2}$$

where $n_1 + n_2 - 2$ is the pooled degrees of freedom from both groups. The first matrix within the parentheses is the sum of squares cross product matrix (SSCP) for the treatment group, and the second matrix is that for the control group. The diagonal elements in both SSCP matrices are the sums of squares for the two outcome variables, and the off-diagonal elements in the matrices are the cross products of the deviation scores for the two outcomes. Had there been more outcome variables, the estimated variance covariance matrix would expand its dimension. If there is only one outcome, the variance covariance matrix $\hat{\Sigma}$ reduces to a scalar: it simplifies to the pooled sample variance in the regular t test, $(\sum (y_{i11} - \bar{y}_{11})^2 + \sum (y_{i12} - \bar{y}_{12})^2)/(n_1 + n_2 - 2)$.

The estimated variance and covariate matrix plays an important part in defining the multivariate effect size. The inverse of $\hat{\Sigma}$ premultiplied and postmultiplied by the difference of the two mean vectors is the Mahalanobis distance D^2,

$$D^2 = (\bar{y}_1 - \bar{y}_2)' \hat{\Sigma}^{-1} (\bar{y}_1 - \bar{y}_2). \tag{6.3}$$

The Mahalanobis distance measures the overall separation between the two contrasted groups, taking into account the correlations among the different outcomes. It is a multivariate measure of the effect size. If we replace the sample estimates by their population parameters in D^2, we obtain the multivariate effect size Δ^2,

$$\Delta^2 = (\mu_1 - \mu_2)' \Sigma^{-1} (\mu_1 - \mu_2), \tag{6.4}$$

where the population mean vectors are $\mu_1' = [\mu_{11}\ \mu_{21}]$ and $\mu_2' = [\mu_{12}\ \mu_{22}]$.

The multivariate effect size Δ^2 can be related to the univariate effect sizes of the individual outcomes. Suppose that we still use two outcome variables. The univariate effect size for the first outcome is $\Delta_1 = \mu_{11} - \mu_{12}$, and the effect size for the second outcome $\Delta_2 = \mu_{21} - \mu_{22}$. We can write the two univariate effect sizes in matrix notation;

$$\begin{bmatrix} \Delta_1 \\ \Delta_2 \end{bmatrix} = \mu_1 - \mu_2. \tag{6.5}$$

The univariate standardized effect sizes are $\delta_1 = \Delta_1/\sigma_1$ and $\delta_2 = \Delta_2/\sigma_2$, where σ_1 and σ_2 are the standard deviations for the first and second outcomes, respectively. In matrix notation, the standardized effect sizes can be expressed as

$$\delta = \begin{bmatrix} \delta_1 \\ \delta_2 \end{bmatrix} = \begin{bmatrix} \sigma_1 & 0 \\ 0 & \sigma_2 \end{bmatrix}^{-1} (\mu_1 - \mu_2) = D^{-1}(\mu_1 - \mu_2). \tag{6.6}$$

The diagonal matrix D is the standard deviation matrix with the diagonal elements being σ_1 and σ_2. Through the standard deviation matrix D, we can express the variance covariance matrix Σ in terms of a correlation matrix R,

$$\Sigma = DRD. \tag{6.7}$$

In our case, the correlation matrix R is a 2-by-2 matrix with the diagonal elements being 1 and the off-diagonal elements being the correlation r_{12} between y_1 and y_2,

$$R = \begin{bmatrix} 1 & r_{12} \\ r_{21} & 1 \end{bmatrix}. \tag{6.8}$$

The multivariate effect size Δ^2 can be expressed in terms of the standardized effect size δ and the correlation matrix R,

$$\begin{aligned} \Delta^2 &= (\mu_1 - \mu_2)'\Sigma^{-1}(\mu_1 - \mu_2) \\ &= (\mu_1 - \mu_2)'(DRD)^{-1}(\mu_1 - \mu_2) \\ &= \left[(\mu_1 - \mu_2)'D^{-1}\right] R^{-1} \left[D^{-1}(\mu_1 - \mu_2)\right]. \end{aligned}$$

Substituting δ for $D^{-1}(\mu_1 - \mu_2)$ in this equation (see Equation 6.6), we can obtain a simplified expression of the multivariate effect size,

$$\Delta^2 = \delta' R^{-1} \delta. \tag{6.9}$$

Equation 6.9 shows a general way to compute the multivariate effect size. When there are p outcomes, the vector δ contains the standardized effect sizes on the p outcomes, $\delta' = [\delta_1\ \delta_2\ ...\ \delta_p]$. The correlation matrix R has a size of p by p,

$$R = \begin{bmatrix} 1 & r_{12} & r_{13} & ... & ... \\ r_{21} & 1 & r_{23} & ... & ... \\ ... & ... & ... & ... & ... \\ r_{p1} & r_{p2} & r_{p3} & ... & 1 \end{bmatrix}. \tag{6.10}$$

A researcher can conjecture the effect size for individual outcomes and then estimate the correlations between individual outcomes when computing the multivariate effect size for statistical power analysis.

Statistical power analysis in the Hotelling T^2 test uses a non-central F distribution because the Hotelling T^2 statistic can be converted to an exact F statistic,

$$\frac{n_1 + n_2 - p - 1}{(n_1 + n_2 - 2)p}T^2 = F(p, n_1 + n_2 - p - 1, \lambda). \tag{6.11}$$

When the null hypothesis is true ($H_0 : \mu_1 = \mu_2$), the non-centrality parameter λ is zero. Under the alternative hypothesis $H_a : \mu_1 \neq \mu_2$, the mean difference $\mu_1 - \mu_2$ is a non-zero vector. The F converted from the Hotelling T^2 is a non-central F'. In this case, the non-centrality parameter is a function of the multivariate effect size Δ^2 (see Equation 6.9),

$$\lambda = \frac{n_1 n_2}{n_1 + n_2} \Delta^2. \tag{6.12}$$

The statistical power for the Hotelling T^2 is, therefore,

$$\begin{aligned} 1 - \beta &= P\left[F(v_1, v_2, \lambda) \geq F_{1-\alpha, v_1, v_2}\right] \\ &= 1 - P\left[F(v_1, v_2, \lambda) < F_{1-\alpha, v_1, v_2}\right], \end{aligned} \tag{6.13}$$

where the two degrees of freedom are $v_1 = p$ and $v_2 = n_1 + n_2 - p - 1$.

For example, an international student adviser at a large state university wants to examine the effectiveness of the GRE preparatory school in helping foreign undergraduate students improve their performance on the GRE. He or she will recruit a sample of foreign undergraduates who expect to graduate from the university and take the GRE for application to graduate schools soon. The students' consent will be obtained to participate in the study, and they will be randomly assigned to either the GRE preparatory school or the business-as-usual condition for two months, during which they prepare to take the GRE exam. A Hotelling T^2 test will be used to compare the two groups of students in their performance on the GRE verbal and quantitative sections. To find the appropriate sample size for the study, the statistical consultant obtains some information from the graduate school admission and the GRE preparatory school. Assume that the GRE preparatory school is expected to improve students' GRE scores by 40 on the verbal section and 70 on the quantitative section when compared with the control students, and that the standard deviations of GRE verbal and quantitative scores are 120 and 150. The ETS publication indicates that the correlation between the GRE verbal and quantitative scores is about .35. The statistical consultant converts the information to relevant parameters for power analysis, that is, $\delta' = [40/120, 70/150]$ and $r_{12} = .35$. After conducting the power analysis, the statistical consultant finds that 79 subjects are required for each group in a balanced design to achieve a power higher than .80 (see the R code and Figure 6.1).

```
# statistical power for Hotelling t
# assume equal group size of n
```

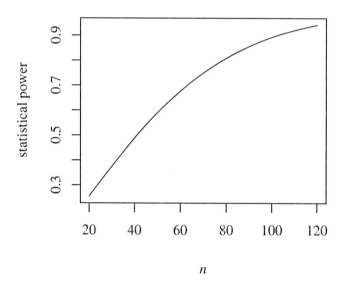

Figure 6.1: Statistical power and group size n in a Hotelling T^2 test

```
p4mt=function(n=30,d,R){
 v1=length(d)
 v2=2*n-v1-1
 a=.05
 f0=qf(1-a,v1,v2)
 lambda= .5*n*t(d)%*%solve(R)%*%d
 power=1-pf(f0,v1,v2, lambda)
}

d=matrix(c(40/120,70/150), nrow=2)
R=matrix( c(1,.35,.35,1),nrow=2)

p=p4mt(79,d,R); p

curve(p4mt(x,d,R),20,120,ylab="Statistical power",xlab="n")
```

The following SAS program can be used to calculate statistical power in the Hotelling T^2 and produce the same power curve. As the computation involves matrices, we will need to use the SAS `proc iml` procedure to handle the matrices. The power function is enclosed in a routine punctuated by the keywords `start` and `finish`.

```
*SAS Hotelling T;
proc iml;

sd={120 150};
mu={40, 70};
d=inv(diag(sd))*mu;
*print d;
R={1 .35, .35 1};

start p4mt(n,d,R);
 v1=nrow(d);
 v2=2*n-v1-1;
 a=.05;
 f0=finv(1-a, v1,v2);
 lambda= .5*n*t(d)*inv(R)*d;
 power=1-probf(f0, v1,v2, lambda);
 return(power);
finish p4mt;
              *compute power for sample size 20-120;
 nmin=20;
 nmax=120;
 power=j(nmax-nmin+1,1,.);
 do n=nmin to nmax;
  power[n-nmin+1,1]=p4mt(n,d,R);
 end;
n=nmin:nmax;
table=t(n)||power;
print table [colname={n power}];

create npower from table[colname={n power}];
append from table;
close npower;

quit;
```

```
                    *plot power against n ;

symbol color=black  interpol=join line=1;
proc gplot data=npower;
plot power*n;
run;
```

The SPSS code for computing power in the Hotelling T^2 uses MATRIX and END MATRIX to wrap the matrix computation. However, the non-central cumulative distribution function does not run within the segment enclosed by MATRIX and END MATRIX. The computed non-centrality within MATRIX and END MATRIX needs to be saved to the data set first by using SAVE within the MATRIX and END MATRIX enclosure. Once the non-centrality parameter (LAMBDA), sample size (N), and degrees of freedom (V1,V2) are saved in the data set, the non-central cumulative distribution function becomes accessible and statistical power can be computed.

```
* HOTELLING T.
SET MXLOOPS=1E3.
MATRIX.
COMPUTE D={40/120; 70/150}.
COMPUTE R={1,.35;.35, 1}.

LOOP N=20 TO 120.
 COMPUTE V1=NROW(D).
 COMPUTE V2=2*N-V1-1.
 COMPUTE LAMBDA=.5*N*T(D)*INV(R)*D.
 COMPUTE CASE={N,V1,V2,LAMBDA}.
 SAVE CASE /OUTFILE=* /VARIABLES= N V1 V2 LAMBDA.
END LOOP.

END MATRIX.

COMPUTE ALPHA=.05.
COMPUTE POWER=1-NCDF.F(IDF.F(1-ALPHA,V1,V2),V1,V2,LAMBDA).
EXECUTE.
```

```
DELETE VARIABLES V1 V2  ALPHA LAMBDA.
EXECUTE.

GRAPH
  /LINE(SIMPLE)=VALUE(POWER) BY N
  /TITLE='Statistical power vs n in Hotelling T^2'.
```

6.2 Multivariate Analysis of Variance

In multivariate analysis of variance (MANOVA), we compare more than two groups on multiple outcomes to see whether the groups differ in their multivariate profiles. If we added another treatment, say, GRE preparatory school plus private tutoring, to the previous example, we would use MANOVA to test whether the three groups perform any differently on the GRE verbal and quantitative sections. The number of outcomes is still the same, but the number of comparison groups increases from two to three.

We will compute two matrices to measure the two sources of variation in the multiple outcomes. One source of variation comes from the between-groups or between-treatment, and the other from the within-group. For simplicity of explanation, we can focus on a particular group or the kth group ($k = 1, 2, ..., K$). Its within-group sum of squares cross product matrix is

$$E_k = \begin{bmatrix} \sum (y_{i1k} - \bar{y}_{1k})^2 & \sum (y_{i1k} \quad \bar{y}_{1k})(y_{i2k} - \bar{y}_{2k}) \\ \sum (y_{i2k} - \bar{y}_{2k})(y_{i1k} - \bar{y}_{1k}) & \sum (y_{i2k} - \bar{y}_{2k})^2 \end{bmatrix}. \quad (6.14)$$

If we sum E_k across the K groups, we will have the within-group sum of squares cross product matrix E,

$$E = \sum_{k=1}^{K} E_k. \quad (6.15)$$

It should be noted that E is equivalent to $(n_1 + n_2 - 2)\hat{\Sigma}$ in the two-group comparison. In other words, we pool the within-group sum of squares cross product matrices from all the groups, much as in the Hotelling T^2 test.

We can obtain the between-treatment sum of squares cross product matrix by drawing an analogy with the univariate ANOVA. In ANOVA, the between-treatment sum of squares is

$$SST = \sum_{k=1}^{K} n(\overline{Y}_{.k} - \overline{Y}_{..})^2.$$

We can rearrange the elements in this formula and write

$$SST = n \sum_{k=1}^{K} (\overline{Y}_{.k} - \overline{Y}_{..})(\overline{Y}_{.k} - \overline{Y}_{..}).$$

Replacing $\overline{Y}_{.k}$ and $\overline{Y}_{..}$ with their multivariate counterparts produces the between-treatment sum of squares cross product matrix H in MANOVA,

$$\boldsymbol{H} = n \sum_{k=1}^{K} (\bar{\boldsymbol{y}}_k - \bar{\boldsymbol{y}})(\bar{\boldsymbol{y}}_k - \bar{\boldsymbol{y}})', \qquad (6.16)$$

where $\bar{\boldsymbol{y}}_k$ is the mean vector for the kth group, and $\bar{\boldsymbol{y}}$ is the grand mean vector. When k starts at 1, $\bar{\boldsymbol{y}}_1$ is the mean vector for the first group. The grand mean $\bar{\boldsymbol{y}}$ contains the grand means for every outcome. In our example, the grand mean vector lists the grand mean score on the GRE verbal and quantitative sections,

$$\bar{\boldsymbol{y}} = \begin{bmatrix} \bar{y}_{1.} \\ \bar{y}_{2.} \end{bmatrix}.$$

The multivariate test in MANOVA involves the determinants of E and H. The test statistic Wilks' Λ compares the determinant of E with the determinant of $E + H$ in a ratio,

$$\Lambda = \frac{|E|}{|E + H|}. \qquad (6.17)$$

The Wilks' Λ can be converted to an approximate F test (Rao, 1951),

$$F = \frac{(1 - \Lambda^{1/t})/df_1}{\Lambda^{1/t}/df_2}, \qquad (6.18)$$

where $df_1 = p\nu_1$, $df_2 = wt - (p\nu_1 - 2)/2$, p is the number of outcome variables, $\nu_1 = K - 1$, and $\nu_2 = N - K$, $w = \nu_1 + \nu_2 - (p + \nu_1 + 1)/2$ and

$$t = \sqrt{\frac{p^2 \nu_1^2 - 4}{p^2 + \nu_1^2 - 5}}.$$

If there is only one dependent variable (i.e., $p = 1$), t becomes one. The ratio $(1 - \Lambda^{1/t})/\Lambda^{1/t}$ in the aforementioned F test indicates the proportion of the between-group sum of squares over the within-group sum of squares in one-way ANOVA. In this case, Rao's F test simplifies to a regular F statistic in one-way ANOVA analysis. When more than one dependent variable is used, the ratio $(1 - \Lambda^{1/t})/\Lambda^{1/t}$ is a multivariate effect size. It shows the between-group variation relative to the within-group variation among all the p dependent variables. This effect size plays an important role in the statistical power for the Wilks' Λ test.

Building on Rao's converted F test, we can use a non-central F distribution to compute the statistical power for the Wilks' Λ test. The non-central F has df_1 in the numerator, df_2 in the denominator, and a non-centrality parameter λ. The statistical power function is, therefore,

$$1 - \beta = P[F^{'}(df_1, df_2, \lambda) \geq F_0], \qquad (6.19)$$

where F_0 is the critical F value or the $100(1 - \alpha)$th quantile of the central F distribution with degrees of freedom df_1 in the numerator and df_2 in the denominator.

The non-centrality parameter for the approximate F test can be derived in a way analogous to its counterpart in a regular F test in univariate ANOVA. In the univariate case, the non-centrality parameter can be deduced from its sample estimate, which equals the degrees of freedom in the numerator (df_1) multiplied by the F statistic in one-way ANOVA (i.e., $\hat{\lambda} = df_1 F$). The non-centrality parameter is obtained by replacing the sample estimates in the F statistics with their population counterparts. The F ratio thus obtained is denoted by F_p;

$$\lambda = df_1 F_p = df_1 \frac{n \sum_{k=1}^{K} \alpha_k^2 / df_1}{\sigma^2}.$$

In the multivariate case, we can follow the same strategy to derive the non-centrality parameter. First, we express the estimated non-centrality parameter in terms of the sample statistic, that is,

$$\hat{\lambda} = df_1 F = df_1 \frac{(1 - \Lambda^{1/t}) df_2}{\Lambda^{1/t} df_1}.$$

Next, we replace the sample estimates in Λ with their population counterparts. The population counterpart for E is the within-treatment SSCP matrix or $\nu_2 \Sigma$; the counterpart for H is the population between-treatment SSCP matrix A. The non-centrality parameter for Rao's F test in MANOVA is, therefore,

$$\lambda = \frac{p\nu_1(1 - L^{1/t})df_2}{L^{1/t}df_1}, \tag{6.20}$$

where

$$L = \frac{|\nu_2\Sigma|}{|\nu_2\Sigma + A|}, \tag{6.21}$$

and

$$A = n \sum_{k=1}^{K} (\mu_k - \mu)(\mu_k - \mu)'. \tag{6.22}$$

The vectors μ_k and μ are the population counterparts of $\bar{y}_k$ and $\bar{y}$, respectively (Rencher, 1998, p.141).

Note that in Rencher (1998) L is defined as $L = |\nu_2\Sigma|/|\nu_2\Sigma + \nu_1 A|$. The extra ν_1 appears to be unnecessary because the formula with ν_1 does not reduce to the correct non-centrality parameter for $p = 1$ in the univariate case. It is easy to see that L is derived from Λ by replacing E and H with their population counterparts. In a sense, the capital L stands for the population value of the statistic Λ. So the ratio $(1 - L^{1/t})/L^{1/t}$ corresponds to $(1 - \Lambda^{1/t})/\Lambda^{1/t}$ in the converted F test. The former is the population parameter; the latter a sample estimate. If we do not need to highlight the effect size in the non-centrality parameter, we can simplify the non-centrality parameter to

$$\lambda = (L^{-1/t} - 1)df_2. \tag{6.23}$$

Cohen (1988) actually refers to $L^{-1/t} - 1$ as the effect size in MANOVA. However, he uses a slightly different non-centrality parameter than that in Equation 6.23. He uses $\lambda = (L^{-1/t} - 1)(df_1 + df_2 + 1)$ as the non-centrality parameter for MANOVA (Cohen, 1988, p.481, Equation 10.3.1). Such a difference is consistent with his treatment of the non-centrality parameter in multiple regression, where his calculation is tantamount to assuming random independent variables (Gatsonis and Sampson, 1989). It is obvious that Rencher's non-centrality parameter is a more conservative estimate than Cohen's. As df_1 is often much smaller than df_2, the two non-centrality parameters will not much differ.

We can continue to use GRE preparation as an example to illustrate the computation of statistical power in MANOVA. Suppose that there are three different ways for foreign students to prepare for the GRE general exam. They can receive self-study GRE materials or self-study GRE materials plus 5 hours coaching or self-study GRE materials plus 24 hours classroom instruction. The three different ways of preparing for the GRE exam require increasing amounts of time commitment and instructional resources. It is natural to ask whether there is any differential exam performance among the three different ways of preparation. To add some complexity to the statistical power analysis, we will look at the GRE verbal, quantitative, and analytical scores together. In other words, the MANOVA analysis will involve three dependent variables (i.e., $p = 3$). Assume that we can obtain students' consent to achieve random assignment in the proposed study (i.e., $K = 3$). We can analyze the data, using one-way MANOVA.

In planning for a one-way MANOVA study, we want to know how many subjects must be recruited into each of the three treatment conditions. We want to find a sufficient sample size n to achieve at least .80 statistical power in the multivariate test. We will need to estimate the possible multivariate effect size L, which portrays the proportion of the performance variation due to treatment, relative to the variation due to error or individual idiosyncrasy. It is very difficult to conjecture this proportion for possible effect size because a substantive researcher rarely thinks of effect size in terms of the proportion of variation due to treatment. The researcher most likely knows how much improvement students can anticipate in each treatment. In other words, he or she will naturally think about simple effect sizes of mean score difference on the dependent variables between the treatment conditions rather than an abstract effect size like the proportion of explained variation due to treatment. Although it is possible to use the rule-of-thumb numbers for small, medium, or large effect sizes, these rule-of-thumb numbers do not capture all the research scenarios. One size does not fit all. Therefore, we need to establish a connection between the abstract multivariate effect size and the simple effect sizes that researchers typically have some knowledge of.

The multivariate effect size $L^{1/t} - 1$ can be computed based on the simple effect sizes of mean differences on the dependent variables and the correlations among the dependent variables. The simple effect sizes and correlations are often readily available to substantive researchers. In the following, we will show that the two matrices A and Σ in the capital L can be expressed in terms of simple effects, standard deviations of the dependent variables, and their correlations.

The between-group sum of squares cross product matrix A can be expressed in terms of the treatment effects on the p dependent variables,

$$
\begin{aligned}
A &= n \sum_{k=1}^{K} (\mu_k - \mu)(\mu_k - \mu)' \\[2mm]
&= n \begin{bmatrix}
\mu_{11} - \mu_{1.} & \mu_{12} - \mu_{1.} & \cdots & \mu_{1K} - \mu_{1.} \\
\mu_{21} - \mu_{2.} & \mu_{22} - \mu_{1.} & \cdots & \mu_{2K} - \mu_{2.} \\
\cdots & \cdots & \cdots & \cdots \\
\mu_{p1} - \mu_{p.} & \mu_{p2} - \mu_{p.} & \cdots & \mu_{pK} - \mu_{p.}
\end{bmatrix} \\[2mm]
&\times \begin{bmatrix}
\mu_{11} - \mu_{1.} & \mu_{21} - \mu_{2.} & \cdots & \mu_{p1} - \mu_{p.} \\
\mu_{12} - \mu_{1.} & \mu_{22} - \mu_{1.} & \cdots & \mu_{p2} - \mu_{p.} \\
\cdots & \cdots & \cdots & \cdots \\
\cdots & \cdots & \cdots & \cdots \\
\mu_{1K} - \mu_{1.} & \mu_{2K} - \mu_{2.} & \cdots & \mu_{pK} - \mu_{p.}
\end{bmatrix} \\[2mm]
&= n \begin{bmatrix} \alpha_1 \\ \alpha_2 \\ . \\ . \\ \alpha_p \end{bmatrix} \begin{bmatrix} \alpha_1' & \alpha_2' & . & .\alpha_p' \end{bmatrix},
\end{aligned}
\tag{6.24}
$$

The row vector α_p contains all the treatment effects associated with K groups on the pth dependent variable,

$$
\begin{aligned}
\alpha_p &= \begin{bmatrix} \mu_{p1} - \mu_{p.} & \mu_{p2} - \mu_{p.} & \cdots & \mu_{pK} - \mu_{p.} \end{bmatrix} \\
&= \begin{bmatrix} \alpha_{p1} & \alpha_{p2} & \cdots & \alpha_{pK} \end{bmatrix},
\end{aligned}
\tag{6.25}
$$

where $\alpha_{p1} = \mu_{p1} - \mu_{p.}, \alpha_{p2} = \mu_{p2} - \mu_{p.}, ..., \alpha_{pK} = \mu_{pK} - \mu_{p.}$.

We can estimate all the treatment effects associated with the K groups on any dependent variable by $K - 1$ simple effects that compare $K - 1$ groups with the last reference group. Suppose that we look at an arbitrary

pth dependent variable. The simple effects are

$$\Delta_{p1} = \mu_{p1} - \mu_{pK}$$
$$\Delta_{p2} = \mu_{p2} - \mu_{pK}$$
$$\vdots = \vdots$$
$$\Delta_{p(K-1)} = \mu_{p(K-1)} - \mu_{pK}. \qquad (6.26)$$

It is quite easy to prove that all the treatment effects on the pth dependent variable can be expressed in $K-1$ simple effects;

$$\alpha_{p1} = \Delta_{p1} - \frac{\Delta_{p1} + \Delta_{p2} + \cdots + \Delta_{p(K-1)}}{K}$$
$$\alpha_{p2} = \Delta_{p2} - \frac{\Delta_{p1} + \Delta_{p2} + \cdots + \Delta_{p(K-1)}}{K}$$
$$\vdots = \vdots$$
$$\alpha_{pK} = -\frac{\Delta_{p1} + \Delta_{p2} + \cdots + \Delta_{p(K-1)}}{K}. \qquad (6.27)$$

For instance, the treatment effect for the first group is

$$\alpha_{p1} = \Delta_{p1} - \frac{\Delta_{p1} + \Delta_{p2} + \cdots + \Delta_{p(K-1)}}{K}$$
$$= \mu_{p1} - \mu_{pK} - \frac{\sum_{k=1}^{K-1}(\mu_{pk} - \mu_{pK})}{K}$$
$$= \mu_{p1} - \frac{K\mu_{pK}}{K} - \frac{\sum_{k=1}^{K-1}\mu_{pk} - (K-1)\mu_{pK}}{K}$$
$$= \mu_{p1} - \frac{\sum_{k=1}^{K-1}\mu_{pk} + \mu_{pK}}{K}$$
$$= \mu_{p1} - \mu_{p\cdot\cdot}. \qquad (6.28)$$

We can prove the treatment effects for the other groups in a similar way.

For the last reference group (K),

$$\alpha_{pK} = -\frac{\Delta_{p1} + \Delta_{p2} + \cdots + \Delta_{p(K-1)}}{K}$$

$$= \mu_{pK} - \frac{K\mu_{pK}}{K} - \frac{\Delta_{p1} + \Delta_{p2} + \cdots + \Delta_{p(K-1)}}{K}$$

$$= \mu_{pK} - \frac{K\mu_{pK}}{K} - \frac{\sum_{k=1}^{K-1} \mu_{pk} - (K-1)\mu_{pK}}{K}$$

$$= \mu_{pK} - \mu_{p\cdot\cdot} \tag{6.29}$$

For example, the researcher can examine the GRE verbal, quantitative, and analytical scores ($p = 3$) between three different methods of exam preparation. The first group uses study GRE materials plus 24 hours classroom instruction ($k = 1$); the second group uses self-study GRE materials plus 5 hours coaching ($k = 2$); and the third group uses self-study GRE materials ($k = 3$). The simple effects for GRE verbal scores are estimated at $\Delta_{11} = 50$ and $\Delta_{12} = 20$, which means that the first group on average will score 50 points higher than the last reference group on the GRE verbal score, and that the second group will outperform the last group by 20 points on the GRE verbal score. The simple effects for GRE quantitative scores can be similarly estimated based on the researchers' knowledge of how the different ways of exam preparation may help students improve on the GRE. Suppose $\Delta_{21} = 70$ and $\Delta_{22} = 20$. The researcher anticipates that the first group and the second group will score 70 and 20 points higher on the GRE quantitative section than the last group, respectively. For the GRE analytical score, the researcher expects that the first group and the second group will on average outperform the last group by .5 and .2 (i.e., $\Delta_{31} = .5$ and $\Delta_{32} = .2$).

We can compute the treatment effects among the three groups for each dependent variable. For the GRE verbal score, the vector that contains the three treatment effects for the three groups is

$$\alpha_1 = \left[50 - \tfrac{50+20}{3}, \quad 20 - \tfrac{50+20}{3}, \quad -\tfrac{50+20}{3}\right].$$

The row vectors for the GRE quantitative and analytical scores are

$$\alpha_2 = \left[70 - \tfrac{70+20}{3}, \quad 20 - \tfrac{70+20}{3}, \quad -\tfrac{70+20}{3}\right] \text{ and}$$
$$\alpha_3 = \left[.5 - \tfrac{.5+.2}{3}, \quad .2 - \tfrac{.5+.2}{3}, \quad -\tfrac{.5+.2}{3}\right], \text{respectively.} \tag{6.30}$$

Substituting the vectors into A produces

$$A = n \begin{bmatrix} \alpha_1 \\ \alpha_2 \\ \alpha_3 \end{bmatrix} \begin{bmatrix} \alpha_1' & \alpha_2' & \alpha_3' \end{bmatrix}$$

$$= n \begin{bmatrix} 1266.67 & 1800 & 12.67 \\ 1800 & 2600 & 18 \\ 12.67 & 18 & 0.13 \end{bmatrix} .$$

(6.31)

In addition to A, we still need to estimate the covariance matrix Σ, which shows the variances and covariances of the dependent variables. When it comes to the relationships among the dependent variables, researchers naturally think about the correlations based on past experience, but do not typically have the covariances in mind. This does not pose a difficulty because the covariance matrix can be derived from the variances of the dependent variables and their correlations,

$$\Sigma = DRD,$$

(6.32)

where the matrix D is a diagonal matrix with the diagonal elements being the standard deviations of the dependent variables and the matrix R is the correlation matrix of the dependent variables. In our example, we may obtain the standard deviations and correlations of the GRE verbal, quantitative, and analytical scores according to *GRE: Guide to the Use of Scores 2007-08* (Educational Testing Service, 2007):

$$D = \begin{bmatrix} 120 & 0 & 0 \\ 0 & 150 & 0 \\ 0 & 0 & 1 \end{bmatrix} ;$$

$$R = \begin{bmatrix} 1.00 & 0.35 & 0.62 \\ 0.35 & 1.00 & 0.22 \\ 0.62 & 0.22 & 1.00 \end{bmatrix} .$$

With the estimated D and R, the covariance matrix Σ can be computed;

$$\Sigma = DRD = \begin{bmatrix} 14400.0 & 6300 & 74.4 \\ 6300.0 & 22500 & 33.0 \\ 74.4 & 33 & 1.0 \end{bmatrix} .$$

Suppose the sample size for each group is sixty ($n = 60$). The multivariate effect size $L^{-1/t} - 1$ is .0333228 according to Equation 6.21. The detailed computation is:

$$L = \frac{|v_2 \Sigma|}{|v_2 \Sigma + A|}$$

$$= \frac{\left| (60 \times 3 - 3) \begin{bmatrix} 14400.0 & 6300 & 74.4 \\ 6300.0 & 22500 & 33.0 \\ 74.4 & 33 & 1.0 \end{bmatrix} \right|}{\left| (60 \times 3 - 3) \begin{bmatrix} 14400.0 & 6300 & 74.4 \\ 6300.0 & 22500 & 33.0 \\ 74.4 & 33 & 1.0 \end{bmatrix} + 60 \begin{bmatrix} 1266.67 & 1800 & 12.67 \\ 1800 & 2600 & 18 \\ 12.67 & 18 & 0.13 \end{bmatrix} \right|}$$

$$= .9365435$$

$$t = \sqrt{\frac{p^2 v_1^2 - 4}{p^2 + v_1^2 - 5}}$$

$$= \sqrt{\frac{3^2(3-1)^2 - 4}{3^2 + (3-1)^2 - 5}}$$

$$= 2$$

The multivariate effect size is $L^{-1/t} - 1 = .9365435^{-1/2} - 1 = .0333228$. It is obvious that the estimated multivariate effect size is a fractional number almost impossible to get right through guessing, and that the rule-of-thumb numbers on multivariate effect size will not necessarily come close. Therefore, it is advisable to start with simple effects, standard deviations, and correlations and then estimate the multivariate effect size. The multivariate effect size thus computed will closely match our expected treatment effects based on past experience. This helps obtain an accurate estimate of statistical power in the proposed research.

When the sample size n is sixty, the statistical power for the Wilks' λ test is .71. The following R code can be used to compute the statistical power. If we seek to achieve power over .80, then we need to increase the sample size n to 71.

```
#manova
#GRE classroom coaching self-study
```

```
D<-matrix( c(120,0,0,0,150,0,0,0,1),nrow=3)
R<-matrix( c(1,.35,.62,.35,1,.22,.62,.22,1), nrow=3)

a1=c(50-(50+20)/3, 20-(50+20)/3, -(50+20)/3)
a2=c(70-(70+20)/3, 20-(70+20)/3, -(70+20)/3)
a3=c(.5-(.5+.2)/3, .2-(.5+.2)/3, -(.5+.2)/3)
a<-matrix(rbind(a1,a2,a3),nrow=3)

E=D%*%R%*%D

p4maov=function(n=30,a,E){

p=nrow(a)
k=ncol(a)

v1=k-1
v2=(n-1)*k

t=sqrt((p^2*v1^2-4)/(p^2+v1^2-5))
w=v1+v2-.5*(p+v1+1)

df1=v1*p
df2=w*t-.5*(p*v1-2)

A=n*a%*%t(a)

L=det(v2*E)/det(v2*E+A)
es=L^(-1/t)-1
lambda=(L^(-1/t)-1)*df2

alpha=.05
1-pf(qf(1-alpha,df1,df2),df1,df2,lambda)
}

p4maov(60,a,E)
p4maov(71,a,E)
```

The SAS program for computing power in MANOVA is as follows:

```
*SAS MANOVA;

proc iml;

sd={120,150,1};
D=diag(sd);
R={ 1  .35 .62,
   .35  1  .22,
   .62 .22  1};

d1={ 50  20  0};
d2={70 20 0};
d3={.5 .2 0};

j=j(1,3,1);

a1=d1-sum(d1)/ncol(d1)*j;
a2=d2-sum(d2)/ncol(d2)*j;
a3=d3-sum(d3)/ncol(d3)*j;
a=a1//a2//a3;

E=D*R*D;

                *power function for MANOVA;
start p4maov(n,a,E);
 p=nrow(a);
 k=ncol(a);
 v1=k-1;
 v2=(n-1)*k;

 t=sqrt((p**2*v1**2-4)/(p**2+v1**2-5));
 w=v1+v2-.5*(p+v1+1);

 df1=v1*p;
 df2=w*t-.5*(p*v1-2);

 aa=a*t(a);
```

```
bigA=n*aa;
L=det(v2*E)/det(v2*E+bigA);
lambda=(L**(-1/t)-1)*df2;

alpha=.05;
power=1-probf(finv(1-alpha,df1,df2),df1,df2,lambda);
return(power);
finish p4maov;

                  *compute power for sample size 35-70;
nmin=35;
nmax=75;
power=j(nmax-nmin+1,1,.);
do n=nmin to nmax;
 power[n-nmin+1,1]=p4maov(n,a,E);
end;

n=nmin:nmax;
table=t(n)||power;
print table [colname={n power}];

quit;
```

The relevant SPSS code for calculating power in MANOVA is:

```
*MANOVA.
SET MXLOOPS=1E3.

MATRIX.
COMPUTE SD={120, 150,1}.
COMPUTE D=MDIAG(SD).
COMPUTE R={1, .35, .62; .35, 1, .22; .62, .22, 1}.
COMPUTE D1={50,20,0}.
COMPUTE D2={70,20,0}.
COMPUTE D3={.5,.2,0}.
COMPUTE J=MAKE(1,3,1).

COMPUTE A1=D1-MSUM(D1)/NCOL(D1)*J.
```

```
COMPUTE A2=D2-MSUM(D2)/NCOL(D2)*J.
COMPUTE A3=D3-MSUM(D3)/NCOL(D3)*J.
COMPUTE A={A1;A2;A3}.

COMPUTE E=D*R*D.
COMPUTE P=NROW(A).
COMPUTE K=NCOL(A).

LOOP N=35 TO 75.
  COMPUTE V1=K-1.
  COMPUTE V2=(N-1)*K.
  COMPUTE T1=SQRT((P**2*V1**2-4)/(P**2+V1**2-5)).
  COMPUTE W=V1+V2-.5*(P+V1+1).
  COMPUTE DF1=V1*P.
  COMPUTE DF2=W*T1-.5*(P*V1-2).

  COMPUTE A2=A*T(A).
  COMPUTE BIGA=N*A2.

  COMPUTE L=DET(V2*E)/DET(V2*E+BIGA).
  COMPUTE NC=(L**(-1/T1)-1)*DF2.
  COMPUTE CASE={N, DF1, DF2, NC}.
  SAVE  CASE /OUTFILE=* /VARIABLES=N DF1 DF2  NC.
END LOOP.

END MATRIX.

COMPUTE ALPHA=.05.
COMPUTE POWER=1-NCDF.F(IDF.F(1-ALPHA,DF1,DF2),DF1,DF2,NC).
EXECUTE.

DELETE VARIABLES DF1 DF2  ALPHA NC.
EXECUTE.
```

6.3 Multivariate Analysis of Covariance

Multivariate analysis of covariance (MANCOVA) includes prognostic variables that may affect the dependent variables. These variables are used as covariates to reduce the unexplained error variation and improve the statistical power. The improvement is due to the reduced covariance matrix for error Σ, which makes the between-group sum of squares cross product matrix A look more prominent. The matrix A to Σ is much like a signal-to-noise ratio. The signal is more salient when the background noise is reduced. In a multivariate test, a prominent A relative to Σ is conducive to achieving statistical significance and high power.

The reduction in Σ depends on how correlated the dependent variables are with the covariates. In the previous example on GRE preparation, we may include foreign students' TOEFL score as a covariate in the multivariate analysis. The TOEFL score is a prognostic measure of foreign students' English language ability, which may affect students' performance in the GRE. Using TOEFL score as a covariate will help reduce the covariance matrix for error because the TOEFL score is known to be correlated with the GRE scores. In other words, students' English proficiency as measured by TOEFL score reflects the prior achievement that may influence the subjects' performance on the GRE. Although random assignment may create comparable groups, there still exist differences in prior achievement among the participating foreign students. If left unaccounted for in the multivariate analysis, the influence of the prior differences will inflate the error variance. Including the prior differences as covariates in the model allows us to identify them and then remove them from the error variance. The more correlated the covariates are with the dependent variables, the smaller the error variances will become. The reduction in error variance is a function of the correlations between the covariates and the dependent variables and the correlations between the dependent variables themselves.

In our example on GRE preparation, the correlations between the GRE scores and the TOEFL score can be obtained from ETS publications. The correlation between TOEFL and the three GRE scores are .64, .34, and .53 (Stricker, 2002);

$$\begin{array}{cccc} & Verb. & Quan. & Anal. \\ \boldsymbol{R}_{XY} = & [.64, & .34, & .53]. \end{array}$$

Had there been more than one covariate, a row of correlations for each additional covariate would be appended to the correlation matrix R_{XY}.

We can remove the influence of the X covariates from the dependent variables, using the correlation matrix R_{XY}. We therefore obtain the conditional covariance matrix of the dependent variables conditional on the X covariates. This is equivalent to regressing the dependent variables on the covariates and computing the covariance matrix of the residuals. The residuals are the adjusted dependent variables, and are much like the adjusted dependent variable in univariate ANCOVA. We can illustrate the idea by drawing an analogy between ANCOVA and MANCOVA. Here, we first review the adjusted dependent variable in univariate ANCOVA and then generalize it to the multivariate dependent variables in MANCOVA.

The regular ANCOVA model is

$$Y = \mu + \alpha + \beta X + e,$$

where Y is the dependent variable; μ is the grand mean; α is the treatment effect; β is the regression coefficient for the covariate X; and e is the normal error term. In computing statistical power in ANCOVA, Cohen (1988) transforms the model into a special case of ANOVA with the adjusted dependent variable $Y - \beta X$,

$$Y - \beta X = \mu + \alpha + e.$$

The transformed model can be conceived of as equivalent to the original model because X is supposed to be independent of the treatment effects α. In the absence of known bias, the treatment effects are not confounded with the covariate. In theory, the treatment groups have equal covariate means. The correlation between group affiliation and covariate means, therefore, should be zero. This assumption is tenable when random assignment is used with sufficient sample size. The transformed model is simple to deal with, for it becomes a special case of regular ANOVA except that e has a reduced error variance ($e \sim N(0, (1 - r^2)\sigma^2)$. The symbol r is the correlation between the dependent variable Y and the covariate X. Power computation for ANCOVA uses the same formulas as that in ANOVA but with a smaller error variance $(1 - r^2)\sigma^2$. This is because $Y - \beta X$ is similar to the residual after Y is regressed on X. In other words the adjusted dependent variable $Y - \beta X$ is the residual portion of the outcome that is unrelated to the covariate predictor X. Therefore, the variance of $Y - \beta X$ is reduced compared with that of the unadjusted Y.

To generalize our model to MANCOVA, we may simply replace the relevant terms in the ANCOVA model by their multivariate counterparts,

$$Y = \mu + \alpha + X\beta + e. \tag{6.33}$$

The term $X\beta$ has the order reversed because of conformity in matrix multiplication. The bold symbols in the MANCOVA model represent matrices that contain p dependent variables. Specifically, we can spell out the individual elements in those matrices;

$$Y = \mu + \alpha + X\beta + e$$
$$\begin{bmatrix} Y_1 & Y_2 & \cdots & Y_p \end{bmatrix} = \begin{bmatrix} \mu_1 & \mu_2 & \cdots & \mu_p \end{bmatrix} + \begin{bmatrix} \alpha_1 & \alpha_2 & \cdots & \alpha_p \end{bmatrix}$$
$$+ \begin{bmatrix} \beta_1 X & \beta_2 X & \cdots & \beta_p X \end{bmatrix} + \begin{bmatrix} e_1 & e_2 & \cdots & e_p \end{bmatrix}. \tag{6.34}$$

The subscripts pertain to the pth dependent variable. So the multivariate model contains p univariate ANCOVA models, one for each dependent variable. They are collated like stacks of paper, with terms of the same nature arranged in the same matrix.

As in the univariate ANCOVA, we can adjust the dependent variables by the covariate, namely,

$$Y - X\beta = \mu + \alpha + e. \tag{6.35}$$

Referring to the univariate case, we can deduce that the adjusted dependent variables $Y - X\beta$ are essentially the residuals. These residuals act as if we have performed a multivariate regression and remove the influence of the covariate from the dependent variables. As in the univariate case, the adjusted dependent variables $Y - X\beta$ will have a reduced error covariance matrix $\Sigma_{Y.X}$.

The reduced error covariance is the conditional covariance matrix after the effect of X has been partialled out from the dependent variables. We can compute the conditional covariance based on the covariance matrix of Y and X (Σ_{YX}), its transpose ($\Sigma'_{YX} = \Sigma_{XY}$), and the covariance matrix of X (Σ_X),

$$\Sigma_{Y.X} = \Sigma - \Sigma_{YX}\Sigma_X^{-1}\Sigma_{XY}. \tag{6.36}$$

In planning a study, the covariances in the matrices may be difficult to determine. Researchers naturally think of correlations rather than covariance in dealing with relationships between variables. Thus, we want to express the covariance matrices in terms of correlation matrices. The covariance Σ can be alternatively written as $\Sigma = DRD$, where D is a diagonal matrix with diagonal elements being standard deviations of the dependent variables, and R is their correlation matrix without covariate adjustment. Likewise, we can obtain $\Sigma_X = D_X R_X D_X$. D_X and R_X are the standard deviation matrix and the correlation matrix for the covariates. The covariance matrix Σ_{YX} can be expressed as $DR_{YX}D_X$. Thus, the conditional covariance matrix $\Sigma_{Y.X}$ can be expressed in terms of the correlation matrices:

$$
\begin{aligned}
\Sigma_{Y.X} &= \Sigma - \Sigma_{YX}\Sigma_X^{-1}\Sigma_{XY} \\
&= DRD - DR_{YX}D_X(D_X R_X D_X)^{-1}D_X R_{XY}D \\
&= D(R \quad R_{YX}R_X R_{XY})D.
\end{aligned}
\tag{6.37}
$$

In our example on GRE preparation, we use only one covariate (i.e., TOEFL score). The correlation matrix for the covariate R_X simplifies to one. The covariance matrix for Y and X is a column vector of size $p \times 1$. It contains the correlations between the three GRE scores and the TOEFL score;

$$
R_{YX} = \begin{bmatrix} .64 \\ .34 \\ .53 \end{bmatrix} \begin{array}{l} Verbal \\ Quantitative \\ Analytical. \end{array}
$$

According to Equation 6.37, the conditional covariance matrix is

$$
\begin{aligned}
\Sigma_{Y.X} =&\, D(R - R_{YX}1R_{XY})D \\
=&\, \begin{bmatrix} 120 & 0 & 0 \\ 0 & 150 & 0 \\ 0 & 0 & 1 \end{bmatrix} \times \left(\begin{bmatrix} 1.00 & 0.35 & 0.62 \\ 0.35 & 1.00 & 0.22 \\ 0.62 & 0.22 & 1.00 \end{bmatrix} - \begin{bmatrix} .64 \\ .34 \\ .53 \end{bmatrix} \begin{bmatrix} .64, & .34, & .53 \end{bmatrix} \right) \\
&\times \begin{bmatrix} 120 & 0 & 0 \\ 0 & 150 & 0 \\ 0 & 0 & 1 \end{bmatrix} \\
=&\, \begin{bmatrix} 8501.760 & 2383.20 & 33.6960 \\ 2383.200 & 19899.00 & 5.9700 \\ 33.696 & 5.97 & 0.7191 \end{bmatrix}.
\end{aligned}
$$

After partialling out the effect of the covariate, the conditional covariance $\Sigma_{Y.X}$ has smaller values in all the elements than the original covariance matrix Σ, namely,

$$\Sigma = DRD = \begin{bmatrix} 14400.0 & 6300 & 74.4 \\ 6300.0 & 22500 & 33.0 \\ 74.4 & 33 & 1.0 \end{bmatrix}.$$

Owing to the smaller covariance matrix, the statistical power in MAN-COVA is expected to be higher than that in MANOVA without the covariate.

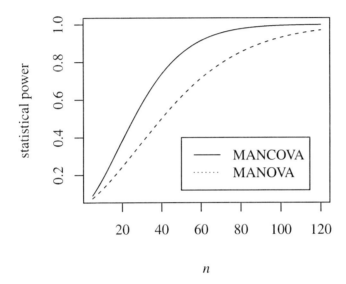

Figure 6.2: Statistical power and n in MANOVA and MANCOVA

The power computation for MANCOVA uses the same formulas as for MANOVA, except that the degrees of freedom v_2 and the covariance matrix Σ need to be changed. The degrees of freedom are now $v_2 = N - K - q$; q is the number of covariates. The covariance matrix Σ is replaced by the conditional covariance matrix $\Sigma_{Y.X}$. We may compare statistical power between MANOVA and MANCOVA in our example on GRE preparation. The statistical power in MANOVA without using the covariate is .71 when the sample size is sixty. After including TOEFL as covariate, MANCOVA analysis increases the statistical power to .91 for the same sample size, $n = 60$. Figure 6.2 shows that MANCOVA uses a smaller sample size than MANOVA to achieve the same level of statistical power. The savings from the reduction in sample size are quite significant in our study on GRE preparation and exam performance.

The relevant R code is:

```
#mancova Rx

D<-matrix( c(120,0,0,0,150,0,0,0,1),nrow=3)
R<-matrix( c(1,.35,.62,.35,1,.22,.62,.22,1), nrow=3)

a1=c(50-(50+20)/3, 20-(50+20)/3, -(50+20)/3)
a2=c(70-(70+20)/3, 20-(70+20)/3, -(70+20)/3)
a3=c(.5-(.5+.2)/3, .2-(.5+.2)/3, -(.5+.2)/3)
a<-matrix(rbind(a1,a2,a3),nrow=3)

Ryx=matrix(c(.64,.34,.53),nrow=1)
Rx=R-t(Ryx)%*%Ryx
Ex=D%*%Rx%*%D

p4macov=function(n=30,a,Ex,q=1){

p=nrow(a)
k=ncol(a)

v1=k-1
v2=(n-1)*k-q

t=sqrt((p^2*v1^2-4)/(p^2+v1^2-5))
w=v1+v2-.5*(p+v1+1)

df1=v1*p
df2=w*t-.5*(p*v1-2)

A=n*(a%*%t(a))
L=det(v2*Ex)/det(v2*Ex+A)
lambda=(L^(-1/t)-1)*df2

a=.05
```

```
1-pf(qf(1-a,df1,df2),df1,df2,lambda)
}


p4macov(60,a,Ex)

#MANCOVA vs MANOVA plot

p<-c(); px<-c()
n=5:120
for (i in n){
 p[i]=p4maov(i,a,E)
 px[i]=p4macov(i,a,Ex)
}

plot(n,px[n],type='l',xlab="n",ylab="statistical power")
lines(n,p[n],lty=2)
legend(50,.4,legend=c("MANCOVA","MANOVA",
     lty=c("solid","dotted"))
```

The corresponding SAS program is:

```
*SAS MANCOVA;

proc iml;

sd={120,150,1};
D=diag(sd);
R={ 1 .35 .62,
    .35  1 .22,
    .62 .22  1};

d1={ 50  20  0};
d2={70 20 0};
d3={.5 .2 0};

j=j(1,3,1);
```

```
a1=d1-sum(d1)/ncol(d1)*j;
a2=d2-sum(d2)/ncol(d2)*j;
a3=d3-sum(d3)/ncol(d3)*j;
a=a1//a2//a3;

Ryx={.64, .34, .53};

Ex=D*(R-Ryx*t(Ryx))*D;
q=ncol(Ryx);
*print sd, D, R, d1,j,a1,a2,a3,a, AA,E;

                        *power function for MANCOVA;
start p4macov(n,a,Ex,q);
 p=nrow(a);
 k=ncol(a);
 v1=k-1;
 v2=(n-1)*k-q;

 t=sqrt((p**2*v1**2-4)/(p**2+v1**2-5));
 w=v1+v2-.5*(p+v1+1);

 df1=v1*p;
 df2=w*t-.5*(p*v1-2);

 aa=a*t(a);
 bigA=n*aa;
 L=det(v2*Ex)/det(v2*Ex+bigA);
 lambda=(L**(-1/t)-1)*df2;

 alpha=.05;
 power=1-probf(finv(1-alpha,df1,df2),df1,df2,lambda);
 return(power);
finish p4macov;
                        *compute power for sample size 30-60;

 nmin=30;
 nmax=60;
```

```
 power=j(nmax-nmin+1,1,.);
 do n=nmin to nmax;
  power[n-nmin+1,1]=p4macov(n,a,Ex,q);
 end;

n=nmin:nmax;
table=t(n)||power;
print table [colname={n power}];

quit;
```

The relevant SPSS code is:

```
* MANCOVA   .

SET MXLOOPS=1E3.

MATRIX.
COMPUTE SD={120, 150,1}.
COMPUTE D=MDIAG(SD).
COMPUTE R={1, .35, .62; .35, 1, .22; .62, .22, 1}.
COMPUTE D1={50,20,0}.
COMPUTE D2={70,20,0}.
COMPUTE D3={.5,.2,0}.
COMPUTE J=MAKE(1,3,1).

COMPUTE A1=D1-MSUM(D1)/NCOL(D1)*J.
COMPUTE A2=D2-MSUM(D2)/NCOL(D2)*J.
COMPUTE A3=D3-MSUM(D3)/NCOL(D3)*J.
COMPUTE A={A1;A2;A3}.

COMPUTE RYX={.64; .34; .53}.
COMPUTE EX=D*(R-RYX*T(RYX))*D.
COMPUTE P=NROW(A).
COMPUTE K=NCOL(A).
COMPUTE Q=NCOL(RYX).

LOOP N=30 TO 60.
```

```
     COMPUTE V1=K-1.
     COMPUTE V2=(N-1)*K-Q.
     COMPUTE T1=SQRT((P**2*V1**2-4)/(P**2+V1**2-5)).
     COMPUTE W=V1+V2-.5*(P+V1+1).
     COMPUTE DF1=V1*P.
     COMPUTE DF2=W*T1-.5*(P*V1-2).

     COMPUTE A2=A*T(A).
     COMPUTE BIGA=N*A2.

     COMPUTE L=DET(V2*EX)/DET(V2*EX+BIGA).
     COMPUTE NC=(L**(-1/T1)-1)*DF2.
     COMPUTE CASE={N, DF1, DF2, NC}.
     SAVE  CASE /OUTFILE=* /VARIABLES=N DF1 DF2  NC.
 END LOOP.

 END MATRIX.

 COMPUTE ALPHA=.05.
 COMPUTE POWER=1-NCDF.F(IDF.F(1-ALPHA,DF1,DF2),DF1,DF2,NC).
 EXECUTE.

 DELETE VARIABLES DF1 DF2  ALPHA NC.
 EXECUTE.
```

Chapter 7

Multi-level Models

In many evaluation studies, the units of randomization may be intact social settings (e.g., communities, neighborhoods, and schools). Individuals situated within the same social setting receive the same intervention because logistic or ethical constraints do not allow individuals to be treated differently in the same social setting. Therefore, the researcher may choose to assign the whole social setting into either the treatment or the control condition. The randomization of aggregate units, however, violates the assumption of independence among individual observations for ordinary statistical analyses.

The observation dependence within aggregate units previously perplexed researchers as the "unit of analysis problem". Individuals in the same aggregate units share backgrounds and tend to produce correlated responses to the same intervention. The correlation among observations in the same aggregate unit violates the independence assumption for ordinary linear model analysis, in which units of randomization are individual people. Ignoring the observation dependence in aggregate units introduces estimation bias and spurious significance. Yet, proper modeling requires simultaneous estimation of multiple variance components, the computation of which posed an insurmountable challenge in the past. The last few decades have seen tremendous advances in estimation algorithms (e.g., expectation maximization, iterative generalized least squares, Fisher's scoring, and the Newton-Raphson algorithm). The development of popular software (i.e., HLM, MLwiN, and SAS proc mixed) has enabled researchers to overcome the computational challenge in handling the unit of analysis problem (Singer, 1998). Researchers can now easily apply multi-level models to analyze data arising from correlated observations.

Multi-level designs can basically be classified into either cross-sectional studies or longitudinal studies. Cross-sectional studies may be further divided into either cluster randomized trials or multi-site randomized trials, depending on whether treatment assignment is crossed with any random effect at a higher level. If the treatment assignment occurs at the school level, then the treatment assignment may not be crossed with the random effects of the school. In this case, the randomly assigned schools are nested in the treatment conditions, forming a cluster randomized trial. On the contrary, if students within schools are randomly assigned to the treatment and control conditions, the treatment assignment is then crossed with the school effect. This forms a multi-site randomized trial.

7.1 Cluster Randomized Trials

Cluster randomized trials, sometimes called group randomized trials, are the best way of measuring the impact of educational interventions implemented at the school level. Randomizing schools avoids a possible "spill over" effect within schools, where the treatment may accidentally spread from the classrooms in the treatment condition to those in the control condition. Such treatment diffusion compromises any causal claim about the effect of the intervention on the educational outcome.

7.1.1 Two Treatment Arms

The data from a cluster randomized trial can be analyzed in a two-level hierarchical linear model. In the level-1 equation, the outcome observation is conceived of as comprising a cluster mean and individual error,

$$Y_{ij} = \beta_{0j} + e_{ij}, \ e_{ij} \sim N(0, \sigma^2). \tag{7.1}$$

The symbol Y_{ij} represents the ith outcome observation in the jth cluster, and e_{ij} is the individual error, which has a normal distribution with a variance σ^2. The level-2 equation regresses the cluster mean β_{0j} on the indicator variable X_j for treatment assignment, which takes .5 for the treatment and $-.5$ for the control. The level-2 regression equation is

$$\beta_{0j} = \gamma_{00} + \gamma_{01}X_j + u_{0j}, \ u_{0j} \sim N(0, \tau). \tag{7.2}$$

The term γ_{00} is the grand mean, and γ_{01} represents the main effect of treatment. The cluster-level random error u_{0j} has a normal distribution with a variance τ.

The multi-level model may appear quite different from the linear regression, although they are closely related. If the design is balanced, with all the clusters of same size n, we can aggregate the data within cluster and collapse the multi-level model into a regular regression equation. Substituting the level-2 Equation 7.2 into the level-1 Equation 7.1, we can obtain a combined model,

$$Y_{ij} = \gamma_{00} + \gamma_{01}X_j + u_{0j} + e_{ij}. \tag{7.3}$$

If we average all the observations within each cluster on both sides of Equation 7.3, we have

$$\frac{1}{n}\sum_{i=1}^{n}Y_{ij} = \frac{1}{n}\sum_{i=1}^{n}(\gamma_{00} + \gamma_{01}X_j + u_{0j} + e_{ij})$$

$$\overline{Y}_j = \gamma_{00} + \gamma_{01}X_j + u_{0j} + \frac{1}{n}\sum_{i=1}^{n}e_{ij}$$

$$\overline{Y}_j = \gamma_{00} + \gamma_{01}X_j + u_{0j} + \bar{e}_j, \ \bar{e}_j \sim N(0, \frac{\sigma^2}{n}). \tag{7.4}$$

We can use one symbol e_j^* to represent the two random terms in Equation 7.4 and simplify the equation to

$$\overline{Y}_j = \gamma_{00} + \gamma_{01}X_j + e_j^*, \ e_j^* \sim N(0, \sigma^{*2}) \tag{7.5}$$

where $e_j^* = u_{0j} + \bar{e}_j$ and $\sigma^{*2} = \tau + \sigma^2/n$. We will use σ^{*2} to denote $Var(e_j^*)$. Thus, Equation 7.5 is a regular regression model except that its error term is slightly more complex than that in a simple regression.

The estimation of the model parameters is straightforward if we assume a balanced design with half the clusters ($J/2$) in the treatment and the other half ($J/2$) in the control. The main effect of treatment is the difference between the averaged cluster mean in the treatment and the averaged cluster mean in the control,

$$\hat{\gamma}_{01} = \frac{\sum\limits_{j=1}^{J/2}\overline{Y}_{ej}}{J/2} - \frac{\sum\limits_{j=J/2+1}^{J}\overline{Y}_{cj}}{J/2}. \tag{7.6}$$

The subscripts e and c indicate whether cluster mean is from the treatment arm or the control arm.

The variance of the main effect of treatment can be easily derived from the variance of the cluster mean $\overline{Y}_{ej}$ and $\overline{Y}_{cj}$, which are independent of each other and have a common variance σ^{*2}. The variance of the main effect of treatment (Raudenbush, 1997) is

$$Var(\hat{\gamma}_{01}) = \frac{4}{J}\sigma^{*2}$$
$$= \frac{4(\tau + \sigma^2/n)}{J}. \tag{7.7}$$

The sample estimate of the variance σ^{*2} is the pooled sum of squares of cluster means divided by the pooled degrees of freedom $J - 2$,

$$\hat{\sigma}^{*2} = \frac{1}{J-2}\left[\sum_{j=1}^{J/2}\left(\overline{Y}_{ej} - \frac{\sum_{j=1}^{J/2}\overline{Y}_{ej}}{J/2}\right)^2 + \sum_{j=J/2+1}^{J}\left(\overline{Y}_{cj} - \frac{\sum_{j=J/2+1}^{J}\overline{Y}_{cj}}{J/2}\right)^2\right]$$
$$= \frac{1}{J-2}[SSW_e + SSW_c]. \tag{7.8}$$

The terms SSW_e and SSW_c are the within-treatment sums of squares of the cluster means for the treatment condition and the control condition, respectively. The variance estimate bears great resemblance to the pooled sample variance in a two sample independent t test. It becomes the same as the pooled sample variance if the symbols for the cluster mean $\overline{Y}_{ej}$ and $\overline{Y}_{cj}$ are replaced by the individual observations in the two sample independent t test. This is because Equation 7.5 suggests a t test for testing the main effect if the cluster means are treated as independent individual observations. The estimated variance of the main effect of treatment is, therefore,

$$\widehat{Var}(\hat{\gamma}_{01}) = \frac{4}{J}\hat{\sigma}^{*2}. \tag{7.9}$$

The test for the main effect of treatment uses a t test with degrees of freedom $J - 2$,

$$T = \frac{\hat{\gamma}_{01}}{\sqrt{\widehat{Var}(\hat{\gamma}_{01})}}. \tag{7.10}$$

When the null hypothesis is true $H_0 : \gamma_{01} = 0$, the test statistic T follows a central t distribution. Under the alternative hypothesis $H_a : \gamma_{01} \neq 0$, the test statistic has a non-central t distribution or T' with degrees of freedom $J - 2$ and a non-centrality parameter λ. Replacing the sample estimates in the test statistic T by their population parameters yields the non-centrality parameter,

$$
\begin{aligned}
\lambda &= \frac{\gamma_{01}}{\sqrt{Var(\hat{\gamma}_{01})}} \\
&= \sqrt{\frac{J}{4}} \frac{\gamma_{01}}{\sigma^*} \\
&= \frac{\gamma_{01}}{\sqrt{\frac{4(\tau + \sigma^2/n)}{J}}}.
\end{aligned}
\tag{7.11}
$$

Equation 7.11 again shows that the non-centrality parameter is related to the non-centrality parameter in the two sample independent t test, which uses σ instead of σ^*.

Statistical power in a two-sided test for the main effect of treatment is

$$
\begin{aligned}
1 - \beta &= P[|T'(J - 2, \lambda)| \geq t_0] \\
&= 1 - P[T'(J - 2, \lambda) < t_0] + P[T'(J - 2, \lambda) \leq -t_0],
\end{aligned}
\tag{7.12}
$$

where the critical value is a t quantile ($t_0 = t_{1-\alpha/2, J-2}$). The power in a one-sided test is

$$
1 - \beta = 1 - P[T'(J - 2, \lambda) < t_0],
\tag{7.13}
$$

where $t_0 = t_{1-\alpha, J-2}$. To compute statistical power in a cluster randomized trial, we start with some estimated parameters to calculate the non-centrality parameter λ.

We can use the intraclass correlation coefficient ρ to estimate the parameter τ because the intraclass correlation coefficient ρ shows the proportion of τ over the total variance $\tau + \sigma^2$, that is,

$$
\rho = \frac{\tau}{\tau + \sigma^2}.
\tag{7.14}
$$

The intraclass correlation coefficient shows how similar the individual subjects within the same cluster are or how correlated the individual observations are within each cluster. The intraclass correlation can, in theory, range from zero to one, and it is often known in a substantive research area. In school-based research, the intraclass class correlation coefficient usually ranges from .10 to .30. If the researcher can estimate the variance of individual error σ^2, he or she can then estimate the variability among schools, or τ, by using an intraclass correlation coefficient often reported in studies on school-based research. The ratio between τ and σ^2 can be expressed in terms of the intraclass correlation coefficient ρ, that is, $\tau : \sigma^2 = \rho : 1 - \rho$.

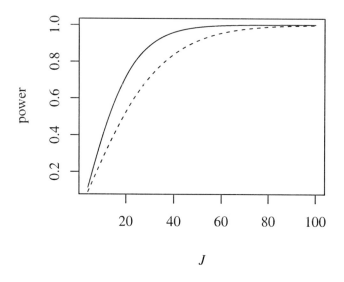

Figure 7.1: Statistical power and J in cluster randomized trial

For example, Englert and her colleagues (1991) developed cognitive strategies for a writing program that helps students with learning disabilities improve their writing skills. The cognitive strategy instruction emphasizes the immersion of writers in a holistic and cognitive process with the teacher engaging writers in the cognitive process. The intervention can be implemented in classrooms where teachers prompt and guide students through a series of think sheets and procedural support. In the study that evaluates the effectiveness of cognitive strategy instruction, classrooms are randomly assigned to the treatment or control condition. The study is a two-level cluster randomized trial, in which classrooms are the clusters and students are nested in different classrooms. The outcome

Table 7.1: Number of clusters and statistical power

J	$1-\beta$	J	$1-\beta$
13	0.5054	22	0.7633
14	0.5414	23	0.7834
15	0.5755	24	0.802
16	0.6078	25	0.8193
17	0.6381	26	0.8352
18	0.6667	27	0.8499
19	0.6934	28	0.8634
20	0.7184	29	0.8758
21	0.7416	30	0.8872

variable is self-perceived competence in writing. Using the estimates from the analysis of the study (Raudenbush and Bryk, 2002), we assume that $\sigma = .258$, $\tau = .019$, and $\gamma_{01} = .188$. Table 7.1 shows that the statistical power is .82 when there are 25 classrooms with 12 students in each classroom ($J = 25$ and $n = 12$). We may change the simple effect size γ_{01} to .15 and compare power between the two scenarios (see Figure 7.1). The solid line in Figure 7.1 represents the power for $\gamma_{01} = .188$; and the dotted line the power for $\gamma_{01} = .15$. We may also explore the power while holding sample sizes constant ($J = 25$ and $n = 12$) and varying the effect size γ_{01} or the intraclass correlation ρ (see Figure 7.2).

The R code is:

```
#two arm cluster randomized trial
#default values from Englert cited in Raudenbush and Bryk 2002

p4crt=function(J=25,n=12,gamma01=.188,
        sd=sqrt(.258^2+.019),rho=.019/(.258^2+.019)){

tau=sd^2*rho
sigma2=sd^2*(1-rho)

lambda=gamma01/sqrt(4*(sigma2/n + tau)/J)
a=.05
```

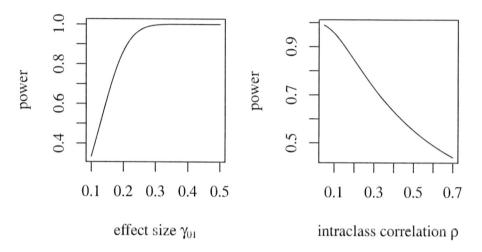

Figure 7.2: Statistical power vs γ_{01} or ρ in cluster randomized trial

```
t0=qt(1-a/2,J-2)
1-pt(t0,J-2,lambda)+pt(-t0,J-2,lambda)
}
p4crt()

curve(p4crt(x),4,100, ylab="power",xlab="J")
#  dashed line for gamma01=.15
curve(p4crt(x, , .15),4,100, ylab="power",
xlab="J",add=TRUE,lty=2)

curve(p4crt(,x,),5,50, ylab="power",
xlab="n")

curve(p4crt(,,x),.1,.5, ylab="power",
xlab="effect size gamma01")

curve(p4crt(,,,,x),.05,.7,
ylab="power",xlab="intraclass correlation rho")
```

The SAS program is:

```
* cluster randomized trial with two arms;
```

```
*default values from Englert cited in Raudenbush and Bryk 2002;
data crt2(keep=J n gamma01 rho p);
n=12;
gamma01=.188;
sd=sqrt(.258**2+.019);
rho=.019/(.258**2+.019);

tau=sd**2*rho;
sigma2=sd**2*(1-rho);
a=.05;

do J=4 to 100;
 lambda=gamma01/sqrt(4*(sigma2/n+tau)/J);
 t0=tinv(1-a/2,J-2);
 p=1-probt(t0,J-2,lambda)+probt(-t0,J-2,lambda);
 output;
end;
run;

*proc print; run;

symbol color=black interpol=join line=1;
proc gplot data=crt2;
 plot p*J;
run;
```

The SPSS code is:

```
NEW FILE.
INPUT PROGRAM.

COMPUTE N=12.
COMPUTE GAMMA01=.188.
COMPUTE SD=SQRT(.258**2+.019).
COMPUTE RHO=.019/(.258**2+.019).

COMPUTE TAU=SD**2*RHO.
COMPUTE SIGMA2=SD**2*(1-RHO).
```

```
COMPUTE A=.05.

LEAVE N TO A.

LOOP J=4 TO 100.
 COMPUTE LAMBDA=GAMMA01/SQRT(4*(SIGMA2/N+TAU)/J).
 COMPUTE T0=IDF.T(1-A/2,J-2).
 COMPUTE POWER=1-NCDF.T(T0,J-2,LAMBDA)+NCDF.T(-T0,J-2,LAMBDA).
 END CASE.
END LOOP.
END FILE.
END INPUT PROGRAM.
EXECUTE.

DELETE VARIABLES SD TAU SIGMA2 A LAMBDA T0.
LIST.

GRAPH
 /LINE(SIMPLE)=VALUE(POWER) BY J.
```

7.1.2   Three Treatment Arms

A cluster randomized trial may occasionally involve three arms (e.g., two treatments and one control), instead of two arms, as in most cases. The statistical model for a cluster randomized trial with three arms can use different coding schemes to differentiate the treatment conditions. For instance, either dummy coding or orthogonal coding may be used to indicate the treatments and the control. We will use orthogonal coding to derive the statistical power function because the non-centrality parameter for the omnibus F test is related to the non-centrality parameters for the orthogonal contrast tests. We will also map the parameters under dummy coding to those under the orthogonal coding, which is slightly more complicated than the dummy coding. In the dummy coding scheme, the treatment arm is usually compared with a reference arm (i.e., the control arm). The relevant parameters for the treatment effects are the simple effects of the contrasts between the treatment and the control conditions. It turns out that the parameters of treatment contrasts in dummy coding have a one-to-one correspondence with the parameters of the orthogonal contrasts in the orthogonal coding.

The statistical model for a cluster randomized trial with three arms uses the same level-1 equation in the hierarchical linear model;

$$Y_{ij} = \beta_{0j} + e_{ij}.$$

The level-2 equation now includes an additional indicator variable for the orthogonal coding,

$$\beta_{0j} = \gamma_{00} + \gamma_{01} X_{1j} + \gamma_{02} X_{2j} + u_{0j}, \; u_{0j} \sim N(0, \tau). \qquad (7.15)$$

The indicator variable X_{1j} takes $1/3$ for the first treatment arm, $1/3$ for the second treatment arm, and $-2/3$ for the control condition. The second indicator X_{2j} assumes $1/2$ for the first treatment arm, $-1/2$ for the second treatment arm, and 0 for the control condition. Such orthogonal coding represents two Helmert comparisons (see Appendix B), which are orthogonal to each other. The estimate of one comparison of the treatment effects is not correlated with the estimate of the other comparison. Although other orthogonal contrasts can be used, they will not change the power computation. We use Helmert coding for illustration because it is frequently used in orthogonal comparisons.

The first indicator X_{1j} is used to compare the average outcome of the two treatment arms with that of the control arm; the second indicator X_{2j} is used to contrast the average outcome between the two treatment arms. The level-2 coefficient γ_{01} estimates the difference between the mean average of the two treatment conditions and the mean of the control condition,

$$\gamma_{01} = \frac{\mu_{e1} + \mu_{e2}}{2} - \mu_c, \qquad (7.16)$$

where μ_{e1}, μ_{e2}, and μ_c represent the mean on outcome performance for the first treatment arm, the second treatment arm, and the control arm, respectively. The coefficient γ_{02} is the mean difference between the two treatment arms,

$$\gamma_{02} = \mu_{e1} - \mu_{e2}. \qquad (7.17)$$

The level-2 intercept γ_{00} is the grand mean for the three arms. It is easy to see why the three level-2 coefficients represent the grand mean and the mean differences. If we substitute the level-2 regression equation (Equation

7.15) into β_{0j} in the level-1 equation, we can obtain the combined model for the cluster randomized trial with three arms,

$$Y_{ij} = \gamma_{00} + \gamma_{01} X_{1j} + \gamma_{02} X_{2j} + u_{0j} + e_{ij}. \tag{7.18}$$

Taking the expectation on both sides for observations in each arm produces the mean for each arm, that is,

$$\mu_{e1} = \gamma_{00} + \frac{1}{3}\gamma_{01} + \frac{1}{2}\gamma_{02} \tag{7.19}$$

$$\mu_{e2} = \gamma_{00} + \frac{1}{3}\gamma_{01} - \frac{1}{2}\gamma_{02} \tag{7.20}$$

$$\mu_{c} = \gamma_{00} - \frac{2}{3}\gamma_{01}. \tag{7.21}$$

The three means can be used to derive the two Helmert contrasts in Equations 7.16 and 7.17.

The Helmert contrasts are useful for power analysis because they represent mean differences. People naturally think of the mean differences between the treatment conditions to gage effect size. In particular, the Helmert contrasts (γ_{01} and γ_{02}) can be expressed in terms of simple effect sizes, which are always meaningful to substantive researchers. The simple effect sizes between the treatment arms and the control arm are

$$\Delta_1 = \mu_{e1} - \mu_c \text{ and } \Delta_2 = \mu_{e2} - \mu_c. \tag{7.22}$$

We can then use the following relationship to convert the simple effects to the parameter values of γ_{01} and γ_{02}:

$$\gamma_{01} = \frac{\mu_{e1} + \mu_{e2}}{2} - \mu_c = \frac{\Delta_1 + \Delta_2}{2}; \tag{7.23}$$

$$\gamma_{02} = \mu_{e1} - \mu_{e2} = \Delta_1 - \Delta_2. \tag{7.24}$$

Therefore, Helmert contrasts make it easy to translate what people normally know about effect size to parameter values in the model for statistical power analysis.

The statistical test and power can be derived from the aggregated model, based on cluster means. Suppose the clusters are of the same size n. As before, we can use one random term e_j^* to represent the two random terms in the aggregated model because the two random terms have a constant variance σ^{*2},

$$\overline{Y}_j = \gamma_{00} + \gamma_{01}X_{1j} + \gamma_{02}X_{2j} + u_{0j} + \bar{e}_j$$
$$= \gamma_{00} + \gamma_{01}X_{1j} + \gamma_{02}X_{2j} + e_j^*, \ e_j^* \sim N(0, \sigma^{*2}). \qquad (7.25)$$

The estimate of the variance σ^{*2} is the pooled within-treatment sum of squares of the cluster means divided by the sum of the within-treatment degrees of freedom,

$$\hat{\sigma}^{*2} = \frac{SSW_{e1} + SSW_{e2} + SSW_c}{J - 3}. \qquad (7.26)$$

The term SSW refers to the within-treatment sum of squares of the cluster means, as in Equation 7.8. The subscripts $e1$, $e2$, and c represent the three treatment arms. The number of degrees of freedom for the estimated variance $\hat{\sigma}^{*2}$ is $J - 3$ if the three arms in the cluster randomized trial contain equal numbers of clusters (i.e., $J/3$). In each arm the number of within-treatment degrees of freedom is $J/3 - 1$. Their sum is equal to $J - 3$.

The estimate of the treatment contrast γ_{01} is the weighted sum of the outcome means for the three treatment arms, with the weights being the contrast coefficients. In our case, the first Helmert contrast uses the contrast coefficients $1/2, 1/2$, and -1 for the first treatment arm, second treatment arm, and control arm, respectively. The estimate of the first Helmert contrast is, therefore,

$$\hat{\gamma}_{01} = \frac{1}{2}\overline{Y}_{e1} + \frac{1}{2}\overline{Y}_{e2} - \overline{Y}_c, \qquad (7.27)$$

where $\overline{Y}_{e1}$, $\overline{Y}_{e2}$, and $\overline{Y}_c$ are the means of the three treatment arms. Specifically, $\overline{Y}_{e1}$ is the average of cluster means in the first treatment arm,

$$\overline{Y}_{e1} = \frac{\sum_{j=1}^{J/3} \overline{Y}_{e1j}}{J/3}.$$

The other two averages of cluster means for the second treatment and control arm are

$$\overline{Y}_{e2} = \frac{\sum_j \overline{Y}_{e2j}}{J/3} \text{ and } \overline{Y}_c = \frac{\sum_j \overline{Y}_{cj}}{J/3}.$$

The averages of the cluster means for each treatment arm share a common variance,

$$Var(\overline{Y}_{e1}) = Var(\overline{Y}_{e2}) = Var(\overline{Y}_c) = \frac{\sigma^{*2}}{J/3}.$$

The variance of $\hat{\gamma}_{01}$ becomes

$$Var(\hat{\gamma}_{01}) = \frac{1}{4}Var(\overline{Y}_{e1}) + \frac{1}{4}Var(\overline{Y}_{e2}) + Var(\overline{Y}_c)$$
$$= \left(\frac{1}{4} + \frac{1}{4} + 1\right)\frac{\sigma^{*2}}{J/3}. \tag{7.28}$$

Substituting $\hat{\sigma}^{*2}$ (Equation 7.26) for σ^{*2} in Equation 7.28, we obtain the estimated variance

$$\widehat{Var}(\hat{\gamma}_{01}) = \frac{3}{2}\frac{\hat{\sigma}^{*2}}{J/3}. \tag{7.29}$$

The orthogonal contrast coefficients are related to the values of the Helmert coding (i.e., $a_k = \frac{3}{2}X_{1j}$). In general, we can have contrast coefficients a_1, a_2, and a_3,

$$a_k = \frac{3}{2}X_{1j}$$
$$a_1 = \frac{3}{2} \times \frac{1}{3} = \frac{1}{2}$$
$$a_2 = \frac{3}{2} \times \frac{1}{3} = \frac{1}{2}$$
$$a_3 = \frac{3}{2} \times -\frac{2}{3} = -1.$$

Note that the contrast coefficients can be combined into a vector $a' = [a_1, a_2, a_3]$, and that the regression coding for X_{1j} uses $1/3, 1/3,$ and $-2/3$ to differentiate the three arms (see Appendix B for Helmert contrasts). The estimate of the Helmert contrast can be written as

$$\hat{\gamma}_{01} = \sum_{k=1}^{3} a_k \overline{Y}_k, \tag{7.30}$$

where the subscript represents the treatment arm, and $\overline{Y}_k$ represents the average of the cluster means for the kth treatment arm. The variance of $\hat{\gamma}_{01}$

is

$$Var(\hat{\gamma}_{01}) = \sum_{k=1}^{3} a_k^2 Var(\overline{Y}_k)$$

$$= \sum_{k=1}^{3} a_k^2 \frac{\sigma^{*2}}{J/3}.$$

The estimated variance is

$$\widehat{Var}(\hat{\gamma}_{01}) = \sum_{k=1}^{3} a_k^2 \frac{\hat{\sigma}^{*2}}{J/3}. \tag{7.31}$$

The test for the first orthogonal treatment contrast uses a t statistic with $J - 3$ degrees of freedom,

$$T_1 = \frac{\hat{\gamma}_{01}}{\sqrt{\widehat{Var}(\hat{\gamma}_{01})}}. \tag{7.32}$$

When the null hypothesis is true, $H_0 : \gamma_{01} = 0$, the t statistic has a central t distribution. When the alternative hypothesis is true, $H_a : \gamma_{10} \geq 0$, the t statistic follows a non-central t distribution T_1' with $J - 3$ degrees of freedom and a non-centrality parameter λ_1,

$$\lambda_1 = \frac{\gamma_{01}}{\sqrt{Var(\hat{\gamma}_{01})}}$$

$$= \frac{\gamma_{01}}{\sqrt{\sum_{k=1}^{3} a_k^2 \frac{\sigma^{*2}}{J/3}}}$$

$$= \frac{\gamma_{01}}{\sqrt{\frac{3(\tau+\sigma^2/n)}{J} \sum_{k=1}^{3} a_k^2}}$$

$$= \frac{\gamma_{01}}{\sqrt{\frac{4.5(\tau+\sigma^2/n)}{J}}}. \tag{7.33}$$

In a similar way, the contrast coefficients for the second contrast γ_{02} are $1, -1$, and 0. Or, we can use $2X_{2j}$ to derive the orthogonal coefficients b_1,

b_2, and b_3 for the means of the three treatment arms,

$$b_k = 2X_{2j}$$
$$b_1 = 2 \times \frac{1}{2} = 1$$
$$b_2 = 2 \times -\frac{1}{2} = -1$$
$$b_3 = 2 \times 0 = 0.$$

Note that the contrast coefficients can be combined into a vector $b' = [b_1, b_2, b_3]$, and that the regression coding for X_{2j} uses $b/||b||^2$ to differentiate the three arms. The estimate of the second orthogonal contrast is

$$\hat{\gamma}_{02} = \sum_{k=1}^{3} b_k \overline{Y}_k. \tag{7.34}$$

Its variance is

$$Var(\hat{\gamma}_{02}) = \sum_{k=1}^{3} b_k^2 \frac{\sigma^{*2}}{J/3}.$$

The estimated variance is

$$\widehat{Var}(\hat{\gamma}_{02}) = \sum_{k=1}^{3} b_k^2 \frac{\hat{\sigma}^{*2}}{J/3}. \tag{7.35}$$

The test for the second contrast also uses a t statistic with $J - 3$ degrees of freedom,

$$T_2 = \frac{\hat{\gamma}_{02}}{\sqrt{\widehat{Var}(\hat{\gamma}_{02})}}. \tag{7.36}$$

It has a central t distribution when the null hypothesis $H_0 : \gamma_{02} = 0$ is true. Under the alternative hypothesis $H_a : \gamma_{02} \neq 0$, the test statistic follows a non-central t distribution T_2' with $J - 3$ degrees of freedom and a non-centrality parameter λ_2,

$$
\begin{aligned}
\lambda_2 &= \frac{\gamma_{02}}{\sqrt{Var(\hat{\gamma}_{02})}} \\
&= \frac{\gamma_{02}}{\sqrt{\sum_{k=1}^{3} b_k^2 \frac{\sigma^{*2}}{J/3}}} \\
&= \frac{\gamma_{02}}{\sqrt{\frac{6(\tau + \sigma^2/n)}{J}}}.
\end{aligned}
\tag{7.37}
$$

The statistical power for testing the orthogonal contrasts can be formulated in one equation with subscript p indicating which contrast is used. The statistical power in a two-sided test is

$$
\begin{aligned}
1 - \beta &= P[|T_p'(J - 3, \lambda_p)| \geq t_0] \\
&= 1 - P[T_p'(J - 3, \lambda_p) < t_0] + P[T_p'(J - 3, \lambda_p) \leq -t_0],
\end{aligned}
\tag{7.38}
$$

where $p = 1$ means the first contrast γ_{01}, $p = 2$ means the second contrast γ_{02}, and t_0 is the critical value. If the orthogonal contrasts are set a posteriori, we can use Bonferroni adjustment to set the critical value to $t_{1-\alpha/4, J-3}$. However, we can forgo the Bonferroni adjustment and use the regular critical value $t_{1-\alpha/2, J-3}$ when the orthogonal contrasts are estimated a priori and without an omnibus F test.

The omnibus F test examines the null hypothesis that the means of the three treatment arms are all equal, $H_0 : \mu_{e1} = \mu_{e2} = \mu_c$, which is equivalent to the orthogonal contrasts being simultaneously zero (i.e., $H_0 : \gamma_{01} = \gamma_{02} = 0$). It can be proven that the overall F is the average of the two squared t statistics for the two orthogonal contrast tests;

$$
F = \frac{1}{2}(T_1^2 + T_2^2).
\tag{7.39}
$$

The F statistic has 2 degrees of freedom in the numerator and $J - 3$ degrees of freedom in the denominator.

It is intuitive to see why the two squared t statistics add up to an F statistic. Squaring T_1 produces an F statistic. By the definition of an F statistic, it is a ratio between two chi squares,

$$
T_1^2 = F(1, J - 3) = \frac{\chi_1^2/1}{\chi_3^2/(J - 3)}.
$$

Likewise, we have

$$T_2^2 = F(1, J - 3) = \frac{\chi_2^2/1}{\chi_3^2/(J-3)}.$$

Note that the two squared T tests share a common χ_3^2 in the denominator, and that χ_1^2 and χ_2^2 are independent, owing to orthogonality between the two contrasts. Adding two independent chi square variables yields a chi square with the degrees of freedom equal to the sum of their respective degrees of freedom (Liu, 2013c). Thus, we have

$$\frac{1}{2}(T_1^2 + T_2^2) = \frac{(\chi_1^2 + \chi_2^2)/2}{\chi_3^2/(J-3)}$$

$$= \frac{\chi_{df=2}^2/2}{\chi_3^2/(J-3)} \sim F(2, J-3). \tag{7.40}$$

When the means of the three treatment arms are not equal, this suggests $H_a : \mu_{e1} \neq \mu_{e2} \neq \mu_c$, or alternatively, $H_a : \gamma_{01} \neq 0$ and/or $\gamma_{02} \neq 0$. The two independent chi squares χ_1^2 and χ_2^2 have a non-centrality parameter λ_1^2 and λ_2^2, respectively. It is easy to see that the non-centrality parameters for the non-central chi squares are the squared non-centrality parameters for the orthogonal contrast tests. The non-centrality parameters among independent chi squares are additive (Johnson et al, 1995). So the non-centrality parameter λ for $\chi_{df=2}^2$ is

$$\lambda = \lambda_1^2 + \lambda_2^2. \tag{7.41}$$

Under H_a the F statistic has a non-central F distribution with 2 degrees of freedom in the numerator, $J - 3$ degrees of freedom in the denominator, and a non-centrality parameter λ (i.e., $F'(2, J-3, \lambda)$). Its statistical power function is

$$1 - \beta = P[F'(2, J-3, \lambda) \geq F_0], \tag{7.42}$$

where F_0 is the critical value for the overall F test.

We may use primary care management as an illustrating example. Suppose that a medical researcher plans to compare two kinds of primary-care-based disease management and regular care in improving glucose control among diabetic patients. The first treatment offers pharmacist-led, primary-care-based disease management; the second treatment arm uses only primary-care-based disease management, including diabetes education, coverage of glucose meters and strips, simplified outcome reporting, and support of clinical leadership. The third arm is the regular care or business-as-usual condition (Rothman et al, 2003; Sidorov et al, 2000). As the intervention can only be implemented through primary-care clinics, a three-arm cluster randomized trial will be a viable study design, in which primary-care clinics are randomly assigned to the three arms. The outcome variable is the reduction in glycated hemoglobin or hemoglobin A1c (HbA1c). Hemoglobin is an oxygen-bearing substance in the red blood cells, which die every three months. The glucose or sugar can bind with hemoglobin, becoming glycated. As the glucose level increases, the concentration of glycated hemoglobin increases in a predictable way. Therefore, HbA1c is a good measure of the average glucose concentration for the previous two or three months. It does not vary as much as finger-stick blood sugar measurements. Suppose that the pharmacist-led, primary-care-based disease management might reduce diabetic patients' HbA1c on average by 1.9% ($\Delta_1 = 1.9$), compared with that in the regular care, and that primary care-based disease management might decrease patients' HbA1c on average by 1% ($\Delta_2 = 1$) over that in the regular care. The standard deviation of HbA1c is estimated to be 2% ($\sqrt{\sigma^2 + \tau} = 2$); the intraclass correlation is .05 or $\rho = .05$ (Parker, Evangelou, and Eaton, 2005). When nine clinics with forty patients each ($J = 9$ and $n = 40$) are recruited into the study, the statistical power for the omnibus test reaches .84. However, the power for comparing the two treatment arms is a meager .27. It requires 24 participating clinics to achieve a power of at least .80 in a comparison test for the two treatment arms, for which the effect size is $\Delta_1 - \Delta_2 = .9$. So statistical power is not evenly distributed among the omnibus test and post-hoc contrast tests. If a particular contrast is of great interest, the researcher needs to calculate power separately for different tests to ensure adequate power for each test.

The R code is:

```
# three arm cluster randomized trial
#HbAC1 %
#Ref Sidorov et al 2000 Am J Manag Care
#    Rothman et al 2003 Am J Med Qual

p4crt3=function(J,n=40,rho=.05,D1=1.9,D2=1,sd=2){
```

```
a=.05
b1=(D1+D2)/2
b2=D1-D2

tau=sd^2*rho
sigma2=sd^2*(1-rho)

lambda1=b1/sqrt(4.5*(tau+sigma2/n)/J)
lambda2=b2/sqrt(6*(tau+sigma2/n)/J)
lambda=lambda1^2 + lambda2^2

f0=qf(1-a,2,J-3)
p=1-pf(f0,2,J-3, lambda)

nc1=D1/sqrt(6*(tau+sigma2/n)/J)
nc2=(D1-D2)/sqrt(6*(tau+sigma2/n)/J)

# p13 is the power for comparing e1 and control
# p12 is the power for comparing e1 and e2
t0=qt(1-a/2/2,J-3)
p13=1-pt(t0,J-3,nc1)+pt(-t0,J-3,nc1)
p12=1-pt(t0,J-3,nc2)+pt(-t0,J-3,nc2)

cat(rho, "\t", J,"\t", p,"\t", p13,"\t", p12,"\n")
}

for(J in seq(5,30,by=1)){p4crt3(J)}
```

The SAS program is:

```
* cluster randomized trial with three arms;
/*HbAC1: default values from
Sidorov et al 2000 Am J Manag Care
Rothman et al 2003 Am J Med Qual
*/
data crt3(keep=J n D1 D2 rho p p13 p12);
a=.05;
n=40;
```

```
D1=1.9; D2=1;
b1=(D1+D2)/2;
b2=D1-D2;

sd=2;
rho=.05;
tau=sd**2*rho;
sigma2=sd**2*(1-rho);

do J=12 to 30;
 lambda1=b1/sqrt(4.5*(tau+sigma2/n)/J);
 lambda2=b2/sqrt(6*(tau+sigma2/n)/J);
 lambda=lambda1**2+lambda2**2;

 f0=finv(1-a,2,J-3);
 p=1-probf(f0,2,J-3,lambda);

 nc1=D1/sqrt(6*(tau+sigma2/n)/J);
 nc2=(D1-D2)/sqrt(6*(tau+sigma2/n)/J);

/* p13 is the power for comparing e1 and control
   p12 is the power for comparing e1 and e2 */
 t0-tinv(1-a/2/2,J 3);
 p13=1-probt(t0,J-3,nc1)+probt(-t0,J-3,nc1);
 p12=1-probt(t0,J-3,nc2)+probt(-t0,J-3,nc2);
 output;
end;
run;

proc print data=crt3;run;
```

The SPSS code is:

```
* cluster randomized trial with three arms
HbAC1  default values from
Sidorov et al 2000 Am J Manag Care
Rothman et al 2003 Am J Med Qual.
```

```
NEW FILE.
INPUT PROGRAM.

COMPUTE N=40.
COMPUTE D1=1.9.
COMPUTE D2=1.
COMPUTE B1=(D1+D2)/2.
COMPUTE B2=D1-D2.

COMPUTE SD=2.
COMPUTE RHO=.05.
COMPUTE TAU=SD**2*RHO.
COMPUTE SIGMA2=SD**2*(1-RHO).
COMPUTE A=.05.

LEAVE N TO A.

LOOP J=6 TO 45.
  COMPUTE LAMBDA1=B1/SQRT(4.5*(SIGMA2/N+TAU)/J).
  COMPUTE LAMBDA2=B2/SQRT(6*(SIGMA2/N+TAU)/J).

  COMPUTE LAMBDA=LAMBDA1**2+LAMBDA2**2.
  COMPUTE P=1-NCDF.F(IDF.F(1-A,2,J-3),2,J-3,LAMBDA).

  COMPUTE NC1=D1/SQRT(6*(TAU+SIGMA2/N)/J).
  COMPUTE NC2=(D1-D2)/SQRT(6*(TAU+SIGMA2/N)/J).

  COMPUTE T0=IDF.T(1-A/2/2,J-3).
  COMPUTE P13=1-NCDF.T(T0,J-3,NC1)+NCDF.T(-T0,J-3,NC1).
  COMPUTE P12=1-NCDF.T(T0,J-3,NC2)+NCDF.T(-T0,J-3,NC2).
  END CASE.
END LOOP.
END FILE.
END INPUT PROGRAM.
EXECUTE.

DELETE VARIABLES SD TAU SIGMA2 A
```

```
LAMBDA1 LAMBDA2 LAMBDA NC1 NC2 TO.
VARIABLE LABELS P 'POWER FOR OMNIBUS TEST'
  P13 'POWER FOR COMPARING TREATMENT 1 AND 3'
  P12 'POWER FOR COMPARING TREATMENT 1 AND 2'.
LIST.

GRAPH
  /LINE(MULTIPLE)=VALUE(P13 P12) BY J.
```

7.2 Multi-site Randomized Trials

A multi-site randomized trial replicates a small randomized trial across different sites. The design is popular because it allows researchers to recruit a large sample in a short period. It is more convenient to obtain a large sample for a study from multiple sites than from a single site. It is also more economical to sample additional participants in each site than to do so from geographically dispersed locations. As a multi-site randomized trial simply replicates the same study across sites, each site follows the same study protocol. Therefore, it becomes relatively easy to manage such a study despite the large sample (Fuller et al., 1994).

The data arising form a multi-site randomized trial can be framed in a hierarchical linear model (HLM), which uses regression equations at multiple levels. Suppose that the multi-site randomized trial randomly assigns subjects into either the treatment or the control condition at each site, and that this is replicated across a number of sites. A two-level HLM model can be used to analyze the data in the multi-site randomized trial. The level-1 regression equation models the relationship between the outcome and the treatment assignment at each site, and the level-2 regression equation relates the treatment effects at sites to the main effect of treatment.

7.2.1 Two Treatment Conditions at Each Site

The level-1 equation is

$$Y_{ij} = \beta_{0j} + \beta_{1j} X_{ij} + e_{ij}, \ i = 1, \cdots, n; \ j = 1, \cdots, J. \qquad (7.43)$$

where Y_{ij} is the outcome observation for the ith subject at the jth site; X_{ij} is the indicator variable for treatment assignment ($X_{ij} = .5$ for the treatment condition and $X_{ij} = -.5$ for the control condition); β_{0j} is the mean of the outcome for the jth site; β_{1j} is the mean difference in outcome between the treatment and control condition at the jth site; and e_{ij} is an individual error term ($e_{ij} \sim N(0, \sigma^2)$). In a balanced design half of the subjects ($n/2$) are randomly assigned to the treatment, and the other half ($n/2$) to the control.

The level-2 equations are

$$\begin{aligned} \beta_{0j} &= \gamma_{00} + u_{0j} \\ \beta_{1j} &= \gamma_{10} + u_{1j} \end{aligned} \qquad \begin{pmatrix} \beta_{0j} \\ \beta_{1j} \end{pmatrix} \sim N\left(0, \begin{bmatrix} \tau_0 & \tau_{01} \\ \tau_{10} & \tau_1 \end{bmatrix}\right), \qquad (7.44)$$

where γ_{00} is the grand mean; u_{0j} is a random deviation of the site mean from the grand mean; γ_{10} is the grand mean difference between the treatment and control across all the sites (i.e., the main effect of treatment); and u_{1j} is a random deviation of the site-specific mean difference from the grand mean difference. The two level-2 random errors are independent of the level-1 individual error e_{ij}, and they assume a multivariate normal distribution. The variances of u_{0j} and u_{1j} are τ_0 and τ_1, respectively; and their covariance is τ_{10}.

The research interest revolves around the main effect of treatment, site variability, and variance of the mean differences among sites, which correspond to the parameters γ_{10}, τ_0, and τ_1. The parameter γ_{10} measures the main effect of treatment, τ_0 reflects the site variability, and τ_1 is the variance of the mean difference among sites. In the following, we will describe the test statistics for each parameter and their power functions.

In a balanced design the estimate of γ_{10} is a weighted least squares estimate. When the normality assumption holds true, it is also a maximum likelihood estimate. We can first estimate the treatment effect at an arbitrary site, say, the jth site, and then average the treatment effect estimates across the sites. Conditional on the jth site, the treatment effect estimate is

$$\begin{aligned} \hat{\beta}_{1j} &= \sum_{i=1}^{n/2} \frac{Y_{eij}}{n/2} + \sum_{i=n/2+1}^{n} \frac{Y_{cij}}{n/2} \\ &= \overline{Y}_{ej} - \overline{Y}_{cj}, \end{aligned} \qquad (7.45)$$

where the subscript e and c indicate the treatment and the control, and $\overline{Y}_{ej}$

and $\overline{Y}_{cj}$ represent the mean outcomes in the treatment and control groups at the jth site. As each site weighs the same in estimating the main effect of treatment, the estimate of γ_{10} is simply the average of all the site-specific treatment effect estimates $\hat{\beta}_{1j}$,

$$\hat{\gamma}_{10} = \frac{\sum\limits_{j=1}^{J} \hat{\beta}_{1j}}{J}. \tag{7.46}$$

The variance of the estimate of the main effect of treatment can be derived easily based on the conditional variance. Conditioning on the site or β_{1j}, we have the variance of $\hat{\beta}_{1j}$,

$$Var(\hat{\beta}_{1j}|\beta_{1j}) = \frac{4\sigma^2}{n}.$$

This is because $\overline{Y}_{ej}$ and $\overline{Y}_{cj}$ are independent and each has a variance $2\sigma^2/n$. By the law of total variance, we can obtain the unconditional variance of $\hat{\beta}_{1j}$,

$$\begin{aligned} Var(\hat{\beta}_{1j}) &= E(Var(\hat{\beta}_{1j}|\beta_{1j})) + Var(E(\hat{\beta}_{1j}|\beta_{1j})) \\ &= \frac{4\sigma^2}{n} + Var(\beta_{1j}) \\ &= \frac{4\sigma^2}{n} + \tau_1. \end{aligned} \tag{7.47}$$

Note that the least squares estimate is unbiased and $E(\hat{\beta}_{1j}|\beta_{1j}) = \beta_{1j}$. As the sites are independent of each other, so are the treatment effect estimates $\hat{\beta}_{1j}$. According to Equation 7.46, the variance of $\hat{\gamma}_{10}$ is

$$Var(\hat{\gamma}_{10}) = Var(\hat{\beta}_{1j})/J \tag{7.48}$$

$$= \frac{4\sigma^2/n + \tau_1}{J}. \tag{7.49}$$

The unbiased estimate of the variance $Var(\hat{\gamma}_{10})$ is $\widehat{Var}(\hat{\gamma}_{10}) = \widehat{Var}(\hat{\beta}_{1j})/J$ according to Equation 7.48. The unbiased estimate $\widehat{Var}(\hat{\beta}_{1j})$ is the sum of squares of $\hat{\beta}_{1j}$ divided by $J - 1$. As the $\hat{\beta}_{1j}$ are independently identically distributed normal variables with a common variance $Var(\hat{\beta}_{1j})$, their sum of squares over $J - 1$ is an unbiased estimate of the common variance $Var(\hat{\beta}_{1j})$, that is,

$$\widehat{Var}(\hat{\beta}_{1j}) = \frac{\sum\limits_{j=1}^{J} (\hat{\beta}_{1j} - \bar{\hat{\beta}}_{1j})^2}{J - 1}, \tag{7.50}$$

where the average $\bar{\hat{\beta}}_{1j}$ is indeed $\hat{\gamma}_{10}$ in Equation 7.46.

The test for the main effect of treatment uses a t statistic with degrees of freedom $J - 1$,

$$T = \frac{\hat{\gamma}_{10}}{\sqrt{\widehat{Var}(\hat{\gamma}_{10})}}. \tag{7.51}$$

In the presence of a non-zero treatment effect $H_a : \gamma_{10} \neq 0$, the t statistic follows a non-central t distribution with degrees of freedom $J - 1$ and a non-centrality parameter λ,

$$\lambda = \frac{\gamma_{10}}{\sqrt{Var(\hat{\gamma}_{10})}} = \frac{\gamma_{10}}{\sqrt{\frac{4\sigma^2/n + \tau_1}{J}}}. \tag{7.52}$$

The non-centrality parameter is obtained through replacing the sample estimates by their corresponding population parameters in Equation 7.51.

The statistical power for the two-sided test is

$$\begin{aligned}
1 - \beta &= P[|T'(J - 1, \lambda)| \geq t_0] \\
&= 1 - P[T'(J - 1, \lambda) < t_0] + P[T'(J - 1, \lambda) \leq -t_0], \tag{7.53}
\end{aligned}$$

where t_0 is the critical value or $t_{1-\alpha/2}$. The statistical power for the one-sided test, say, $H_a : \gamma_{10} > 0$, is

$$1 - \beta = 1 - P[T'(J - 1, \lambda) < t_0], \tag{7.54}$$

where $t_0 = t_{1-\alpha}$.

For example, a medical researcher plans to conduct a multi-site randomized trial to examine the effect of behavioral therapy and fluoxetine on recovering from anorexia. At each clinic, 30 anorexic girls will be randomly assigned to the treatment of behavioral therapy and fluoxetine or to the business-as-usual condition for three months. To choose a sufficient number of participating clinics for the study, a statistical consultant is

Table 7.2: Number of sites and statistical power

J	$1 - \beta$	J	$1 - \beta$
15	0.6806	23	0.8706
16	0.7127	24	0.8854
17	0.7422	25	0.8986
18	0.7691	26	0.9104
19	0.7936	27	0.9209
20	0.8159	28	0.9303
21	0.8361	29	0.9387
22	0.8542	30	0.9461

hired to conduct power analysis for testing the main effect of treatment based on the estimated parameters for the multi-site randomized trial. The researcher knows from past experience that the range of body mass index (BMI) for anorexic girls is between 12 and 18 kg/m^2 (Bouten et al., 1996). Using four standard deviations for 95%, the researcher estimates that the variance for individual error is $\sigma^2 = [(18 - 12)/4]^2 = 2.25$. Further, the ratio between σ^2 and τ_1 is set at $9 : 1$, that is, $\sigma^2 : \tau_1 = 9 : 1$. The minimum effect size that is of some clinical importance is set to a difference of .5 in change of BMI in five months after the subjects have undergone the treatment ($\gamma_{10} = .5$). Using the parameter estimates and Equation 7.53, the statistical consultant finds that the statistical power reaches .8159 when twenty clinics are recruited into the multi-site trial (see Table 7.2).

The R code for computing the statistical power is:

```
# multi-site randomized trial with two treatments
# behavioral therapy and fluoxetine on anorexia

p4mst2=function(J=20,n=30,gamma10=.5,
sigma2=1.5^2,tau1=1.5^2/9){
a=.05
lambda=gamma10/sqrt((4*sigma2/n + tau1)/J)

t0=qt(1-a/2,J-1)
1-pt(t0,J-1,lambda)+pt(-t0,J-1,lambda)
```

```
}

p4mst2()
#[1] 0.8158948

for(J in 15:30) cat(J,"\t",p4mst2(J,),"\n")
```

The SAS program is:

```
*multi-site randomized trial with two treatments at site;
data mst2(keep=J n gamma10 sigma2 tau1 p);
a=.05;
n=30;

gamma10=.5;
sigma2=1.5**2;
tau1=1.5**2/9;

do J=10 to 30;
 lambda=gamma10/sqrt((4*sigma2/n+tau1)/J);
 t0=tinv(1-a/2,J-1);
 p=1-probt(t0,J-1,lambda)+probt(-t0,J-1,lambda);
 output;
end;
run;

proc print data=mst2;run;
```

The SPSS code is:

```
*multi-site randomized trial with two treatments at site.
NEW FILE.
INPUT PROGRAM.

COMPUTE N=30.
COMPUTE GAMMA10=.5.
COMPUTE SIGMA2=1.5**2.
COMPUTE TAU1=SIGMA2/9.
COMPUTE A=.05.
```

```
LEAVE N TO A.

LOOP J=5 TO 80.
 COMPUTE LAMBDA=GAMMA10/SQRT((4*SIGMA2/N+TAU1)/J).
 COMPUTE T0=IDF.T(1-A/2,J-1).
 COMPUTE POWER=1-NCDF.T(T0,J-1,LAMBDA)+NCDF.T(-T0,J-1,LAMBDA).
 END CASE.
END LOOP.
END FILE.
END INPUT PROGRAM.
EXECUTE.

DELETE VARIABLES  TAU1 A LAMBDA T0.
LIST.

GRAPH
 /LINE(SIMPLE)=VALUE(POWER) BY J.
```

The parameter τ_0 measures site variability, which shows how sites vary in the average outcome performance. The average outcome performance is $\hat{\beta}_{0j}$. Its variance can be derived in a similar way as in Equation 7.47, namely, $Var(\hat{\beta}_{0j}) = \tau_0 + \sigma^2/n$. The estimate of β_{0j} is

$$\hat{\beta}_{0j} = \frac{\sum_{i=1}^{n} Y_{ij}}{n} = \overline{Y}_j. \tag{7.55}$$

As $\hat{\beta}_{0j}$ is independently and identically normally distributed, the unbiased estimate of its variance is the sample variance of $\hat{\beta}_{0j}$,

$$\widehat{Var}(\hat{\beta}_{0j}) = \frac{\sum_{j=1}^{J} (\hat{\beta}_{0j} - \sum_{j=1}^{J} \hat{\beta}_{0j}/J)^2}{J-1}. \tag{7.56}$$

The expectation of $\widehat{Var}(\hat{\beta}_{0j})$ equals $Var(\hat{\beta}_{0j}) = \tau_0 + \sigma^2/n$, and $\widehat{Var}(\hat{\beta}_{0j})$ is related to a chi square distribution with degrees of freedom $J-1$,

$$(J-1)\widehat{Var}(\hat{\beta}_{0j})/Var(\hat{\beta}_{0j}) \sim \chi^2_{J-1}. \tag{7.57}$$

To test site variability, we can use an F statistic,

$$F = \frac{n\widehat{Var}(\beta_{0j})}{\hat{\sigma}^2}. \tag{7.58}$$

The variance of individual error σ^2 can be estimated by summing the pooled within-treatment sum of squares at each site and then dividing the sum by the total within-treatment degrees of freedom. Each site contains an independent two-group comparison study similar to the regular two sample independent t test. At each site the pooled within-treatment sums of squares is

$$SSW_j = \sum_{i=1}^{n/2} (Y_{eij} - \overline{Y}_{ej})^2 + \sum_{i=n/2+1}^{n} (Y_{cij} - \overline{Y}_{cj})^2, \tag{7.59}$$

with $df_{wj} = n - 2$ degrees of freedom. We learn from the two sample independent t test that the SSW_j are independent of the site mean $\hat{\beta}_{0j}$, and that they yield an unbiased estimate of the error variance σ^2 ($df_{wj}SSW_j/\sigma^2 \sim \chi^2_{df_{wj}}$). As the sites are independent of each other, so are the site-specific within-treatment sums of squares, SSW_j. Thus, summing the SSW_j and dividing the sum by the total degrees of freedom $\sum_{j=1}^{J} df_{wj} = J(n-2)$ yields an unbiased estimate of σ^2,

$$\hat{\sigma}^2 = \frac{\sum_{j=1}^{J} SSW_j}{J(n-2)}. \tag{7.60}$$

Based on the formulas for $\hat{\sigma}^2$, we can see that the F test for site variability follows a central F distribution with the numerator degrees of freedom $J - 1$ and denominator degrees of freedom $J(n-2)$ under the null hypothesis $H_0 : \tau_0 = 0$.

The F statistic multiplied by $E(\hat{\sigma}^2)/E(n\widehat{Var}(\beta_{0j}))$ also has a central F distribution when the alternative hypothesis is true. The statistical power for testing site variability can be computed in a similar way to that in random-effects ANOVA (see Chapter 4). The expectations of the numerator and denominator of the F statistic form a ratio

$$\frac{E(n\widehat{Var}(\beta_{0j}))}{E(\hat{\sigma}^2)} = \frac{n\tau_0 + \sigma^2}{\sigma^2}. \tag{7.61}$$

The F statistic is related to an F distribution,

$$F \sim \frac{E(n\widehat{Var}(\beta_{0j}))}{E(\hat{\sigma}^2)} F(J-1, J(n-2)).$$

The ratio is one when τ_0 is zero under the null hypothesis. The F statistic has a central F distribution. When τ_0 is not zero under the alternative hypothesis, the ratio is not one. We denote the F statistic as F_a under the alternative hypothesis, which no longer has a central F distribution. However, multiplying the reciprocal of that ratio converts F_a back to a central F,

$$F_a \frac{\sigma^2}{n\tau_0 + \sigma^2} \sim F(J-1, J(n-2)). \tag{7.62}$$

Therefore, statistical power for testing τ_0 is

$$\begin{aligned}
1 - \beta &= P[F_a \geq F_0] \\
&= P\left[F_a \frac{\sigma^2}{n\tau_0 + \sigma^2} \geq F_0 \frac{\sigma^2}{n\tau_0 + \sigma^2}\right] \\
&= P\left[F(J-1, J(n-2)) \geq F_0 \frac{\sigma^2}{n\tau_0 + \sigma^2}\right]. \tag{7.63}
\end{aligned}$$

The parameter τ_1 assesses the variance of treatment effects among different sites. Substantial variation of treatment effects means that the magnitude of the treatment effect may depend on some site characteristics (e.g., better facilities at certain sites). Thus, it is of great interest to test the variation of treatment effects among sites. The sample variance of $\hat{\beta}_{1j}$ (i.e., $\widehat{Var}(\hat{\beta}_{1j})$ in Equation 7.47) measures the variance of treatment effects among sites. Its expectation is equal to $E(\widehat{Var}(\hat{\beta}_{1j})) = Var(\hat{\beta}_{1j}) = 4\sigma^2/n + \tau_1$, and it is related to a chi square distribution with degrees of freedom $J-1$, $(J-1)\widehat{Var}(\hat{\beta}_{1j})/(4\sigma^2/n + \tau_1) \sim \chi_{J-1}^2$.

When the null hypothesis is true, there is no variation in treatment effects among sites ($H_0 : \tau_1 = 0$). The expectation $E(\widehat{Var}(\hat{\beta}_{1j}))$ reduces to $4\sigma^2/n$. The ratio between $n/4\widehat{Var}(\hat{\beta}_{1j})$ and $\hat{\sigma}^2$ (Equation 7.60) has a central F distribution,

$$F = \frac{\frac{n}{4}\widehat{Var}(\hat{\beta}_{1j})}{\hat{\sigma}^2}. \tag{7.64}$$

When the alternative hypothesis holds true, the ratio becomes F_a. It has a central F distribution if it is multiplied by $E(\hat{\sigma}^2)/E(\frac{n}{4}\widehat{Var}(\hat{\beta}_{1j}))$, that is,

$$F_a \frac{E(\hat{\sigma}^2)}{E(\frac{n}{4}\widehat{Var}(\hat{\beta}_{1j}))} = F_a \frac{\sigma^2}{\sigma^2 + n\tau_1/4} \sim F(J-1, J(n-2)). \qquad (7.65)$$

Statistical power can be computed as

$$1 - \beta = P[F_a \geq F_0]$$

$$= P\left[F_a \frac{\sigma^2}{\sigma^2 + n\tau_1/4} \geq F_0 \frac{\sigma^2}{\sigma^2 + n\tau_1/4}\right]$$

$$= P\left[F(J-1, J(n-2)) \geq F_0 \frac{\sigma^2}{\sigma^2 + n\tau_1/4}\right], \qquad (7.66)$$

where the critical value is an F quantile, $F_0 = F_{1-\alpha, J-1, J(n-2)}$.

7.2.2   Multiple Treatment Conditions at Each Site

The multi-site randomized trials may involve more than the treatment and control condition at each site. The multiple treatment conditions are easily accommodated because they do not change the major feature of the design. Participants at each site can be randomly assigned to the multiple treatment conditions, and the ensuing statistical analysis can proceed without any difficulty. We will use three treatment conditions at each site for illustration without loss of generality.

The level-1 model uses orthogonal coding to differentiate the three treatment conditions, say, two different inventions plus the business-as-usual condition. The orthogonal coding can be created such that the level-1 regression coefficients represent Helmert contrasts, which are commonly utilized to compare treatment means among more than two treatment conditions. Helmert contrasts can expand systematically as the number of treatment conditions increases. So the methodology described here is also applicable to more than three treatment conditions.

The level-1 equation is

$$Y_{ij} = \beta_{0j} + \beta_{1j}X_{1ij} + \beta_{2j}X_{2ij} + e_{ij}, \quad i = 1, \cdots, n; \quad j = 1, \cdots, J. \qquad (7.67)$$

At the jth site, the subjects are randomly assigned to the two treatments and the control. The indicator variable X_{1ij} takes $1/3$ for the subjects in the first treatment ($e1$), $1/3$ for the subjects in the second treatment ($e2$), and $-2/3$ for those in the control condition (c). The second indicator X_{2j} assumes $1/2$ for the first treatment, $-1/2$ for the second treatment, and 0 for those in the control condition.

The orthogonal coding allows us to represent the least squares estimates of the level-1 regression coefficients in simple formulas. We can easily see this if we limit our attention to the data produced at the jth site. Note first that the correlation between the two indicator variables X_{1ij} and X_{2ij} is zero. This suggests that the effect of the predictor X_{1ij} on the outcome Y_{ij} is independent of the effect of X_{2ij} on Y_{ij}. Therefore, we can ignore the predictor X_{2ij} when we estimate the regression coefficient β_{1j} for X_{1ij}. We can obtain the least squares estimate of β_{1j} in a simple regression analysis of Y_{ij} and X_{1ij} as if X_{2ij} does not exist in the data. The formula for the simple regression estimate of β_{1j} is

$$\hat{\beta}_{1j} = \frac{\sum_{i=1}^{n} (X_{1ij} - \overline{X}_{1j}) Y_{ij}}{\sum_{i=1}^{n} (X_{1ij} - \overline{X}_{1j})^2}$$

$$= \frac{\sum_{i=1}^{n} X_{1ij} Y_{ij}}{\sum_{i=1}^{n} X_{1ij}^2}, \tag{7.68}$$

where $\overline{X}_{1j}$ is the mean of the indicator variable X_{1ij}. The mean $\overline{X}_{1j}$ is zero because the orthogonal coding adds up to zero, $\sum_{i=1}^{n} X_{1ij} = 0$.

Assume that we use equal numbers of subjects among the treatment conditions at every site. At the jth site, the number of subjects in each condition is $n/3$. So the group sizes are the same. The least squares estimate $\hat{\beta}_{1j}$ can be expressed in terms of the group means at the jth site. We use $\overline{Y}_{e1j}$, $\overline{Y}_{e2j}$, and $\overline{Y}_{cj}$ to represent the group means for the first and second treatment and the control, respectively. The numerator of $\hat{\beta}_{1j}$ in Equation 7.68 becomes

$$\sum_{i=1}^{n} X_{1ij} Y_{ij} = \frac{2}{3} \frac{n}{3} \left(\frac{1}{2} \overline{Y}_{e1j} + \frac{1}{2} \overline{Y}_{e2j} - \overline{Y}_{cj} \right).$$

The denominator of $\hat{\beta}_{1j}$ in Equation 7.68 is

$$\sum_{i=1}^{n} X_{1ij}^2 = \frac{n}{3}\left(\left(\frac{1}{3}\right)^2 + \left(\frac{1}{3}\right)^2 + \left(-\frac{2}{3}\right)^2\right) = \frac{n}{3}\frac{2}{3}.$$

Taking the ratio of the numerator and denominator yields

$$\hat{\beta}_{1j} = \frac{1}{2}\overline{Y}_{e1j} + \frac{1}{2}\overline{Y}_{e2j} - \overline{Y}_{cj}. \tag{7.69}$$

Thus, the least squares estimate $\hat{\beta}_{1j}$ compares the average mean of the two treatments with the group mean of the control.

The least squares estimate of the intercept β_{0j} is

$$\hat{\beta}_{0j} = \overline{Y}_j - \hat{\beta}_{1j}\overline{X}_{1j} = \overline{Y}_j, \tag{7.70}$$

where $\overline{X}_{1j}$ is zero. So the least squares estimate of the intercept represents the site mean $\overline{Y}_j$. Similarly, we can obtain the least squares estimate of the regression coefficient β_{2j} in a simple regression of Y_{ij} on X_{2ij},

$$\begin{aligned}
\hat{\beta}_{2j} &= \frac{\sum\limits_{i=1}^{n}(X_{2ij} - \overline{X}_{2j})Y_{ij}}{\sum\limits_{i=1}^{n}(X_{2ij} - \overline{X}_{2j})^2} \\
&= \frac{\sum\limits_{i=1}^{n} X_{2ij}Y_{ij}}{\sum\limits_{i=1}^{n} X_{2ij}^2},
\end{aligned} \tag{7.71}$$

where $\overline{X}_{2j}$ is the mean of the indicator variable X_{2ij}. The mean of X_{2ij} is zero because the orthogonal variable sums up to zero. Further, we find that

$$\begin{aligned}
\hat{\beta}_{2j} &= \frac{\sum\limits_{i=1}^{n} X_{2ij}Y_{ij}}{\sum\limits_{i=1}^{n} X_{2ij}^2} \\
&= \frac{\frac{n}{3}\left(\frac{1}{2}\overline{Y}_{e1j} - \frac{1}{2}\overline{Y}_{e2j} + 0 \times \overline{Y}_{cj}\right)}{\frac{n}{3}\left(\left(\frac{1}{2}\right)^2 + \left(-\frac{1}{2}\right)^2 + (0)^2\right)} \\
&= \overline{Y}_{e1j} - \overline{Y}_{e2j}.
\end{aligned} \tag{7.72}$$

The orthogonal coding scheme makes it easy to interpret the meaning of the regression coefficients. Taking the expectation of the three equations (Equation 7.70, 7.68, and 7.72) changes the group means into the population means. The intercept β_{0j} is the outcome mean at the jth site. The regression coefficient β_{1j} represents the difference between the average mean of the two treatments and the mean of the control condition at the jth site. The coefficient β_{2j} is the mean difference between the two treatment conditions.

Another nice property of these least squares estimates is that they are independent of each other, even though they are based on data from the same site. Each site produces a set of level-1 regression coefficient estimates that are independent within the set or the site. There are J sites or J sets of level-1 regression coefficients. As sites are independent of each other, the J sets of level-1 regression coefficients are, therefore, independent too. This greatly facilitates the derivation of the test statistics for testing the level-2 regression coefficients, which are the key parameters of interest. The level-2 regression coefficients can be estimated in a similar way by treating the level-1 regression coefficient estimates as the outcome observations in the level-2 equations.

The number of level-2 equations is three because of an additional level-1 coefficient β_{2j}. At level 2, the model equations are

$$\beta_{0j} = \gamma_{00} + u_{0j} \tag{7.73}$$
$$\beta_{1j} = \gamma_{10} + u_{1j} \tag{7.74}$$
$$\beta_{2j} = \gamma_{20} + u_{2j}. \tag{7.75}$$

The γ_{00} represents the grand mean across all the sites; γ_{10}, the contrast between the average of the two treatments and the control across all the sites; γ_{20}, the contrast between the two treatment conditions. The level-2 equations are the unconditional models or the null models with no level-2 predictors. Treating the βs from individual sites as outcome observations in the null models, we can obtain the estimates of the γs by averaging the relevant βs over all the sites. That is exactly how we estimate the intercept or the grand mean in a null model of linear regression.

The estimate of γ_{00} is

$$\hat{\gamma}_{00} = \frac{\sum\limits_{j=1}^{J} \hat{\beta}_{0j}}{J}. \tag{7.76}$$

Likewise, we can find the estimates of γ_{10} and γ_{20}. The estimated difference between the average of the two treatments and the control across all the sites is

$$\hat{\gamma}_{10} = \frac{\sum\limits_{j=1}^{J} \hat{\beta}_{1j}}{J}. \tag{7.77}$$

The estimated difference between the two treatment conditions across sites is

$$\hat{\gamma}_{20} = \frac{\sum\limits_{j=1}^{J} \hat{\beta}_{2j}}{J}. \tag{7.78}$$

It should be noted that $\hat{\gamma}_{00}$, $\hat{\gamma}_{10}$, and $\hat{\gamma}_{20}$ are indeed the maximum likelihood estimates (Liu, 2013b).

The variances of the estimated γs are the variances of the corresponding $\hat{\beta}$s divided by J because those estimated γs are simple averages of those $\hat{\beta}$s, that is,

$$Var(\hat{\gamma}_{00}) = \frac{Var(\hat{\beta}_{0j})}{J}; \ \ Var(\hat{\gamma}_{10}) = \frac{Var(\hat{\beta}_{1j})}{J}; \ \ Var(\hat{\gamma}_{20}) = \frac{Var(\hat{\beta}_{2j})}{J}. \tag{7.79}$$

The variances of the βs can be derived in a similar way as in the previous section on two treatment conditions at each site. They are

$$Var(\hat{\beta}_{0j}) = \frac{\sigma^2}{n} + \tau_0,$$

$$Var(\hat{\beta}_{1j}) = \frac{9\sigma^2}{2n} + \tau_1,$$

$$\text{and } Var(\hat{\beta}_{2j}) = \frac{6\sigma^2}{n} + \tau_2. \tag{7.80}$$

The variance τ_0 represents site variability; τ_1 is the variance of the first Helmert contrasts among sites; and τ_2 is the variance of the second Helmert contrasts among sites.

To estimate the variances of the $\hat{\beta}$s, we may resort to the same strategy as for two treatments per site. Those $\hat{\beta}$s are all independently identically distributed with a common variance. The unbiased estimate of the common variance is the sample variance of the $\hat{\beta}$s. For example, the estimate of

$Var(\hat{\beta}_{1j})$ is the sum of squares of J number of $\hat{\beta}_{1j}$ divided by the degrees of freedom $J - 1$, or

$$\widehat{Var}(\hat{\beta}_{1j}) = \frac{\sum_{j=1}^{J} (\hat{\beta}_{1j} - \sum_{j=1}^{J} \hat{\beta}_{1j}/J)^2}{J - 1}. \qquad (7.81)$$

We can compute $\widehat{Var}(\hat{\beta}_{0j})$ and $\widehat{Var}(\hat{\beta}_{2j})$ in a similar fashion.

The estimated variances of the βs can then be substituted to Equation 7.79 to estimate the variance of the γs. Knowing the estimated variance of the γs, we can construct statistical tests to compare means among the treatments and the control. To test the null hypothesis $H_0 : \gamma_{10} = 0$, we can use a t statistic

$$T_1 = \frac{\hat{\gamma}_{10}}{\sqrt{\widehat{Var}(\hat{\gamma}_{10})}}, \qquad (7.82)$$

where

$$\widehat{Var}(\hat{\gamma}_{10}) = \frac{\widehat{Var}(\hat{\beta}_{1j})}{J}. \qquad (7.83)$$

The t statistic has a central t distribution with $J - 1$ degrees of freedom. When the alternative hypothesis $H_a : \gamma_{10} \neq 0$ is true, the t statistic follows a non-central t distribution T_1' with $J - 1$ degrees of freedom and a non-centrality parameter λ_1. The non-centrality parameter can be found by replacing the estimates in the T_1 with the relevant population parameters;

$$\lambda_1 = \frac{\gamma_{10}}{\sqrt{Var(\hat{\gamma}_{10})}}$$
$$= \frac{\gamma_{10}}{\sqrt{(\frac{9\sigma^2}{2n} + \tau_1)/J}}. \qquad (7.84)$$

A t statistic can also be used to test the mean difference between the two treatment conditions across sites;

$$T_2 = \frac{\hat{\gamma}_{20}}{\sqrt{\widehat{Var}(\hat{\gamma}_{20})}}, \qquad (7.85)$$

where

$$\widehat{Var}(\hat{\gamma}_{20}) = \frac{\widehat{Var}(\hat{\beta}_{2j})}{J}. \qquad (7.86)$$

The statistic T_2 has a t distribution with $J-1$ degrees of freedom and a non-centrality parameter λ_2. The non-centrality parameter is

$$
\begin{aligned}
\lambda_2 &= \frac{\gamma_{20}}{\sqrt{Var(\hat{\gamma}_{20})}} \\
&= \frac{\gamma_{20}}{\sqrt{\left(\frac{6\sigma^2}{n}+\tau_2\right)/J}}.
\end{aligned}
\tag{7.87}
$$

The components in the two t tests can be combined into an F statistic, which is the omnibus test for the existence of any mean difference among the three study conditions across sites. The null hypothesis for the omnibus test states that there is no mean difference among the three conditions across sites or $H_0 : \gamma_{10} = \gamma_{20} = 0$. The null hypothesis $\gamma_{10} = \gamma_{20} = 0$ suggests two orthogonal contrasts among the multiple treatment conditions. The parameter γ_{10} compares the average of the first two conditions with the control. The corresponding contrast coefficients are .5, .5, and -1 for the means of the two treatment conditions and the mean of the control. In general, we can write c_{1m} to denote the coefficients for the implied mean contrast. The subscript 1 indicates that it is the first mean contrast, and the subscript m means the treatment condition to which the coefficient is applied (i.e., $m = e1, e2, \cdots, c$). We will use M to stand for the total number of treatment conditions. Likewise, the parameter γ_{20} implies another set of contrast coefficients c_{2m}. In our example, $c_{2e1} = 1$, $c_{2e2} = -1$, and $c_{2c} = 0$. The F statistic for the omnibus test is

$$
F = \frac{\left(J\hat{\gamma}_{10}^2 / \sum_m^M c_{1m}^2 + J\hat{\gamma}_{20}^2 / \sum_m^M c_{2m}^2\right)/2}{\left((J-1)\widehat{Var}(\hat{\beta}_{1j}) / \sum_m^M c_{1m}^2 + (J-1)\widehat{Var}(\hat{\beta}_{2j}) / \sum_m^M c_{2m}^2\right)/(2J-2)}.
\tag{7.88}
$$

The F statistic has a central F distribution with $M-1$ degrees of freedom in the numerator and $(M-1)(J-1)$ degrees of freedom in the denominator under the null hypothesis $H_0 : \gamma_{10} = \gamma_{20} = 0$. When the alternative hypothesis is true, the F statistic follows a non-central F distribution F' with degrees of freedom $M-1$ and $(M-1)(J-1)$. The non-centrality parameter λ for the non-central F' is the sum of the squared non-centrality parameters from the contrast t tests, that is,

$$
\lambda = \lambda_1^2 + \lambda_2^2.
\tag{7.89}
$$

Thus, the statistical power for the omnibus F test is

$$1 - \beta = 1 - P[F'(2, 2(J-1), \lambda) \geq F_{1-\alpha,2,2(J-1)}]. \qquad (7.90)$$

We can use the study of cognitive behavioral therapy to illustrate the power analysis. A psychiatrist intends to examine the effects of cognitive behavioral therapy, individual peer support, and regular care (business-as-usual) in treating postnatal depression among high-risk women, who are likely to experience a wide range of distressing symptoms following childbirth (Dennis et al, 2009; Stevenson et al, 2010). Cognitive behavioral therapy helps clients challenge their thinking distortions by "reality testing" to see the errors in their thinking. Patients typically need to go to a mental health professional to receive cognitive behavioral therapy but resources are limited and waiting times long: proactive individualized telephone-based (mother-to-mother) peer support offers an accessible alternative. In running the study, patients at each participating clinic are randomly assigned to the three treatment conditions. The study is a multi-site randomized trial with three study conditions at each site. The outcome is the change in rating on the Edinburgh Postnatal Depression Scale (EPDS), which has been widely used in many countries. The psychiatrist is interested in comparing the average effect of the two treatments with that of the control. As a typical patient who suffers postnatal depression might receive treatment that falls somewhere between intensive counseling and peer support, the average effect of the two treatments is somewhat comparable to the average treatment that a patient might usually receive. It is of interest to know whether treatment is better than control (business as usual) at all. This corresponds to the first Helmert contrast. The second Helmert contrast compares the two treatments: cognitive behavioral therapy and telephone peer support. Previous research suggests that cognitive behavioral therapy might outperform the business-as-usual treatment by 3.4 on the EPDS scale ($\Delta_1 = 3.4$), and that the individual peer support is better than the business-as-usual by 1.1 on the EPDS scale ($\Delta_2 = 1.1$). Note that the two simple effect sizes are related to the model parameters;

$$\gamma_{10} = \frac{\Delta_1 + \Delta_2}{2}$$
$$\gamma_{20} = \Delta_1 - \Delta_2. \qquad (7.91)$$

The standard deviation of the EPDS score is 4.6 ($\sqrt{\sigma^2 + \tau} = 4.6$). The ratio between τ and σ^2 is estimated as $1 : 10$ (i.e., $\tau : \sigma^2 = 1 : 10$). Suppose that about forty-five patients will participate at each clinic ($n = 45$). If seven clinics are used ($J = 7$), the statistical power for the omnibus F test will be .82. However, the power for the first and second Helmert contrasts are .62 and .52, respectively. If the number of participating clinics is increased to twelve ($J = 12$), the power for the two Helmert contrasts will reach .898 and .817 instead.

The R code is:

```
# multi-site randomized trial with three treatments at site

#postpartum depression psychotherapy/peer support/control
#ref Dennis et al 2009 BMJ
#     Stevenson et al 2010 Health Tech Assessment
# total variance=sigma2+tau=4.6^2
# tau : sigma2 = 1 :10

p4mst3=function(J=12,n=45,D1=3.4,D2=1.1,
        sigma2=4.6^2/1.1,tau=4.6^2/1.1*.1){
c1=c(.5,.5,-1)
c2=c(1,-1,0)
sc1=sum(c1^2)
sc2=sum(c2^2)

tau1=sc1*tau
tau2=sc2*tau

gamma10=(D1+D2)/2
gamma20=D1-D2

lambda1=sqrt(J)*gamma10/sqrt(sc1*3*sigma2/n+tau1)
lambda2=sqrt(J)*gamma20/sqrt(sc2*3*sigma2/n+tau2)

lambda=lambda1^2+lambda2^2

#power for omnibus test
a=.05
```

```
f0=qf(1-a,2,2*(J-1))
p=1-pf(f0,2,2*(J-1),lambda)

#power for orthogonal contrast
t0=qt(1-a/2,J-1)
p1=1-pt(t0,J-1,lambda1)+pt(-t0,J-1,lambda1)
p2=1-pt(t0,J-1,lambda2)+pt(-t0,J-1,lambda2)

#power for comparing e1 and control
t00=qt(1-a/2/2,J-1)
nc13=sqrt(J)*D1/sqrt(sc2*3*sigma2/n+tau2)
p13=1-pt(t00,J-1,nc13)+pt(-t00,J-1,nc13)

#power for comparing e2 and control
nc23=sqrt(J)*D2/sqrt(sc2*3*sigma2/n+tau2)
p23=1-pt(t00,J-1,nc23)+pt(-t00,J-1,nc23)

cat(J, "\t",p,"\t", p1,"\t", p2, "\t",p13,"\t",p23,"\n")
}

p4mst3(7,)
p4mst3()

for(J in 6:35){p4mst3(J)}
```

The SAS program is:

```
*multi-site randomized trial with three treatments at site;
/*
postpartum depression psychotherapy/peer support/control
default values from
Dennis et al 2009 BMJ
Stevenson et al 2010 Health Tech Assessment
total variance=sigma2+tau=4.6^2
tau : sigma2 = 1 :10
*/
data mst3(keep=n J sigma2 tau p p1 p2);
a=.05;
```

```
n=45;
Delta1=3.4;
Delta2=1.1;
sigma2=4.6**2/1.1;
tau=4.6**2/1.1*.1;

c11=.5;  c12=.5;  c13=-1;
c21=1;   c22=-1;  c23=0;
sc1=c11**2+c12**2+c13**2;
sc2=c21**2+c22**2+c23**2;

gamma10=(Delta1+Delta2)/2;
gamma20=Delta1-Delta2;

tau1=sc1*tau;
tau2=sc2*tau;

do J=6 to 35;
 lambda1=sqrt(J)*gamma10/sqrt(sc1*3*sigma2/n+tau1);
 lambda2=sqrt(J)*gamma20/sqrt(sc2*3*sigma2/n+tau2);
 lambda=lambda1**2+lambda2**2;

 f0=finv(1-a,2,2*(J-1));
 p=1-probf(f0,2,2*(J-1),lambda);

 *power for orthogonal contrasts;
 t0=tinv(1-a/2,J-1);
 p1=1-probt(t0,J-1,lambda1)+probt(-t0,J-1,lambda1);
 p2=1-probt(t0,J-1,lambda2)+probt(-t0,J-1,lambda2);

 output;
end;
run;
```

The SPSS code is:

```
*multi-site randomized trial with three treatments at site
    postpartum depression psychotherapy/peer support/control
```

```
      default values from
      Dennis et al 2009 BMJ
      Stevenson et al 2010 Health Tech Assessment
      total variance=sigma2+tau=4.6^2
      tau : sigma2 = 1 :10.

NEW FILE.
INPUT PROGRAM.

COMPUTE N=45.
COMPUTE DELTA1=3.4.
COMPUTE DELTA2=1.1.
COMPUTE SIGMA2=4.6**2/1.1.
COMPUTE TAU=4.6**2/1.1*.1.

COMPUTE GAMMA10=(DELTA1+DELTA2)/2.
COMPUTE GAMMA20=DELTA1-DELTA2.

COMPUTE SC1=.5**2+.5**2+(-1)**2.
COMPUTE SC2=1**2+(-1)**2+0**2.
COMPUTE TAU1=SC1*TAU.
COMPUTE TAU2=SC2*TAU.

COMPUTE A=.05.

LEAVE N TO A.

LOOP J=6 TO 60.
  COMPUTE LAMBDA1=SQRT(J)*GAMMA10/SQRT(SC1*3*SIGMA2/N+TAU1).
  COMPUTE LAMBDA2=SQRT(J)*GAMMA20/SQRT(SC2*3*SIGMA2/N+TAU2).
  COMPUTE LAMBDA=LAMBDA1**2+LAMBDA2**2.
  COMPUTE P=1-NCDF.F(IDF.F(1-A,2,2*(J-1)),2,2*(J-1),LAMBDA).
    *power for Helmert contrasts.
  COMPUTE T0=IDF.T(1-A/2,J-1).
  COMPUTE P1=1-NCDF.T(T0,J-1,LAMBDA1)+NCDF.T(-T0,J-1,LAMBDA1).
  COMPUTE P2=1-NCDF.T(T0,J-1,LAMBDA2)+NCDF.T(-T0,J-1,LAMBDA2).
  END CASE.
```

```
END LOOP.
END FILE.
END INPUT PROGRAM.
EXECUTE.

DELETE VARIABLES SC1 SC2 TAU1 TAU2 A LAMBDA LAMBDA1 LAMBDA2.
LIST.
```

7.2.3　Derivation of the F Statistic

This section contains mathematical derivation of the F statistic in Equation 7.88 for the omnibus test. Readers who are not interested in the technical details may skip it without any disruption in reading.

The numerator of the F ratio comprises two sums of squares due to the two contrasts,

$$SSB_1 = \frac{J\hat{\gamma}_{10}^2}{\sum_m^M c_{1m}^2}; SSB_2 = \frac{J\hat{\gamma}_{20}^2}{\sum_m^M c_{2m}^2}. \tag{7.92}$$

The contrast estimate $\hat{\gamma}_{10}$ has a normal distribution,

$$\hat{\gamma}_{10} \sim N\left(\gamma_{10}, \frac{\frac{3\sigma^2}{n}\sum_m^M c_{1m}^2 + \tau_1}{J}\right).$$

The variance τ_1 can be related to the variance of the interaction between the treatment and the site τ in a simplified mixed effects ANOVA model, where the variance of the observation Y_{ij} can be decomposed into three parts: the variance of sites τ_0, the variance of site by treatment interaction τ, and the residual variance σ^2,

$$Var(Y_{ij}) = \tau_0 + \tau + \sigma^2. \tag{7.93}$$

The variance of the mean of the mth treatment at the jth site is

$$Var(\overline{Y}_{mj}) = \tau_0 + \tau + \frac{M\sigma^2}{n}. \tag{7.94}$$

Assume that there are n subjects at each site with equal numbers of subjects in the M treatment conditions n/M (e.g., $M = 3$ in our example). In our example, the mean contrast estimate at the jth site is $\hat{\beta}_{1j}$, and its variance is

$$Var(\hat{\beta}_{1j}) = Var(\sum_m^3 c_{1m}\overline{Y}_{mj})$$

$$= \sum_m^3 c_{1m}^2 \tau + \sum_m^3 c_{1m}^2 \frac{3\sigma^2}{n}, \qquad (7.95)$$

where $\sum_m^3 c_{1m}^2 \tau = \tau_1$.

The variance of $\hat{\gamma}_{10}$ can be expressed in terms of the variance of the interaction common to both contrast tests, that is,

$$\hat{\gamma}_{10} \sim N\left(\gamma_{10}, \frac{\frac{3\sigma^2}{n}\sum_m^M c_{1m}^2 + \sum_m^M c_{1m}^2 \tau}{J}\right). \qquad (7.96)$$

It is easy to see that

$$\tau_1 = \sum_m^3 c_{1m}^2 \tau. \qquad (7.97)$$

Likewise, we can obtain the variance of the second contrast for γ_{20},

$$\hat{\gamma}_{20} \sim N\left(\gamma_{20}, \frac{\frac{3\sigma^2}{n}\sum_m^M c_{2m}^2 + \sum_m^M c_{2m}^2 \tau}{J}\right), \qquad (7.98)$$

where $\tau_2 = \sum_m^3 c_{2m}^2 \tau$.

The denominator of the F ratio includes two sums of squares,

$$SSE_1 = (J-1)\widehat{Var}(\hat{\beta}_{1j})/\sum_m^M c_{1m}^2; \; SSE_2 = (J-1)\widehat{Var}(\hat{\beta}_{2j})/\sum_m^M c_{2m}^2. \quad (7.99)$$

It can be proven that SSE_1 is related to a chi-square random variate,

$$SSE_1 \sim \left(\frac{3\sigma^2}{n} + \tau\right)\chi_{J-1}^2. \qquad (7.100)$$

Similarly, SSE_2 contains a chi-square random variate,

$$SSE_2 \sim \left(\frac{3\sigma^2}{n} + \tau\right)\chi_{J-1}^2. \qquad (7.101)$$

The two chi square variates are independent because SSE_1 and SSE_2 are orthogonal to each other.

Dividing the numerator and denominator of the F ratio in Equation 7.88 by $3\sigma^2/n + \tau$ shows that it has an F distribution,

$$F = \frac{\left(Z_1^2(\lambda_1^2) + Z_2^2(\lambda_2^2)\right)/2}{\left(\chi_{J-1}^2 + \chi_{J-1}^2\right)/(2J-2)}, \tag{7.102}$$

where Z_1^2 and Z_2^2 are two squared normal random variates with mean λ_1 and λ_2. Thus, the F ratio has an F distribution with non-centrality parameter $\lambda = \lambda_1^2 + \lambda_2^2$ (Liu, 2013b).

Chapter 8

Complex Multi-level Models

Complex multi-level models may involve three levels or covariate adjustment. We will deal with two kinds of three-level model in this chapter: three-level cluster randomization trials and multi-site cluster randomized trials. The two designs differ in the level at which random assignment is formed. If the random assignment occurs at level 3, it is a cluster randomized trial. If the randomization occurs at level 2 across multiple sites, it will be a multi-site cluster randomized trial. In addition, we will find how to consider covariate adjustment and sample allocation and their implications for statistical power in multi-level analysis.

8.1 Three-level Cluster Randomized Trial

In school-based studies, schools are randomly assigned into treatment and control conditions. The study design is a cluster randomized trial with schools viewed as clusters. If we consider those classrooms nested within each school, we can represent the cluster randomized trial in a three-level HLM model. The level-1 equation is

$$Y_{ijk} = \pi_{0jk} + e_{ijk}, \; e_{ijk} \sim N(0, \sigma^2)$$
$$i = 1, 2, \cdots, n; \; j = 1, 2, \cdots, J; k = 1, 2, \cdots, K. \quad (8.1)$$

The observation Y_{ijk} is an outcome measure for the ith student in the jth classroom nested in the kth school. The outcome observation Y_{ijk} is conceived of as comprising a classroom mean π_{0jk} and individual error e_{ijk}, the latter of which is assumed to be normally distributed with a zero mean and a variance σ^2. The classroom mean π_{0jk} is the average of the observations pertaining to the jth classroom in the kth school, and it becomes the outcome in the regression equation at level 2.

The level-2 equation is

$$\pi_{0jk} = \beta_{00k} + r_{0jk}, \; r_{0jk} \sim N(0, \tau_\pi), \tag{8.2}$$

where β_{00k} is the school mean of the kth school, and r_{0jk} is the level-2 random error specific to the jth classroom. The level-2 equation is a null regression model, in which the classroom mean π_{0jk} in the kth school is a linear function of the school mean of the kth school β_{00k} and a random deviation from the school mean or level-2 random error. As the level-2 regression equation applies to every one of the K schools in the study, there will be K school means β_{00k}. The K school means become the outcome observations in the regression equation at level 3, which includes an indicator variable W_k on random assignment.

The level-3 equation is

$$\beta_{00k} = \gamma_{000} + \gamma_{001} W_k + u_{00k}, \; u_{00k} \sim N(0, \tau_\beta), \tag{8.3}$$

where γ_{000} is the grand mean, W_k takes .5 for a school in the treatment group and $-.5$ for a school in the control group, γ_{001} is the average difference in outcome between schools in the treatment group and those in the control group, and u_{00k} is the level-3 random error. The parameter γ_{001} represents the differential in outcome between the treated schools and the untreated controls (i.e., the main effect of treatment).

We can test the main effect of treatment in a similar way as in a two-level cluster randomized trial. First, we find the combined model for the three-level cluster randomized trial. Second, we aggregate the combined model to simplify it. To find the combined model, we substitute the level-3 equation into the level-2 equation,

$$\pi_{0jk} = \gamma_{000} + \gamma_{001} W_k + u_{00k} + r_{0jk}.$$

We then substitute the expanded level-2 equation into the level-1 equation to get the combined model,

$$Y_{ijk} = \gamma_{000} + \gamma_{001} W_k + u_{00k} + r_{0jk} + e_{ijk}. \tag{8.4}$$

The combined model can be simplified when the observations are aggregated over the subscripts i and j. In effect, we aggregate all the observations within each of the K schools and work with K sample school means $\bar{Y}_{..k}$.

$$\bar{Y}_{..k} = \gamma_{000} + \gamma_{001}W_k + u_{00k} + \bar{r}_{.k} + \bar{e}_{..k}, \tag{8.5}$$

where the aggregated level-2 random error is $\bar{r}_{.k} = \sum_{j=1}^{J} r_{0jk}/J$, the variance of which is

$$Var(\bar{r}_{.k}) = \frac{\tau_\pi}{J}. \tag{8.6}$$

Likewise, the aggregated level-1 random error is $\bar{e}_{..k} = \sum_{j=1}^{J}\sum_{i=1}^{n} e_{ijk}/(Jn)$; its variance is

$$Var(\bar{e}_{..k}) = \frac{\sigma^2}{Jn}. \tag{8.7}$$

As the random errors across levels are independent, the variance of the aggregated school mean is the sum of the respective variances of the three random effects u_{00k}, $\bar{r}_{.k}$, and $\bar{e}_{..k}$;

$$\begin{aligned} Var(\bar{Y}_{..k}) &= Var(\gamma_{000} + \gamma_{001}W_k + u_{00k} + \bar{r}_{.k} + \bar{e}_{..k}) \\ &= Var(u_{00k} + \bar{r}_{.k} + \bar{e}_{..k}) \\ &= Var(u_{00k}) + Var(\bar{r}_{.k}) + Var(\bar{e}_{..k}) \\ &= \tau_\beta + \frac{\tau_\pi}{J} + \frac{\sigma^2}{Jn}. \end{aligned} \tag{8.8}$$

The combined model can be viewed as a special case of a regular linear model with a complex error;

$$\bar{Y}_{..k} = \gamma_{000} + \gamma_{001}W_k + e_k^*, \tag{8.9}$$

where the three random errors are wrapped in one complex error e_k^* (i.e., $e_k^* = u_{00k} + \bar{r}_{.k} + \bar{e}_{..k}$). The variance of the complex error is equal to the variance of the school mean because the fixed effects γ_{000} and $\gamma_{001}W_k$ do not contribute any variance;

$$
\begin{aligned}
Var(\bar{Y}_{..k}) &= Var(\gamma_{000} + \gamma_{001}W_k + e_k^*) \\
&= Var(e_k^*) \\
&= Var(u_{00k} + \bar{r}_{.k} + \bar{e}_{..k}) \\
&= Var(u_{00k}) + Var(\bar{r}_{.k}) + Var(\bar{e}_{..k}) \\
&= \tau_\beta + \frac{\tau_\pi}{J} + \frac{\sigma^2}{Jn}.
\end{aligned}
$$

In short, the complex error e_k^* is an independently identically distributed (i.i.d.) normal variate with a common variance

$$
Var(e_k^*) = \tau_\beta + \frac{\tau_\pi}{J} + \frac{\sigma^2}{Jn}. \tag{8.10}
$$

As the K school means have i.i.d. normal errors and are regressed on the predictor of treatment assignment W_k, Equation 8.9 is simply a regular linear model. We can estimate γ_{000} and γ_{001} in Equation 8.9, using maximum likelihood estimation.

The maximum likelihood (ML) estimate of the grand mean γ_{000} is

$$
\hat{\gamma}_{000} = \sum_{k=1}^{K} \bar{Y}_{..k}. \tag{8.11}
$$

It is obvious that the ML estimate of the grand mean is the grand average of the sample school mean $\bar{Y}_{..k}$. The ML estimate of the main effect of treatment γ_{001} is

$$
\hat{\gamma}_{001} = \sum_{k=1}^{K/2} \bar{Y}_{..k} - \sum_{k=K/2+1}^{K} \bar{Y}_{..k}, \tag{8.12}
$$

$$
\{k: 1, 2, \cdots, K/2\} \in \text{treatment} \quad \{k: K/2+1, \cdots, K\} \in \text{control},
$$

where the first half of the schools are in the treatment group, and the second half in the control group.

The variance of the ML estimate of the main effect of treatment $\hat{\gamma}_{001}$ is

$$
\begin{aligned}
Var(\hat{\gamma}_{001}) &= \frac{4Var(\bar{Y}_{..k})}{K} \\
&= \frac{4\left(\tau_\beta + \frac{\tau_\pi}{J} + \frac{\sigma^2}{Jn}\right)}{K}. \tag{8.13}
\end{aligned}
$$

The estimated variance is based on the fact that the school means are i.i.d. normal with a common variance $Var(\overline{Y}_{..k})$. The restricted maximum likelihood estimate of the common variance $Var(\overline{Y}_{..k})$ is

$$\widehat{Var}(\overline{Y}_{..k}) = \frac{\sum_{k=1}^{K/2} (\overline{Y}_{..k} - \frac{\sum_{k=1}^{K/2} \overline{Y}_{..k}}{K/2})^2 + \sum_{k=K/2+1}^{K} (\overline{Y}_{..k} - \frac{\sum_{k=K/2+1}^{K} \overline{Y}_{..k}}{K/2})^2}{K - 2}. \quad (8.14)$$

The estimated variance of the main effect of treatment, therefore, is

$$\widehat{Var}(\hat{\gamma}_{001}) = \frac{4\widehat{Var}(\overline{Y}_{..k})}{K}. \quad (8.15)$$

The test for the main effect of treatment uses a t statistic with degrees of freedom $K - 2$,

$$T = \frac{\hat{\gamma}_{001}}{\sqrt{\widehat{Var}(\hat{\gamma}_{001})}}. \quad (8.16)$$

In the absence of any main effect of treatment ($H_0 : \gamma_{001} = 0$), the t statistic follows a central t distribution. When the alternative hypothesis is true $H_a : \gamma_{001} \neq 0$, the t statistic has a non-central t distribution with $K - 2$ degrees of freedom and non-centrality parameter λ,

$$\lambda = \frac{\gamma_{001}}{\sqrt{Var(\hat{\gamma}_{001})}}$$

$$= \frac{\gamma_{001}}{\sqrt{\frac{4Var(\overline{Y}_{..k})}{K}}}$$

$$= \frac{\gamma_{001}}{\sqrt{\frac{4\left(\tau_\beta + \frac{\tau_\pi}{J} + \frac{\sigma^2}{Jn}\right)}{K}}}. \quad (8.17)$$

The statistical power for testing the main effect of treatment is

$$1 - \beta = P[|T'(K - 2, \lambda)| \geq t_0]$$
$$= 1 - P[T'(K - 2, \lambda) < t_0] + P[T'(K - 2, \lambda) \leq -t_0], \quad (8.18)$$

where t_0 is the critical t value ($t_{1-\alpha/2,K-2}$), and $P[T'(K - 2, \lambda) < t_0]$ is the cumulative distribution function of a non-central t.

The statistical power function in a three-level cluster randomized trial bears resemblance to that in a two-level cluster randomized trial in the previous chapter. The number of degrees of freedom in the t test depends on the number of schools or clusters (i.e., $K - 2$), and it is identical between the two-level and three-level cluster randomized trials. In addition, we can rearrange the elements in the non-centrality parameter in the three-level cluster randomized trial (Equation 8.17) to make it resemble its counterpart in the two-level cluster randomized trial,

$$\lambda = \frac{\gamma_{001}}{\sqrt{\frac{4\left(\tau_\beta + \frac{\tau_\pi + \sigma^2/n}{J}\right)}{K}}}. \tag{8.19}$$

The numerator in the non-centrality parameter represents the main effect of treatment, and it is the same between a two-level model and a three-level model. In the denominator, τ_β is comparable to the level-2 variance τ in a two-level model, and $\tau_\pi + \sigma^2/n$ to the level-1 variance in a two-level model. This is because the three-level model is related to the two-level model.

The three-level model for a cluster randomized trial can be folded into a two-level model without losing any useful data (Liu, 2003). If we collapse the data within each school into J class means $\overline{Y}_{.jk}$, we can write those J class means in K schools in a two-level model:

$$\text{Level-1: } \overline{Y}_{.jk} = \beta_{00k} + (r_{0jk} + \bar{e}_{..k});$$
$$\text{Level-2: } \beta_{00k} = \gamma_{000} + \gamma_{001}W_k + u_{00k}.$$

The combined model is

$$\overline{Y}_{.jk} = \gamma_{000} + \gamma_{001}W_k + u_{00k} + (r_{0jk} + \bar{e}_{..k}), \ (r_{0jk} + \bar{e}_{..k}) \sim N(0, \tau_\pi + \sigma^2/n), \tag{8.20}$$

where $r_{0jk} + \bar{e}_{.k}$ is lumped together and made comparable to the level-1 variance in a two-level model. The combined model differs from its counterpart in a two-level cluster randomized trial by a complex level-1 error variance. Although a two-level model is an option for representing the data in a three-level cluster randomized trial, we need to use a three-level model anyway to include covariates at both level 2 and level 3. It is easy to represent those covariates at different levels in a three-level model.

We can use a study of school reform to demonstrate how to calculate statistical power for a three-level cluster randomized trial. Many school reform initiatives are implemented at district level, such as the development of data-driven accountability (Carlson, Borman, and Robinson, 2011) or teacher incentive pay for student performance. The schools in the same district will be assigned to receive the same intervention. This gives rise to a three-level cluster randomized trial, in which schools are nested in districts and students are nested in schools. The student achievement variable is typically the outcome measure. The research questions whether the reform efforts bring any substantial improvement in student achievement, compared with those in the control group. The main effect of treatment is the average difference in student achievement between the treatment and control groups (i.e., simple effect size). There is not a consensus on how to standardize such a simple effect size. In planning a three-level cluster randomized trial, the researcher might start with an estimated simple effect size (γ_{001}) and then estimate the total variance of the student achievement variable (i.e., $\sigma^2 + \tau_\pi + \tau_\beta$). The latter can be done by investigating the range of the student achievement scores. Using four and six standard deviations for 95% and 99%, the researcher can estimate the standard deviation of the student achievement variable (i.e., $\sqrt{\sigma^2 + \tau_\pi + \tau_\beta}$). To run statistical power analysis, the researcher needs to specify the relative size of the variance components (σ^2, τ_π, and τ_β). People usually define these relative sizes by using intraclass correlation. In a two-level cluster randomized trial, there is only one way to define the intraclass correlation, which actually means the correlation between two observations within the same cluster. A three-level cluster randomized trial has two intraclass correlations. There are at least two different ways to define the two intraclass correlations (Teerenstra, Moerbeek, van Achterber, Pelzer, and Borm, 2008). As intraclass correlation connotes correlation, we will use two intraclass correlations to represent two correlations. The first intraclass correlation ρ_1 is the correlation between two observations in the smaller cluster. In our example, it is the correlation between two student observations in the same smaller cluster,

$$\rho_1 = \frac{\tau_\beta + \tau_\pi}{\tau_\beta + \tau_\pi + \sigma^2}. \tag{8.21}$$

We use the second intraclass correlation ρ_2 to represent the correlation between two means of smaller clusters within the same larger cluster,

$$\rho_2 = \frac{\tau_\beta}{\tau_\beta + \tau_\pi}. \tag{8.22}$$

The two intraclass correlations ρ_1 and ρ_2 show the relative size of the three variance components. They are actually correlations between the observations in the model. For simplicity of illustration, we scale the simple effect size γ_{001} relative to the standard deviation $\sqrt{\sigma^2 + \tau_\pi + \tau_\beta}$. The standard deviation is set to one, and the simple effect size is .3 ($\gamma_{001} = .3$). The two intraclass correlations are .3 and .2, respectively (i.e., $\rho_1 = .3$ and $\rho_2 = .2$). This implies that students' observations in the same school are slightly more correlated than two school means in the same district. Suppose that the average number of schools in a district is about 5 ($J = 5$), and that twelve 5th grade students will be sampled from each school ($n = 12$). If forty-four districts ($K = 44$) are recruited into the study, statistical power for testing the main effect of treatment will reach .80.

The R code is:

```
# 3 level cluster randomized trial
#rho1 correlation btw obs within
#smaller cluster (school)
#rho2 correlation btw obs (sch means) within
#larger cluster (district)

p3crt=function(K=44,J=5,n=12,gamma001=.3,sd=1,
rho1=.3,rho2=.2){
a=.05
sigma2=sd^2*(1-rho1)
tau_pi=sd^2*rho1*(1-rho2)
tau_b=sd^2*rho1*rho2

lambda=gamma001/sqrt(4*(tau_b+(tau_pi+sigma2/n)/J)/K)
t0=qt(1-a/2,K-2)
1-pt(t0,K-2,lambda)+pt(-t0,K-2,lambda)
}

p3crt()
```

The SAS program is:

```
/*
3-level cluster randomized trial
rho1 correlation btw obs within smaller cluster
rho2 correlation btw sch means within larger cluster
*/
data l3crt(keep=J n K gamma001 sd rho1 rho2 power);
a=.05;
J=5;
n=12;
gamma001=.3;
sd=1;
rho1=.3;
rho2=.2;

sigma2=sd**2*(1-rho1);
tau_pi=sd**2*rho1*(1-rho2);
tau_b=sd**2*rho1*rho2;

do K=6 to 50 by 2;
 lambda=gamma001/sqrt(4*(tau_b+(tau_pi+sigma2/n)/J)/K);
 t0=tinv(1-a/2,K-2);
 power=1-probt(t0,K-2,lambda)+probt(-t0,K-2,lambda);
 output;
end;
run;
```

The SPSS is:

```
* 3-level cluster randomized trial
rho1 correlation btw obs within smaller cluster
rho2 correlation btw sch means within larger cluster.

NEW FILE.
INPUT  PROGRAM.

COMPUTE A=.05.
```

```
COMPUTE J=5.
COMPUTE N=12.
COMPUTE GAMMA001=.3.
COMPUTE SD=1.
COMPUTE RHO1=.3.
COMPUTE RHO2=.2.

COMPUTE SIGMA2=SD**2*(1-RHO1).
COMPUTE TAU_PI=SD**2*RHO1*(1-RHO2).
COMPUTE TAU_B=SD**2*RHO1*RHO2.

LEAVE A TO TAU_B.

LOOP K=6 TO 50 BY 2.
COMPUTE LAMBDA=GAMMA001/SQRT(4*(TAU_B+(TAU_PI+SIGMA2/N)/J)/K).
COMPUTE T0=IDF.T(1-A/2,K-2).
COMPUTE POWER=1-NCDF.T(T0,K-2,LAMBDA)+NCDF.T(-T0,K-2,LAMBDA).
END CASE.
END LOOP.
END FILE.
END INPUT PROGRAM.

DELETE VARIABLES A SD SIGMA2 TAU_PI TAU_B LAMBDA T0.
LIST.
```

We will postpone addressing covariate adjustment in multi-level models until after we have dealt with another complex multi-level design; the multi-site cluster randomized trial. Covariate adjustment is common to both three-level cluster randomized trials and multi-site cluster randomized trials. It will be convenient to address covariates after we have introduced both designs.

8.2   Multi-site Cluster Randomized Trial

The multi-site cluster randomized trial combines a multi-site trial with cluster randomized trials by replicating cluster randomized trials across multiple sites. For example, schools can be randomly assigned to a treatment or control group (a cluster randomized trial) in one district or locale, and the same study protocol can be followed in different districts or locales, which gives rise to a multi-site cluster randomized trial. Using the multiple sites makes it easy to recruit a large sample into the study and strengthen the generality of the potential findings about the treatment. We can analyze the data in a multi-site cluster randomized trial, using multi-level modeling.

The level-1 equation is

$$Y_{ijk} = \pi_{0jk} + e_{ijk}, \; e_{ijk} \sim N(0, \sigma^2) \tag{8.23}$$

$$i = 1, 2, \cdots, n; \; j = 1, 2, \cdots, J; k = 1, 2, \cdots, K,$$

where the observation Y_{ijk} is the outcome measure for the ith individual in the jth cluster at the kth site, π_{0jk} is the jth cluster mean at the kth site, and e_{ijk} is the individual error, which is normally distributed with a zero mean and a variance σ^2.

The level-2 equation is the regression of the cluster mean π_{0jk} on an indicator variable of treatment assignment X_{jk}, which takes .5 for treatment and $-.5$ for control,

$$\pi_{0jk} = \beta_{00k} + \beta_{01k} X_{jk} + r_{0jk}, \; r_{0jk} \sim N(0, \tau_\pi), \tag{8.24}$$

where β_{00k} is the site mean, β_{01k} is the treatment effect specific to the kth site, and r_{0jk} is the level-2 random error, which is normally distributed.

The level-3 equations are

$$\begin{aligned}\beta_{00k} &= \gamma_{000} + u_{00k}; \\ \beta_{01k} &= \gamma_{010} + u_{01k}.\end{aligned} \qquad \begin{pmatrix} u_{00k} \\ u_{01k} \end{pmatrix} \sim N\left(\mathbf{0}, \begin{bmatrix} \tau_{u0} & \tau_{01} \\ \tau_{10} & \tau_{u1} \end{bmatrix}\right). \tag{8.25}$$

Equation 8.25 shows that each of the K site means β_{00k} is conceived of as comprising a grand mean γ_{000} and a random deviation of the site mean from the grand mean (i.e., level-3 random error $u_{00k} \sim N(0, \tau_{u_0})$). Likewise, the site-specific treatment effect β_{01k} is made of the grand average of treatment effects γ_{010} and a random deviation of the site-specific treatment effect from the grand average (i.e., level-3 random error $u_{01k} \sim N(0, \tau_{u_1})$).

The grand average of treatment effects γ_{010} represents the main effect of treatment. It is the key parameter of interest in a multi-site cluster randomized trial. The estimation of the main effect of treatment can be based on the K site-specific treatment effects β_{01k}, which can be individually estimated from the sample mean difference between the treatment and control arms in the cluster randomized trial at the kth site. The estimation of β_{01k} uses the same formulas as in a regular two-level cluster randomized trial (see Chapter 7). The sample mean difference between the two arms at the kth site is

$$\hat{\beta}_{01k} = \frac{\sum\limits_{j=1}^{J/2} \overline{Y}_{.jk}}{J/2} - \frac{\sum\limits_{j=J/2+1}^{J} \overline{Y}_{.jk}}{J/2}, \tag{8.26}$$

where $\overline{Y}_{.jk}$ is the cluster mean at the kth site. The first half of the clusters are in the treatment arm ($\{j : 1, 2, \cdots, J/2\}$), and the second half are in the control arm ($\{j : J/2+1, J/2+2, \cdots, J\}$). There are K $\hat{\beta}_{01k}$ from the K sites. Each site-specific treatment effect $\hat{\beta}_{01k}$ weighs the same in estimating the grand average of treatment effects or the main effect of treatment. The estimated main effect of treatment $\hat{\gamma}_{010}$ is the average of the estimated site-specific treatment effects $\hat{\beta}_{01k}$,

$$\hat{\gamma}_{010} = \frac{\sum\limits_{k=1}^{K} \hat{\beta}_{01k}}{K}. \tag{8.27}$$

The variance of $\hat{\gamma}_{010}$ is

$$Var(\hat{\gamma}_{010}) = \frac{Var(\hat{\beta}_{01k})}{K}. \tag{8.28}$$

The variance of the estimated site-specific treatment effect $Var(\hat{\beta}_{01k})$ can be obtained by applying the well-known formulas for variance decomposition. The variance comprises the expectation of the conditional variance of $\hat{\beta}_{01k}$ at the kth site and the variance of the expectation of $\hat{\beta}_{01k}$ at the kth site,

$$Var(\hat{\beta}_{01k}) = E(Var(\hat{\beta}_{01k}|k\text{th site})) + Var(E(\hat{\beta}_{01k}|k\text{th site}))$$
$$= \frac{4(\tau_\pi + \sigma^2/n)}{J} + Var(\beta_{01k})$$
$$= \frac{4(\tau_\pi + \sigma^2/n)}{J} + \tau_{u_1}. \tag{8.29}$$

Estimating $Var(\hat{\gamma}_{010})$ uses the sample variance of $\hat{\beta}_{01k}$. The K site-specific treatment effects $\hat{\beta}_{01k}$ are independently estimated, and they are i.i.d. random variables with a common variance $Var(\hat{\beta}_{01k})$. So the sample variance of $\hat{\beta}_{01k}$ is an unbiased estimate of $Var(\hat{\beta}_{01k})$,

$$\widehat{Var}(\hat{\beta}_{01k}) = \frac{\sum\limits_{k=1}^{K} \left(\hat{\beta}_{01k} - \frac{\sum_{k=1}^{K}\hat{\beta}_{01k}}{K} \right)^2}{K-1}. \tag{8.30}$$

Using the estimated variance, we have the estimated variance of the main effect of treatment;

$$\widehat{Var}(\hat{\gamma}_{010}) = \frac{\widehat{Var}(\hat{\beta}_{01k})}{K}. \tag{8.31}$$

We can form a t statistic to test the main effect of treatment with its estimate and variance (Equations 8.27 and 8.31),

$$T = \frac{\hat{\gamma}_{010}}{\sqrt{\widehat{Var}(\hat{\gamma}_{010})}}. \tag{8.32}$$

The t statistic has $K-1$ degrees of freedom. When the null hypothesis holds true, $H_0 : \gamma_{010} = 0$, the t statistic follows a central t distribution. When the alternative hypothesis is true, the t statistic follows a non-central t distribution with a non-centrality parameter λ or $T'(K-1,\lambda)$,

$$\lambda = \frac{\gamma_{010}}{\sqrt{Var(\hat{\gamma}_{010})}}$$

$$= \frac{\gamma_{010}}{\sqrt{\frac{Var(\hat{\beta}_{01k})}{K}}}$$

$$= \frac{\gamma_{010}\sqrt{K}}{\sqrt{\frac{4(\tau_\pi + \sigma^2/n)}{J} + \tau_{u_1}}}. \tag{8.33}$$

The statistical power for testing the main effect of treatment uses the cumulative distribution function of a non-central t,

$$1 - \beta = P[|T'(K-1,\lambda)| \geq t_0]$$
$$= 1 - P[T'(K-1,\lambda) < t_0] + P[T'(K-1,\lambda) \leq -t_0], \tag{8.34}$$

where t_0 is the critical t value ($t_0 = t_{1-\alpha/2, K-1}$), and $P[T'(K-1,\lambda) < t_0]$ is the cumulative distribution function of a non-central t.

In addition to testing the main effect of treatment, researchers are often interested in examining the site variability τ_{u_0} and the variance of treatment effects among sites τ_{u_1}. Testing the two variances uses the same principle as in the random-effects model. The null hypothesis posits that the variance τ_{u_0} or τ_{u_1} is zero . We form an F test by calculating a ratio of two variances V_1 and V_2, the expectations of which differ in τ_{u_0} or τ_{u_1}. The ratio of the two variances is a central F multiplied by the ratio of the expectations of the two variances,

$$\frac{V_1}{V_2} \sim \frac{E(V_1)}{E(V_2)} F.$$

If τ_{u_0} or τ_{u_1} is indeed zero under the null hypothesis, the ratio of the expectations of the two variances will become one. In this case, the ratio of the two variances will have a central F distribution. Under the alternative hypothesis, the ratio of the expectations of the two variances in the F is no longer one. The expectations of one variance in the ratio will contain a non-zero τ_{u_0} or τ_{u_1}. However, if we multiply the ratio by the reciprocal of the expectations of the two variances, the transformed F will revert to a central F distribution;

$$H_a : \frac{E(V_2)}{E(V_1)} \frac{V_1}{V_2} \sim \frac{E(V_2)}{E(V_1)} \frac{E(V_1)}{E(V_2)} F \sim F.$$

The statistical power for testing the variance τ_{u_0} or τ_{u_1} can, still, be based on a central F.

The test for site variability τ_{u_0} compares the variances $\tau_{u_0} + (\tau_\pi + \sigma^2/n)/J$ and $\tau_\pi + \sigma^2/n$ in an F ratio. The former is the variance of the site mean $\overline{Y}_{..k}$ (i.e., $Var(\overline{Y}_{..k})$); the latter the conditional variance of the cluster mean $\overline{Y}_{.jk}$ conditional on a specific site (i.e., $Var(\overline{Y}_{.jk}|k\text{th site})$). They differ only by a variance τ_{u_0}. When τ_{u_0} is zero under the null hypothesis, the numerator and denominator of the F ratio, which differ only by a variance τ_{u_0}, will be equal in their expectations. The F ratio will follow a central F distribution with $K - 1$ degrees of freedom in the numerator and $K(J - 2)$ degrees of freedom in the denominator,

$$F = \frac{J\widehat{Var}(\overline{Y}_{..k})}{\widehat{Var}(\overline{Y}_{.jk}|k\text{th site})}. \tag{8.35}$$

The numerator of the F ratio $\widehat{Var}(\overline{Y}_{..k})$ is the sample variance of $\overline{Y}_{..k}$; and the denominator $\widehat{Var}(\overline{Y}_{.jk}|k\text{th site})$ is the total within-site sample variance of $\overline{Y}_{.jk}$.

The numerator of the F ratio $\widehat{Var}(\overline{Y}_{..k})$ is an unbiased estimate of the variance $\tau_{u_0} + (\tau_\pi + \sigma^2/n)/J$ because the site means $(\overline{Y}_{..k})$ are i.i.d. normal with a common variance $\tau_{u_0} + (\tau_\pi + \sigma^2/n)/J$. The sample variance of $\overline{Y}_{..k}$ is, therefore, an unbiased estimate of $Var(\overline{Y}_{..k})$;

$$\widehat{Var}(\overline{Y}_{..k}) = \frac{\sum\limits_{k=1}^{K} \left(\overline{Y}_{..k} - \sum_{k-1}^{K} \overline{Y}_{..k}/K\right)^2}{K-1}. \tag{8.36}$$

The sample variance $\widehat{Var}(\overline{Y}_{..k})$ is distributed as the population variance multiplied by a chi square variate with $K-1$ degrees of freedom,

$$(K-1)\widehat{Var}(\overline{Y}_{..k}) \sim \left(\tau_{u_0} + \frac{\tau_\pi + \sigma^2/n}{J}\right) \chi^2_{K-1}.$$

The denominator of the F ratio uses the total within-site sample variance of $\overline{Y}_{.jk}$ to estimate the conditional variance $Var(\overline{Y}_{.jk}|k\text{th site})$. In computing the within-site sample variance of $\overline{Y}_{.jk}$, we pool together all the within-treatment sums of squares of $\overline{Y}_{.jk}$ (SSW_k) and divide the pooled sums of squares $(\sum_{k=1}^{K} SSW_k)$ by their total degrees of freedom, $K(J-2)$.

$$SSW_k = \sum_{j=1}^{J/2} \left(\overline{Y}_{.jk} - \frac{\sum_{j=1}^{J/2} \overline{Y}_{.jk}}{J/2}\right)^2 + \sum_{j=J/2+1}^{J} \left(\overline{Y}_{.jk} - \frac{\sum_{j=J/2+1}^{J} \overline{Y}_{.jk}}{J/2}\right)^2 \tag{8.37}$$

$$\widehat{Var}(\overline{Y}_{.jk}|k\text{th site}) = \frac{\sum_{k=1}^{K} SSW_k}{K(J-2)}. \tag{8.38}$$

The statistical power for testing τ_{u_0} uses the cumulative distribution of a central F. Under the alternative hypothesis $H_a : \tau_{u_0} \neq 0$, we use F_a to represent the F statistic,

$$\frac{\tau_\pi + \sigma^2/n}{J\tau_{u_0} + \tau_\pi + \sigma^2/n} F_a \sim F(K-1, K(J-2)). \tag{8.39}$$

The statistical power is the probability of F_a being larger than or equal to the critical value $F_0 = F_{1-\alpha,\,K-1,\,K(J-2)}$;

$$1 - \beta = P[F_a \geq F_0]$$

$$= 1 - P\left[\frac{\tau_\pi + \sigma^2/n}{J\tau_{u_0} + \tau_\pi + \sigma^2/n}\, F_a < \frac{\tau_\pi + \sigma^2/n}{J\tau_{u_0} + \tau_\pi + \sigma^2/n}\, F_0\right]$$

$$= 1 - P\left[F(K-1, K(J-2)) < \frac{\tau_\pi + \sigma^2/n}{J\tau_{u_0} + \tau_\pi + \sigma^2/n}\, F_0\right]. \qquad (8.40)$$

This power function is for testing the site variability in the average outcome. The variability among sites may also be manifest in the treatment effects, which may vary across different sites.

The variability of treatment effects among sites τ_{u_1} is of great interest in a multi-site cluster randomized trial. If a significant amount of variation exists in treatment effects across sites, the researcher may proceed to investigate why some sites produce larger treatment effects than others. A site characteristic may be added to the model to explain why some sites outperform others in treatment effect. So τ_{u_1} is often tested in the data analysis of a multi-site cluster randomized trial.

The test for τ_{u_1} uses a F ratio, like its counterpart for testing τ_{u_0}. The numerator of the F ratio measures the variance of the site-specific treatment effect $Var(\hat{\beta}_{01k})$. Its unbiased estimate is the sample variance of $\hat{\beta}_{01k}$,

$$\widehat{Var}(\hat{\beta}_{01k}) = \frac{\sum\limits_{k=1}^{K}\left(\hat{\beta}_{01k} - \frac{\sum_{k=1}^{K}\hat{\beta}_{01k}}{K}\right)^2}{K-1}. \qquad (8.41)$$

The denominator of the F ratio measures the conditional variance of the class mean $\overline{Y}_{.jk}$ conditional on a specific site (i.e., $Var(\overline{Y}_{.jk}|k\text{th site})$). Its unbiased estimate is the total within-site sample variance of $\overline{Y}_{.jk}$ in Equation 8.38, namely, $\widehat{Var}(\overline{Y}_{.jk}|k\text{th site}) = \sum_{k=1}^{K} SSW_k/(K(J-2))$. So the F ratio for testing τ_{u_1} is

$$F = \frac{\frac{J}{4}\widehat{Var}(\hat{\beta}_{01k})}{\widehat{Var}(\overline{Y}_{.jk}|k\text{th site})}. \qquad (8.42)$$

The multiplicative factor $J/4$ is necessary because the numerator and denominator of the F ratio thus computed have equal expectations under the null hypothesis $H_0 : \tau_{u_1} = 0$. As both $\widehat{Var}(\hat{\beta}_{01k})$ and $\widehat{Var}(\overline{Y}_{.jk}|k\text{th site})$ are unbiased estimates, their expectations are

$$E(\widehat{Var}(\hat{\beta}_{01k})) = \frac{4(\tau_\pi + \sigma^2/n)}{J} + \tau_{u_1}$$

$$E(\widehat{Var}(\overline{Y}_{.jk}|k\text{th site})) = \tau_\pi + \sigma^2/n.$$

The F statistic is distributed as

$$F \sim \frac{E(\frac{J}{4}\widehat{Var}(\hat{\beta}_{01k}))}{E(\widehat{Var}(\overline{Y}_{.jk}|k\text{th site}))} \, F(K-1, K(J-2)). \tag{8.43}$$

When τ_{u_1} is zero under H_0, the ratio of the two expectations becomes one;

$$\frac{E(\frac{J}{4}\widehat{Var}(\hat{\beta}_{01k}))}{E(\widehat{Var}(\overline{Y}_{.jk}|k\text{th site}))} = \frac{\tau_\pi + \sigma^2/n + J\tau_{u_1}/4}{\tau_\pi + \sigma^2/n} = \frac{\tau_\pi + \sigma^2/n + J \times 0/4}{\tau_\pi + \sigma^2/n} = 1.$$

Thus, the F ratio simplifies to a central F with $K-1$ degrees of freedom in the numerator and $K(J-2)$ degrees of freedom in the denominator (i.e., $F(K-1, K(J-2))$). When the alternative hypothesis $H_a : \tau_{u_1} \neq 0$ is true, the F is not exactly a central F, namely,

$$F_a = \frac{\tau_\pi + \sigma^2/n + J\tau_{u_1}/4}{\tau_\pi + \sigma^2/n} \, F(K-1, K(J-2)).$$

The numerator and denominator of the F ratio do not have equal expectations. However, F_a will revert to a central F once it is multiplied by the reciprocal of the two expectations;

$$\frac{\tau_\pi + \sigma^2/n}{\tau_\pi + \sigma^2/n + J\tau_{u_1}/4} F_a$$

$$= \frac{\tau_\pi + \sigma^2/n}{\tau_\pi + \sigma^2/n + J\tau_{u_1}/4} \frac{\tau_\pi + \sigma^2/n + J\tau_{u_1}/4}{\tau_\pi + \sigma^2/n} F(K-1, K(J-2))$$

$$= F(K-1, K(J-2)).$$

Computing the statistical power for the test of τ_{u_1} uses the reverted F;

$$1 - \beta = P[F_a \geq F_0]$$

$$= P\left[\frac{\tau_\pi + \sigma^2/n}{\tau_\pi + \sigma^2/n + J\tau_{u_1}/4}F_a \geq \frac{\tau_\pi + \sigma^2/n}{\tau_\pi + \sigma^2/n + J\tau_{u_1}/4}F_0\right]$$

$$= 1 - P[F(K-1, K(J-2)) < \frac{\tau_\pi + \sigma^2/n}{\tau_\pi + \sigma^2/n + J\tau_{u_1}/4}F_0], \qquad (8.44)$$

where F_0 is the critical F value, and $P[F(K-1, K(J-2)) < F_0]$ is the cumulative distribution function of a central F with $K-1$ degrees of freedom in the numerator and $K(J-2)$ degrees of freedom in the denominator.

For example, a clinical psychologist wants to study the effect of motivational interviewing on changing adolescents' perception of cannabis use (McCambridge and Strang, 2004). The study will be conducted across different geographical locations (e.g., cities and states). At each geographical location (site), several youth counseling centers will be recruited, and they will be randomly assigned to provide the treatment (motivational interviewing) or business as usual. The eligible subjects in the treatment centers will receive motivational interviewing. Each site produces a cluster randomized trial, which is replicated across different sites. The outcome variable is the change in perception of cannabis use. Suppose that the effect size is .45 ($\gamma_{010} = .45$), and that the total variance at one location is one ($\sigma^2 + \tau_\pi = 1$). We group σ^2 and τ_π as the total variance within a site because there is a cluster randomized trial at each site, which basically forms an independent study on its own. Using the within-site total variance, we may define the intraclass correlation ρ in the cluster randomized trial;

$$\rho = \frac{\tau_\pi}{\sigma^2 + \tau_\pi}. \qquad (8.45)$$

This intraclass correlation means the correlation between two observations in the same counseling center or cluster at a particular site. The conditional total variance $\sigma^2 + \tau_\pi$ represents the within-site variance. As in a multi-site trial, we may specify the proportion of between-site variance by defining a ratio, $\sigma^2 + \tau_\pi : \tau_{u_1} = 1 : p$. Suppose that $\rho = .1$ and $p = .1$. We can compute the statistical power for testing the main effect of treatment γ_{010}. Assume that there are on average eight counseling centers at each site and twelve participating subjects at each counseling center ($J = 8$ and $n = 12$). If ten sites are used ($K = 10$), the statistical power will reach .83.

The R code for computing power is:

```
#multisite cluster randomized trial
# rho: intraclass correlation conditional on site
# rho=tau_pi /( tau_pi +sigma2)
# sd^2=sigma2 + tau_pi: within-site total variance
# sd^2 : tau_u1 = 1 : p
# within-site variance vs between-site variance

p4mcrt=function(K=10,J=8,n=12,gamma010=.45,sd=1, rho=.1,p=.1){
a=.05
sigma2=sd^2*(1-rho)
tau_pi=sd^2*rho
tau_u1=sd^2*p

lambda=gamma010*sqrt(K)/sqrt(4*(tau_pi + sigma2/n)/J + tau_u1)
t0=qt(1-a/2,K-1)
1-pt(t0,K-1,lambda)+pt(-t0,K-1,lambda)
}

p4mcrt()
```

The SAS program is:

```
/*multisite cluster randomized trial

rho: intraclass correlation conditional on site
rho=tau_pi /( tau_pi +sigma2)
sd^2=sigma2 + tau_pi: within-site variance
sd^2 : tau_u1 = 1 : p
*/

data mcrt(keep=J n K gamma010 sd rho p power);
a=.05;
J=8;
n=12;
gamma010=.45;
sd=1;
```

```
rho=.1;
p=.1;

sigma2=sd**2*(1-rho);
tau_pi=sd**2*rho;
tau_u1=sd**2*p;

do K=4 to 20;
 lambda=gamma010*sqrt(K)/sqrt(4*(tau_pi+sigma2/n)/J+tau_u1);
 t0=tinv(1-a/2,K-1);
 power=1-probt(t0,K-1,lambda)+probt(-t0,K-1,lambda);
 output;
end;
run;
```

The SPSS code is:

```
*  multisite cluster randomized trial
       rho: intraclass correlation conditional on site
       rho=tau_pi /( tau_pi +sigma2)
       sd^2=sigma2 + tau_pi: within cluster variance
       sd^2 : tau_u1 = 1 : p.

NEW FILE.
INPUT  PROGRAM.

COMPUTE A=.05.
COMPUTE J=8.
COMPUTE N=12.
COMPUTE GAMMA010=.45.
COMPUTE SD=1.
COMPUTE RHO=.1.
COMPUTE P=.1.

COMPUTE SIGMA2=SD**2*(1-RHO).
COMPUTE TAU_PI=SD**2*RHO.
COMPUTE TAU_U1=SD**2*P.
```

```
LEAVE A TO TAU_U1.

LOOP K=4 TO 20.
  COMPUTE LAMBDA=GAMMA010*SQRT(K)/
  SQRT(4*(TAU_PI+SIGMA2/N)/J +TAU_U1).
  COMPUTE T0=IDF.T(1-A/2,K-1).
  COMPUTE POWER=1-NCDF.T(T0,K-1,LAMBDA)+
                NCDF.T(-T0,K-1,LAMBDA).
  END CASE.
END LOOP.
END FILE.
END INPUT PROGRAM.

DELETE VARIABLES A SD SIGMA2 TAU_PI TAU_U1 LAMBDA T0.
LIST.
```

8.3 Covariate Adjustment

Covariates may be added to multi-level models to reduce error variance and improve statistical power, although it is generally difficult to compute statistical power for covariate adjustment. The current approach uses Cohen's method, which replaces the dependent variable with the adjusted dependent variable. The parameters in the statistical power function will be changed accordingly. The effect size of the adjusted dependent variable remains the same as that of the unadjusted dependent variable. However, the error variance of the adjusted dependent variable is reduced over the original variance by a fraction that is related to the correlation between the dependent variable and covariates. The approach generally works for sufficiently large sample sizes, but may not be accurate for small sample sizes. We will compare the multi-level models with and without covariate adjustment, showing how to adjust the parameters in the power function. We will start with a cluster randomized trial and then proceed to a multi-site randomized trial.

The combined model for a two-level cluster randomized trial without covariates is

$$Y_{ij} = \gamma_{00} + \gamma_{01} X_{1j} + u_{0j} + e_{ij}, \tag{8.46}$$

where i represents an ith individual in the jth cluster, X_{1j} is an indicator variable for treatment assignment (.5 for treatment and $-.5$ for control), u_{0j} is the level-2 random error, and e_{ij} is the level-1 error. The main effect of treatment is represented by γ_{01}. As before, we average on both sides of the combined model equation and obtain the aggregated model,

$$\overline{Y}_j = \gamma_{00} + \gamma_{01} X_{1j} + u_{0j} + \bar{e}_{.j}.$$

Grouping the error terms into one, we can simplify the aggregated model into

$$\overline{Y}_j = \gamma_{00} + \gamma_{01} X_{1j} + e_j^*, \tag{8.47}$$

where $e_j^* = u_{0j} + \bar{e}_{.j}$ and $e_j^* \sim N(0, \tau + \sigma^2/n)$.

Now suppose that we have access to a level-2 covariate that describes the characteristic of the clusters (e.g., the percentage of free or subsidized lunch at school). The level-2 covariate is often used because it is convenient and economical to measure such a characteristic at the cluster level (school level). The covariate may potentially remove unaccounted error and improve statistical power without increasing sample size. In the multi-level model, a level-2 covariate is denoted by X_{2j},

$$Y_{ij} = \beta_{0j} + e_{ij}$$
$$\beta_{0j} = \gamma_{00} + \gamma_{01}' X_{1j} + \gamma_{02} X_{2j} + u_{0j}',$$

where γ_{02} is the regression coefficient for the level-2 covariate X_{2j}. The term γ_{01}' represents the covariate-adjusted main effect of treatment. We use a prime to differentiate it from the unadjusted main effect of treatment γ_{01}, and we do the same with the level-2 error u_{0j}'. The combined model with a level-2 covariate is

$$Y_{ij} = \gamma_{00} + \gamma_{01}' X_{1j} + \gamma_{02} X_{2j} + u_{0j}' + e_{ij}. \tag{8.48}$$

To simplify the combined model, we can use an aggregated model by averaging both sides of the equation over subscript i. In effect we take the average of all the observations within clusters and use the cluster mean as the dependent variable. The aggregated model is

$$\overline{Y}_{.j} = \gamma_{00} + \gamma_{01}' X_{1j} + \gamma_{02} X_{2j} + u_{0j}' + \bar{e}_{.j}. \tag{8.49}$$

The error term $u'_{0j} + \bar{e}_{.j}$ can be wrapped into one e'_j for conciseness. The aggregated model becomes

$$\overline{Y}_{.j} = \gamma_{00} + \gamma'_{01}X_{1j} + \gamma_{02}X_{2j} + e'_j, \tag{8.50}$$

where $e'_j = u'_{0j} + \bar{e}_{.j}$.

The error e'_j has a smaller variance than its counterpart e^*_j in the model without the covariate. This is because the covariate X_{2j} in Equation 8.50 explains some unaccounted error variance in e^*_j. We can illustrate this point by using the adjusted dependent variable $\overline{Y}'_{j}$. Moving $\gamma_{02}X_{2j}$ to the left side of Equation 8.50 changes the dependent variable to the covariate-adjusted dependent variable $\overline{Y}'_{j}$,

$$\overline{Y}_{.j} - \gamma_{02}X_{2j} = \gamma_{00} + \gamma'_{01}X_{1j} + e'_j,$$

$$\overline{Y}'_{.j} = \gamma_{00} + \gamma'_{01}X_{1j} + e'_j, \tag{8.51}$$

where $\overline{Y}'_{.j} = \overline{Y}_{.j} - \gamma_{02}X_{2j}$. The adjusted dependent variable $\overline{Y}'_{.j}$ is essentially the residual of the dependent variable after it has been regressed on the covariate, which removes the effect of the covariate from the dependent variable. Thus, the adjusted dependent variable $\overline{Y}'_{.j}$ has a smaller error variance than the unadjusted dependent variable $\overline{Y}_{.j}$, that is, $Var(e'_j) < Var(e^*_j)$.

The reduction in error variance due to covariate adjustment depends on the correlation r between the cluster mean $\overline{Y}_{.j}$ and the covariate X_{1j}. The reduced error variance is

$$Var(e'_j) = (1 - r^2)Var(e^*_j) = (1 - r^2)\left(\tau + \frac{\sigma^2}{n}\right). \tag{8.52}$$

Cohen (1988) uses the same approach in computing statistical power for covariate adjustment, but he does not explain that such an approach works well when there is no correlation between X_{1j} and X_{2j} in Equation 8.50. This is generally true if random assignment is used with a sufficient number of clusters (J). The treatment group and control group are equalized in the covariate mean on X_{2j}. In other words, there is no collinearity between X_{2j} and X_{1j}. We can regress the dependent variable $\overline{Y}_{.j}$ on X_{2j} and then regress the residual $\overline{Y}_j'$ on the treatment assignment variable X_{1j}. The results will be the same as regressing $\overline{Y}_{.j}$ on both X_{1j} and X_{2j} all at once.

The statistical power for testing the main effect with covariate(s) uses the adjusted mean difference γ_{01}' and the reduced error variance $(1 - r^2)(\tau + \sigma^2/n)$. In a two-sided test, the power function becomes

$$1 - \beta = 1 - P[T'(J - 3, \lambda') < t_0] + P[T'(J - 3, \lambda') \leq -t_0], \qquad (8.53)$$

where t_0 is the right-side critical value ($t_0 = t_{1-\alpha/2, J-3}$), and λ' is the non-centrality parameter. When a right-sided alternative hypothesis is used, the statistical power in the one-sided test simplifies to

$$1 - \beta = 1 - P[T'(J - 3, \lambda') < t_0], \qquad (8.54)$$

where $t_0 = t_{1-\alpha, J-3}$;

$$\lambda' = \frac{\gamma_{01}'}{\sqrt{\frac{4(1 - r^2)(\tau + \sigma^2/n)}{J}}}. \qquad (8.55)$$

The variance $\tau + \sigma^2/n$ in the non-centrality parameter reduces by r^2, owing to the covariate adjustment, which increases the non-centrality parameter and, in turn, the statistical power. However, the covariate consumes one degree of freedom. The t test now has $J - 3$ degrees of freedom instead of $J - 2$. This will negatively affect statistical power, although such a negative effect is often eclipsed by the error reduction in the non-centrality parameter. The gain in error reduction more than compensates for the loss in the degrees of freedom. For practical purposes, the change in degrees of freedom is negligible. The change in statistical power is primarily attributed to the increased non-centrality parameter, which has the error variance in its denominator shrink by $100r^2$ percent.

The reduction in error variance can increase further when multiple covariates are used in the analysis. The multiple correlation coefficient R between the cluster mean and q covariates replaces the correlation r in the non-centrality parameter. The number of degrees of freedom for the t test is now $J - 2 - q$. Statistical power for testing the main effect in a two-sided test becomes

$$1 - \beta = 1 - P[T'(J - 2 - q, \lambda') < t_0] + P[T'(J - 2 - q, \lambda') \leq -t_0], \quad (8.56)$$

where $t_0 = t_{1-\alpha/2, J-2-q}$, and

$$\lambda' = \frac{\gamma'_{01}}{\sqrt{\frac{4(1-R^2)(\tau+\sigma^2/n)}{J}}}. \tag{8.57}$$

When the multiple correlation coefficient R is larger than the simple correlation r, statistical power will increase further.

However, including covariates does not always improve statistical power when the number of clusters J is small. We can use one covariate to illustrate the point without loss of generality. Covariate imbalance might distort the main effect of treatment (i.e., the adjusted mean difference γ'_{01} between the treatment and control). Cohen would simply equate the adjusted mean difference γ'_{01} to the unadjusted mean difference γ_{01} without covariates in power analysis . In doing so, he implicitly makes an assumption that a large sample size is used and that the covariate imbalance is small. People often overlook this implicit assumption and erroneously associate higher power with covariate adjustment when random assignment involves a limited sample size. We will see that higher power due to covariates is far less certain than people tend to think.

The adjusted mean difference γ'_{01} in the numerator of the non-centrality parameter can be larger or smaller than the unadjusted mean difference γ_{01}, depending on the covariate imbalance or covariate mean difference. The covariate mean difference between the treatment and control condition affects the adjusted mean difference,

$$\gamma'_{01} = \gamma_{01} - \gamma_{02}(\overline{X}_{2e} - \overline{X}_{2c}), \tag{8.58}$$

where $\overline{X}_{2e}$ and $\overline{X}_{2c}$ are the covariate means for the treatment and control groups, respectively. When the number of clusters is large, random assignment balances the covariate means between the treatment and control groups. The covariate means tend to be close or equal in this case ($\overline{X}_{2e} = \overline{X}_{2c}$). The unadjusted mean difference γ_{01} can be used to substitute for the adjusted mean difference γ'_{01} in the non-centrality parameter in the power function, which now has the same numerator in the non-centrality parameter but a smaller denominator due to covariate adjustment, compared with the power function without using covariates. Consequently, the statistical power will be higher with covariate adjustment than without covariate adjustment. Yet, it is not always true when the number of randomly assigned clusters is small. When the number of clusters is limited, random assignment will not produce covariate balance between the treatment and control groups. There may be a substantial covariate mean difference in $\overline{X}_{2e} - \overline{X}_{2c}$. Suppose that the covariate (school socioeconomic status) is positively related to the dependent variable (academic achievement), that is, $\gamma_{02} > 0$. If schools in the treatment group are better off than those in the control group, the adjustment term $\gamma_{02}(\overline{X}_{2e} - \overline{X}_{2c})$ in Equation 8.58 would be positive, which makes the adjusted mean difference smaller than an unadjusted mean difference or $\gamma'_{01} < \gamma_{01}$. In this case, the non-centrality in the power function has a decreased numerator and denominator. Compared with that obtained without using a covariate, there may not be any gain in statistical power.

We can find how likely a covariate will improve statistical power by comparing the non-centrality parameter with and without covariate adjustment;

$$\frac{\lambda'}{\lambda} = \frac{\dfrac{\gamma'_{01}}{\sqrt{\dfrac{4(1-r^2)(\tau+\sigma^2/n)}{J}}}}{\dfrac{\gamma_{01}}{\sqrt{\dfrac{4(\tau+\sigma^2/n)}{J}}}} = \frac{\gamma_{01} - \gamma_{02}(\overline{X}_{2e} - \overline{X}_{2c})}{\gamma_{01}\sqrt{1-r^2}}.$$

Note that the regression coefficient γ_{02} can be expressed in terms of the correlation r or $\gamma_{02} = \sigma_{\overline{Y}_j}/\sigma_X r$, where $\sigma_{\overline{Y}_j}$ and σ_X are the standard deviations of the variable $\overline{Y}_j$ and the covariate X, respectively. Also, we observe that $\overline{X}_{2e} - \overline{X}_{2c}$ on school socioeconomic status is related to a normal Z ($(\sqrt{J/4}(\overline{X}_{2e} - \overline{X}_{2c})/\sigma_X \sim Z$), and that $\delta = \gamma_{01}/\sigma_{\overline{Y}_j}$ is the standardized effect size (for notational brevity).

$$\begin{aligned}
\frac{\lambda'}{\lambda} &= \frac{\gamma_{01} - \dfrac{\sigma_{\overline{Y}_j}}{\sigma_X} r(\overline{X}_{2e} - \overline{X}_{2c})}{\gamma_{01}\sqrt{1-r^2}} \\[2mm]
&= \frac{1 - \dfrac{\sigma_{\overline{Y}_j}}{\gamma_{01}} r\sqrt{4/J}\sqrt{J/4}(\overline{X}_{2e} - \overline{X}_{2c})/\sigma_X}{\sqrt{1-r^2}} \\[2mm]
&= \frac{1 - (2r\delta^{-1}/\sqrt{J})Z}{\sqrt{1-r^2}}
\end{aligned} \tag{8.59}$$

The statistical power gains when the non-centrality parameter λ' in the covariate-adjusted analysis is larger than its counterpart λ in the unadjusted analysis, or $\lambda'/\lambda > 1$;

$$\frac{\lambda'}{\lambda} > 1$$

$$\frac{1 - (2r\delta^{-1}/\sqrt{J})Z}{\sqrt{1-r^2}} > 1$$

$$\frac{\delta(1 - \sqrt{1-r^2})\sqrt{J}}{2r} > Z. \tag{8.60}$$

We can calculate the probability of having $\lambda'/\lambda > 1$, using a normal cumulative distribution function Φ,

$$P\left[\frac{\lambda'}{\lambda} > 1\right] = P\left[Z < \frac{\delta(1 - \sqrt{1-r^2})\sqrt{J}}{2r}\right] = \Phi\left(\frac{\delta(1 - \sqrt{1-r^2})\sqrt{J}}{2r}\right). \tag{8.61}$$

Suppose that the correlation r between the cluster mean and covariate is .4 and the standardized effect size δ is .5. When four schools are randomly assigned into the treatment or control group, the chance of gaining power is little better than a coin toss.

$$P\left[\frac{\lambda'}{\lambda} > 1\right] = \Phi\left(\frac{.5(1 - \sqrt{1-.4^2})\sqrt{4}}{2 \times .4}\right) = .54 \tag{8.62}$$

In a multi-site randomized trial, site characteristics can be included as covariates. It is often quite easy to observe or access site characteristics, such as school socioeconomic status, percentage of free or subsidized lunch, etc. Adding site-level covariates can remove some otherwise unexplained error variance and increase the statistical power for testing the main effect. The same principles used in cluster randomized trials can be applied to multi-site randomized trials.

The site-specific treatment effect estimate will have a reduced variance due to the inclusion of site-level covariates. The level-2 equation for the site-specific treatment effect is

$$\beta_{1j} = \gamma_{10} + u_{1j}.$$

Conditioning on the jth site, we can estimate the site-specific treatment effect β_{1j} by calculating the mean difference between the treatment and control within the site $\hat{\beta}_{1j}$. Since this is an unbiased estimate, it deviates from the true parameter β_{1j} by a normal error $\bar{e}_j$ with mean zero and variance $4\sigma^2/n$,

$$\hat{\beta}_{1j} - \beta_{1j} = \bar{e}_j, \; \bar{e}_j \sim N\left(0, \frac{4\sigma^2}{n}\right).$$

We thereby obtain

$$\hat{\beta}_{1j} = \gamma_{10} + \bar{e}_j + u_{1j}.$$

If we wrap the two error terms into one, we have a regular linear model,

$$\hat{\beta}_{1j} = \gamma_{10} + e_j^*,$$

where $e_j^* - \bar{e}_j + u_{1j}$ and $e_j^* \sim N(0, \tau_1 \mid 4\sigma^2/n)$. When we add a site-level covariate W_j, the level-2 equation becomes

$$\hat{\beta}_{1j} = \gamma_{10} + \gamma_{11}(W_j - \overline{W}) + e_j', \; e_j' \sim N(0, (1-r^2)(\tau_1 + 4\sigma^2/n)), \quad (8.63)$$

where r is the correlation between the site-specific treatment effect and the site-level covariate. The covariate W_j is centered around its mean $\overline{W}$. The centering makes it meaningful to interpret γ_{10}, which is the treatment effect for a site with a mean score on the covariate. Without centering, γ_{10} is the treatment effect for a site with a zero score on the covariate. The zero score on the covariate does not necessarily have a clear meaning because it may not exist at all (e.g., zero on school socioeconomic status). The error variance will decrease by $100r^2$ percent, which helps boost statistical power.

The statistical power for testing the main effect in a two-sided test then becomes

$$1 - \beta = 1 - P[T'(J-2, \lambda') < t_0] + P[T'(J-2, \lambda') < -t_0], \quad (8.64)$$

where t_0 is a t quantile $t_{1-\alpha/2, J-2}$, and λ' is the regular non-centrality parameter λ without covariate adjustment multiplied by $1/\sqrt{1-r^2}$,

$$\lambda' = \frac{\lambda}{\sqrt{1-r^2}}$$
$$= \frac{\gamma_{10}}{\sqrt{\frac{4(1-r^2)(\tau_1+\sigma^2/n)}{J}}}. \quad (8.65)$$

The number of degrees of freedom is $J - 2$ rather than $J - 1$ because the covariate consumes one degree of freedom in the test. As long as the covariate is substantially correlated with the site-specific treatment effect, covariate adjustment may improve statistical power in multi-site randomized trials.

8.4   Optimal Sample Allocation

Multi-level models involve large sampling units and small sampling units that are nested in the large sampling units. The total sample size depends on the number of large sampling units as well as the number of small sampling units. For example, in a cluster randomized trial, the large sampling units may be J schools, and the small sampling units n students in each of the J schools. The total sample size N is the product of n and J ($N = nJ$). Likewise, in a multi-site randomized trial the total sample size is the number of sites, J, multiplied by the number of participants, n, in each of the J sites. A researcher may opt to choose different values of n and J for the same total sample size N. For instance, $n = 50$ and $J = 10$ produce a total sample size $N = 500$; so do $n = 25$ and $J = 20$. A researcher can, therefore, choose different n and J without changing the total sample size. How to allocate the sample size to n and J becomes an interesting issue because the sample allocation affects the statistical power. An optimal sample allocation can maximize statistical power and minimize sampling costs.

Optimal sample allocation works in a similar fashion to sample size optimization in survey sampling because cluster randomized trials and multi-site randomized trials resemble cluster random sampling and stratified random sampling. In cluster random sampling, J clusters (e.g., schools) are chosen, and then n small sampling units (e.g., students) in each cluster are randomly selected. The sample size of the large sampling units, J, and the sample size of the small sampling units, n, can be optimized to minimize the variance of the sample estimate whether that sample estimate is a mean or a total value. The optimal sample sizes return the minimum variance under the constraint of a total cost. Likewise, in stratified random sampling, the population is divided into J strata, which correspond to the multiple sites in a multi-site randomized trial. Within each stratum, n small sampling units are randomly selected. The optimal sample sizes J and n return a minimum variance of the sample estimate for a fixed total cost. We shall first introduce the basic principles in optimizing sample sizes J and n in survey sampling. The same principles can later be applied to cluster randomized trials and multi-site randomized trials.

8.4.1   Cluster Randomized Trial

Optimal sample sizes n and J need to be proportional to the within-cluster and between-cluster variance in a cluster random sample. It is intuitive to understand this because a large sample size reduces the variance of the sample estimate. In the formulas for the variance of the sample mean, sample size serves as a divisor to cut the variance. The divisor for the within-cluster variance is n, and the divisor for the between-cluster variance is J. If the within-cluster variance appears to be prominent, a larger sample size n needs to be used. In a similar vein, a prominent between-cluster variance calls for a large sample size J.

Optimal sample sizes also depend on sampling costs in cluster random sampling. There are two sampling costs. One is the overhead cost for accessing a cluster (e.g., travel cost); the other, the cost for using each small sampling unit in the clusters. If the overhead cost for sampling clusters is relatively more expensive, then it is economical to recruit more small sampling units into each cluster. Likewise, a relatively high cost for using a small sampling unit means that it is economical to use a smaller sample size n (Cochran, 1977). We apply these well-known principles to cluster randomized trial in determining sample sizes J and n.

The total cost C for a cluster randomized trial can be represented in a simple function,

$$C = J(c_0 + c_1 n). \tag{8.66}$$

The overhead cost for using a cluster is c_0; the cost for a small sampling unit within a cluster is c_1. Under the cost constraint C we want to find the optimal sample sizes to maximize the statistical power for testing the main effect of treatment. Although the statistical power function is rather complex, its most influential determinant is the non-centrality parameter. Other things being equal, the larger the non-centrality parameter is, the higher the statistical power gets. So maximizing the statistical power is tantamount to finding the maximum value of the non-centrality parameter under the cost constraint.

The non-centrality parameter λ comprises the main effect γ_{01} and the variance of the effect estimate $Var(\hat{\gamma}_{01})$,

$$\lambda = \frac{\gamma_{01}}{\sqrt{Var(\hat{\gamma}_{01})}}.$$

The main effect γ_{01} is a population quantity, and it does not change with respect to the sample sizes. Maximizing λ is equivalent to minimizing the variance $Var(\hat{\gamma}_{01})$, and is similar to sample size optimization in survey sampling, which too seeks to minimize the variance. The variance $Var(\hat{\gamma}_{01})$ depends on the within-cluster variance σ^2, the between-cluster variance τ, and the sample sizes n and J;

$$Var(\hat{\gamma}_{01}) = \frac{4(\tau + \sigma^2/n)}{J}. \tag{8.67}$$

For a fixed total cost C, the sample size J can be expressed in terms of n in Equation 8.66;

$$J = \frac{C}{c_0 + c_1 n}.$$

Substituting this expression for J into Equation 8.67 produces the variance or V,

$$V = \frac{4(\tau + \sigma^2/n)(c_0 + c_1 n)}{C}.$$

The variance V reaches its extreme (i.e., minimum) when its derivative with respect to n evaluates to zero, $dV/dn = 0$,

$$\frac{dV}{dn} = \frac{4}{C}\left(-\frac{c_0\sigma^2}{n^2} + c_1\tau\right) = 0.$$

Solving this equation yields the optimal sample size n_o for n (Cochran, 1977; Raudenbush, 1997; Snijders and Bosker, 1993),

$$n_o = \sqrt{\frac{c_0}{c_1}\frac{\sigma^2}{\tau}}. \tag{8.68}$$

The optimal sample size n_o is proportional to the overhead cost c_0 but to the reciprocal of c_1. This suggests that the more costly the overhead is, the more small sampling units should be used in each cluster, and that the less expensive the small sampling unit is, the more of them should be used. Also, the optimal sample size n_o increases with the within-cluster variance σ^2 but decreases with the between-cluster variance τ. In other words, a large n won't help much when variability lies more in between clusters than within clusters. This can be made obvious by using intra-class correlation ρ in Equation 8.68,

$$n_o = \sqrt{\frac{c_0}{c_1} \frac{1-\rho}{\rho}},$$
(8.69)

where the intraclass correlation is $\rho = \tau/(\tau + \sigma^2)$. The higher the intraclass correlation is, the fewer small sampling units should be used to minimize the variance.

The optimal sample size n_o determines the optimal sample size J_o for J. Under the cost constraint C, the optimal sample size J_o is

$$J_o = \frac{C}{c_0 + c_1 n_o}.$$
(8.70)

The optimal sample sizes n_o and J_o will minimize the variance of the main effect and maximize the statistical power for testing the main effect.

Sample size optimization can be extended to a three-level cluster randomized trial, e.g. one which involves schools, classrooms, and students. The number of schools and the number of classrooms in each school can be optimized in a similar way. The variance for the main effect estimate $\hat{\gamma}_{001}$ in the non-centrality parameter in Equation 8.17 is

$$Var(\hat{\gamma}_{001}) = \frac{4\left(\tau_\beta + \frac{\tau_\pi + \sigma^2/n}{J}\right)}{K}.$$
(8.71)

Suppose that all the n students in the chosen classroom will participate in the study, for logistic convenience. We only need to determine the optimal sample sizes for J and K. We can minimize the variance $Var(\hat{\gamma}_{001})$, or V for short, under the cost constraint C,

$$C = K(c_0 + c_1 J),$$
(8.72)

where c_0 is the overhead cost of sampling a school, and c_1 is the cost of using a classroom. Taking the derivative of V with respect to J and solving $dV/dJ = 0$ produces the optimal sample size J_o;

$$J_o = \sqrt{\frac{c_0}{c_1} \frac{\tau_\pi + \sigma^2/n}{\tau_\beta}}.$$ (8.73)

The optimal sample size K_o for K is then

$$K_o = \frac{C}{c_0 + c_1 J_o}.$$ (8.74)

One may observe that the optimal sample sizes are similar between the two-level and three-level cluster randomized trials, the latter of which can be folded into a special case of the former design. Their design features are similar, as are their optimal sample sizes.

8.4.2 Multi-site Randomized Trial

Multi-site randomized trials use the same principle in optimal sample allocation as stratified random sampling. The strata in a stratified random sample parallel the different sites in a multi-site randomized trial. It is well known that the optimal number of strata is proportional to the between-strata variance but inversely proportional to the within-strata variance. The optimal number of small sampling units, on the contrary, is proportional to the within-strata variance but inversely proportional to the between-strata variance. In short, sample size allocation goes toward where most variance lies. If the between-strata variance appears to be prominent relative to the within-strata variance, then more strata should be used. Otherwise, more small sampling units within strata should be chosen. The sampling principle applies to the multi-site randomized trial.

The non-centrality parameter λ for the test of the main effect in a multi-site randomized trial is the main effect divided by the variance of its estimate,

$$\lambda = \frac{\gamma_{10}}{\sqrt{\frac{4\sigma^2/n + \tau_1}{J}}},$$ (8.75)

where σ^2 is the within-site variance, and τ_1 is the between-site variance. The variance of the main effect estimate is in the denominator of the non-centrality parameter.

$$Var(\hat{\gamma}_{10}) = \frac{4\sigma^2/n + \tau_1}{J} \tag{8.76}$$

Minimizing the variance in effect produces the maximum statistical power under the cost constraint C,

$$C = J(c_0 + c_1 n), \tag{8.77}$$

where c_0 is the overhead cost of adding a site, and c_1 is the cost of using a small sampling unit within a site. As before, we express J in n and substitute this into the variance $Var(\hat{\gamma}_{10})$. We use V to stand for $Var(\hat{\gamma}_{10})$ and take the derivative of V with respect to n,

$$\frac{dV}{dn} = \left(-\frac{4c_0\sigma^2}{n^2} + c_1\tau_1 \right) / C.$$

Solving $dV/dn = 0$ yields the optimal sample size n_o for n (Raudenbush and Liu, 2000),

$$n_o = 2\sqrt{\frac{c_0\,\sigma^2}{c_1\,\tau_1}}. \tag{8.78}$$

The optimal sample size J_o for J follows from Equation 8.77;

$$J_o = \frac{C}{c_0 + c_1 n_o}. \tag{8.79}$$

Optimal sample sizes can be similarly derived in a multi-site cluster randomized trial, which shares basic design features with multi-site randomized trials. The non-centrality parameter λ for testing the main effect is provided in Equation 8.33,

$$\lambda = \frac{\gamma_{010}\sqrt{K}}{\sqrt{\frac{4(\tau_\pi + \sigma^2/n)}{J} + \tau_{u_1}}}.$$

The between-site variance is τ_{u_1}, and the within-site variance is $\tau_\pi + \sigma^2/n$. Suppose that the cluster size n is fixed. The optimal sample sizes J_o, for the number of clusters in each site, and K_o, for the number of sites, can be easily obtained by substituting the between-site and within-site variance into Equation 8.78,

$$J_o = 2\sqrt{\frac{c_0}{c_1} \frac{\tau_\pi + \sigma^2/n}{\tau_{u_1}}},\tag{8.80}$$

where c_0 is the overhead cost of using a site, and c_1 is the cost of sampling a cluster within each site. The total cost is C,

$$C = K(c_0 + c_1 J).\tag{8.81}$$

The optimal sample size K_o is

$$K_o = \frac{C}{c_0 + c_1 J_o}.\tag{8.82}$$

8.4.3   Unequal Costs Per Unit of Randomization

Our description of optimal sample allocation assumes that the cost of sampling units in the treatment group is the same as that in the control group. More often than not, the cost of using sampling units is not the same in the two groups. It can take more resources to treat the subjects in the treatment group than to simply observe the subjects in the control group because treatment itself may incur substantial costs in training and administration.

A balanced design with equal sample sizes in the treatment and control groups will not return the maximum statistical power for a fixed total cost. An unbalanced design that allocates more samples to the control group than to the treatment group actually produces a higher statistical power than a balanced design with equal sample sizes. The optimal sample allocation to the treatment and control groups depends on the cost ratio of using a sampling unit between the two groups. The more expensive it is to use a sampling unit in the treatment group, the fewer sampling units should be allocated to it. The savings from using a smaller sample in the treatment group can be used to increase the sample size in the control group. The total sample size will increase, and so will the statistical power.

The optimum sample allocation ratio depends only on the cost ratio between the treatment and control groups, regardless of whether the randomization of sampling units occurs at level 1, 2, or 3. For example, randomization takes place at level 1 in a multi-site randomized trial, at level 2 in a cluster randomized trial, and at level 3 in a three-level cluster randomized trial. We shall illustrate the optimal sample allocation in all three designs.

In a multi-site randomized trial, random assignment takes place within site or at level 1. We can allocate more subjects to the control group than to the treatment group at each site. The total cost C is

$$C = J(c_0 + c_1 n_1 + c_2 n_2), \tag{8.83}$$

where c_0 is the overhead cost per site, and c_1 and c_2 are the costs of using a small sampling unit in the treatment and control groups, respectively. The sample sizes, n_1 for the treatment group and n_2 for the control group, at each site are allowed to be unequal to achieve maximum statistical power under the cost constraint.

The statistical power for testing the main effect in a two-sided test is now

$$1 - \beta = 1 - P[T'(J - 1, \lambda) < t_0] + P[T'(J - 1, \lambda) < -t_0], \tag{8.84}$$

where the critical t value t_0 is $t_{1-\alpha/2, J-1}$. The non-centrality parameter is

$$\lambda = \frac{\gamma_{10}}{\sqrt{\frac{\sigma^2(1/n_1 + 1/n_2) + \tau_1}{J}}}. \tag{8.85}$$

In a balanced design that has the same number of sampling units in the treatment and control groups at each site, the sample sizes n_1 and n_2 are equal. They are half the site size n or $n_1 = n_2 = n/2$. Substituting $n/2$ for n_1 and n_2 in λ produces the same non-centrality parameter as that in a balanced multi-site randomized trial. Since the sampling cost varies between the two groups, we need to use unequal sample sizes n_1 and n_2 to maximize the statistical power.

We seek values of n_1 and n_2 that minimize the variance V in the denominator of the non-centrality parameter λ under the cost constraint C,

$$V = \frac{\sigma^2(1/n_1 + 1/n_2) + \tau_1}{J}. \tag{8.86}$$

Using Lagrange multipliers, we can find the minimum value of the variance V under the cost constraint C (Liu, 2003). The optimal ratio between sample sizes n_1 and n_2 is inversely related to the square root of their respective costs,

$$\frac{n_1}{n_2} = \sqrt{\frac{c_2}{c_1}}. \tag{8.87}$$

Applying the optimal ratio, we can obtain the optimal sample sizes for n_1, n_2, and J:

$$n_1 = \sqrt{\frac{c_0\sigma^2}{c_1\tau_1}}$$

$$n_2 = \sqrt{\frac{c_0\sigma^2}{c_2\tau_1}}$$

$$J = \frac{C}{\sqrt{\frac{c_0\sigma^2}{\tau_1}}\left(\sqrt{c_1} + \sqrt{c_2}\right) + c_0}. \tag{8.88}$$

The optimal ratio $\sqrt{c_2/c_1}$ basically holds true between the treatment and control groups, regardless of the level at which randomization occurs. We shall see it in later designs, where random assignment takes place at level 2 and level 3.

We can allocate the number of clusters to the treatment and control groups according to the optimal ratio $\sqrt{c_2/c_1}$ in a cluster randomized trial, which has random assignment take place at level 2. Suppose that the cluster size is fixed at n. The total cost C is

$$C = J_1 c_1 + J_2 c_2, \tag{8.89}$$

where the costs of using a cluster in the treatment and control groups are c_1 and c_2, respectively. The number of clusters in the treatment and control groups are J_1 and J_2. If we allocate clusters according to $J_1/J_2 = \sqrt{c_2/c_1}$, we will be able to maximize the statistical power for testing the main effect under the cost contrast C.

The statistical power for testing the main effect is

$$1 - \beta = 1 - P[T'(J_1 + J_2 - 2, \lambda) < t_0] + P[T'(J_1 + J_2 - 2, \lambda) < -t_0], \tag{8.90}$$

where t_0 is $t_{1-\alpha/2, J_1+J_2-2}$, and the non-centrality parameter is

$$\lambda = \frac{\gamma_{01}}{\sqrt{\left(\frac{1}{J_1} + \frac{1}{J_2}\right)\left(\frac{\sigma^2}{n} + \tau\right)}}. \tag{8.91}$$

To maximize the statistical power, we will need to minimize the variance V in the denominator of the non-centrality parameter λ;

$$V = \left(\frac{1}{J_1} + \frac{1}{J_2}\right)\left(\frac{\sigma^2}{n} + \tau\right). \tag{8.92}$$

The variance V reaches its minimum under the cost constraint C when J_1 and J_2 are allocated as

$$J_1 = \frac{C}{c_1 + \sqrt{c_1 c_2}}$$

$$J_2 = \frac{C}{c_2 + \sqrt{c_1 c_2}}. \tag{8.93}$$

It is easy to verify that sample allocation follows the optimal ratio $J_1/J_2 = \sqrt{c_2/c_1}$. The same holds true in a three-level cluster randomized trial, where random assignment takes place at level 3. The sample allocation among clusters at level 3 uses the same optimal ratio to achieve maximum statistical power for testing the main effect (Liu, 2003, p. 246).

Chapter 9

Meta-analysis

Meta-analysis combines effect size measures from independent but related studies. Karl Pearson (1904) conducted the first meta-analysis in an attempt to remedy the shortcoming of insufficient statistical power in a small study by grouping studies of similar nature and improving the data analysis. Each individual study might not have enough data to test the population effect size with sufficient statistical power and reach a conclusive decision on the existence of a treatment effect. However, the accumulated evidences from those studies can overcome the limitation of an individual study and achieve high statistical power in examining the same issue. So meta-analysis mirrors the natural process of any scientific discovery, which is greatly facilitated by the accumulation of evidence collected on several occasions. Although the evidence on one occasion might not be strong enough, the combined evidence from multiple studies might portray a clear picture of the phenomenon.

Meta-analysis can use either a fixed-effects model or a random-effects model, depending on how effect size measures from individual studies are treated in the analytical procedure. The fixed-effects model treats the population effect sizes from individual studies as unknown constants. The estimated effect sizes from individual studies may be different in magnitude, but the corresponding population effect sizes are assumed to be homogeneous, that is, the population effect sizes from individual studies are equal. The random-effects model treats the population effect sizes from individual studies as a random sample of all the possible effect sizes, which has an underlying distribution (e.g., a normal distribution). In the following, we will introduce statistical power analysis for both models.

9.1   Fixed-Effects Meta-analysis

9.1.1   Test for Main Effect

The fixed-effects model assumes that the effect size estimates d_i from individual studies have underlying population effect sizes θ_i . The effect size estimate uses the standardized mean difference between the treatment and control groups,

$$d_i = \frac{\overline{Y}_e - \overline{Y}_c}{s_p}, \tag{9.1}$$

where $\overline{Y}_e$ and $\overline{Y}_c$ are the means for the treatment and control groups, and s_p is the pooled standard deviation, as for that in a two sample independent t test. If we denote t_i as the reported t statistic of the ith individual study in a meta-analysis, the effect size estimate d_i is functionally related to the reported t statistic,

$$d_i = t_i \sqrt{\frac{1}{n_{ei}} + \frac{1}{n_{ci}}}, \tag{9.2}$$

where n_{ei} and n_{ci} are the group sizes for the treatment and control groups, respectively. The effect size estimate d_i is assumed to have a normal distribution $d_i \sim N(\theta_i, v_i)$. Its variance (Hedges and Olkin, 1985) is known to be

$$v_i \approx \frac{n_{ei} + n_{ci}}{n_{ei} n_{ci}} + \frac{d_i^2}{2(n_{ei} + n_{ci})}. \tag{9.3}$$

The null hypothesis in the meta-analysis stipulates that the population effect sizes from individual studies are all equal to θ, say, zero under H_0. In this case, the null hypothesis is $H_0 : \theta_1 = \theta_2 = ...\theta_i... = \theta_I = \theta = 0$. The fixed-effects model becomes

$$d_i = \theta + e_i, e_i \sim N(0, v_i). \tag{9.4}$$

The estimate of the common effect size θ is a weighted average ($\hat{\theta} = \bar{d}$),

$$\bar{d} = \frac{\sum\limits_{i=1}^{I} w_i d_i}{\sum\limits_{i=1}^{I} w_i}, \tag{9.5}$$

where the weight w_i is the reciprocal of the variance v_i ($w_i = 1/v_i$). So the weights used are the precision of the individual effect size estimate or the inverse of the variance v_i. The variance of the weighted average is denoted by v (i.e., $v = Var(\bar{d})$),

$$v = \frac{1}{\sum\limits_{i=1}^{I} w_i}. \tag{9.6}$$

An approximate Z test can be used to test the null hypothesis,

$$Z = \frac{\bar{d} - 0}{\sqrt{Var(\bar{d})}} = \frac{\bar{d} - 0}{\sqrt{v}}. \tag{9.7}$$

Under the alternative hypothesis, the common effect size θ equals a non-zero constant θ_a. The Z test follows a non-central normal distribution $Z(\lambda)$ with a non-centrality parameter λ (Hedges and Pigott, 2001),

$$\lambda = \frac{\theta_a}{\sqrt{v}}. \tag{9.8}$$

Statistical power analysis can be done just as in a regular Z test, except that the difficulty lies in determining the variance v. The current approach is to assume a common sample size for individual studies and simplify the variance v. Suppose that the sample sizes are about the same in the individual studies in the prospective meta-analysis, that is, $v_1 = v_2 = ...v_i... = v_I$. The variance v has a simple form

$$v = \bar{v}_i / I, \tag{9.9}$$

where

$$\bar{v}_i = \frac{\bar{n}_{ei} + \bar{n}_{ci}}{\bar{n}_{ei} \bar{n}_{ci}} + \frac{\theta_a^2}{2(\bar{n}_{ei} + \bar{n}_{ci})}. \tag{9.10}$$

In current practice, one assumes the average sample sizes for n_{ei} and n_{ci} in a typical individual study and conjectures an effect size $d_i = \theta_a$ common to the individual studies in the meta-analysis. Using Equation 9.3, one can calculate v_i and v for the power analysis. The variance thus computed is a conservative estimate of the variance, based on varying sample sizes in the actual meta-analysis (Hedges and Pigott, 2001).

The power function for the two-sided test is

$$1 - \beta \approx P[|Z(\lambda)| \geq z_0] \tag{9.11}$$
$$= 1 - \Phi(z_0 - \lambda) + \Phi(-z_0 - \lambda),$$

where z_0 is the critical value for the Z test ($z_0 = z_{1-\alpha/2}$). The non-centrality parameter is

$$\lambda = \frac{\theta_a}{\sqrt{v}} \approx \frac{\theta_a}{\sqrt{\bar{v}_i/I}} = \frac{\sqrt{I}\theta_a}{\sqrt{\bar{v}_i}}. \tag{9.12}$$

For a one-sided test, say, $H_a : \theta > 0$, the power is

$$1 - \beta \approx P[Z(\lambda) \geq z_0] \tag{9.13}$$
$$= 1 - \Phi(z_0 - \lambda),$$

where the critical value z_0 is $z_{1-\alpha}$.

The non-centrality parameter λ shows why meta-analysis can overcome the limitation of insufficient statistical power in an individual study with a small sample size. We can make this obvious by relating it to the non-centrality parameter in a single study. For simplicity of explanation, we can set the group sizes for the treatment and control groups to be equal ($\bar{n}_{ei} = \bar{n}_{ci} = n$). The non-centrality parameter in the meta-analysis becomes

$$\lambda = \frac{\sqrt{I}\theta_a}{\sqrt{\frac{2}{n} + \frac{\theta_a^2}{4n}}}. \tag{9.14}$$

Note that the term $\theta_a^2/4n$ under the square root is often negligible when the population effect size θ_a is small, say, .2. The term $\theta_a^2/4n$ has a significant digit in the fourth decimal place (i.e., $\theta_a^2/4n = .2^2/(4 \times 15) = .000\dot{6}$) when the sample size n is set to a meager number of 15. Of course, any larger sample size will make $\theta_a^2/4n$ even smaller. Dropping the negligible term $\theta_a^2/4n$ in λ yields

$$\lambda \approx \sqrt{I} \left(\theta_a \sqrt{\frac{n}{2}} \right). \tag{9.15}$$

As θ_a is the standardized mean difference common to all individual studies, it equals the standardized effect size δ in a single study using a Z test (i.e., $\theta_a = \delta$). Thus, the quantity within the parentheses in Equation 9.15 is the non-centrality parameter for the Z test in an individual study. In essence, the non-centrality parameter in a meta-analysis is the square root of the number of combined studies I multiplied by the non-centrality parameter for a single study $\delta\sqrt{n/2}$. As the number of combined studies I increases, so does the non-centrality parameter for the meta-analysis. Other things being equal, the larger the non-centrality parameter is, the higher the statistical power for the significance test. Thus, a meta-analysis has a higher statistical power than does a single study on the same issue.

For example, a researcher wants to initiate a meta-analysis on intervention programs aimed at reducing the incidence of juvenile delinquency. The effect size for the impact of intervention programs on juvenile delinquency is estimated to be .17 (Lipsey, 1992). Previous studies on juvenile delinquency treatment show that the average sample size is about 100 (i.e., $\bar{n}_{ei}$=50 and $\bar{n}_{ci} = 50$). The estimated non-centrality parameter is 2.814053, according to Equation 9.12.

$$\lambda = \frac{\sqrt{I}\theta_a}{\sqrt{\bar{v}_i}}$$

$$= \frac{\sqrt{11} \times .17}{\sqrt{\frac{50+50}{50\times50} + \frac{.17^2}{2(50+50)}}}$$

$$= \frac{\sqrt{11} \times .17}{\sqrt{.04 + .0001445}}$$

$$= 2.814053$$

The statistical power reaches .8035 when 11 studies are used in the meta-analysis,

$$1 - \beta = 1 - \Phi(z_0 - \lambda) + \Phi(-z_0 - \lambda)$$
$$= 1 - \Phi(1.96 - 2.814) + \Phi(-1.96 - 2.814)$$
$$\approx .80.$$

If we use the simpler formula in Equation 9.15, the results will be almost identical. The non-centrality parameter is 2.819131, based on Equation

9.15, and the statistical power is then .8048. The difference between the two methods of computing power is inconsequential. The simpler formulas in Equation 9.15 can be used without losing any accuracy in power computation.

The R code for computing statistical power is as follows:

```
#fixed-effects meta-analysis

p4fma=function(I=11,ne=50,nc=50,es=.17){
a=.05
vi=(ne+nc)/(ne*nc) + .5*es^2/(ne+nc)

lambda=sqrt(I)*es/sqrt(vi)
1-pnorm(qnorm(1-a/2)-lambda)+pnorm(qnorm(a/2)-lambda)
}
p4fma()
```

The SAS program is:

```
/* fixed-effects meta-analysis*/

data fma(drop=a lambda vi);
a=.05;
ne=50;
nc=50;
es=.17;
vi=(ne+nc)/(ne*nc) + .5*es**2/(ne+nc);

do I=5 to 20;
 lambda=sqrt(I)*es/sqrt(vi);
 power=1-probnorm(probit(1-a/2)-lambda)
        +probnorm(probit(a/2)-lambda);
 output;
end;
run;

proc print data=fma;
run;
```

The SPSS code is:

```
*fixed-effects meta-analysis .

NEW FILE.
INPUT PROGRAM.
COMPUTE A=.05.
COMPUTE N1=50.
COMPUTE N2=50.
COMPUTE ES=.17.
COMPUTE VI=(N1+N2)/(N1*N2) +.5*ES**2/(N1+N2).

LEAVE A TO VI.

LOOP I=5 TO 20.
  COMPUTE LAMBDA=SQRT(I)*ES/SQRT(VI).
  COMPUTE POWER=1-CDFNORM(PROBIT(1-A/2)-LAMBDA) +
               CDFNORM(PROBIT(A/2)-LAMBDA) .
  END CASE.
END LOOP.
END FILE.
END INPUT PROGRAM.
EXECUTE.

DELETE VARIABLES A VI LAMBDA.
LIST.
```

9.1.2   Test for Homogeneity of Individual Effect Sizes

In testing the main effect, we assume that the effect sizes from individual studies share a common effect size. This assumption is called homogeneity of effect sizes, that is, $H_0 : \theta_1 = \theta_2 = ...\theta_i... = \theta_I$. In other words, a common effect size underlies all the individual studies and their effect sizes. We can use a test statistic to check the homogeneity assumption about individual effect sizes.

The statistic for testing the homogeneity of effect sizes uses a weighted sum of squares:

$$Q = \sum_{i=1}^{I} w_i (d_i - \bar{d}.)^2, \tag{9.16}$$

where the weight w_i is the reciprocal of the variance of the effect size from the ith study ($w_i = 1/v_i$), and $\bar{d}.$ is the weighted mean with the weights being w_i (Hedges and Olkin, 1985).

The Q statistic measures the variation of the effect sizes among individual studies. When the null hypothesis is true, the Q statistic has a central chi square distribution with $I - 1$ degrees of freedom. If the homogeneity of individual effect sizes does not hold true, the Q statistic will follow a non-central chi square distribution with $I - 1$ degrees of freedom and non-centrality parameter λ. The non-centrality parameter can be obtained by replacing the sample effect sizes in Q with their population counterparts,

$$\lambda = \sum_{i=1}^{I} w_i (\theta_i - \bar{\theta}.)^2, \tag{9.17}$$

where $\bar{\theta}.$ is the weighted mean of $\theta_1, \theta_2, \cdots, \theta_I$ with the weights being w_i ($\bar{\theta}. = \sum_i^I w_i \theta_i / \sum_i^I w_i$).

The statistical power for testing the homogeneity of effect sizes, therefore, uses the cumulative distribution function of a non-central chi square $\chi^2_{I-1}(\lambda)$. The probability of having a Q statistic exceeding the critical value at five percent $\chi^2_{.95,I-1}$ is the statistical power,

$$\begin{aligned} 1 - \beta &= P[Q \geq \chi^2_{.95,I-1}] \\ &= P[\chi^2_{I-1}(\lambda) \geq \chi^2_{.95,I-1}] \\ &= 1 - P[\chi^2_{I-1}(\lambda) < \chi^2_{.95,I-1}], \end{aligned} \tag{9.18}$$

where $P[\chi^2_{I-1}(\lambda) < \chi^2_{.95,I-1}]$ is the cumulative distribution function of a non-central chi square (Hedges and Pigott, 2001).

9.2   Random-Effects Meta-analysis

9.2.1   Test for Main Effect

In the random-effects model, the effect size estimates from individual studies have an underlying distribution with a population mean, which can have its prior distribution. Specifically, the effect size estimate d_i follows a normal distribution $d_i \sim N(\theta_i, v_i)$, and θ_i also has its own distribution $\theta_i \sim N(\theta, \tau)$. This means that the population effect sizes θ_i from individual studies have a prior normal distribution. So effect sizes θ_i may fall above or below the mean θ of the prior distribution. Unlike the fixed-effects model, which assumes equal θ_i for the individual studies (homogeneity of effect sizes), random-effects meta-analysis suggests that effect sizes may bounce around the grand average effect size θ. For instance, it is not unusual to observe a negative impact even though the grand average effect size θ is positive. In other words, the effect size estimates are presumably more varied than that in a fixed-effects meta-analysis. The model for the effect size estimate d_i can be written as

$$d_i = \theta_i + e_i \tag{9.19}$$
$$= \theta + \alpha_i + e_i,$$

where θ_i is random and is conceived of as comprising a population mean θ and a random deviation α_i from θ. The random effect α_i is due to the ith study, and its variance is τ. The last term in the model e_i refers to the sampling error of d_i, and its variance is v_i.

The significance test can proceed in a similar way as for the fixed-effects meta-analysis. We only need to reformulate the model so that we can use the same procedure as in the fixed-effects meta-analysis. If we combine the random effect α_i and sampling error e_i into a single error e_i^*, we can make the random-effects model a special case of the fixed-effects model.

$$d_i = \theta + \alpha_i + e_i = \theta + e_i^*, \tag{9.20}$$

where $e_i^* = \alpha_i + e_i$, and

$$v_i^* = Var(e_i^*) = \tau + v_i. \tag{9.21}$$

It is easy to see that the random-effects model in Equation 9.20 is essentially the same as the fixed-effects model in Equation 9.4, except that the random-effects model has an error e_i^* with a slightly more complex variance v_i^*. The estimate of the population mean or the grand average effect size θ is a weighted mean of d_i with the weight equal to the reciprocal of the variance $1/v_i^*$. We will denote the weights in the random-effects model as

$$w^* = 1/v_i^*. \tag{9.22}$$

Substituting the new weight w^* into Equation 9.5 yields the weighted mean $\bar{d}$ in the random-effects meta-analysis,

$$\bar{d} = \frac{\sum\limits_{i=1}^{I} w_i^* d_i}{\sum\limits_{i=1}^{I} w_i^*}. \tag{9.23}$$

The variance of the weighted mean $\bar{d}$ uses the same formula as in Equation 9.6, except that the weights are w_i^*. We use v^* to represent the variance $Var(\bar{d})$ in the random-effects model,

$$v^* = \frac{1}{\sum\limits_{i=1}^{I} w_i^*}. \tag{9.24}$$

The null hypothesis states that the population effect size θ is a constant θ_0, say, zero. We can use a Z statistic to test the null hypothesis $H_0 : \theta = 0$, as in the fixed-effects model,

$$Z = \frac{\bar{d} - 0}{\sqrt{v^*}}. \tag{9.25}$$

When the alternative hypothesis is true, the grand average effect size θ is a non-zero constant θ_a. In this case, the Z test follows a non-central normal distribution with a non-centrality parameter λ (Hedges and Pigott, 2001),

$$\lambda = \frac{\theta_a}{\sqrt{v^*}} \tag{9.26}$$

Again, we will use some approximation to conjecture v^* in estimating the non-centrality parameter λ. Specifically, we will estimate the average sample sizes ($\bar{n}_{ei}$ and $\bar{n}_{ci}$) in the experiment and control groups. Using the average sample sizes, we can get the average of v_i^* (i.e., $\bar{v}_i^*$). This allows us to compute its reciprocal or the average weight $\bar{w}_i^* = 1/\bar{v}_i^*$. The variance v^* is then calculated as

$$v^* \approx \frac{1}{\sum\limits_{i=1}^{I} \bar{w}_i^*} = \frac{\bar{v}_i^*}{I}, \tag{9.27}$$

where

$$\bar{v}_i^* = \bar{v}_i + \tau$$

$$= \frac{\bar{n}_{ei} + \bar{n}_{ci}}{\bar{n}_{ei}\bar{n}_{ci}} + \frac{\theta_a^2}{2(\bar{n}_{ei} + \bar{n}_{ci})} + \tau. \tag{9.28}$$

The non-centrality parameter in the random-effects meta-analysis is deflated because its denominator contains the between-study variance τ in addition to the error variance $\bar{v}_i$. We can highlight the change in non-centrality parameter when we switch from a fixed-effects model to a random-effects model,

$$\lambda = \frac{\theta_a}{\sqrt{v^*}}$$

$$= \frac{\sqrt{I}\theta_a}{\sqrt{\bar{v}_i^*}}$$

$$= \frac{\sqrt{I}\theta_a}{\sqrt{\bar{v}_i + \tau}}. \tag{9.29}$$

The non-centrality parameter in the random-effects model is smaller than its counterpart in the fixed-effects model (Equation 9.12). Note that $\bar{v}_i + \tau$ represents the total variance of d_i. The portion $\bar{v}_i$ represents the within-study variance, and τ the between-study variance. Researchers may estimate the ratio of the between-study and within-study variances, based on their knowledge of the subject area. The ratio can be denoted by $p = \tau/\bar{v}_i$. The non-centrality parameter can be expressed in terms of $\bar{v}_i$ and p,

$$\lambda = \frac{\sqrt{I}\theta_a}{\sqrt{\bar{v}_i(1+p)}} = \left(\frac{\sqrt{I}\theta_a}{\sqrt{\bar{v}_i}}\right)\frac{1}{\sqrt{1+p}}. \tag{9.30}$$

The non-centrality parameter reduces by a factor $1/\sqrt{1+p}$, compared with its value in the fixed-effects model. Although the random-effects model makes it easy to generalize the research findings to a broader context than the fixed-effects model, the statistical power in the random-effects meta-analysis tends to be lower than that in the fixed-effects analysis.

The statistical power in the random-effects meta-analysis uses the same formula as that for fixed-effects analysis except that the non-centrality parameter changes slightly (see Equation 9.30). For a two-sided test, the power is

$$1 - \beta \approx P[|Z(\lambda)| \geq z_0]$$
$$= 1 - \Phi(z_{1-\alpha/2} - \lambda) + \Phi(z_{\alpha/2} - \lambda). \tag{9.31}$$

For a one-sided test, the power can be simplified to

$$1 - \beta \approx P[Z(\lambda) \geq z_0]$$
$$= 1 - \Phi(z_{1-\alpha} - \lambda). \tag{9.32}$$

For example, a medical researcher is interested in studying the overall effect of using antibiotics on reducing infection after a certain surgical procedure. The estimated overall effect size is .20. Suppose that the average sample size for randomized controlled trials (RCT) on antibiotics use after the surgical procedure is about 50 (i.e., $\bar{n}_{ei}=25$ and $\bar{n}_{ci} = 25$). Further, the researcher assumes that the between-study variance and the within-study variance has a ratio of 1 to 3 ($\tau : \bar{v}_i = 1 : 3$ or $p \approx .3\dot{3}$). When twenty-two RCT studies are used in the random-effects meta-analysis ($I = 22$), the non-centrality parameter is 2.8651 (Equation 9.30):

$$\bar{v}_i = \frac{\bar{n}_{ei} + \bar{n}_{ci}}{\bar{n}_{ei}\bar{n}_{ci}} + \frac{\theta_a^2}{2(\bar{n}_{ei} + \bar{n}_{ci})}$$
$$= \frac{25 + 25}{25 \times 25} + \frac{.2^2}{2 \times (25 + 25)}$$
$$= .0804$$

$$\lambda = \left(\frac{\sqrt{I}\theta_a}{\sqrt{\bar{v}_i}}\right) \frac{1}{\sqrt{1 + p}}$$
$$= \frac{\sqrt{22} \times .2}{\sqrt{.0804}} \frac{1}{\sqrt{1 + 1/3}}$$
$$= 2.8651.$$

The statistical power is .8173 (Equation 9.31);

$$1 - \beta = 1 - \Phi(1.96 - 2.8651) + \Phi(-1.96 - 2.8651)$$
$$= .8173.$$

The R code for computing power in random-effects meta-analysis is:

```
#random-effects meta-analysis

p4rma=function(I=22,ne=25,nc=25,es=.2,p=1/3){
a=.05
vi=(ne+nc)/(ne*nc) + .5*es^2/(ne+nc)

lambda=sqrt(I)*es/sqrt(vi)/sqrt(1+p)
1-pnorm(qnorm(1-a/2)-lambda)+pnorm(qnorm(a/2)-lambda)
}

p4rma()
```

The corresponding SAS program is:

```
/* random-effects meta-analysis */

data rma(drop=a lambda vi);
a=.05;
ne=25;
nc=25;
es=.20;
p=1/3;

vi=(ne+nc)/(ne*nc) + .5*es**2/(ne+nc);

do I=5 to 30;
 lambda=sqrt(I)*es/sqrt(vi)/sqrt(1+p);
 power=1-probnorm(probit(1-a/2)-lambda)
        +probnorm(probit(a/2)-lambda);
 output;
end;
run;
```

The SPSS code is:

```
*random-effects meta-analysis.

NEW FILE.
INPUT PROGRAM.
```

```
COMPUTE A=.05.
COMPUTE N1=25.
COMPUTE N2=25.
COMPUTE ES=.20.
COMPUTE VI=(N1+N2)/(N1*N2) +.5*ES**2/(N1+N2).
COMPUTE P=1/3.

LEAVE A TO P.

LOOP I=5 TO 30.
  COMPUTE LAMBDA=SQRT(I)*ES/SQRT(VI)/SQRT(1+P).
  COMPUTE POWER=1-CDFNORM(PROBIT(1-A/2)-LAMBDA) +
               CDFNORM(PROBIT(A/2)-LAMBDA) .
  END CASE.
END LOOP.
END FILE.
END INPUT PROGRAM.
EXECUTE.

DELETE VARIABLES A VI LAMBDA.
LIST.
```

9.2.2 Test for the Variance of Individual Effect Sizes

The variance of effect sizes from individual studies τ can be tested with the same Q statistic. When the null hypothesis about the variance ($H_0 : \tau = 0$) is true, the Q statistic has a central chi square distribution with degrees of freedom $I - 1$. Under the null hypothesis, there is no random variation in effect size between individual studies. The variation in effect size is only attributable to the variance of the sampling error, which would change the estimated effect size if the same individual study were to be replicated in the same circumstance. When the variance of effect sizes τ is not zero ($H_a : \tau \neq 0$), the Q statistic has a complex distribution.

The Q statistic under the alternative hypothesis can be related to a central chi square distribution with degrees of freedom $I - 1$. The expected value of Q under the alternative hypothesis is approximately $(v^*/v)(I-1)$,

$$E(Q) \approx \frac{v^*}{v}(I-1). \tag{9.33}$$

Note that the variance v^* in the random-effects model contains a non-zero variance τ, and that v is the variance of effect sizes due only to the sampling error. Under the null hypothesis H_0, τ is zero and v^*/v is just one. In this case, the expected value of the Q statistic is simply the expected value of a central chi square variate with $I-1$ degrees of freedom. Using the ratio v^*/v, we can convert the Q statistic to a central chi square with $I-1$ degrees of freedom under the alternative hypothesis $H_a : \tau \neq 0$:

$$Q \sim \frac{v^*}{v}\chi^2_{I-1}$$
$$\frac{v}{v^*}Q \sim \chi^2_{I-1}. \tag{9.34}$$

The conversion is reminiscent of the similar operation on the F statistic in a one-way random-effects ANOVA in Chapter 4.

The statistical power for testing the variance τ, therefore, can be based on the cumulative distribution function of a central chi square (Hedges and Pigott, 2001).

$$
\begin{aligned}
1 - \beta &= P[Q \geq \chi^2_{.95,I-1}] \\
&= P[\frac{v}{v^*}Q \geq \frac{v}{v^*}\chi^2_{.95,I-1}] \\
&= P[\chi^2_{I-1} \geq \frac{v}{v^*}\chi^2_{.95,I-1}] \\
&= 1 - P[\chi^2_{I-1} < \frac{v}{v^*}\chi^2_{.95,I-1}], \tag{9.35}
\end{aligned}
$$

where $P[\chi^2_{I-1} < v/v^*\chi^2_{.95,I-1}]$ is the cumulative distribution of a central chi square with $I-1$ degrees of freedom. For simplicity of planning, we may assume that the variances of effect size due to sampling error among individual studies v_i are about the same. We can use their average $\bar{v}_i$ to replace those v_i in v. The variance v is then $v = \bar{v}_i/I$, and v^* is $(\bar{v}_i + \tau)/I$. Thus, the ratio v/v^* can be simplified to $\bar{v}_i/(\bar{v}_i + \tau)$. The statistical power function can be expressed in terms of the ratio $p = \tau/\bar{v}_i$,

$$
\begin{aligned}
1 - \beta &= 1 - P[\chi^2_{I-1} < \frac{v}{v^*}\chi^2_{.95,I-1}] \\
&\approx 1 - P[\chi^2_{I-1} < \frac{\bar{v}_i}{\bar{v}_i + \tau}\chi^2_{.95,I-1}] \\
&= 1 - P[\chi^2_{I-1} < \frac{1}{1 + \tau/\bar{v}_i}\chi^2_{.95,I-1}] \\
&= 1 - P[\chi^2_{I-1} < \frac{1}{1 + p}\chi^2_{.95,I-1}].
\end{aligned}
\tag{9.36}
$$

Chapter 10

Structural Equation Models

Structural equation modeling (SEM) describes the dependence among a set of latent variables in a path diagram. The path diagram portrays the relationships among those latent variables. Some of the latent variables are viewed as causes or exogenous, and others as effects or endogenous. Although a structural equation model implies causality among the latent variables, the causal relationships are mostly postulated according to a substantive theory. The fit of the model does not prove the causal relationship, but it lends support to the implied causality.

Structural equation modeling uses two kinds of models: the structural model and the measurement model. The structural model defines the relationships among the latent variables that are presumably unobserved but can be measured using other observed variables. For instance, a personality trait, such as extroversion, is a latent variable that cannot be directly assessed. It can nevertheless be measured from individual variables on related observable characteristics (e.g., being talkative, enthusiastic, gregarious). The measurement model is related to factor analysis, in which latent variables are viewed as factors underlying observed variables. The latent variables are then modeled as outcomes in a set of simultaneous equations that form the structural model. The path diagram of the structural model is rendered in the same way as in path analysis.

We will start with path analysis, a simplified structural equation model, because the exogenous and endogenous variables in the path analysis can be measured without an underlying measurement model. Sample size affects the statistical power in testing the path coefficients between the exogenous and endogenous variables in a path model. We will then examine sample size for the measurement model in SEM. As the measurement model is based on factor analysis, sample size affects the reliabilities of the factors or latent variables. Finally, we will examine sample size and statistical power in SEM, which combines path analysis with factor analysis. We will study how sample size impacts statistical power in the structural model, taking into account the reliabilities of the latent variables in the measurement models.

10.1 Path Analysis

Path analysis comprises a set of multiple regressions of endogenous variables. Some of the endogenous variables may also be regressed on the other endogenous variables. The relationships among exogenous and endogenous variables can be shown in a path diagram, and the multiple regression equations can be represented in matrix notation,

$$y = \alpha + By + \Gamma x + \zeta, \tag{10.1}$$

where $\alpha = [\alpha_1, \alpha_2, \cdots, \alpha_p]$ gives the constants or intercepts for the multiple regressions, $y' = [y_1, y_2, \cdots, y_p]$ represents the endogenous variables, $x' = [x_1, x_2, \cdots, x_q]$ represents the exogenous variables, and $\zeta' = [\zeta_1, \zeta_2, \cdots, \zeta_p]$ is the random error or disturbance. The matrices B and Γ contain the path regression coefficients (direct effects) that relate the exogenous and endogenous variables, as shown in the path diagram. We will consider recursive models in which the relationships are of one direction and the path regression coefficients are estimable. To simplify the model, we may use the deviation scores from the means for the exogenous and endogenous variables. For brevity, we do not change the notation for the mean centered variables, and we still use y and x to represent those mean centered endogenous and exogenous variables. The simplified model will not contain the intercepts α for the multiple regressions:

$$y = By + \Gamma x + \zeta. \tag{10.2}$$

Note that the mean centered y and x will not change the meaning of the path regression coefficients.

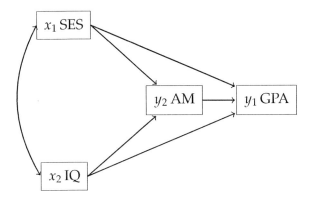

Figure 10.1: Path diagram

The path model implies a set of multiple regression equations. For instance, let us use the example on college students' grade point average (GPA) in Pedhazur (1997). The college students' GPA is an endogenous variable, and it is presumably affected by another endogenous variable, achievement motivation (AM). Socioeconomic status (SES) and IQ are exogenous variables that are supposed to affect GPA and achievement motivation. The relationship between the two exogenous variables is left unanalyzed (see Figure 10.1). We will use y_1 to stand for GPA, y_2 for AM, x_1 for SES, and x_2 for IQ. Their relationships can be represented in two multiple regression equations.

Two simultaneous multiple regression equations are

$$
\begin{aligned}
y_1 &= b_{12}y_2 + \gamma_{11}x_1 + \gamma_{12}x_2 + \zeta_1 \\
y_2 &= \phantom{b_{12}y_2 +} \gamma_{21}x_1 + \gamma_{22}x_2 + \zeta_2.
\end{aligned}
$$

The matrices B and Γ for the path regression coefficients are

$$
B = \begin{bmatrix} 0 & b_{12} \\ 0 & 0 \end{bmatrix} \quad \text{and} \quad \Gamma = \begin{bmatrix} \gamma_{11} & \gamma_{12} \\ \gamma_{21} & \gamma_{22} \end{bmatrix}.
$$

The path regression coefficients can be obtained by running the two multiple regressions separately. The regression coefficients are the path regression coefficients in the path analysis. If standardized exogenous and endogenous variables are used in the multiple regressions, the regression coefficients are standardized regression coefficients, and are called path coefficients in the path analysis. In summary, we run a set of related multiple regressions to estimate the path coefficients (direct effects) in path analysis. When the model is correct and its assumptions (i.e., normality and homoscedasticity) hold true, the path coefficient estimates from the multiple regressions coincide with the maximum likelihood estimates (Land, 1973; Bollen, 1989).

10.1.1   Statistical Power for Testing Individual Equations and Direct Effects

To find the statistical power for testing the direct effects, we can follow the same method as in multiple regression. As the variables can be measured on different scales, they add to the complexity of the analysis. To make it simple, we will standardize y and x variables. We will not change the notation for y and x, but they now represent standardized variables.

The path analysis involves two multiple regression equations. We can start with the first equation,

$$y_1 = b_{12}y_2 + \gamma_{11}x_1 + \gamma_{12}x_2 + \zeta_1.$$

This is just a multiple regression equation with y_1 as the outcome variable and y_2, x_1, and x_2 as predictors. Since these variables are all standardized, their relationships can be represented through the correlations among them. We can examine two general kinds of test in multiple regression analysis. The first one asks whether y_1 is significantly related to y_2, x_1, and x_2; the second, whether a particular predictor among y_2, x_1, and x_2 is significantly related to y_1.

For the first kind of test, we want to check whether y_2, x_1, and x_2 together explain a significant amount of variance in y_1. This relationship is represented by the multiple correlation between y_1 and y_2, x_1, and x_2, or $R_{y_1,y_2x_1x_2}$. We use a comma to separate the endogenous variable y_1 from its predictors because the predictors may contain other endogenous variables that can be outcomes in other multiple regression equations in the path model. To test the multiple correlation coefficient $R_{y_1,y_2x_1x_2}$, we will use the methodology in Chapter 5 and run an F test. Statistical power in the F test is

$$1 - \beta = 1 - P[F(3, n - 4, \lambda) < F_{1-\alpha,3,n-4}], \tag{10.3}$$

where $F_{1-\alpha,3,n-4}$ is the critical F value, and the non-centrality parameter is

$$\lambda = \frac{nR^2_{y_1,y_2x_1x_2}}{1 - R^2_{y_1,y_2x_1x_2}}. \qquad (10.4)$$

The multiple correlation coefficient $R_{y_1,y_2x_1x_2}$ can be computed from the correlations among y_1, y_2, x_1, and x_2.

$$R^2_{y_1,y_2x_1x_2} = \boldsymbol{R}'_{Xy}\boldsymbol{R}_X^{-1}\boldsymbol{R}_{Xy}, \qquad (10.5)$$

where $\boldsymbol{R}_{Xy}$ is a column of correlations between the endogenous variable y_1 and its predictors y_2, x_1, and x_2, and $\boldsymbol{R}_X$ is the correlation matrix for y_2, x_1, and x_2.

For the second kind of test, we are interested in checking a significant direct effect on y_1. We are essentially testing one predictor, say, y_2 in the multiple regression. The F test has one degree of freedom in the numerator and the same number of degrees of freedom in the denominator as before. The statistical power for testing the direct effect is

$$1 - \beta = 1 - P[F(1, n - 4, \lambda) < F_{1-\alpha,1,n-4}], \qquad (10.6)$$

where

$$\lambda = \frac{n(R^2_{y_1,y_2x_1x_2} - R^2_{y_1,x_1x_2})}{1 - R^2_{y_1,y_2x_1x_2}}, \qquad (10.7)$$

and R_{y_1,x_1x_2} is the multiple correlation coefficient without y_2 in the multiple regression. We can calculate this multiple correlation coefficient in a similar way as before, using the correlations among y_1, x_1, and x_2;

$$R^2_{y_1,x_1x_2} = \boldsymbol{R}'_{X\_y}\boldsymbol{R}_{X\_}^{-1}\boldsymbol{R}_{X\_y},$$

where the underscore in $X\_$ indicates that y_2 is excluded in the multiple regression.

10.1.2 Statistical Power in Path Analysis

Model Fit

The fit of the path model can be defined in two different ways. One way is to find how far the path model is different from the ideal model that can reproduce the variance covariance matrix of all the observed variables. The measure of the discrepancy between the path model and the ideal model is a chi square statistic. A large chi square statistic allows us to reject the null hypothesis that the path model is as good as the ideal one. So failure to reject the null actually means that the model is fit. The other way is to assess whether the path model has explained a significant amount of variance in the endogenous variables. Although the latter approach is seldom referred to in the software package for SEM, it appears to be in alignment with how we examine the model fit of multiple regression. In running multiple regression, we check how much variance in the outcome has been explained by the multiple regression. The standard measure for the percentage of explained variance is the squared multiple correlation. It can be generalized to the case of path analysis, which involves a set of multiple regression equations. Each regression equation has an endogenous variable as the outcome variable.

To combine the variance in several endogenous variables, we need to find a general measure of the variance among more than one variable. We will first introduce the generalized variance measure and then apply it to path analysis.

The generalized variance is the determinant of the variance covariance matrix of all the variables, whether they are exogenous or endogenous (Specht, 1975; Wilks, 1932). If there is one variable involved, the generalized variance reduces to a scalar or the variance of the only variable. When there is more than one variable, we will use the determinant of variance covariance matrix as the generalized variance. We can illustrate the idea of generalized variance with two variables y and x, which form the simple regression analysis. Under the null hypothesis H_0 we assume that the dependent variable y has nothing to do with the predictor or the independent variable x. Their correlation is zero. The variance covariance matrix of all the variables Σ_0 is

$$\Sigma_0 = \begin{bmatrix} \sigma_x^2 & 0 \\ 0 & \sigma_y^2 \end{bmatrix}.$$

Its determinant is $|\Sigma_0| = \sigma_x^2 \sigma_y^2$; it is the generalized variance of all the variables under H_0.

This generalized variance can be used to define the squared multiple correlation coefficient R^2, which is the ratio of the explained variance over the total variance. It can be redefined in terms of the generalized variance

$|\Sigma_0|$ under the null hypothesis H_0 and the generalized variance $|\Sigma_a|$ under the alternative hypothesis H_a, which suggests that the dependent variable y is related to the independent variable x. Under H_a, there is covariance between y and x. The variance covariance matrix Σ_a is

$$\Sigma_a = \begin{bmatrix} \sigma_x^2 & \sigma_{xy} \\ \sigma_{yx} & \sigma_y^2 \end{bmatrix}.$$

Its determinant is $|\Sigma_a| = \sigma_x^2 \sigma_y^2 - \sigma_{xy}^2$. It is easily verifiable that the squared multiple correlation coefficient R^2 is one minus the ratio of the two generalized variances $|\Sigma_a|$ and $|\Sigma_0|$ under the alternative and null hypothesis;

$$
\begin{aligned}
R^2 &= 1 - \frac{|\Sigma_a|}{|\Sigma_0|} \\
&= 1 - \frac{\sigma_x^2 \sigma_y^2 - \sigma_{xy}^2}{\sigma_x^2 \sigma_y^2} \\
&= 1 - \left(1 - \frac{\sigma_{xy}^2}{\sigma_x^2 \sigma_y^2}\right) \\
&= \rho_{xy}^2.
\end{aligned}
\tag{10.8}
$$

The squared correlation ρ_{xy}^2 for x and y is R^2 in simple regression analysis. This formula also applies to multiple regression with more than one predictor.

The variance covariance matrix involving more than one predictor under H_0 is

$$\Sigma_0 = \begin{bmatrix} \Sigma_{xx} & \mathbf{0} \\ \mathbf{0} & \sigma_y^2 \end{bmatrix},$$

where Σ_{xx} is the variance covariance matrix of the predictors. For instance, the covariance matrix for two predictors x_1 and x_2 is

$$\Sigma_{xx} = \begin{bmatrix} \sigma_{x_1}^2 & \sigma_{x_1 x_2} \\ \sigma_{x_2 x_1} & \sigma_{x_2}^2 \end{bmatrix}.$$

Under the null hypothesis, the dependent variable is not related to the predictors. There is no covariance between the dependent variable y and its predictors x_1 and x_2. Their covariance matrix is a zero vector, that is,

$\Sigma_{yx} = 0$. Under the alternative hypothesis, the covariance matrix Σ_{yx} is not a zero matrix. The variance covariance matrix of all the variables is, therefore,

$$\Sigma_a = \left[\begin{array}{cc} \Sigma_{xx} & \Sigma_{xy} \\ \Sigma_{yx} & \sigma_y^2 \end{array} \right].$$

Using Equation 10.8, we can express the squared multiple correlation coefficient in terms of the determinants of Σ_0 and Σ_a, which are the generalized variances of all variables under the null and alternative models. The determinant of Σ_0 is $|\Sigma_{xx}|\,\sigma_y^2$. The determinant of Σ_a is

$$|\Sigma_{xx}| \left| \sigma_y^2 - \Sigma_{yx}\Sigma_{xx}^{-1}\Sigma_{xy} \right|,$$

which we will prove shortly. Using Equation 10.8, we can find the squared multiple correlation coefficient R^2,

$$
\begin{aligned}
R^2 &= 1 - \frac{|\Sigma_a|}{|\Sigma_0|} \\
&= 1 - \frac{|\Sigma_{xx}| \left| \sigma_y^2 - \Sigma_{yx}\Sigma_{xx}^{-1}\Sigma_{xy} \right|}{|\Sigma_{xx}|\,\sigma_y^2} \\
&= \frac{\Sigma_{yx}\Sigma_{xx}^{-1}\Sigma_{xy}}{\sigma_y^2}.
\end{aligned}
$$

$$(10.9)$$

It is easily verifiable that $\Sigma_{yx}\Sigma_{xx}^{-1}\Sigma_{xy}$ represents the variance of the predicted y. Thus, R^2 is the squared multiple correlation coefficient.

We can apply the idea of generalized variance to path analysis, where there is more than one multiple regression equation. We can partition the variance and covariance matrix Σ into four submatrices.

$$\Sigma = \left[\begin{array}{cc} \Sigma_{xx} & \Sigma_{xy} \\ \Sigma_{yx} & \Sigma_{yy} \end{array} \right], \qquad (10.10)$$

where Σ_{yy} is the variance covariance matrix of the endogenous variables; Σ_{xx} is the variance covariance matrix of the exogenous variables; and Σ_{yx} is the covariance matrix between the endogenous and exogenous variables.

In a null path model (Figure 10.2), the endogenous variables are not related to the exogenous variables. There are no paths that link the exogenous variables to the endogenous variables. The null path model implies that there is neither covariance between the exogenous and endogenous variables ($\Sigma_{yx} = 0$) nor covariance between the two endogenous variables, that is,

$$\Sigma_{yy} = \begin{bmatrix} \sigma_{y_1}^2 & 0 \\ 0 & \sigma_{y_2}^2 \end{bmatrix}.$$

The variance covariance matrix of all the variables in the null path model is denoted by Σ_0,

$$\Sigma_0 = \begin{bmatrix} \Sigma_{xx} & 0 & 0 \\ 0 & \sigma_{y_1}^2 & 0 \\ 0 & 0 & \sigma_{y_2}^2 \end{bmatrix}.$$

Its determinant $|\Sigma_0|$ is the generalized variance under the null path model, which does not explain any relationship among the variables. We therefore use a hypothesized path model, as shown in Figure 10.1, to better explain the relationship among the variables. In doing so, we can reduce the amount of unexplained variance in $|\Sigma_0|$. The reduced overall variance can be measured by the generalized variance under the hypothesized model, which is the determinant of the variance covariance matrix of all the variables under the hypothesized model (i.e., $|\Sigma|$). The percentage change in generalized variance due to path analysis is

$$\frac{|\Sigma_0| - |\Sigma|}{|\Sigma_0|} = 1 - \frac{|\Sigma|}{|\Sigma_0|}.$$

It is obvious that the right side of the equation is the same as Equation 10.8 for the squared multiple correlation except that the variance covariance matrix in path analysis involves more than one dependent variable (i.e., endogenous variables). We will call it the generalized R square in path analysis or GR^2 for short;

$$GR^2 = 1 - \frac{|\Sigma|}{|\Sigma_0|}. \tag{10.11}$$

We may interpret the generalized R square in a similar way as the regular R square. It basically shows the proportion of generalized variance

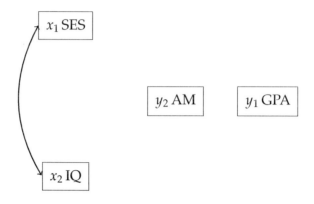

Figure 10.2: Null path model

explained in the path analysis. The generalized R square ranges from zero to one. If the determinant $|\Sigma|$ is the same as the determinant $|\Sigma_0|$, the generalized R square is zero. This means that the hypothesized path model in Figure 10.1 does not explain the relationship among the variables any better than the null path model in Figure 10.2. The determinant $|\Sigma_0|$ represents the total generalized variance to be explained. The determinant $|\Sigma|$ shows the remaining generalized variance after some portion of the total generalized variance in $|\Sigma_0|$ has been accounted for in the path analysis. The maximum value of GR^2 is bounded by one, which means that all the generalized variance has been explained in the path analysis. Thus, the generalized GR^2 offers a more straightforward index of model fit in path analysis than does the chi square statistic. It unifies the approach to model fit between path analysis and multiple regression, the latter of which can be viewed as a special case of path analysis.

The generalized GR^2 can be used to facilitate statistical power analysis because it can be expressed as a function of the regular R^2 for the regression equations in a recursive path model. Researchers can think of R^2 for the regression equations in the path model and then estimate the overall model fit GR^2 for power analysis. We shall now find how to express GR^2 in terms of R^2 of individual regression equations in the recursive path model. We will utilize a general matrix lemma about the determinant of a partitioned matrix.

Suppose that a partitioned matrix M is

$$M = \begin{bmatrix} A & B \\ C & D \end{bmatrix}.$$

Its determinant is $|M| = |A| |D - CA^{-1}B|$. Using this lemma, we can rewrite the generalized variances $|\Sigma_0|$ and $|\Sigma|$,

$$|\Sigma_0| = |\Sigma_{xx}| \sigma_{y_1}^2 \sigma_{y_2}^2.$$

If there are p endogenous variables, we will have

$$|\Sigma_0| = |\Sigma_{xx}| (\sigma_{y_1}^2 \sigma_{y_2}^2 \cdots \sigma_{y_p}^2).$$

The generalized variance under the hypothesized model is

$$|\Sigma| = |\Sigma_{xx}| \left| \Sigma_{yy} - \Sigma_{yx} \Sigma_{xx}^{-1} \Sigma_{xy} \right|.$$

Note that Σ_{yy} simplifies to a scalar σ_y^2 in a multiple regression with one y, and that $|\Sigma_{yy} - \Sigma_{yx} \Sigma_{xx}^{-1} \Sigma_{xy}|$ reduces to $|\sigma_y^2 - \Sigma_{yx} \Sigma_{xx}^{-1} \Sigma_{xy}|$ or the residual variance, which proves the early results about R^2 in the multiple regression.

Now we want to express the variance covariance matrices in terms of the parameters in the path model. The path model in Equation 10.2 can be rewritten as

$$y = (I - B)^{-1} \Gamma x + (I - B)^{-1} \zeta.$$

The covariance matrix between y and x is

$$\Sigma_{yx} = (I - B)^{-1} \Gamma \Sigma_{xx}.$$

The variance covariance matrix of y is

$$\Sigma_{yy} = (I - B)^{-1} \Gamma \Sigma_{xx} \Gamma' (I - B)^{'-1} + (I - B)^{-1} \Psi (I - B)^{'-1},$$

where Ψ is the variance covariance matrix of ζ, $cov(\zeta) = \Psi$. These results can be used to define GR^2.

The generalized R square is

$$GR^2 = 1 - \frac{|\boldsymbol{\Sigma}|}{|\boldsymbol{\Sigma}_0|}$$

$$= 1 - \frac{|\boldsymbol{\Sigma}_{xx}| \left| \boldsymbol{\Sigma}_{yy} - \boldsymbol{\Sigma}_{yx} \boldsymbol{\Sigma}_{xx}^{-1} \boldsymbol{\Sigma}_{xy} \right|}{|\boldsymbol{\Sigma}_{xx}| \left(\sigma_{y_1}^2 \sigma_{y_2}^2 \cdots \sigma_{y_p}^2 \right)}$$

$$= 1 - \frac{\left| (\boldsymbol{I} - \boldsymbol{B})^{-1} \boldsymbol{\Psi} (\boldsymbol{I} - \boldsymbol{B})'^{-1} \right|}{\sigma_{y_1}^2 \sigma_{y_2}^2 \cdots \sigma_{y_p}^2}. \tag{10.12}$$

This formula for GR^2 holds true for all the path models. However, the GR^2 for a recursive path model can be greatly simplified because the matrix $(\boldsymbol{I} - \boldsymbol{B})$ is triangular with ones on the diagonal. The determinant of the matrix $(\boldsymbol{I} - \boldsymbol{B})^{-1}$ is, therefore, one. Further, the variance matrix $\boldsymbol{\Psi}$ is diagonal in a recursive model.

$$\boldsymbol{\Psi} = \begin{bmatrix} \psi_{11} & 0 & \cdots & 0 \\ 0 & \psi_{22} & \cdots & 0 \\ 0 & \cdots & \cdots & 0 \\ 0 & 0 & \cdots & \psi_{pp} \end{bmatrix},$$

where ψ_{pp} is the variance of the residual ζ_p for the pth endogenous variable in the pth regression equation. The generalized R square in a recursive model (Specht, 1975) simplifies to

$$GR^2 = 1 - \frac{|\boldsymbol{\Psi}|}{\sigma_{y_1}^2 \sigma_{y_2}^2 \cdots \sigma_{y_p}^2}$$

$$= 1 - \frac{\psi_{11} \psi_{22} \cdots \psi_{pp}}{\sigma_{y_1}^2 \sigma_{y_2}^2 \cdots \sigma_{y_p}^2}$$

$$= 1 - (1 - R_1^2)(1 - R_2^2) \cdots (1 - R_p^2), \tag{10.13}$$

where R_p^2 is the R square in the pth regression equation in the path model, and $R_p^2 = 1 - \psi_{pp}/\sigma_{y_p}^2$.

The test for the generalized R square has an asymptotic chi square distribution with degrees of freedom d (Specht, 1975, p. 124),

$$W = -(N - d)\ln(1 - GR^2), \tag{10.14}$$

where N is the total sample size; d is the difference in the number of path coefficients between the null model and the alternative model; and ln is the natural logarithmic function. In our example, the null hypothesis suggests an empty model, as shown in Figure 10.2. The alternative hypothesis represents a full recursive model, as shown in Figure 10.1, where the number of path coefficients is $pq + p(p-1)/2$. The symbol q counts the number of exogenous variables in the path model. In our example, the number of degrees of freedom d is $2 \times 2 + 2(2-1)/2 = 5$. When the alternative hypothesis is indeed true, the test statistic W follows a non-central chi square distribution with a non-centrality parameter λ. It is difficult to express the non-centrality parameter, but we can estimate it using

$$\hat{\lambda} = \hat{W} - d, \tag{10.15}$$

where

$$\hat{W} = -(N-d)\ln(1 - \widehat{GR}^2).$$

The estimated $\widehat{GR}^2$ is

$$1 - (1 - \hat{R}_1^2)(1 - \hat{R}_2^2)\cdots(1 - \hat{R}_p^2). \tag{10.16}$$

The estimate $\hat{\lambda}$ thus computed is unbiased. Since $W \sim \chi_d^2(\lambda)$ or W' for short, we find that $E(W') = \lambda + d$ (Saxena and Alam, 1982). The statistical power for testing the model fit is

$$1 - \beta = P[\chi_d^2(\lambda) \geq \chi_{1-\alpha,d}^2], \tag{10.17}$$

where $\chi_{1-\alpha,d}^2$ is the critical value at significance level α.

We can compute the statistical power for testing the full path model in Figure 10.1 against the null path model in Figure 10.2. We can estimate the generalized R square, using two multiple correlations for the two regression equations in the full path model. The two estimated R^2 may be obtained from their sample data in Pedhazur (1997): $\hat{R}_{y_1,y_2x_1x_2}^2 = .49647$ and $\hat{R}_{y_2,x_1x_2}^2 = .1696$.

$$\widehat{GR}^2 = 1 - (1 - .49647)(1 - .1696) = .5818687$$

The estimated non-centrality parameter is

$$\hat{\lambda} = \hat{W} - d$$
$$= -(N-d)\ln(1 - \widehat{GR}^2) - d$$
$$= -(N-5)\ln(1 - .5818687) - 5.$$

$$(10.18)$$

When the sample size N is 38, the estimated non-centrality parameter is 20.03075.

$$\hat{\lambda} = -(38-5)\ln(1 - .5818687) - 5 = 23.77467$$

The statistical power for testing the fit of the full path model is .9797 or

$$P[\chi_5^2(\lambda = 23.77467) \geq \chi_{.95,5}^2] = .9797.$$

The R code for computing the power is:

```
# testing a full path model against a null model
R2y1=.49647
R2y2=.1696
p=2;  q=2

GR2=1-(1-R2y1)*(1-R2y2)
N=38
d=p*q+p*(p-1)/2
W=-(N-d)*log(1-GR2)

a=.05
lambda=W-d
1-pchisq(qchisq(1-a,d),d,lambda)
```

The SAS program is:

```
*power in path analysis;
*power for testing model fit;
data null;
R2y1=.49647;
R2y2=.1696;
```

```
p=2;  q=2;

GR2=1-(1-R2y1)*(1-R2y2);
N=38;
d=p*q+p*(p-1)/2;
W=-(N-d)*log(1-GR2);

a=.05;
lambda=W-d;
power=1-probchi(cinv(1-a,d),d,lambda);
put power=;
run;
```

Comparing Path Models

A similar chi square test can be developed to compare two path models. One path model will have a smaller number of path coefficients to estimate than the other path model. We name the first model 1 and the other model 2. The two path models are often nested, with model 2 being less restrictive than model 1. Model 1 does not have to be an empty model like that in Figure 10.2. We use d_1 for the number of path coefficients in model 1 and d_2 for the number of path coefficients in model 2. The difference between d_2 and d_1 can be one or more, depending how different the two models are. We can use a chi square statistic W to compare the two path models (Specht, 1975, p. 125; Jöreskog, 1969).

$$
\begin{aligned}
W &= -(N-d)\ln\frac{1-GR_2^2}{1-GR_1^2} \\
&= -(N-d)\ln\frac{|\Sigma_2|}{|\Sigma_1|},
\end{aligned}
\tag{10.19}
$$

where $d = d_2 - d_1$; GR_2^2 and GR_1^2 are the generalized variances for models 2 and 1; and Σ_2 and Σ_1 are the variance covariance matrices in models 2 and 1. The null hypothesis suggests that the fit of model 1 is as good as that of model 2. Under the null hypothesis, the W statistic has an asymptotic chi square distribution with d degrees of freedom. The alternative hypothesis means that the fit of model 1 is not as good as that of model 2. Under the alternative hypothesis, the statistic W has a non-central chi-square

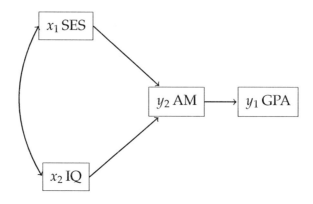

Figure 10.3: Path model 1

distribution with a non-centrality parameter λ. As before, we use $\hat{\lambda} = \hat{W} - d$ to estimate the non-centrality parameter.

$$\hat{W} = -(N-d)\ln\frac{1-\widehat{GR}_2^2}{1-\widehat{GR}_1^2}$$

The statistical power for the model comparison test uses a similar formula except that the degrees of freedom and non-centrality parameter take different values,

$$1 - \beta = P[\chi_d^2(\lambda) \geq \chi_{1-\alpha,d}^2].$$

When calculating power, we will substitute $\hat{\lambda}$ for λ in this formula.

For example, we want to compare the full path model in Figure 10.1 with a model in Figure 10.3. The latter model suggests that GPA is not directly affected by socioeconomic status or IQ. These two exogenous variables exert their influence on GPA only through the other endogenous variable, AM. We can use hypothesis testing to compare the two models, which represent competing theories about GPA and its determinants. We name the latter model model 1 and the full path model model 2 because the full path model is less restrictive than the model in Figure 10.3.

To calculate power, we need to know the generalized R squares for the two competing models. We have previously calculated the generalized R square for the full path model in Figure 10.1: $\widehat{GR}_2^2 = .5818687$. We can estimate the generalized R square for model 1 in Figure 10.3 in a similar way, using multiple correlations for the two regression equations in model 1, that is,

$$y_1 = b_{12}y_2 + \zeta_1$$
$$y_2 = \gamma_{21}x_1 + \gamma_{22}x_2 + \zeta_2.$$

The two R squares are $\hat{R}^2_{y_1,y_2} = .25$ and $\hat{R}^2_{y_2,x_1x_2} = .1696$ (Pedhazur, 1997). The generalized R square for model 1 is, therefore,

$$\widehat{GR}^2_1 = 1 - (1 - .25)(1 - .1696) = .3772.$$

The estimated non-centrality parameter is

$$\hat{\lambda} = -(N - d)\ln\frac{1 - \widehat{GR}^2_2}{1 - \widehat{GR}^2_1} - d$$
$$= -(N - 2)\ln\frac{1 - .5818687}{1 - .3772} - 2.$$

When the sample size N is 38, the estimated non-centrality parameter is

$$\hat{\lambda} = -(38 - 2)\ln\frac{1 - .5818687}{1 - .3772} - 2 = 12.34348.$$

The statistical power evaluates to .8923,

$$P[\chi^2_2(12.34348) \geq \chi^2_{.95,2}] = .8923.$$

The following R code produces the power value:

```
# power for comparing two models
R2y1_1=.5^2
R2y2_1=.1696

R2y1_2=.49647
R2y2_2=.1696

GR2_1=1-(1-R2y1_1)*(1-R2y2_1)
GR2_2=1-(1-R2y1_2)*(1-R2y2_2)

d=2
```

```
N=38
W=-(N-d)*log( (1-GR2_2)/(1-GR2_1))

a=.05
lambda=W-d
1-pchisq(qchisq(1-a,d),d,lambda)
```

The relevant SAS program is:

```
*power for comparing path models;
data null;
R2y1_1=.5**2;
R2y2_1=.1696;

R2y1_2=.49647;
R2y2_2=.1696;

GR2_1=1-(1-R2y1_1)*(1-R2y2_1);
GR2_2=1-(1-R2y1_2)*(1-R2y2_2);

d=2;
N=38;
W=-(N-d)*log((1-GR2_2)/(1-GR2_1));

a=.05;
lambda=W-d;
power=1-probchi(cinv(1-a,d),d,lambda);
put power=;
run;
```

10.2   Factor Analysis

The measurement model in SEM is based on factor analysis, although it is not exactly the same as an exploratory factor analysis, in which factors are siphoned from all the variables without prejudice. In some cases factor analysis may not produce the same set of factors, owing to different estimation methods. This is not the case in SEM analysis, where factors are predetermined to be related to certain observed variables according to a substantive theory. The factors in SEM are conceived of as being measured by those observed variables. The aim of the SEM analysis is to determine how the observed variables contribute to the relevant factors. This simplifies our treatment of factor analysis in the context of SEM.

We are mostly interested in how much variance in each predetermined factor is retained from the observed variables and how much variance there is in the factor relative to its own error variance. In other words, we want to know the reliability measure of the predetermined factors in SEM. We will use one factor to illustrate our approach to calculating the reliability measure of the factor because the same approach is applicable to any other factor in SEM analysis, regardless of whether it is an exogenous or endogenous latent variable.

The general model for factor analysis is

$$y = \Lambda \eta + \epsilon. \tag{10.20}$$

We will use an endogenous variable in the factor analysis to show how to estimate the reliability of latent variables. The same process can be extended to exogenous latent variables. For simplicity of illustration, we limit our attention to one endogenous latent variable η_1 and three observed variables y_1, y_2, and y_3,

$$y = \Lambda \eta_1 + \epsilon.$$

The reliability of any other latent variable follows the same computational process.

The reliability of a factor or latent variable uses the formulas developed by Kaiser and Michael (1977):

$$\rho_{\eta_1}^2 = \frac{I}{I-1}\left(1 - \sum_{i=1}^{I} w_i^2\right), \tag{10.21}$$

where I is the number of observed variables related to the latent variable η_1, and w_i is the weight for the ith observed variable in the linear combination of the I observed variables for the factor score on the latent variable η_1. For example, the latent variable η_1 may be based on three observable variables y_1, y_2, and y_3. The linear combination of the three observed variables will be

$$\eta_1 = w_1 y_1 + w_2 y_2 + w_3 y_3.$$

In matrix notation, the one endogenous variable is

$$\eta_1 = y'w,$$

where $w' = [w_1, w_2, w_3]$ contains the weights. If standardized variables are used in factor analysis, we have

$$w = R^{-1}\Lambda. \tag{10.22}$$

The symbol R represents the correlation matrix of the three observed variables y_1, y_2, and y_3. The matrix Λ now contains the standardized regression coefficients in the regression of the observed variables on the latent variable.

For example, we may use three observed variables on reading, writing, and arithmetic to measure a latent variable on students' academic achievement. Suppose that we know the correlation matrix of the three observed variables,

$$R = \begin{bmatrix} 1 & .64 & .66 \\ .64 & 1 & .68 \\ .66 & .68 & 1 \end{bmatrix}.$$

Using the correlation matrix, we can run a factor analysis and obtain the matrix Λ,

$$\Lambda' = \begin{bmatrix} .87045 & .87951 & .88821 \end{bmatrix}.$$

We can then calculate the matrix w,

$$w = R^{-1}\Lambda = \begin{bmatrix} .3751799 \\ .3790789 \\ .3828176 \end{bmatrix}.$$

According to Equation 10.21, we have the reliability $\rho_{\eta_1}^2 = .85$ for the latent variable on academic achievement.

The reliability is no more than one. It always attenuates the variance of the factor or the latent variable. It makes the relationship between latent variables less clear than they are when the latent variables are measured without error. The reliabilities can be used to adjust statistical power for testing structural equation models, in which exogenous and endogenous variables are latent variables measured with error.

10.3 Structural Equation Model

We will first describe the general structural equation model, and then we will introduce our approach to statistical power with a simple SEM model. Using the same approach, we may conduct power analysis to compare any two competing SEM models.

The general structural equation model comprises three sets of equations: the measurement model for exogenous latent variables ξ, the measurement model for endogenous latent variables η, and the structural model that relates η to ξ in a set of regression equations. The two measurement models are based on factor analysis,

$$x = \Lambda_x \xi + \delta, \tag{10.23}$$

where x contains a q number of observed variables; Λ_x is a $q \times n$ matrix of coefficients of the regression of x on ξ; and δ is a $q \times 1$ vector of measurement errors for x. The variance covariance matrix of δ is $Cov(\delta) = \Theta_\delta$;

$$y = \Lambda_y \eta + \epsilon, \tag{10.24}$$

where y contains p number of observed variables related to the endogenous latent variables η; Λ_y is a $p \times m$ matrix of coefficients of the regression of y on η; and ϵ is a $p \times 1$ vector of measurement errors for y. The variance covariance matrix of ϵ is $Cov(\epsilon) = \Theta_\epsilon$.

The structural model is

$$\eta = B\eta + \Gamma\xi + \zeta. \tag{10.25}$$

The symbol B is a $m \times m$ matrix, but it is not necessarily full of non-zero coefficients. In a recursive model B is triangular with zero diagonals. The matrix Γ has a size of $m \times n$. It contains the regression coefficients for the exogenous latent variables ξ. The matrix ζ holds the regression errors. The variance covariance matrix for the regression errors ζ is $Cov(\zeta) = \Psi$. If it is a recursive model, Ψ is a diagonal matrix.

We will use a simple approach to statistical power analysis in structural equation modeling, although there are other ways to analyze power in SEM (Hancock, 2001; MacCallum, Browne, and Sugawara, 1996; Satorra and Saris, 1985). Our approach is to treat the structural model in SEM as a path model except that the exogenous and endogenous latent variables

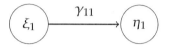

Figure 10.4: Path diagram

are now assumed to have measurement error as indicated by their reliabilities. The correlations between exogenous and endogenous latent variables can be computed from their true correlations and reliabilities. Once the correlations among the latent variables have been computed, the statistical power for the structural equations in SEM can be calculated using the same method as in path analysis. We can illustrate the approach, using the simplest SEM model, with one exogenous latent variable ξ_1 and one endogenous latent variable η_1 (see Figure 10.4). We leave out the observed variables in the figure for simplicity of presentation, although the observed variables are implied by the SEM model. We now look at the structural model of η_1 and ξ_1.

Testing this simplest SEM model is equivalent to testing the coefficient γ_{11} in the structural model. This is the same as testing the correlation $\rho_{\eta_1 \xi_1}$ between η_1 and ξ_1. If η_1 and ξ_1 are measured without error, then we can use linear regression to analyze the data on η_1 and ξ_1. The statistical power can be calculated following the same approach as in Chapter 5 on linear regression. The test for a correlation uses a t statistic. As the sample size is typically large in SEM analysis, squaring the t statistic approximately produces a chi square statistic with one degree of freedom, χ_1^2. The non-centrality parameter for the chi square statistic is

$$\lambda = \frac{N\rho_{\eta_1 \xi_1}^2}{1 - \rho_{\eta_1 \xi_1}^2}.$$

When η_1 and ξ_1 are measured with error, we can modify the non-centrality parameter with the reliabilities. The correlation between η_1 and ξ_1 is

$$\rho_{\eta_1 \xi_1} = \rho_{t\eta_1 t\xi_1} \sqrt{\rho_{\eta_1}^2 \rho_{\xi_1}^2},$$

where $\rho_{t\eta_1 t\xi_1}$ is the true correlation between η_1 and ξ_1, and $\rho_{\eta_1}^2$ and $\rho_{\xi_1}^2$ are the reliabilities for η_1 and ξ_1, respectively. Thus, the non-centrality parameter for the chi square test in this simplest SEM model is

$$\lambda = \frac{N\rho_{t\eta_1 t\xi_1}^2 \rho_{\eta_1}^2 \rho_{\xi_1}^2}{1 - \rho_{t\eta_1 t\xi_1}^2 \rho_{\eta_1}^2 \rho_{\xi_1}^2}. \tag{10.26}$$

Note that the reliabilities can be estimated according to Equation 10.21 in the previous section on factor analysis. When computing the non-centrality parameter and statistical power, researchers can estimate the true correlations and attenuate the true correlations by reliabilities obtained from the factor analyses.

We will use a similar strategy to compute the correlations among more than two latent variables in an SEM model. The correlations among those latent variables define the structural model, on which power analysis is based. The structural model is viewed as a path model. So power in path analysis will apply. As the exogenous and endogenous latent variables are measured with error, we will factor in the reliabilities of the latent variables for power analysis.

10.3.1   Statistical Power in SEM

We treat the structural model as a path model in calculating statistical power in SEM. We will examine statistical power in testing model fit and in comparing structural models. We assume that there are m endogenous latent variables and m equations for each endogenous latent variable in the structural equations,

$$\eta = B\eta + \Gamma\xi + \zeta.$$

The generalized R square GR^2 for the fit of the structural model is

$$GR^2 = 1 - \frac{\left|(I - B)^{-1}\Psi(I - B)'^{-1}\right|}{\sigma_{\eta_1}^2 \sigma_{\eta_2}^2 \cdots \sigma_{\eta_m}^2}. \tag{10.27}$$

Again, GR^2 can be derived from the generalized variances of the structural model under the null hypothesis (empty model) and the alternative hypothesis (hypothesized model),

$$GR^2 = 1 - \frac{|\Sigma_a|}{|\Sigma_0|}.$$

Note that $\boldsymbol{\Sigma}_0$ is the variance covariance matrix of $[\boldsymbol{\eta}'\ \boldsymbol{\xi}']$ under the null model or $cov(\boldsymbol{\eta}'\ \boldsymbol{\xi}') = \boldsymbol{\Sigma}_0$, and that $\boldsymbol{\Sigma}_a$ is the variance covariance matrix of the endogenous and exogenous latent variables in the hypothesized model.

In a recursive structural equations, the generalized R square can be greatly simplified to

$$GR^2 = 1 - (1 - R_1^2)(1 - R_2^2) \cdots (1 - R_m^2).$$

The R_m^2 for the mth regression equation in the structural model can be expressed in terms of the correlations among the endogenous and exogenous latent variables;

$$R_m^2 = \boldsymbol{R}'_{\eta_m} \boldsymbol{R}^{-1} \boldsymbol{R}_{\eta_m}, \tag{10.28}$$

where $\boldsymbol{R}_{\eta_m}$ is a column vector of correlations between the mth endogenous latent variable η_m and its predictors, and $\boldsymbol{R}$ is the correlation matrix of the predictors. The R_m^2 is essentially the same as that in a regular regression except that the outcome is η_m and the predictors are now the exogenous latent variables or endogenous latent variables. As the latent variables are measured with error, they have their reliabilities. We can figure in the reliabilities of the latent variables for the above correlation matrices,

$$\boldsymbol{R} = \boldsymbol{\rho}\boldsymbol{R}_T\boldsymbol{\rho} + \boldsymbol{I} - \boldsymbol{\rho}\boldsymbol{\rho}, \tag{10.29}$$

where $\boldsymbol{\rho}$ is a diagonal matrix with the diagonals being the square root of the reliabilities of the predictor latent variables. For instance, the predictor latent variables may include η_2 and ξ_1 through ξ_n. The matrix $\boldsymbol{\rho}$ is

$$\boldsymbol{\rho} = \begin{bmatrix} \rho_{\eta_2} & 0 & \cdots & 0 \\ 0 & \rho_{\xi_1} & \cdots & 0 \\ 0 & 0 & \cdots & 0 \\ 0 & 0 & \cdots & \rho_{\xi_n} \end{bmatrix}.$$

The symbol $\boldsymbol{R}_T$ is the correlation matrix of the true scores on the predictor latent variables. The correlations of the true scores are often theorized to exist between latent variables according to a substantive theory, and they can take hypothesized values for power analysis. Likewise, we can relate the correlation matrix $\boldsymbol{R}_{\eta_m}$ to the reliabilities of the latent variables,

$$\boldsymbol{R}_{\eta_m} = \boldsymbol{\rho}\boldsymbol{R}_{t\eta_m}\boldsymbol{\rho}_{\eta_m}, \tag{10.30}$$

where $R_{t\eta_m}$ is the correlation matrix of true scores on η_m and its predictors, and $\rho_{\eta_m}^2$ is the reliability of the mth endogenous latent variable. Once the reliabilities have been estimated, we can fill out their square roots in ρ_{η_m} and ρ. The generalized R square GR^2 can then be computed for statistical power analysis.

The statistical power for testing a SEM model is calculated in a similar way as in path analysis. The test statistic for the fit of the model is a chi square statistic based on a large sample approximation. The chi square statistic compares the hypothesized structural equations in the SEM with an empty model under the null hypothesis, which leaves all the variance of endogenous latent variables unexplained. The generalized R square GR^2 shows how much the generalized variance of the latent variables is explained through SEM modeling under the alternative hypothesis. When the alternative hypothesis holds true, the chi square statistic is a non-central chi square with d degrees of freedom and a non-centrality parameter λ. The number of degrees of freedom d is the difference in the number of estimated path coefficients between the hypothesized SEM model and the null empty SEM model. We can estimate the non-centrality parameter λ by using the fact that the chi square statistic minus its degrees of freedom is an unbiased estimate of the non-centrality parameter,

$$\hat{\lambda} = -(N-d)\ln(1-\widehat{GR}^2) - d. \tag{10.31}$$

The statistical power is, therefore,

$$1 - \beta = P[\chi_d^2(\hat{\lambda}) \geq \chi_{1-\alpha,d}^2].$$

The estimated generalized R square $\widehat{GR}^2$ is based on Equation 10.27. If the SEM is a recursive model, $\widehat{GR}^2$ can be easily computed from the R squares for individual regression equations in the structural model.

The statistical power for comparing two competing SEM models is calculated using the same approach. We will estimate the generalized R square $\widehat{GR}^2$ for both models. We name the more restrictive model under the null hypothesis model 1, and the less restrictive model under the alternative hypothesis model 2. The generalized R square $\widehat{GR}_1^2$ is for model 1, and $\widehat{GR}_2^2$ is for model 2. The test for comparing the two models is still an asymptotic chi square statistic, which has a central distribution under the null hypothesis. Under the alternative hypothesis it has a non-central distribution with d degrees of freedom and non-centrality parameter λ. The degrees of freedom d equal the difference in the number of path coefficients between the two SEM models.

When the alternative hypothesis is true, model 1 is not so good as the less restrictive model 2. The discrepancy between the competing models is captured by the ratio of their generalized R squares

$$\frac{1 - GR_2^2}{1 - GR_1^2},$$

and this ratio can be used to estimate the non-centrality parameter,

$$\hat{\lambda} = -(N - d)\ln\frac{1 - \widehat{GR}_2^2}{1 - \widehat{GR}_1^2} - d. \tag{10.32}$$

We can calculate the statistical power, using the formula

$$1 - \beta = P[\chi_d^2(\hat{\lambda}) \geq \chi_{1-\alpha,d}^2].$$

Example

Let us use a management study on job satisfaction by way of illustration. The two endogenous latent variables are job satisfaction η_1 and job competency η_2; the two exogenous latent variables are motivation ξ_1 and self-esteem ξ_2. These latent variables can be measured by survey instruments with certain reliabilities. Suppose that we have some knowledge of the relationships among the latent variables based on previous research. We can think of the correlation of true scores between the latent variables. The correlations of the true scores are then estimated and presented in the lower triangle of the following matrix with their reliabilities at the bottom:

	satisfaction	competency	motivation	self-esteem
η_1 satisfaction	1			
η_2 competency	.4	1		
ξ_1 motivation	.3	.3	1	
ξ_2 self-esteem	.3	.5	.2	1
reliability	.8	.9	.75	.75

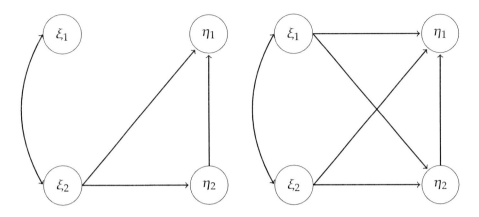

Figure 10.5: SEM model 1   Figure 10.6: SEM model 2

We plan to compare two structural equation models, with model 1 being more restrictive than model 2. Model 2 is a full model; model 1 a reduced one (see Figures 10.5 and 10.6). We are interested in testing the latent variable on motivation ξ_1 by comparing the two models. To have sufficient power for testing the effects of ξ_1, we need to find the necessary sample size N. For this purpose, we need to calculate the generalized R squares for the two models.

The generalized R squares for the two models are functions of the R squares of the regression equations in the structural model. In model 2, we have two regression equations;

$$
\begin{aligned}
\eta_1 &= b_{12}\eta_2 + \gamma_{11}\xi_1 + \gamma_{12}\xi_2 + \zeta_1 \\
\eta_2 &= \qquad\quad \gamma_{21}\xi_1 + \gamma_{22}\xi_2 + \zeta_2 .
\end{aligned}
$$

The R_1^2 corresponds to the regression equation with η_1 as the outcome; the R_2^2 to the regression equation with η_2 as the outcome. According to Equation 10.28, we have

$$
R_1^2 = R_{\eta_1}' R^{-1} R_{\eta_1} .
$$

The matrices in this formula are the observed correlation matrices, which can be computed from the correlations of true scores and reliabilities. Using

Equation 10.29, we obtain

$$R = \rho R_T \rho + I - \rho\rho$$

$$= \begin{bmatrix} \sqrt{.9} & 0 & 0 \\ 0 & \sqrt{.75} & 0 \\ 0 & 0 & \sqrt{.75} \end{bmatrix} \begin{bmatrix} 1 & .3 & .5 \\ .3 & 1 & .2 \\ .5 & .2 & 1 \end{bmatrix} \begin{bmatrix} \sqrt{.9} & 0 & 0 \\ 0 & \sqrt{.75} & 0 \\ 0 & 0 & \sqrt{.75} \end{bmatrix}$$

$$+ \begin{bmatrix} 1 & 0 & 0 \\ 0 & 1 & 0 \\ 0 & 0 & 1 \end{bmatrix} - \begin{bmatrix} \sqrt{.9} & 0 & 0 \\ 0 & \sqrt{.75} & 0 \\ 0 & 0 & \sqrt{.75} \end{bmatrix} \begin{bmatrix} \sqrt{.9} & 0 & 0 \\ 0 & \sqrt{.75} & 0 \\ 0 & 0 & \sqrt{.75} \end{bmatrix}.$$

According to Equation 10.30, we have

$$R_{\eta_1} = \rho R_{t\eta_1} \rho_{\eta_1}$$

$$= \begin{bmatrix} \sqrt{.9} & 0 & 0 \\ 0 & \sqrt{.75} & 0 \\ 0 & 0 & \sqrt{.75} \end{bmatrix} \begin{bmatrix} .4 \\ .3 \\ .3 \end{bmatrix} \sqrt{.8} .$$

The R_1^2 evaluates to .147515. The R_2^2 is computed in a similar way, $R_2^2 = .2037084$. The generalized R square for model 2 is

$$GR_2^2 = 1 - (1 - .147515)(1 - .2037084) = .3211734.$$

Likewise, we can obtain the generalized R square for Model 1,

$$GR_1^2 = 1 - (1 - .125594)(1 - .16875) = .27315.$$

We can obtain the non-centrality parameter by substituting GR_1^2 and GR_2^2 into Equation 10.32;

$$\hat{\lambda} = -(N - 2)\ln\frac{1 - .3211734}{1 - .27315} - 2 .$$

If we choose a sample size $N = 172$, we will achieve .8 statistical power in comparing the two SEM models (see the following R code).

```
# power in sem

R2eta1_2=.147515
R2eta2_2=.2037084
```

```
GR2_2=1-(1-R2eta1_2)*(1-R2eta2_2)

R2eta1_1=.125594
R2eta2_1=.16875
GR2_1=1-(1-R2eta1_1)*(1-R2eta2_1)

d=2
N=172
W=-(N-d)*log( (1-GR2_2)/(1-GR2_1))

a=.05
lambda=W-d
p=1-pchisq(qchisq(1-a,d),d,lambda)
p
```

The SAS program is:

```
proc iml;
*full model 2;
*eta1 ~ eta2 xi1 xi2;
Rte1={.4, .3, .3};
Rt_1={1 .3 .5,
   .3 1 .2,
   .5 .2 1};
rho2_1=diag({.9,.75, .75});
rho_1=sqrt(rho2_1);

R_1=rho_1*Rt_1*rho_1+I(nrow(Rt_1))-rho_1*rho_1;
Re1=rho_1*Rte1*sqrt(.8);
R2_1=t(Re1)*inv(R_1)*Re1;
print R2_1[label="model 2: R^2 for eta1"];

*eta2 ~ xi1 xi2;
Rte2={.3, .5};
Rt_2={1 .2,
   .2 1 };
rho2_2=diag({.75, .75});
rho_2=sqrt(rho2_2);
```

```
R_2=rho_2*Rt_2*rho_2+I(nrow(Rt_2))-rho_2*rho_2;
Re2=rho_2*Rte2*sqrt(.9);
R2_2=t(Re2)*inv(R_2)*Re2;
print R2_2[label="model 2: R^2 for eta2"];

GR2_2=1-(1-R2_1)*(1-R2_2);
print GR2_2[label="model 2: GR^2"];

*reduced model 1;

* eta1 ~ eta2 + xi2;
Rte1={.4, .3};
Rt_1={1 .5,
      .5  1};
rho2_1=diag({.9,.75});
rho_1=sqrt(rho2_1);

R_1=rho_1*Rt_1*rho_1+I(nrow(Rt_1))-rho_1*rho_1;
Re1=rho_1*Rte1*sqrt(.8);
R2_1=t(Re1)*inv(R_1)*Re1;
print R2_1[label="model 1: R^2 for eta1"];

*eta2 ~ xi2;
R2_2=.75*.5**2*.9;
print R2_2[label="model 1: R^2 for eta2"];

GR2_1=1-(1-R2_1)*(1-R2_2);
print GR2_1[label="model 1: GR^2"];
*power;
ratio= (1-GR2_2)/(1-GR2_1);
*print ratio;
d=2; a=.05; N=172;
lambda=-(N-d)*log(ratio) -d;
power=1-probchi(cinv(1-a,d),d,lambda);
print power;
quit iml;
```

Chapter 11

Longitudinal Studies

Longitudinal studies involve repeated observations of subjects over an extended period. The repeated measures can also be observations made under different treatment conditions (e.g., dosages), but the data have the same structure, in which observations made on different occasions come from the same individual subject. Such data structures call for a different kind of analysis than the cross-sectional data analyses discussed in the previous chapters (see Singer and Willett, 2003).

The simplest repeated measures design may include only a pretest and posttest. The difference between the pretest and posttest can be used as the only outcome in the statistical model. The ensuing analysis can be framed as a special case of a cross-sectional study. For example, a matched pairs t test can be used to analyze the difference between the pretest and posttest measured on the same group of subjects. Although it is a simple repeated measures design, the data analysis is not that different from the one sample t test.

Most of the time, the repeated measures involve more than two observations on the same subject. The analysis can become rather complicated, depending on the modeling techniques used. In the past, repeated measures on a group of subjects were analyzed as ANOVA in the randomized block design. In this method, the subjects are treated as blocks and are assumed to be random effects. The fixed effects are the outcome means in analysis of variance. The outcome means on different occasions or under different treatments (e.g., dosage) can be weighted with different coefficients according to a certain hypothesized pattern (e.g., linear and quadratic trend). An F statistic can be used to test the linear or quadratic trend. Two groups of subjects in the study give rise to a split-plot design. As the randomized block design analysis requires balanced design and strict assumptions, it has largely been superseded by new modeling techniques (e.g., multivariate analysis, random coefficients model).

Multivariate analysis uses fewer assumptions about the data than the randomized block design analysis. The repeated measures are deemed to be multiple outcomes on the same subject, and are allowed to have a complex variance covariance structure under the framework of multivariate analysis. The underlying population means of the repeated measures can be tested for a linear or quadratic trend by checking the relationship among those population means. Multivariate analysis still requires even spacing between occasions and balanced data. To accommodate uneven spacing and a flexible data structure, people have resorted to linear mixed models, which are sometimes called random coefficients models in longitudinal studies.

There have been great developments in the analysis of longitudinal studies using random coefficients models. The random coefficients model is used more often than ANOVA and multivariate analysis because it can accommodate uneven time points and unbalanced data. The random coefficients model can easily be formulated as an HLM model. In fact, the randomized block design can be subsumed under the random coefficients model with a random intercept and a fixed slope. In the following, we will describe first the power in the multivariate analysis of longitudinal data and then the power in the random coefficients models.

11.1 Multivariate Analysis of Repeated Measures

11.1.1 Linear Change

In multivariate analysis of repeated measures, we work with the population means of the repeated measures made on different occasions or under different treatment conditions. To motivate the power analysis, we can start with a general example of five repeated measures ($p = 5$) on a group of n subjects. The individual observation can be represented by Y_{ij}. The subscript i denotes the subject, and j the occasion or treatment condition. The corresponding population means are μ_1, μ_2, μ_3, μ_4, and μ_5. If the average response changes with occasions or treatment conditions, say, increasing dosage, then there might be a linear trend among the population means. For instance, the subjects' average response might improve as the dosage increases, that is, $\mu_1 < \mu_2 < \mu_3 < \mu_4 < \mu_5$. To check the linear trend, we can simply take the difference between two consecutive means and test whether the pair-wise mean differences are equal to some constant. If all the means are equal, they fall on a flat line. In other words, all the means do not change over time. There is no linear change at all. Their mean differences become all zeros. The multivariate null hypothesis is

$$H_0 : \begin{bmatrix} \mu_{d1} \\ \mu_{d2} \\ \mu_{d3} \\ \mu_{d4} \end{bmatrix} = \begin{bmatrix} \mu_2 - \mu_1 \\ \mu_3 - \mu_2 \\ \mu_4 - \mu_3 \\ \mu_5 - \mu_4 \end{bmatrix} = \begin{bmatrix} 0 \\ 0 \\ 0 \\ 0 \end{bmatrix}. \tag{11.1}$$

When the alternative hypothesis is true, the mean differences are equal to a constant, say, β_1. If the repeated measures are evenly spaced over time, β_1 is the amount of change in the outcome between two consecutive time points, which often mark one elapsed time unit (e.g., a month or year). The constant β_1, therefore, is the linear change of outcome per time unit. The means can be expressed in terms of time point t and β_1,

$$\mu_j = \beta_0 + \beta_1 t,$$

where time point t ranges from 0 to $p - 1$, μ_j is the mean at time point t ($j = t + 1$ or $j = 1, 2, \cdots, p$), and β_0 is the mean at the initial time point $t = 0$. The more β_1 deviates from zero; the steeper the linear change. Thus, the alternative hypothesis for linear change is

$$H_a : \begin{bmatrix} \mu_{d1} \\ \mu_{d2} \\ \mu_{d3} \\ \mu_{d4} \end{bmatrix} = \begin{bmatrix} \mu_2 - \mu_1 \\ \mu_3 - \mu_2 \\ \mu_4 - \mu_3 \\ \mu_5 - \mu_4 \end{bmatrix} = \begin{bmatrix} \beta_1 \\ \beta_1 \\ \beta_1 \\ \beta_1 \end{bmatrix}. \tag{11.2}$$

A multivariate Hotelling T^2 can be used to test the null hypothesis about the linear change because the sample estimates of the mean differences have a multivariate normal distribution,

$$\hat{\mu}_d = \begin{bmatrix} \overline{Y}_2 - \overline{Y}_1 \\ \overline{Y}_3 - \overline{Y}_2 \\ \overline{Y}_4 - \overline{Y}_3 \\ \overline{Y}_5 - \overline{Y}_4 \end{bmatrix} = C_1 \overline{Y}, \tag{11.3}$$

where $\hat{\mu}_d$ estimates μ_d ($\mu'_d = [\mu_{d1}, \mu_{d2}, \mu_{d3}, \mu_{d4}]$),

$$C_1 = \begin{bmatrix} -1 & 1 & 0 & 0 & 0 \\ 0 & -1 & 1 & 0 & 0 \\ 0 & 0 & -1 & 1 & 0 \\ 0 & 0 & 0 & -1 & 1 \end{bmatrix}, \tag{11.4}$$

and

$$\overline{Y}' = [\overline{Y}_1, \overline{Y}_2, \overline{Y}_3, \overline{Y}_4, \overline{Y}_5]. \tag{11.5}$$

The sample means of the repeated measures $\overline{Y}$ have a multivariate normal distribution, and so do their mean differences $\hat{\mu}_d$.

$$\overline{Y} \sim N\left(\mu, \frac{\Sigma}{n}\right),$$

where Σ is the covariance matrix of the repeated measures.

$$\hat{\mu}_d \sim N(\mu_d, \Sigma_{\hat{\mu}_d}), \tag{11.6}$$

where $\mu_d = C_1 \mu$ and $\Sigma_{\hat{\mu}_d} = C_1 \Sigma C'_1 / n$. Under the null hypothesis $C_1 \mu$ is a null vector $\mathbf{0}$; under the alternative hypothesis $\mu'_d = [\beta_1, \beta_1, \beta_1, \beta_1] = \beta_1 \mathbf{1}'$. The symbol $\mathbf{1}$ is a unit vector that contains a column of ones. The one sample Hotelling T^2 test is

$$T^2 = (\hat{\mu}_d - \mathbf{0})' \hat{\Sigma}_{\hat{\mu}_d}^{-1} (\hat{\mu}_d - \mathbf{0})$$
$$= n\hat{\mu}'_d (C_1 \hat{\Sigma} C'_1)^{-1} \hat{\mu}_d, \tag{11.7}$$

where $\hat{\Sigma}_{\hat{\mu}_d} = C_1 \hat{\Sigma} C'_1 / n$, and $\hat{\Sigma}$ is the estimated within-group covariance matrix (see Chapter 6).

The statistical power for the one sample Hotelling T^2 test can be based on a non-central F,

$$\frac{n-p+1}{(n-1)(p-1)} T^2 = F'(p-1, n-p+1, \lambda), \tag{11.8}$$

where the non-centrality parameter λ is

$$\lambda = n\mu_d'(C_1\Sigma C_1')^{-1}\mu_d$$
$$= n\beta_1^2 \mathbf{1}'(C_1\Sigma C_1')^{-1}\mathbf{1}. \tag{11.9}$$

The power function is

$$1 - \beta = P[F'(p-1, n-p+1, \lambda) \geq F_{1-\alpha,p-1,n-p+1}]$$
$$= 1 - P[F'(p-1, n-p+1, \lambda) < F_{1-\alpha,p-1,n-p+1}]. \tag{11.10}$$

This power function can be adapted in testing the difference in linear change between a treatment group and a control group. The power function for testing the difference in linear change will be

$$1 - P[F'(p-1, n_1 + n_2 - p, \lambda) < F_{1-\alpha,p-1,n_1+n_2-p}], \tag{11.11}$$

where n_1 and n_2 are the sample sizes for the treatment and control groups, and the non-centrality parameter λ now contains a difference in linear change β_d between the treatment and control groups.

$$\lambda = \frac{n_1 n_2}{n_1 + n_2} \beta_d^2 \mathbf{1}'(C_1\Sigma C_1')^{-1}\mathbf{1}, \tag{11.12}$$

where $\beta_d = \beta_{1e} - \beta_{1c}$, and β_{1e} and β_{1c} are the linear change rates for the treatment and control groups, respectively.

For example, let us try to replicate a study on the distance between the pituitary gland and the pterygomaxillary fissure (a small opening in a bony cavity at the base of the human skull). The distance has some significance for orthodontics, and the increase in this distance may differ between boys and girls. We will measure the distance between the pituitary gland and the pterygomaxillary fissure for a sample of boys and girls at ages 8, 10, 12, and 14 ($p = 4$). The original study was reported in Potthoff and Roy (1964). As we want to plan a similar study, we can use their data set to estimate the parameter value for β_d and the covariance matrix Σ. The distance, on average, increases by .95 mm every two years among boys, and by 1.65 mm every two years among girls. If we use boys as a reference, we have $\beta_{e1} = 1.65$ and $\beta_{c1} = .95$. The difference in linear growth between the two sexes is, therefore, $\beta_d = \beta_{e1} - \beta_{c1} = .7$ mm every two years. We may use the estimated covariance matrix in the original study for Σ,

$$\Sigma = \begin{bmatrix} 5.4154545 & 2.7168182 & 3.9102273 & 2.7102273 \\ 2.7168182 & 4.1847727 & 2.9271591 & 3.3171591 \\ 3.9102273 & 2.9271591 & 6.4557386 & 4.1307386 \\ 2.7102273 & 3.3171591 & 4.1307386 & 4.9857386 \end{bmatrix}.$$

Since there are four repeated measures, we have a 3 by 4 matrix for C_1:

$$C_1 = \begin{bmatrix} -1 & 1 & 0 & 0 \\ 0 & -1 & 1 & 0 \\ 0 & 0 & 1 & 1 \end{bmatrix}.$$

If we recruit eleven boys and sixteen girls, as in the original study ($n_e = 16$ and $n_c = 11$), we have a non-centrality parameter of 7.383, according to Equation 11.12. We will have about .54 in statistical power for testing the difference in linear growth of the distance between boys and girls. If the number of boys and girls is increased to forty-four ($n_e = 22$ and $n_c = 22$), statistical power will reach .82.

In practice, people will have difficulty in estimating individual elements in the covariance matrix Σ. If we are willing to make some assumption about the covariance matrix, we can greatly reduce the number of parameters in estimating Σ. Note that the covariance matrix can be expressed in terms of correlation matrix and standard deviations,

$$\Sigma = DRD,$$

where R is the correlation matrix and D is a diagonal matrix, with the diagonals being standard deviations of the repeated measures (see Chapter 6). In our example, we may use the original data of the dental study to compute the actual correlation matrix between the four repeated measures,

$$R = \begin{bmatrix} 1 & 0.5706991 & 0.6613199 & 0.5215831 \\ 0.5706991 & 1 & 0.5631673 & 0.7262157 \\ 0.6613199 & 0.5631673 & 1 & 0.7280983 \\ 0.5215831 & 0.7262157 & 0.7280983 & 1 \end{bmatrix}.$$

The correlation matrix does not deviate far from compound symmetry,

$$R = \begin{bmatrix} 1 & \rho & \rho & \rho \\ \rho & 1 & \rho & \rho \\ \rho & \rho & 1 & \rho \\ \rho & \rho & \rho & 1 \end{bmatrix}.$$

We may use the median of the correlations in R (i.e., .6) to replace ρ in the compound symmetry correlation matrix. In addition, we can find the median of the four standard deviations of the four repeated measures (i.e., 2.3) to construct D. The four standard deviations can be obtained by taking the square root of the four diagonal elements in the estimated covariance matrix for Σ in the original study. For instance, the pooled standard deviation of the first measure taken at age 8 is $\sqrt{5.4154545}$. The other three standard deviations can be similarly obtained, and the median of the four standard deviations is 2.3. Using the median standard deviation of the repeated measures, 2.3, and the median correlation, .6, for ρ, we can compute the covariance matrix Σ,

$$\Sigma = \begin{bmatrix} 2.3 & 0 & 0 & 0 \\ 0 & 2.3 & 0 & 0 \\ 0 & 0 & 2.3 & 0 \\ 0 & 0 & 0 & 2.3 \end{bmatrix} \begin{bmatrix} 1 & .6 & .6 & .6 \\ .6 & 1 & .6 & .6 \\ .6 & .6 & 1 & .6 \\ .6 & .6 & .6 & 1 \end{bmatrix} \begin{bmatrix} 2.3 & 0 & 0 & 0 \\ 0 & 2.3 & 0 & 0 \\ 0 & 0 & 2.3 & 0 \\ 0 & 0 & 0 & 2.3 \end{bmatrix}.$$

It is obvious that we only need two numbers to estimate the entire co-variance matrix Σ. Had we used this estimated covariance in our power analysis, we would get almost identical power values as before. In short, researchers may use a similar strategy to estimate the covariance matrix, assuming a simplified correlation matrix (e.g., Toeplitz matrix). Nevertheless, the assumption about the simplified correlations needs to be based on substantive theory or empirical evidence. There is not a universal way to estimate the covariance matrix Σ for power analysis.

The R code for power analysis in the example is:

```
# multivariate analysis of linear change btw two groups

C1=matrix(c(-1,1,0,0,0,
            0,-1,1,0,0,
            0,0,-1,1,0,
```

```
                 0,0,0,-1,1),nrow=4,byrow=TRUE)
S=diag(5)

C1=matrix(c(-1,1,0,0,
            0,-1,1,0,
            0,0,-1,1),nrow=3,byrow=TRUE)

S=matrix(
c(5.4154545,2.7168182,3.9102273,2.7102273,
  2.7168182,4.1847727,2.9271591,3.3171591,
  3.9102273,2.9271591,6.4557386,4.1307386,
  2.7102273,3.3171591,4.1307386,4.9857386),
nrow=4,byrow=TRUE)


#approximate correlation matrix of compound symmetry
#sd=2.3 ; r=0.6

#D=diag(rep(sd,4))
#R=matrix( c(1, r, r, r,
#            r, 1, r, r,
#            r, r, 1, r,
#            r, r, r, 1), nrow=4,byrow=TRUE)
#S=D%*%R%*%D

CSC=C1%*%S%*%t(C1)

p4maovl=function(n1=16,n2=11,beta_d=.70,CSC){
a=.05
p=nrow(CSC)+1

j=matrix(rep(1,p-1),nrow=p-1)
lambda=n1*n2/(n1+n2)*beta_d^2*(t(j)%*%solve(CSC)%*%j)

f0=qf(1-a,p-1,n1+n2-p)
1-pf(f0,p-1,n1+n2-p,lambda)
}
p4maovl(,,,CSC)
```

The SAS program is:

```
proc iml;
C1={-1 1 0 0 ,
    0 -1 1 0 ,
0 0 -1 1 };

E={135.3863636 67.92045455 97.75568182 67.75568182,
67.92045455 104.6193182 73.17897727 82.92897727,
97.75568182 73.17897727 161.3934659 103.2684659,
67.75568182 82.92897727 103.2684659 124.6434659};
S=E/(16+11-2);

CSC=C1*S*t(C1);

a=.05;
n1=22; n2=22;
beta_d=.7;
p=nrow(CSC)+1;

j=J(p-1,1,1);
lambda=n1*n2/(n1+n2)*beta_d**2*(t(j)*inv(CSC)*j);

f0=finv(1-a,p-1,n1+n2-p);
power=1-probf(f0,p-1,n1+n2-p,lambda);
print power;

quit;
```

The SPSS code is:

```
*multivariate analysis of linear change btw two groups .

MATRIX.
COMPUTE C1={-1,1,0,0;
            0,-1,1,0;
            0,0,-1,1}.
COMPUTE E={
```

```
135.3863636,67.92045455,97.75568182,67.75568182 ;
67.92045455,104.6193182,73.17897727,82.92897727;
97.75568182,73.17897727,161.3934659,103.2684659;
67.75568182,82.92897727,103.2684659,124.6434659}.
COMPUTE S=E/(16+11-2).
COMPUTE CSC=C1*S*T(C1).

COMPUTE N1=22.
COMPUTE N2=22.
COMPUTE BETA_D=.7.
COMPUTE P=NROW(CSC)+1.
COMPUTE J=MAKE(P-1,1,1).
COMPUTE LAMBDA=N1*N2/(N1+N2)*BETA_D**2*(T(J)*INV(CSC)*J).

SAVE {N1,N2,P, BETA_D, LAMBDA} /OUTFILE=*/VARIABLES=N1
N2 P  BETA_D LAMBDA .
END MATRIX.

COMPUTE A=.05.
COMPUTE F0=IDF.F(1-A,P-1,N1+N2-P).
COMPUTE POWER=1-NCDF.F(F0,P-1,N1+N2-P,LAMBDA).
EXECUTE.
```

11.1.2   Quadratic Change

We can test any type of curvature in the change among repeated measures. The most common form of curvature is the quadratic change, which modulates the linear change β_1 over time. In the presence of quadratic change, the means can be expressed as

$$\mu_j = \beta_0 + \beta_1 t + \beta_2 t^2, \tag{11.13}$$

where β_2 represents the quadratic change. Because of β_2, the linear change per unit time does not remain constant over time. Taking the derivative of μ_j with respect to t yields the linear change per unit time $d\mu_j/dt$,

$$\frac{d\mu_j}{dt} = \beta_1 + 2\beta_2 t. \tag{11.14}$$

If the quadratic change were absent or β_2 were zero, the linear change $d\mu_j/dt$ would stay at β_1 over the entire period. Since β_2 is not zero, the linear change rate $d\mu_j/dt$ will either accelerate or decelerate. When β_2 is greater than zero, the linear change accelerates over time. We will see a convex function curve among the repeated measures. When β_2 is negative, the linear change tapers off over time. Hence, we will see a concave function curve among the repeated measures. The amount of acceleration or deceleration in linear change rate between two consecutive times is $2\beta_2$.

The quadratic change $2\beta_2$ represents the differential in linear change rates, which are mean differences between two consecutive time points. According to Equation 11.13, we may express the means at time points 0, 1, 2, 3, and 4 in terms of the linear and quadratic change rates β_1 and β_2. The means spanning five time points are

$$
\mu = \begin{bmatrix} \mu_1 \\ \mu_2 \\ \mu_3 \\ \mu_4 \\ \mu_5 \end{bmatrix} = \begin{bmatrix} \beta_0 \\ \beta_0 + \beta_1 + \beta_2 \\ \beta_0 + 2\beta_1 + 4\beta_2 \\ \beta_0 + 3\beta_1 + 9\beta_2 \\ \beta_0 + 4\beta_1 + 16\beta_2 \end{bmatrix}.
$$

We can calculate the mean differences between two consecutive time points and obtain the linear change rates;

$$
C_1\mu = \begin{bmatrix} -1 & 1 & 0 & 0 & 0 \\ 0 & -1 & 1 & 0 & 0 \\ 0 & 0 & -1 & 1 & 0 \\ 0 & 0 & 0 & -1 & 1 \end{bmatrix} \begin{bmatrix} \mu_1 \\ \mu_2 \\ \mu_3 \\ \mu_4 \\ \mu_5 \end{bmatrix}
$$

$$
= \begin{bmatrix} \mu_2 - \mu_1 \\ \mu_3 - \mu_2 \\ \mu_4 - \mu_3 \\ \mu_5 - \mu_4 \end{bmatrix} = \begin{bmatrix} \mu_{d1} \\ \mu_{d2} \\ \mu_{d3} \\ \mu_{d4} \end{bmatrix} = \begin{bmatrix} \beta_1 + \beta_2 \\ \beta_1 + 3\beta_2 \\ \beta_1 + 5\beta_2 \\ \beta_1 + 7\beta_2 \end{bmatrix}.
$$

We can concisely write this as

$$
\mu_d = \begin{bmatrix} \mu_{d1} \\ \mu_{d2} \\ \mu_{d3} \\ \mu_{d4} \end{bmatrix} = \begin{bmatrix} \beta_1 + \beta_2 \\ \beta_1 + 3\beta_2 \\ \beta_1 + 5\beta_2 \\ \beta_1 + 7\beta_2 \end{bmatrix}.
$$

The last column shows the linear change rates, which differ over time, owing to the quadratic change β_2. The differentials between two consecutive linear change rates are $2\beta_2$,

$$
C_2\mu_d = \begin{bmatrix} -1 & 1 & 0 & 0 \\ 0 & -1 & 1 & 0 \\ 0 & 0 & -1 & 1 \end{bmatrix} \begin{bmatrix} \mu_{d1} \\ \mu_{d2} \\ \mu_{d3} \\ \mu_{d4} \end{bmatrix} = \begin{bmatrix} \mu_{d2} - \mu_{d1} \\ \mu_{d3} - \mu_{d2} \\ \mu_{d4} - \mu_{d3} \end{bmatrix} = \begin{bmatrix} 2\beta_2 \\ 2\beta_2 \\ 2\beta_2 \end{bmatrix}.
$$

Since $\mu_d = C_1\mu$, we can write the quadratic changes as

$$
C_2C_1\mu = \begin{bmatrix} 2\beta_2 \\ 2\beta_2 \\ 2\beta_2 \end{bmatrix}. \tag{11.15}
$$

We may estimate the quadratic changes through the sample means $\hat{\mu}$, which assume a multivariate normal distribution.

The test for the quadratic change is a Hotelling T^2 statistic because its estimate also has a multivariate normal distribution,

$$
\begin{bmatrix} 2\hat{\beta}_2 \\ 2\hat{\beta}_2 \\ 2\hat{\beta}_2 \end{bmatrix} = C_2C_1\hat{\mu} \sim N(C_2C_1\mu, (C_2C_1)\Sigma(C_2C_1)'). \tag{11.16}
$$

The Hotelling T^2 test for the quadratic change in one-group study is

$$
T^2 = n(C\hat{\mu})'(C\Sigma C')^{-1}(C\hat{\mu}), \tag{11.17}
$$

where $C = C_2C_1$.

The statistical power for testing a non-zero quadratic change β_2 is calculated by converting the Hotelling T^2 to a non-central F.

$$
\frac{n-p+2}{(n-1)(p-2)}T^2 = F'(p-2, n-p+2, \lambda), \tag{11.18}
$$

where the non-centrality parameter λ is

$$
\begin{aligned}
\lambda &= n(C_2C_1\mu)'(C_2C_1\Sigma(C_2C_1)')^{-1}(C_2C_1\mu) \\
&= 4n\beta_2^2 \mathbf{1}'(C\Sigma C')^{-1}\mathbf{1}. \tag{11.19}
\end{aligned}
$$

In computing statistical power, we evaluate the cumulative distribution function of the non-central F,

$$1 - \beta = 1 - P[F'(p-2, n-p+2, \lambda) < F_{1-\alpha, p-2, n-p+2}]. \qquad (11.20)$$

For example, a researcher wants to examine the change in calcium loss among older women. In the study, calcium measurements of dominant elbow bone will be taken initially and then after one year, two years, and three years. There are four repeated measures of calcium altogether ($p = 4$). The researcher intends to test whether the change among the four repeated measures exhibits quadratic curvature. A previous study of similar nature (see Table 6.5, Johnson and Wichern, 2002) shows that the quadratic change is -1.96 ($\beta_2 = -1.96$). The estimated covariance matrix Σ is

$$\Sigma = \begin{bmatrix} 92.118857 & 86.110571 & 73.362286 & 74.589 \\ 86.110571 & 89.076381 & 72.955524 & 71.772762 \\ 73.362286 & 72.955524 & 71.890667 & 63.591762 \\ 74.589 & 71.772762 & 63.591762 & 75.444095 \end{bmatrix}.$$

If there are nine older women in the study ($n = 9$), the statistical power for testing the quadratic change will be .86. Alternatively, we can assume compound symmetry for the covariance matrix Σ, which appears tenable in view of the actual correlation matrix. We will use the median of the correlations .9 and the median standard deviation of the four repeated measures 9.0 to compute the covariance matrix Σ. We will obtain a very similar power value, .84.

$$\Sigma = \begin{bmatrix} 9 & 0 & 0 & 0 \\ 0 & 9 & 0 & 0 \\ 0 & 0 & 9 & 0 \\ 0 & 0 & 0 & 9 \end{bmatrix} \begin{bmatrix} 1 & .9 & .9 & .9 \\ .9 & 1 & .9 & .9 \\ .9 & .9 & 1 & .9 \\ .9 & .9 & .9 & 1 \end{bmatrix} \begin{bmatrix} 9 & 0 & 0 & 0 \\ 0 & 9 & 0 & 0 \\ 0 & 0 & 9 & 0 \\ 0 & 0 & 0 & 9 \end{bmatrix}$$

The relevant R code is:

```
# multivariate analysis of quadratic change in one group

C1=matrix(c(-1,1,0,0,
            0,-1,1,0,
            0,0,-1,1),
```

```
                  nrow=3,byrow=TRUE)
C2=matrix(c(-1,1,0,
               0,-1,1),
            nrow=2,byrow=TRUE)


C=C2%*%C1


E=matrix(c(1289.664, 1205.548, 1027.072, 1044.246,
            1205.548, 1247.069333, 1021.377333, 1004.818667,
     1027.072, 1021.377333, 1006.469333, 890.2846667,
     1044.246, 1004.818667, 890.2846667, 1056.217333),
         nrow=4,byrow=TRUE)


S=E/(15-1)


#approximate correlation matrix of compound symmetry


#sd=9; r=0.9


#D=diag(rep(sd,4))
#R=matrix( c(1, r, r, r,
#              r, 1, r, r,
#              r, r, 1, r,
#              r, r, r, 1), nrow=4,byrow=TRUE)


#S=D%*%R%*%D


CSC=C%*%S%*%t(C)


p4maovq=function(n=9,beta2=-1.96,CSC){
a=.05
p=nrow(CSC)+2

j=matrix(rep(1,p-2),nrow=p-2)
lambda=4*n*beta2^2*(t(j)%*%solve(CSC)%*%j)

f0=qf(1-a,p-2,n-p+2)
```

```
1-pf(f0,p-2,n-p+2,lambda)
}

p4maovq(,,CSC)
```

The SAS program is:

```
*multivariate analysis of quadratic change in one group;

proc iml;
C1={-1 1 0 0 ,
    0 -1 1 0 ,
0 0 -1 1 };
C2={-1 1 0,
    0 -1 1};
C=C2*C1;

E={
1289.664 1205.548 1027.072 1044.246,
1205.548 1247.069333 1021.377333 1004.818667,
1027.072 1021.377333 1006.469333 890.2846667,
1044.246 1004.818667 890.2846667 1056.217333};
S=E/14;

CSC=C*S*t(C);

n=9;
beta2=-1.96;
a=.05;
p=nrow(CSC)+2;

j=J(p-2,1,1);
lambda=4*n*beta2**2*(t(j)*inv(CSC)*j);

f0=finv(1-a,p-2,n-p+2);
power=1-probf(f0,p-2,n-p+2,lambda);
print power;
```

```
quit;
```

The SPSS code is:

```
* multivariate analysis of quadratic change in one group.

MATRIX.
COMPUTE C1={-1,1,0,0;
            0,-1,1,0;
            0,0,-1,1}.
COMPUTE C2={-1,1,0;
            0,-1,1}.
COMPUTE C=C2*C1.

COMPUTE E={
1289.664,1205.548,1027.072,1044.246;
1205.548,1247.069333,1021.377333,1004.818667;
1027.072,1021.377333,1006.469333,890.2846667;
1044.246,1004.818667,890.2846667,1056.217333}.
COMPUTE S=E/14.
COMPUTE CSC=C*S*T(C).

COMPUTE N=9.
COMPUTE BETA2=-1.96.
COMPUTE P=NROW(CSC)+2.
COMPUTE J=MAKE(P-2,1,1).
COMPUTE LAMBDA=4*N*BETA2**2*(T(J)*INV(CSC)*J).

SAVE {N,P,BETA2,LAMBDA}
     /OUTFILE=*/VARIABLES=N P BETA2 LAMBDA.
END MATRIX.

COMPUTE A=.05.
COMPUTE F0=IDF.F(1-A,P-2,N-P+2).
COMPUTE POWER=1-NCDF.F(F0,P-2,N-P+2,LAMBDA).
EXECUTE.
```

11.2 HLM: Fixed Coefficient for Slope

Linear change is the basic trend of interest in longitudinal studies because it appeals to our common sense. When we inquire about longitudinal studies, we want to know what increase or decrease in the outcome measure corresponds to the change in time or treatment conditions. For instance, an educational researcher might ask how much learning has taken place since a student progressed from one grade to another. A medical researcher might want to learn by how much the patients' testosterone level can be elevated on average for an increase in the intake dosage.

The repeated measures on an individual subject can be regressed on the predictor of time t, and the regression coefficient for the predictor time represents the average outcome change for each unit increment in time, specific to an individual subject. This becomes the level-1 equation in the HLM formation. At level 1, the regression equation is

$$Y_{ti} = \pi_{0i} + \pi_{1i}t + e_{ti}, \ e_{ti} \sim N(0, \sigma^2), \tag{11.21}$$

where Y_{ti} is the observation on the ith subject at the tth time point or treatment, π_{0i} is the intercept, π_{1i} is the slope or the linear change rate, and e_{ti} is the residual error. The predictor t can represent either different time points or different treatments administered to the same subject over time. For illustration, we can assume five time points or five increasing levels of dosage. The predictor t can take 0, 1, 2, 3, and 4 for the five occasions. It is obvious that the slope β_{1i} measures the linear change rate in the outcome for one unit progress in time.

For the ith subject, the level-1 regression in matrix notation is simply

$$y_i = A\pi_i + e_i \tag{11.22}$$

$$\begin{bmatrix} Y_{0i} \\ Y_{1i} \\ Y_{2i} \\ Y_{3i} \\ Y_{4i} \end{bmatrix} = \begin{bmatrix} 1 & 0 \\ 1 & 1 \\ 1 & 2 \\ 1 & 3 \\ 1 & 4 \end{bmatrix} \begin{bmatrix} \pi_{0i} \\ \pi_{1i} \end{bmatrix} + \begin{bmatrix} e_{0i} \\ e_{1i} \\ e_{2i} \\ e_{3i} \\ e_{4i} \end{bmatrix}. \tag{11.23}$$

The first column of the matrix A is a unit column; the second column of the matrix A contains the constants for t. The two columns are not orthogonal to each other.

We can change the constants for t and make it orthogonal to the first column. By doing so, we can obtain the least squares estimate of π_{1i} in a simpler form without changing its meaning. Specifically, we can let $\mathbf{1}$ stand for the first column of A and use t for the second column. We can obtain the following z_1 to replace the second column t,

$$z_1 = t - \frac{\sum\limits_{t=0}^{4} t}{5} \mathbf{1} \tag{11.24}$$

$$= \begin{bmatrix} 0-2 \\ 1-2 \\ 2-2 \\ 3-2 \\ 4-2 \end{bmatrix} = \begin{bmatrix} -2 \\ -1 \\ 0 \\ 1 \\ 2 \end{bmatrix}. \tag{11.25}$$

The new matrix Z with the second column z_1 is

$$Z = \begin{bmatrix} 1 & -2 \\ 1 & -1 \\ 1 & 0 \\ 1 & 1 \\ 1 & 2 \end{bmatrix}. \tag{11.26}$$

The two columns are now orthogonal to each other. The level-1 equation in matrix form becomes

$$y_i = Z\pi_i + e_i \tag{11.27}$$

$$= \begin{bmatrix} \mathbf{1} & z_1 \end{bmatrix} \pi_i + e_i \tag{11.28}$$

$$\begin{bmatrix} Y_{0i} \\ Y_{1i} \\ Y_{2i} \\ Y_{3i} \\ Y_{4i} \end{bmatrix} = \begin{bmatrix} 1 & -2 \\ 1 & -1 \\ 1 & 0 \\ 1 & 1 \\ 1 & 2 \end{bmatrix} \begin{bmatrix} \pi_{0i} \\ \pi_{1i} \end{bmatrix} + \begin{bmatrix} e_{0i} \\ e_{1i} \\ e_{2i} \\ e_{3i} \\ e_{4i} \end{bmatrix}. \tag{11.29}$$

In effect, we have just centered the second column around its own mean. The centered column is orthogonal to the first column, but the slope π_{1i} still represents the linear change rate for a unit increase in time.

The least squares estimate of the slope based on the data from the ith subject is

$$\hat{\beta}_{1i} = (z_1'z_1)^{-1}z_1'y_i \qquad (11.30)$$

$$= \frac{\sum\limits_{t=0}^{4} z_{t1}Y_{ti}}{\sum\limits_{t=0}^{4} z_{t1}^2}, \qquad (11.31)$$

where the z_{t1} are the constants in the column z_1. The level-1 equation expressed in centered values z_{t1} is

$$Y_{ti} = \pi_{0i} + \pi_{1i}z_{t1} + e_{ti}. \qquad (11.32)$$

In the simplest HLM model, we can assume that the linear change, π_{1i}, is fixed for every subject, and that the random intercept varies from one subject to the other. The level-2 equations are

$$\pi_{0i} = \beta_{00} + r_{0i}, \; r_{0i} \sim N(0, \tau) \qquad (11.33)$$
$$\pi_{1i} = \beta_{10}. \qquad (11.34)$$

The random intercept comprises a grand mean β_{00} and a subject-specific random effect r_{0i}, which has a normal distribution with a zero mean and a variance τ. The linear change rate is fixed at β_{10} for every subject.

Substituting the level-2 equations into the level-1 equation yields the combined model,

$$Y_{ti} = \beta_{00} + \beta_{10}z_{t1} + r_{0i} + e_{ti}. \qquad (11.35)$$

We can group the two random effects into a single term. Although the single random term is complex, the combined model can be deemed a special case of the regular linear model, that is,

$$Y_{ij} = \beta_{00} + \beta_{10}z_{t1} + e_{ti}^*, \qquad (11.36)$$

where $e_{ti}^* = r_{0i} + e_{ti}$. It is obvious that the new combined model is subsumed under a linear model. We can therefore use the weighted least squares estimation to estimate β_{00} and β_{10} if we know the variance covariance matrix of y_i.

The variance covariance matrix of y_i has compound symmetry, with diagonal elements $\sigma^2 + \tau$ and off-diagonal elements τ. The diagonal elements are the variance of Y_{ti}, that is,

$$Var(Y_{ti}) = Var(r_{0i} + e_{ti}) = \tau + \sigma^2. \tag{11.37}$$

The off-diagonal elements are the covariance between Y_{ti} and $Y_{t'i}$, which are repeated measures on the tth and t'th occasions or treatment conditions,

$$
\begin{aligned}
Cov(Y_{ti}, Y_{t'i}) &= Cov(e_{ti}^*, e_{t'i}^*) \\
&= Cov(r_{0i} + e_{ti}, r_{0i} + e_{t'i}) \\
&= \tau.
\end{aligned} \tag{11.38}
$$

Note that the covariance between r_{0i} and itself is the variance of r_{0i} or $Cov(r_{0i}, r_{0i}) = \tau$. The two residual errors e_{ti} and $e_{t'i}$ are not correlated. In other words, they have no covariance. The correlation between Y_{ti} and $Y_{t'i}$ is the covariance divided by their respective standard deviations ($\sqrt{Var(Y_{ti})} = \sqrt{\tau + \sigma^2}$ and $\sqrt{Var(Y_{t'i})} = \sqrt{\tau + \sigma^2}$). The correlation between Y_{ti} and $Y_{t'i}$ is, therefore,

$$\rho = \frac{Cov(Y_{ti}, Y_{t'i})}{\sqrt{Var(Y_{ti})Var(Y_{t'i})}} = \frac{\tau}{\tau + \sigma^2}. \tag{11.39}$$

Suppose that there are five time points or five treatments administered on five different occasions. We let V_i stand for the variance covariance matrix of y_i;

$$V_i = \begin{bmatrix} \tau + \sigma^2 & \tau & \tau & \tau & \tau \\ \tau & \tau + \sigma^2 & \tau & \tau & \tau \\ \tau & \tau & \tau + \sigma^2 & \tau & \tau \\ \tau & \tau & \tau & \tau + \sigma^2 & \tau \\ \tau & \tau & \tau & \tau & \tau + \sigma^2 \end{bmatrix} \tag{11.40}$$

$$= (\tau + \sigma^2) \begin{bmatrix} 1 & \rho & \rho & \rho & \rho \\ \rho & 1 & \rho & \rho & \rho \\ \rho & \rho & 1 & \rho & \rho \\ \rho & \rho & \rho & 1 & \rho \\ \rho & \rho & \rho & \rho & 1 \end{bmatrix}. \tag{11.41}$$

The variance covariance matrix V_i is the same for every subject, and it makes it easy to present the weighted least squares estimates in a simple form. The weighted least square estimates of β_{00} and β_{10} (see proof in Liu, 2013b) are

$$\begin{bmatrix} \hat{\beta}_{00} \\ \hat{\beta}_{10} \end{bmatrix} = \left(\sum_{i=1}^{n} Z' V_i^{-1} Z \right)^{-1} \left(\sum_{i=1}^{n} Z' V_i^{-1} y_i \right) \tag{11.42}$$

$$= \frac{1}{n} \sum_{i=1}^{n} (Z'Z)^{-1} Z' y_i. \tag{11.43}$$

The estimators $\hat{\beta}_{00}$ and $\hat{\beta}_{10}$ are invariant to the variance covariance matrix V_i. It is easy to see that $(Z'Z)^{-1} Z' y_i$ is simply the least squares estimates of π_{0i} and π_{1i},

$$\begin{bmatrix} \hat{\pi}_{0i} \\ \hat{\pi}_{1i} \end{bmatrix} = (Z'Z)^{-1} Z' y_i. \tag{11.44}$$

In particular,

$$\hat{\beta}_{10} = \frac{1}{n} \sum_{i=1}^{n} \hat{\pi}_{1i} \tag{11.45}$$

$$= \frac{1}{n} \sum_{i=1}^{n} \frac{\sum_{t=0}^{4} z_{t1} Y_{ti}}{\sum_{t=0}^{4} z_{t1}^2}. \tag{11.46}$$

The variance of $\hat{\beta}_{10}$ can be derived from the variance of $\hat{\pi}_{1i}$,

$$Var(\hat{\beta}_{10}) = \frac{1}{n} Var(\hat{\pi}_{1i}). \tag{11.47}$$

Since

$$\hat{\pi}_{1i} = \frac{\sum_{t=0}^{4} z_{t1} Y_{ti}}{\sum_{t=0}^{4} z_{t1}^2}$$

in Equation 11.31, we have

$$Var(\hat{\pi}_{1i}) = \frac{\sum\limits_{t=0}^{4} z_{t1}^2 Var(Y_{ti}) + 2 \sum\limits_{t \neq t'}^{4} z_{t1} z_{t'1} Cov(Y_{ti}, Y_{t'i})}{\left(\sum\limits_{t=0}^{4} z_{t1}^2 \right)^2}. \tag{11.48}$$

The numerator of the variance of $\hat{\pi}_{1i}$ can be expressed concisely in matrix notation;

$$z_1' V_i z_1 = \sum\limits_{t=0}^{4} z_{t1}^2 Var(Y_{ti}) + 2 \sum\limits_{t \neq t'}^{4} z_{t1} z_{t'1} Cov(Y_{ti}, Y_{t'i}) \tag{11.49}$$

$$= \sum\limits_{t=0}^{4} z_{t1}^2 \sigma^2. \tag{11.50}$$

The variance of $\hat{\pi}_{1i}$ is

$$Var(\hat{\pi}_{1i}) = \frac{\sigma^2}{\sum\limits_{t=0}^{m} z_{t1}^2}.$$

Therefore, we can obtain the variance of $\hat{\beta}_{10}$,

$$Var(\hat{\beta}_{10}) = \frac{\sigma^2}{n \sum\limits_{t=0}^{m} z_{t1}^2}, \tag{11.51}$$

where $m + 1$ is the total number of repeated measures per subject. The estimator of $Var(\hat{\beta}_{10})$ can be based on the maximum likelihood estimator of the residual variance $\hat{\sigma}^2$, which is the residual sum of squares divided by its degrees of freedom,

$$\hat{\sigma}^2 = \frac{\sum\limits_{i=1}^{n} \sum\limits_{t=0}^{m} (Y_{ti} - \hat{Y}_{ti})^2}{(n-1)m}. \tag{11.52}$$

It follows that

$$\widehat{Var}(\hat{\beta}_{10}) = \frac{\hat{\sigma}^2}{n \sum\limits_{t=0}^{m} z_{t1}^2}. \tag{11.53}$$

The statistic for testing the linear change rate β_{10} uses a t test,

$$T = \frac{\hat{\beta}_{10}}{\sqrt{\widehat{Var}(\hat{\beta}_{10})}}. \tag{11.54}$$

The t statistic has a central t distribution with $(n-1)m$ degrees of freedom when the null hypothesis is true. The null hypothesis states that there is no linear change present ($H_0 : \beta_{10} = 0$). If the t statistic is squared, it becomes an F test with one degree of freedom in the numerator and $(n-1)m$ degrees of freedom in the denominator. This is the same F test for a linear trend as in the randomized block design. So the randomized block design is a special case of the random coefficients model, in which the slope is fixed but the intercept is allowed to vary randomly from one subject to the other.

In the presence of a linear change, the alternative hypothesis will hold true ($H_a : \beta_{10} \neq 0$). Under the alternative hypothesis, the t statistic follows a non-central t distribution T' with $(n-1)m$ degrees of freedom and non-centrality parameter λ. The non-centrality parameter is obtained by replacing the estimates in the t statistic with their population counterparts;

$$\lambda = \frac{\beta_{10}}{\sqrt{Var(\hat{\beta}_{10})}}$$

$$= \frac{\beta_{10}}{\sqrt{\frac{\sigma^2}{n \sum_{t=0}^{m} z_{t1}^2}}}. \tag{11.55}$$

The statistical power for testing the linear change in a two-sided test is the probability of obtaining a t statistic exceeding the critical value,

$$1 - \beta = P[|T'((n-1)m, \lambda)| \geq t_0], \tag{11.56}$$

where the critical t value is $t_0 = t_{1-\alpha/2,(n-1)m}$. For a one-sided test with a positive linear trend in the alternative hypothesis, the power is

$$1 - \beta = P[T'((n-1)m, \lambda) \geq t_{1-\alpha,(n-1)m}]. \tag{11.57}$$

This discussion concerned the linear change in one group of subjects. When there are two groups, the key interest lies in a comparison of linear change between the two groups. For example, a group of students might receive extra help in their academic studies, while another group of students do not get such help. An educational researcher might wonder if the extra help improves students' learning, as measured by the change or progress in students' academic achievement. In a drug test, a medical researcher will want to learn whether the absorption rate of the chemical contents differs between the reference and generic drug formulations as the dosage increases. These questions essentially call for a comparison of linear change rates between the two groups.

We can extend the one-group situation to the comparison of two groups because the two groups can often be assumed to be independent of each other in a randomized controlled trial. The estimator of the linear change rate in each group follows the same approach as that in the one-group situation. Suppose that there are two groups involved in the repeated measures design. One group is in the treatment condition, and the other in the control condition. The two groups are formed by random assignment, with each having an equal number of subjects. For simplicity of explanation, we assume that the group sizes are both equal to $n/2$. The linear change rate for the treatment group is denoted $\hat{\beta}_{10e}$, and the linear change rate for the control group is $\hat{\beta}_{10c}$. The two estimators are independent but share a common variance,

$$Var(\hat{\beta}_{10e}) = Var(\hat{\beta}_{10c}) = \frac{\sigma^2}{\frac{n}{2} \sum_{t=0}^{m} z_{t1}^2}. \tag{11.58}$$

To compare the linear change rate between the two groups, we can take the difference between $\hat{\beta}_{10e}$ and $\hat{\beta}_{10c}$,

$$\hat{\beta}_{11} = \hat{\beta}_{10e} - \hat{\beta}_{10c}. \tag{11.59}$$

The parameter β_{11} represents difference in linear change between the two groups in the level-2 equation in the HLM model. The level-2 equations now become

$$\pi_{0i} = \beta_{00} + r_{0i}, \; r_{0i} \sim N(0, \tau) \tag{11.60}$$

$$\pi_{1i} = \beta_{10} + \beta_{11} X_i, \tag{11.61}$$

where the level-2 predictor X_i shows whether the subject is randomly assigned to the treatment or the control condition. The variable X_i takes .5

for a subject in the treatment condition and $-.5$ for a subject in the control condition. The variance of the estimated difference in linear change is

$$Var(\hat{\beta}_{11}) = Var(\hat{\beta}_{10e}) + Var(\hat{\beta}_{10c})$$

$$= \frac{4\sigma^2}{n \sum\limits_{t=0}^{m} z_{t1}^2}. \tag{11.62}$$

The estimator of $Var(\hat{\beta}_{11})$ can be obtained by finding an estimator for the residual variance σ^2.

To estimate σ^2, we can calculate the residual sum of squares for each group, pool the two sums of squares together, and divide the pooled sums of squares by the sum of their respective degrees of freedom,

$$\hat{\sigma}^2 = \frac{(\frac{n}{2} - 1)m\hat{\sigma}_e^2 + (\frac{n}{2} - 1)m\hat{\sigma}_c^2}{(n-2)m} = \frac{\hat{\sigma}_e^2 + \hat{\sigma}_c^2}{2}, \tag{11.63}$$

where $\hat{\sigma}_e^2$ and $\hat{\sigma}_c^2$ are the residual sums of squares over the degrees of freedom for the treatment and control group, respectively (see Equation 11.52). Replacing σ^2 with its estimator in $Var(\hat{\beta}_{11})$ yields

$$\widehat{Var}(\hat{\beta}_{11}) = \frac{4\hat{\sigma}^2}{n \sum\limits_{t=0}^{m} z_{t1}^2}. \tag{11.64}$$

Since we have found the estimate of the difference in linear change and its variance, we can compute a t test to examine whether the two groups differ in the linear trend. The t test is the ratio of $\hat{\beta}_{11}$ and its estimated standard error $\sqrt{\widehat{Var}(\hat{\beta}_{11})}$,

$$T = \frac{\hat{\beta}_{11}}{\sqrt{\widehat{Var}(\hat{\beta}_{11})}}. \tag{11.65}$$

The t statistic has a central t distribution with $(n-2)m$ degrees of freedom when the null hypothesis is true ($H_0 : \beta_{11} = 0$). Under the alternative hypothesis, the t test has a non-central t distribution T' with a non-centrality parameter λ,

$$\lambda = \frac{\beta_{11}}{\sqrt{Var(\hat{\beta}_{11})}}. \tag{11.66}$$

The statistical power in a two-sided test for the difference in linear change is

$$1 - \beta = P[|T'((n-2)m, \lambda)| \geq t_0]$$
$$= 1 - P[T'((n-2)m, \lambda) < t_0] + P[T'((n-2)m, \lambda) \leq -t_0], \quad (11.67)$$

where the critical value t_0 is $t_{1-\alpha/2,(n-2)m}$. The statistical power in a one-sided test with a positive difference ($H_a : \beta_{11} > 0$) is

$$1 - \beta = 1 - P[T'((n-2)m, \lambda) < t_{1-\alpha,(n-2)m}]. \quad (11.68)$$

11.3   HLM: Random Coefficients Model

We will start with repeated measures of one group and then extend it to two-group comparison in testing a linear change. Quadratic and cubic changes (i.e., higher-order polynomial changes) will be introduced afterwards.

The general hierarchical linear model (HLM) for growth curves can be represented in a multi-level fashion. The level-1 equation models the repeated measures Y_{ti} over time for the ith individual,

$$Y_{ti} = \pi_{0i} + \pi_{1i}t + \pi_{2i}t^2 + \pi_{3i}t^3 + e_{ti}, \quad (11.69)$$

where π_{0i} is the intercept, and π_{1i}, π_{2i}, and π_{3i} represent the linear, quadratic, and cubic changes. The predictor is the time point $t = 0, 1, 2, \cdots, m$. The linear, quadratic, and cubic changes can be regressed on the level-2 predictor X_{qi} (e.g., treatment assignment),

$$\pi_{pi} = \beta_{p0} + \sum_{q=1}^{Q_p} \beta_{pq} X_{qi} + r_{pi}, \quad (11.70)$$

where the subscript p indicates the order of the change (π_{1i} for linear change, π_{2i} for quadratic change, and π_{3i} for cubic change), β_{pq} is the regression coefficient for the qth level-2 predictor in the level-2 equation for the pth order change. For example, the level-2 equation for the linear change is

$$\pi_{1i} = \beta_{10} + \beta_{11} X_{1i} + r_{1i}.$$

The level-2 predictor X_{1i} can be treatment assignment, which differentiates individuals in the treatment group from those in the control group. The level-2 residual error is r_{1i}. If there is only one group, the level-2 equation can be simplified to

$$\pi_{1i} = \beta_{10} + r_{1i}.$$

11.3.1 Linear Change

The fixed slope or linear change is not as common as the random slope, which varies from one individual to another. This befits what we often observe in our data. For instance, students can learn at different rates. Their cognitive development may vary from person to person. The random slope or linear change naturally reflects such individual differences in human development. So the random slope is used more often than the fixed linear change.

The random slope uses the same level-1 equation, $Y_{ti} = \pi_{0i} + \pi_{1i}t + e_{ti}$. For consistency, we will center the time points t.

$$\text{At level 1:} \quad Y_{ti} = \pi_{0i} + \pi_{1i}z_{t1} + e_{ti}, \; e_{ti} \sim N(0, \sigma^2)$$
$$t: 0, 1, 2, \cdots, m, \tag{11.71}$$

where $z_{1t} = t - \sum_{t=0}^{m} t/m$. In matrix notation, the level-1 equation becomes

$$y_i = \begin{bmatrix} 1 & z_1 \end{bmatrix} \begin{bmatrix} \pi_{0i} \\ \pi_{1i} \end{bmatrix} + e_i. \tag{11.72}$$

When there are five repeated observations ($m = 4$), the vector z_1 becomes $z_1' = [-2 \; -1 \; 0 \; 1 \; 2]$. As the vector $\mathbf{1}$ is orthogonal to the vector z_1, this greatly simplifies the formulas for estimating its coefficient π_{1i}.

The least squares estimate of the linear change for the ith individual is

$$\hat{\pi}_{1i} = \frac{z_1' y_i}{\|z_1\|^2}$$

$$= \frac{\displaystyle\sum_{t=0}^{m} z_{t1} Y_{ti}}{\displaystyle\sum_{t=0}^{m} z_{t1}^2}. \tag{11.73}$$

The variance of the least squares estimate $\hat{\pi}_{1i}$ is

$$Var(\hat{\pi}_{1i}|i) = \frac{\sigma^2}{\sum\limits_{t=0}^{m} z_{t1}^2}. \tag{11.74}$$

This is a conditional variance conditioning on the ith individual. The conditional variance shows how much the estimate $\hat{\pi}_{1i}$ varies from the true linear change π_{1i} of the ith individual, $Var(\hat{\pi}_{1i}|i) = Var(\hat{\pi}_{1i} - \pi_{1i})$.

The true linear change π_{1i} of the ith individual is the outcome of the level-2 equation with a level-2 predictor of treatment assignment X_{1i}.

At level 2: $\pi_{1i} = \beta_{10} + \beta_{11}X_{1i} + r_{1i}, \; r_{1i} \sim N(0, \tau_1),$ (11.75)

where X_{1i} takes .5 for an individual in the treatment condition and $-.5$ for an individual in the control condition. The average linear change is β_{10}, and β_{11} represents the average difference in linear change (e.g., cognitive growth) between the treatment and control conditions.

To estimate the average linear change, we can compute the mean of the linear change rates for all the individuals,

$$\hat{\beta}_{10} = \frac{\sum\limits_{i=1}^{n} \hat{\pi}_{1i}}{n}. \tag{11.76}$$

The variance of the estimate is

$$Var(\hat{\beta}_{10}) = \frac{Var(\hat{\pi}_{1i})}{n}. \tag{11.77}$$

To find the variance $Var(\hat{\pi}_{1i})$, we note (Raudenbush and Liu, 2001, p.390) that

$$\hat{\pi}_{1i} = \pi_{1i} + (\hat{\pi}_{1i} - \pi_{1i})$$
$$= \beta_{10} + \beta_{11}X_{1i} + r_{1i} + (\hat{\pi}_{1i} - \pi_{1i})$$

Thus, we have the variance $Var(\hat{\pi}_{1i})$,

$$Var(\hat{\pi}_{1i}) = Var(r_{1i}) + Var(\hat{\pi}_{1i} - \pi_{1i})$$
$$= Var(r_{1i}) + Var(\hat{\pi}_{1i}|i)$$
$$= \tau_1 + \frac{\sigma^2}{\sum\limits_{t=0}^{m} z_{t1}^2}. \tag{11.78}$$

The unbiased estimate of $Var(\hat{\pi}_{1i})$ in a balanced design is

$$\widehat{Var}(\hat{\pi}_{1i}) = \frac{\sum_{i=1}^{n/2}\left(\hat{\pi}_{1i} - \frac{\sum_{i=1}^{n/2}\hat{\pi}_{1i}}{n/2}\right)^2 + \sum_{i=n/2+1}^{n}\left(\hat{\pi}_{1i} - \frac{\sum_{i=n/2+1}^{n}\hat{\pi}_{1i}}{n/2}\right)^2}{n-2}.$$

(11.79)

The test for $H_0 : \beta_{10} = 0$ uses a t statistic with $n - 2$ degrees of freedom,

$$T = \frac{\hat{\beta}_{10}}{\sqrt{\frac{\widehat{Var}(\hat{\pi}_{1i})}{n}}}.$$

(11.80)

When the alternative hypothesis $H_a : \beta_{10} \neq 0$ is true, the t statistic has a non-central t distribution with $n - 2$ degrees of freedom and non-centrality parameter λ,

$$\begin{aligned}
\lambda &= \frac{\sqrt{n}\beta_{10}}{\sqrt{Var(\hat{\pi}_{1i})}} \\
&= \frac{\sqrt{n}\beta_{10}}{\sqrt{\tau_1 + \frac{\sigma^2}{\sum_{t=0}^{m} z_{1t}^2}}}.
\end{aligned}$$

(11.81)

The statistical power for testing β_{10} is

$$1 - \beta = P[|T'(n-2,\lambda)| \geq t_{1-\alpha/2,n-2}].$$

(11.82)

However, the key interest lies in the average difference in linear change between the treatment and control conditions or β_{11}. To estimate β_{11}, we average the linear change rates of all the individuals in the treatment group and then average the linear change rates of those in the control group. Their difference is $\hat{\beta}_{11}$,

$$\hat{\beta}_{11} = \frac{\sum_{i=1}^{n/2}\hat{\pi}_{1i}}{n/2} - \frac{\sum_{i=n/2+1}^{n}\hat{\pi}_{1i}}{n/2}.$$

(11.83)

$\{i : 1, 2, \cdots, n/2\} \in$ treatment $\{i : n/2+1, 2, \cdots, n\} \in$ control.

Its variance is

$$Var(\hat{\beta}_{11}) = \frac{4Var(\hat{\pi}_{1i})}{n}. \tag{11.84}$$

Using the sample estimate $\widehat{Var}(\hat{\pi}_{1i})$ in Equation 11.79, we can obtain the sample estimate of the variance of the difference in linear change between the treatment and control condition,

$$\widehat{Var}(\hat{\beta}_{11}) = \frac{4\widehat{Var}(\hat{\pi}_{1i})}{n}.$$

The test for the difference in linear change uses a t statistic,

$$T = \frac{\hat{\beta}_{11}}{\sqrt{\widehat{Var}(\hat{\beta}_{11})}}. \tag{11.85}$$

The t statistic has a central t distribution with $n - 2$ degrees of freedom when there is no difference in linear change between the treatment and control conditions ($H_0 : \beta_{11} = 0$). When the alternative hypothesis is true ($H_a : \beta_{11} \neq 0$), the t statistic follows a non-central t distribution, namely, $T'(n - 2, \lambda)$. Its non-centrality parameter is

$$\lambda = \frac{\beta_{11}}{\sqrt{Var(\hat{\beta}_{11})}}$$

$$= \sqrt{\frac{n}{4}} \frac{\beta_{11}}{\sqrt{\tau_1 + \frac{\sigma^2}{\sum\limits_{t=0}^{m} z_{1t}^2}}}. \tag{11.86}$$

Under the alternative hypothesis $H_a : \beta_{11} \neq 0$, the statistical power in a two-sided test is

$$1 - \beta = 1 - P[T'(n - 2, \lambda) < t_{1-\alpha/2,n-2}] + P[T'(n - 2, \lambda) < t_{\alpha/2,n-2}]. \tag{11.87}$$

For example, an educational researcher plans to design a longitudinal study on children's cognitive growth in the US Head Start Program. The researcher is interested in examining whether non-English speaking children benefit more than English-speaking children in the Head Start Program, despite the fact that non-English speaking children might start with lower achievement than English-speaking children. All the participating children in the study will be tested on their natural science knowledge on four different occasions ($m = 3$) evenly spaced during a one-year study. The measures will be obtained using item response theory analysis of test items, and are represented in a logit metric, which defines the subject's ability as the log of the odds ratio of a correct response to test items (Raudenbush and Bryk, 2002, p.164). The logit metric can be viewed as approximately continuous and normal. We may obtain the parameter estimates from Tables 6.1, 6.2, and 6.3 in Raudenbush and Bryk (2002). The difference in linear growth rates between non-English and English speaking children averages about .187 between two consecutive time points ($\beta_{11} = .187$). The effect size amounts to a difference $.187 \times 3 = .561$ in logit metric at the end of the study, which has three time periods punctuated by four occasions of measurement. We may also obtain the variance estimates, $\sigma^2 = .42$ and $\tau_1 = .04$. The ratio between τ_1 and σ^2 is $p_1 = .04/.42$. If we recruit one hundred twelve children ($n = 112$) in the study, we will have .80 statistical power in testing the difference in linear growth rate.

The relevant R code is:

```
# HLM random coefficients: linear change
# two-group

p4hlm2l=function(n=112,m=3,beta11=.187,sigma2=.42,p1=.04/.42){
a=.05
tau1=sigma2*p1

t0=rep(1,m+1)
t1=0:m
z1=t1-t(t1)%*%t0/sum(t0^2)*t0

lambda=sqrt(n/4)*beta11/sqrt(tau1+sigma2/sum(z1^2))
t0=qt(1-a/2,n-2)
1-pt(t0,n-2,lambda)+pt(-t0,n-2,lambda)
}

p4hlm2l()
```

The SAS program is:

```
/* HLM random coefficients model:
comparing linear change btw 2 groups*/

proc iml;
 m=3;
 t0=j(m+1,1,1);
 t1=t(0:m);

 z1=t1-t(t1)*t0/t0[##,]*t0;

 a=.05;
 n=112;
 beta11=.187;
 sigma2=.42;
 p1=.04/.42;

 tau1=sigma2*p1;
 lambda=sqrt(n/4)*beta11/sqrt(tau1+sigma2/z1[##,]);
 power=1-probt(tinv(1-a/2,n-2),n-2,lambda)+
       probt(tinv(a/2,n-2),n-2,lambda);
 print power;
quit;
```

The SPSS code is:

```
* HLM random coefficients:
compare linear change between two groups .

MATRIX.
COMPUTE M=3.
COMPUTE T0=MAKE(M+1,1,1).
COMPUTE T1=T({0:M}).
COMPUTE Z1=T1-T(T1)*T0/CSSQ(T0)*T0.

COMPUTE N=112.
COMPUTE BETA11=.187.
```

```
COMPUTE SIGMA2=.42.
COMPUTE P1=.04/.42.

COMPUTE TAU1=SIGMA2*P1.
COMPUTE LAMBDA=SQRT(N/4)*BETA11/SQRT(TAU1+SIGMA2/CSSQ(Z1)).

SAVE {M,N,BETA11,SIGMA2,P1, LAMBDA }
/OUTFILE=* /VARIABLES= M N BETA11 SIGMA2 P1 LAMBDA.
END MATRIX.

COMPUTE A=.05.
COMPUTE T0=IDF.T(1-A/2,N-2).
COMPUTE POWER=1-NCDF.T(T0,N-2,LAMBDA)+NCDF.T(-T0,N-2,LAMBDA).
PRINT /POWER.
EXECUTE.
```

11.3.2 Quadratic Change

A polynomial equation can represent a complex growth curve. We sometimes use polynomial equations to model the curvature in linking repeated measures over time. The order of the polynomial equation is commonly either quadratic or cubic; higher orders are theoretically possible but rare in practice. We will first examine the quadratic change and then the cubic change.

The quadratic change can be represented in a polynomial equation of second order. The repeated measure Y_{ti} is conceived of as a function of the time point t and its square t^2. The polynomial equation is

$$Y_{ti} = \pi_{0i} + \pi_{1i}t + \pi_{2i}t^2 + e_{ti}. \tag{11.88}$$

The $\pi_{2i}t^2$ is the quadratic term in the polynomial equation. The coefficient π_{2i} represents the quadratic change. Its meaning may not be obvious at first sight, but it can be made obvious by taking the derivative of the polynomial equation with respect to time t. For simplicity, we can take the expectation of both sides of the polynomial equation to eliminate the error e_{ti}, which is normal with a zero mean and a constant variance σ^2.

$$\mu_{Y_{ti}} = \pi_{0i} + \pi_{1i}t + \pi_{2i}t^2$$

The expectation on the left side is $\mu_{Y_{ti}}$, and it is the mean outcome at time point t. Taking the derivative of $\mu_{Y_{ti}}$ with respect to time t produces the linear change in outcome per unit time,

$$\frac{d\mu_{Y_{ti}}}{dt} = \pi_{1i} + 2\pi_{2i}t. \tag{11.89}$$

The first derivative $d\mu_{Y_{ti}}/dt$ shows the linear change from time point $t-1$ to time point t. If the coefficient π_{2i} is zero, the linear change from one time point to the next stays constant at π_{1i}. In other words, the means of the repeated measures run through a simple straight line. However, a non-zero π_{2i} suggests that the linear change from one time point to the next may either accelerate or decelerate. The rate of acceleration or deceleration is the derivative of $d\mu_{Y_{ti}}/dt$ with respect to time t, namely, the second derivative of $\mu_{Y_{ti}}$;

$$\frac{d^2\mu_{Y_{ti}}}{dt^2} = 2\pi_{2i}. \tag{11.90}$$

The second derivative $2\pi_{2i}$ shows the amount of acceleration or deceleration per time unit. To simplify the interpretation of π_{2i}, we scale t^2 in the polynomial equation by $1/2$, that is,

$$Y_{ti} = \pi_{0i} + \pi_{1i}t + \pi_{2i}t^2/2 + e_{ti}. \tag{11.91}$$

That way, the second derivative simplifies to

$$\frac{d^2\mu_{Y_{ti}}}{dt^2} = \pi_{2i}. \tag{11.92}$$

So π_{2i} represents the quadratic change or the amount of acceleration or deceleration in linear change from one time point to the next.

As before, we can use orthogonal vectors z_1 and z_2 in the polynomial equation to simplify the formulas for the estimate of the quadratic change π_{2i}. The two orthogonal vectors replace the two columns of data for time t and its square $t^2/2$, and the two orthogonal vectors can be obtained through the Gram-Schmidt process. The Gram-Schmidt process can be thought of as a series of regression. In the first step of the Gram-Schmidt process, the column of data on t is regressed on a vector of ones $\mathbf{1}$ implied by the intercept π_{0i} in the polynomial equation or

$$y_i = \begin{bmatrix} \mathbf{1} & t & t^2/2 \end{bmatrix} \begin{bmatrix} \pi_{0i} \\ \pi_{1i} \\ \pi_{2i} \end{bmatrix} + e_i.$$

$$z_1 = t - \frac{t'\mathbf{1}}{\|\mathbf{1}\|^2}\mathbf{1} \qquad (11.93)$$

The orthogonal vector z_1 contains the residuals in the regression of t on the unit vector $\mathbf{1}$. The prediction due to regression is the mean of t, that is, $t'\mathbf{1}\|\mathbf{1}\|^{-2}\mathbf{1}$. In other words, we obtain the orthogonal vector z_1 by centering t around its mean in the first step of the Gram-Schmidt process. In the second step of the Gram-Schmidt process, we regress $t^2/2$ on $\mathbf{1}$ and z_1. The residuals from the regression form the orthogonal vector z_2,

$$z_2 = t^2/2 - \frac{(t^2/2)'\mathbf{1}}{\|\mathbf{1}\|^2}\mathbf{1} - \frac{(t^2/2)'z_1}{\|z_1\|^2}z_1. \qquad (11.94)$$

For example, there may be five repeated measures over time ($m = 4$). The three original vectors in the original polynomial equation are

$$\mathbf{1} = \begin{bmatrix} 1 \\ 1 \\ 1 \\ 1 \\ 1 \end{bmatrix}, \ t = \begin{bmatrix} 0 \\ 1 \\ 2 \\ 3 \\ 4 \end{bmatrix}, \ t^2/2 = \begin{bmatrix} 0 \\ 1/2 \\ 4/2 \\ 9/2 \\ 16/2 \end{bmatrix}.$$

The three orthogonal vectors from the Gram-Schmidt process are

$$\mathbf{1} = \begin{bmatrix} 1 \\ 1 \\ 1 \\ 1 \\ 1 \end{bmatrix}, \ z_1 = \begin{bmatrix} -2 \\ -1 \\ 0 \\ 1 \\ 2 \end{bmatrix}, \ z_2 = \begin{bmatrix} 1 \\ -.5 \\ -1 \\ -.5 \\ 1 \end{bmatrix}.$$

If we substitute the orthogonal vectors for the three original vectors ($\mathbf{1}$, t, and $t^2/2$), we will obtain the orthogonal polynomial model,

$$y_i = \begin{bmatrix} \mathbf{1} & z_1 & z_2 \end{bmatrix} \begin{bmatrix} \pi_{0i} \\ \pi_{1i} \\ \pi_{2i} \end{bmatrix} + e_i. \qquad (11.95)$$

Using this orthogonal polynomial model, we can greatly simplify the estimation formulas for π_{2i}.

The least squares estimate of π_{2i} for the ith individual is

$$
\begin{aligned}
\hat{\pi}_{2i} &= \frac{z_2' y_i}{\|z_2\|^2} \\
&= \frac{\sum\limits_{t=0}^{m} z_{t2} Y_{ti}}{\sum\limits_{t=0}^{m} z_{t2}^2}.
\end{aligned}
\tag{11.96}
$$

Conditioning on the ith individual, we can obtain the variance of the least squares estimate $\hat{\pi}_{2i}$,

$$
Var(\hat{\pi}_{2i}|i) = \frac{\sigma^2}{\sum\limits_{t=0}^{m} z_{t2}^2}.
\tag{11.97}
$$

It is obvious that the least squares estimate and its variance only depend on the orthogonal vector z_{2i}. The least squares estimate $\hat{\pi}_{2i}$ thus computed is the same as we will obtain in regressing Y_{ti} on t and $t^2/2$.

The quadratic change π_{2i} can vary from one individual to another in a level-2 equation.

$$
\text{At level 2:} \quad \pi_{2i} = \beta_{20} + r_{2i}, \ r_{2i} \sim N(0, \tau_2),
\tag{11.98}
$$

where β_{20i} is the average quadratic change, and r_{2i} is a random deviation for the ith individual. The estimate of β_{20} can be obtained by averaging the individual-specific quadratic change $\hat{\pi}_{2i}$,

$$
\hat{\beta}_{20} = \frac{\hat{\pi}_{2i}}{n}.
\tag{11.99}
$$

The variance of the estimate $\hat{\beta}_{20}$ is

$$
Var(\hat{\beta}_{20}) = \frac{Var(\hat{\pi}_{2i})}{n}.
\tag{11.100}
$$

The sample estimate of the variance $Var(\hat{\beta}_{20})$ is

$$
\widehat{Var}(\hat{\beta}_{20}) = \frac{\widehat{Var}(\hat{\pi}_{2i})}{n},
$$

where

$$\widehat{Var}(\hat{\pi}_{2i}) = \frac{\sum\limits_{i=1}^{n} (\hat{\pi}_{2i} - \sum_{i=1}^{n} \hat{\pi}_{2i}/n)^2}{n-1}. \tag{11.101}$$

The test for the quadratic change β_{20} uses a t statistic with $n-1$ degrees of freedom,

$$T = \frac{\hat{\beta}_{20}}{\sqrt{\widehat{Var}(\hat{\beta}_{20})}}. \tag{11.102}$$

When the alternative hypothesis $H_a : \beta_{20} \neq 0$ is true, the t statistic has a non-central t distribution or T'. The statistical power for testing β_{20} is based on this non-central T';

$$1 - \beta = 1 - P[T'(n-1,\lambda) < t_{1-\alpha/2,n-1}] + P[T'(n-1,\lambda) \leq t_{\alpha/2,n-1}]. \tag{11.103}$$

The non-centrality parameter λ is

$$\lambda = \frac{\sqrt{n}\beta_{20}}{\sqrt{Var(\hat{\pi}_{2i})}}.$$

Note that $\hat{\pi}_{2i} = \pi_{2i} + (\hat{\pi}_{2i} - \pi_{2i})$. We have the variance of $\hat{\pi}_{2i}$ as

$$Var(\hat{\pi}_{2i}) = Var(\pi_{2i}) + Var(\hat{\pi}_{2i} - \pi_{2i})$$
$$= Var(\pi_{2i}) + Var(\hat{\pi}_{2i}|i)$$
$$= \tau_2 + \frac{\sigma^2}{\sum\limits_{t=0}^{m} z_{2t}^2}. \tag{11.104}$$

So the non-centrality parameter λ is

$$\lambda = \frac{\sqrt{n}\beta_{20}}{\sqrt{\tau_2 + \frac{\sigma^2}{\sum\limits_{t=0}^{m} z_{2t}^2}}}. \tag{11.105}$$

If n individuals are randomly assigned to treatment and control conditions of equal size, the level-2 equation will involve a predictor of treatment assignment X_{1i}, which takes .5 for someone in the treatment group and $-.5$ for someone in the control group. The level-2 equation becomes

$$\pi_{2i} = \beta_{20} + \beta_{21}X_{1i} + r_{2i}. \tag{11.106}$$

The t test for β_{20} loses one degree of freedom, owing to the estimation of the parameter β_{21}. The statistical power for testing β_{20} is, therefore,

$$1 - \beta = 1 - P[T'(n-2,\lambda) < t_{1-\alpha/2,n-2}] + P[T'(n-2,\lambda) \leq t_{\alpha/2,n-2}]. \tag{11.107}$$

The non-centrality parameter remains the same as before.

The test for β_{21} uses a t statistic, which examines whether there is any significant difference in quadratic change between the treatment and control groups,

$$T = \frac{\hat{\beta}_{21}}{\sqrt{\widehat{Var}(\hat{\beta}_{21})}}. \tag{11.108}$$

When the alternative hypothesis $H_a : \beta_{21} \neq 0$ holds true, the t statistic follows a non-central t distribution with $n - 2$ degrees of freedom and a non-centrality parameter λ. We can obtain the non-centrality parameter by replacing the estimates in the T formulas with their population counterparts,

$$\begin{aligned}
\lambda &= \frac{\beta_{21}}{\sqrt{Var(\hat{\beta}_{21})}} \\
&= \frac{\beta_{21}}{\sqrt{\frac{n}{4}Var(\hat{\pi}_{2i})}} \\
&= \sqrt{\frac{n}{4}} \frac{\beta_{21}}{\sqrt{\tau_2 + \frac{\sigma^2}{\sum\limits_{t=0}^{m} z_{2t}^2}}}.
\end{aligned} \tag{11.109}$$

The statistical power for testing β_{21} is the probability of having the non-central T' exceed the critical value or $P[|T'(n-2,\lambda)| \geq t_{1-\alpha/2,n-2}]$.

For example, a study is intended to examine the curvature in a plot of the change in girls' length up to 24 months of age. A quadratic curve is expected to fit the growth plot of girls between birth and 24 months. All the subjects' lengths will be measured at birth and then every four months for 24 months. There are seven repeated observations ($m = 6$), and the unit of time for the linear and quadratic change is 4 months. The quadratic change is expected to be $-.707$ cm/(4 months)^2 ($\beta_{20} = -.707$), according to Perrin et al (2007). To calculate the power for testing the quadratic change, we need to estimate τ_2 and σ^2. The former is the variance of the quadratic change, and the latter the level-1 residual variance. There are, of course, different ways to make an educated guess of these two variance components. We will use a simple way to estimate the two variances. The variance τ_2 can be estimated from the confidence interval of the quadratic change based on the relevant literature. We will use the formula $\hat{\beta} \pm 1.96\sqrt{\tau_2/n}$ for the reported 95% confidence interval. The estimated variance τ_2 is $.24^2$ (Perrin et al, 2007). Suppose that the residual e_{ti} can range from 0 cm to 15 cm 95% of the time. Using four standard deviations for 95% of the cases, we estimate the level-1 residual variance to be $\sigma^2 = (15/4)^2 = 3.75^2$. If we recruit fourteen girls into the study, we will have a .82 statistical power in detecting the quadratic change.

The relevant R code is:

```
# HLM random coefficients: quadratic change
# one group

# Perrin et al, BJ Psychiatry
# p2=tau2/sigma^2

p4hlm2q=function(n=14,m=6,beta20=-.707,
sigma=3.75,p2=(.24/3.75)^2){
a=.05
tau2=sigma^2*p2

t0=rep(1,m+1)
t1=0:m
t2=t1^2/2
z1=t1-t(t1)%*%t0/sum(t0^2)*t0
z2=t2-t(t2)%*%t0/sum(t0^2)*t0-t(t2)%*%z1/sum(z1^2)*z1

lambda=sqrt(n)*beta20/sqrt(tau2+sigma^2/sum(z2^2))
t0=qt(1-a/2,n-1)
1-pt(t0,n-1,lambda)+pt(-t0,n-1,lambda)
}

p4hlm2q()
```

The SAS program is:

```
/* HLM random coefficients model:
quadratic change in one group*/

proc iml;
 m=6;
 t0=j(m+1,1,1);
 t1=t(0:m);
 t2=t1##2/2; *print t0 t1 t2;
 z1=t1-t(t1)*t0/t0[##,]*t0;
 z2=t2-t(t2)*t0/t0[##,]*t0-t(t2)*z1/z1[##,]*z1;
 *print z1 z2;

 a=.05;
 n=14;
 beta20=-.707;
 sigma=3.75;
 p2=(.24/3.75)**2;

 tau2=sigma**2*p2;
 lambda=sqrt(n)*beta20/sqrt(tau2+sigma**2/z2[##,]);
 power=1-probt(tinv(1-a/2,n-1),n-1,lambda)
        +probt(tinv(a/2,n-1),n-1,lambda);
 print power;
quit;
```

The SPSS code is:

```
* HLM random coefficients: quadratic change in one group.

MATRIX.
COMPUTE M=6.
COMPUTE T0=MAKE(M+1,1,1).
COMPUTE T1=T({0:M}).
COMPUTE T2=T1&**2/2.
COMPUTE Z1=T1-T(T1)*T0/CSSQ(T0)*T0.
COMPUTE Z2=T2-T(T2)*T0/CSSQ(T0)*T0-T(T2)*Z1/CSSQ(Z1)*Z1.
```

```
COMPUTE N=14.
COMPUTE BETA20=-.707.
COMPUTE SIGMA=3.75.
COMPUTE P2=(.24/3.75)**2.

COMPUTE TAU2=SIGMA**2*P2.
COMPUTE LAMBDA=SQRT(N)*BETA20/SQRT(TAU2+SIGMA**2/CSSQ(Z2)).

SAVE {M,N,BETA20,SIGMA,P2, LAMBDA }
/OUTFILE=* /VARIABLES= M N BETA20 SIGMA P2 LAMBDA .
END MATRIX.

COMPUTE A=.05.
COMPUTE TO=IDF.T(1-A/2,N-1).
COMPUTE POWER=1-NCDF.T(TO,N-1,LAMBDA)+NCDF.T(-TO,N-1,LAMBDA).
PRINT /POWER.
EXECUTE.
```

11.3.3 Orthogonal Polynomial Model

We shall now discuss the relationship between the orthogonal and regular polynomial models, but readers who are only interested in power analysis can skip this section and proceed to the next section on cubic change.

We will represent the models in matrix notation for brevity, and we will use five repeated measures ($m = 4$) to illustrate the involved matrices. The regular polynomial model in matrix notation is

$$y_i = Ab_i + e_i,$$

where

$$A = \begin{bmatrix} 1 & t & t^2/2 \end{bmatrix}$$

$$= \begin{bmatrix} 1 & 0 & 0 \\ 1 & 1 & 1/2 \\ 1 & 2 & 4/2 \\ 1 & 3 & 9/2 \\ 1 & 4 & 16/2 \end{bmatrix};$$

$$b'_i = \begin{bmatrix} b_{0i} & b_{1i} & b_{2i} \end{bmatrix}.$$

Using the Gram-Schmidt process, we can replace **1**, t, and $t^2/2$ in the regular polynomial model with three orthogonal vectors **1**, z_1, and z_2.

$$Z = \begin{bmatrix} \mathbf{1} & z_1 & z_2 \end{bmatrix}$$

$$= \begin{bmatrix} 1 & -2 & 1 \\ 1 & -1 & -.5 \\ 1 & 0 & -1 \\ 1 & 1 & -.5 \\ 1 & 2 & 1 \end{bmatrix};$$

We now have the orthogonal polynomial model,

$$y_i = Z\pi_i + e_i,$$

where

$$\pi'_i = \begin{bmatrix} \pi_{0i} & \pi_{1i} & \pi_{2i} \end{bmatrix}.$$

The design matrices A and Z are related in the two models, and so are their coefficients b_i and π_i. We can express the design matrix A in terms of its counterpart Z in the orthogonal polynomial model.

$$A = Z\Gamma,$$

where

$$\Gamma = \left(Z'Z \right)^{-1} Z'A.$$

It is quite easy to verify $A = Z\Gamma$ because

$$Z\left(Z'Z \right)^{-1} Z'A = A.$$

The matrix $Z(Z'Z)^{-1}Z'$ is the projection matrix spanned by A, for Z is the orthogonal basis of A. The projection of A on its own space is itself. Substituting Γ into the regular polynomial model, we will have

$$\begin{aligned} y_i &= Ab_i + e_i \\ &= Z\Gamma b_i + e_i \\ &= Z\pi_i + e_i, \end{aligned}$$

where $\pi_i = \Gamma b_i$. Alternatively, we can express b_i in terms of π_i,

$$b_i = \Gamma^{-1}\pi_i.$$

The matrix Γ is an upper triangular matrix with ones in the diagonals. Its inverse is also an upper triangular matrix with ones in the diagonals, which explains why the last coefficient in b_i and π_i is the same (i.e., $b_{pi} = \pi_{pi}$). The estimate of b_i is, therefore,

$$\hat{b}_i = \Gamma^{-1}\hat{\pi}_i.$$

The estimate of the last coefficient in $\hat{b}_i$ is always the same as that in $\hat{\pi}_i$. This is true of any orthogonal polynomial model of higher order. In our case, the estimated quadratic change in the orthogonal polynomial model of second order is the same as would be obtained by running a regular polynomial model of second order. The other estimated coefficients in the orthogonal polynomial model of second order, however, will differ from their counterparts in the regular polynomial model of second order.

We can illustrate the relationship in regression coefficients between the regular polynomial model and the orthogonal polynomial model with a mock data set of five repeated measures. The five repeated measures are represented by a vector $y_i' = [3\ 5\ 7\ 11\ 20]$. We can regress y_i on z_1 and z_2 in an orthogonal polynomial model of second order, that is,

$$y_i = \pi_{0i}\mathbf{1} + \pi_{1i}z_1 + \pi_{2i}z_2 + e_i$$

The estimated linear and quadratic effects are $\hat{\pi}_{1i} = 4.0$ and $\hat{\pi}_{2i} = 2.29$. If we regress y_i on t, and $t^2/2$, we will still get the same estimate of the regression coefficient for the quadratic term in the regular polynomial model of second order. The regular polynomial model is

$$y_i = b_{0i}\mathbf{1} + b_{1i}t + b_{2i}t^2/2 + e_i.$$

The estimated regression coefficient for the quadratic term is $\hat{b}_{2i} = 2.29$, which is equal to its counterpart in the polynomial model $\hat{\pi}_{2i} = 2.29$. The estimates of other regression coefficients, however, do not match between the orthogonal polynomial model and the regular polynomial model (i.e., $\hat{\pi}_{0i} \neq \hat{b}_{0i}$ and $\hat{\pi}_{1i} \neq \hat{b}_{1i}$). If we switch to a regular polynomial model of first order, we will get the same estimate of the regression coefficient for the

linear term as for the polynomial model. The regular polynomial model of
first order is

$$y_i = b_{0i}1 + b_{1i}t + e_i.$$

Using the mock data in y_i, we will obtain $\hat{b}_{1i} = 4.0$ in the regular polynomial model of first order. It is the same as its counterpart $\hat{\pi}_{1i} = 4.0$ in the
orthogonal polynomial model. The R code is:

```
y=c(3, 5, 7, 11, 20)

t0=rep(1,5)
t1=0:4
t2=t1^2/2

lm(y~t1)
lm(y~t1+t2)

z1=t1-t(t1)%*%t0/sum(t0^2)*t0
z2=t2-t(t2)%*%t0/sum(t0^2)*t0-t(t2)%*%z1/sum(z1^2)*z1

lm(y~z1+z2)

# R output
Call:
lm(formula = y ~ t1)

Coefficients:
(Intercept)               t1
       1.2              4.0

Call:
lm(formula = y ~ t1 + t2)

Coefficients:
(Intercept)               t1                  t2
     3.486           -0.571               2.29

Call:
```

```
lm(formula = y ~ z1 + z2)

Coefficients:
(Intercept)            z1              z2
      9.20           4.00            2.29
```

Thus, we can test both the linear change in the regular polynomial model of first order and the quadratic change in the regular polynomial model of second order in one go by analyzing an orthogonal polynomial model of second order. This is why orthogonal polynomial models are preferred in analyzing data from longitudinal studies. It is tantamount to building a series of regular polynomial models of increasing orders and consecutively testing the linear, quadratic, and cubic changes in those regular polynomial models.

11.3.4 Cubic Change

The cubic change can be defined in a regular polynomial model of third order,

$$Y_{ti} = \pi_{0i} + \pi_{1i}t + \pi_{2i}t^2/2 + \pi_{3i}t^3 + e_{ti}.$$

The cubic change depends on the coefficient π_{3i} for the cubic term t^3, and it is defined as the rate of acceleration or deceleration in the quadratic change or the third derivative of the outcome over time, d^3Y_{ti}/dt^3;

$$\frac{d^3Y_{ti}}{dt^3} = 6\pi_{3i}.$$

If we scale the cubic term t^3 in the polynomial model by $1/6$, we will be able to simplify the cubic change to π_{3i},

$$Y_{ti} = \pi_{0i} + \pi_{1i}t + \pi_{2i}t^2/2 + \pi_{3i}t^3/6 + e_{ti}. \qquad (11.110)$$

The third derivative or cubic change simplifies to π_{3i}, that is,

$$\frac{d^2Y_{ti}}{dt^2} = \pi_{2i} + \pi_{3i}t; \quad \frac{d^3Y_{ti}}{dt^3} = \pi_{3i}. \qquad (11.111)$$

To estimate the cubic change π_{3i}, we continue the Gram-Schmidt process to find the orthogonal vector z_{t3}, which is the residual from the regression of the scaled cubic term $t^3/6$ on the orthogonal vectors $\mathbf{1}$, z_1,

z_2;

$$z_3 = t^3/6 - \frac{(t^3/6)'\mathbf{1}}{\|\mathbf{1}\|^2}\mathbf{1} - \frac{(t^3/6)'z_1}{\|z_1\|^2}z_1 - \frac{(t^3/6)'z_2}{\|z_2\|^2}z_2. \qquad (11.112)$$

The orthogonal vector is $z_3' = \begin{bmatrix} -.2 & .4 & 0 & -.4 & .2 \end{bmatrix}$.

The corresponding orthogonal polynomial model is

$$y_i = \begin{bmatrix} \mathbf{1} & z_1 & z_2 & z_3 \end{bmatrix} \begin{bmatrix} \pi_{0i} \\ \pi_{1i} \\ \pi_{2i} \\ \pi_{3i} \end{bmatrix} + e_i. \qquad (11.113)$$

The four orthogonal vectors in the orthogonal polynomial model (Rauden-bush and Liu, 2001, p. 389) are

$$\mathbf{1} = \begin{bmatrix} 1 \\ 1 \\ 1 \\ 1 \\ 1 \end{bmatrix} \quad z_1 = \begin{bmatrix} -2 \\ -1 \\ 0 \\ 1 \\ 2 \end{bmatrix} \quad z_2 = \begin{bmatrix} 1 \\ -.5 \\ -1 \\ -.5 \\ 1 \end{bmatrix} \quad z_3 = \begin{bmatrix} -.2 \\ .4 \\ 0 \\ -.4 \\ .2 \end{bmatrix}. \qquad (11.114)$$

The orthogonal vectors can be easily generated in R:

```
#orthogonal coding in Raudenbush and Liu 2001
#t0;z1;z2;z3

m=4
t0=rep(1,m+1)
t1=0:m
t2=t1^2/2
t3=t1^3/6

z1=t1-t(t1)%*%t0/sum(t0^2)*t0
z2=t2-t(t2)%*%t0/sum(t0^2)*t0-t(t2)%*%z1/sum(z1^2)*z1
z3=t3-t(t3)%*%t0/sum(t0^2)*t0-
t(t3)%*%z1/sum(z1^2)*z1-t(t3)%*%z2/sum(z2^2)*z2
```

The cubic change is represented by the coefficient π_{3i} in the orthogonal polynomial model. Its estimate is obtained in the same way as in running the regular polynomial model of third order (see the previous section), but the formulas for estimating π_{3i} may be concisely presented in terms of z_3.

The least squares estimate of π_{3i} is obtained by regressing Y_{ti} on z_{t3} because z_{t3} is independent of other predictors in the orthogonal polynomial model;

$$\hat{\pi}_{3i} = \frac{z_3' y_i}{\|z_3\|^2}$$

$$= \frac{\sum\limits_{t=0}^{m} z_{t3} Y_{ti}}{\sum\limits_{t=0}^{m} z_{t3}^2}. \tag{11.115}$$

We can find the conditional variance of the least squares estimate $\hat{\pi}_{3i}$ conditioning on the ith individual,

$$Var(\hat{\pi}_{3i}|i) = \frac{\sigma^2}{\sum\limits_{t=0}^{m} z_{t3}^2}. \tag{11.116}$$

The individuals' cubic changes become the outcome in a level-2 equation,

$$\pi_{3i} = \beta_{30} + r_{3i}, \ r_{3i} \sim N(0, \tau_3), \tag{11.117}$$

where β_{30} is the average cubic change, and r_{3i} is a random deviation for the ith individual. These estimated individuals' cubic changes $\hat{\pi}_{3i}$ form one independent sample, and they can be used to test the average cubic change β_{30} in a t test, which has $n - 1$ degrees of freedom. The statistical power for testing β_{30} in a two-sided t test is

$$1 - P[T'(n-1, \lambda) < t_{1-\alpha/2, n-1}] + P[T'(n-1, \lambda) \leq t_{\alpha/2, n-1}]. \tag{11.118}$$

The non-centrality parameter is

$$\lambda = \frac{\sqrt{n}\beta_{30}}{\sqrt{\tau_3 + \frac{\sigma^2}{\sum\limits_{t=0}^{m} z_{3t}^2}}}. \tag{11.119}$$

Had the n individuals been randomly assigned to treatment and control groups of equal size, we would use a level-2 predictor of treatment assignment X_{1i} to model the individuals' cubic changes π_{3i} in the level-2 equation.

$$\text{At level 2:}\quad \pi_{3i} = \beta_{30} + \beta_{31}X_{1i} + r_{3i}, \; r_{3i} \sim N(0, \tau_3) \qquad (11.120)$$

The test for the average cubic change β_{30} still uses a t statistic but with one less degree of freedom. It has $n - 2$ degrees of freedom. The power function basically remains the same except that there are now $n - 2$ degrees of freedom instead of $n - 1$.

The test for the group difference in cubic change β_{31} uses a t statistic that has $n - 2$ degrees of freedom. Its statistical power in a two-sided test is

$$1 - P[T'(n - 2, \lambda) < t_{1-\alpha/2, n-2}] + P[T'(n - 2, \lambda) \leq t_{\alpha/2, n-2}], \qquad (11.121)$$

where

$$\lambda = \sqrt{\frac{n}{4}} \frac{\beta_{31}}{\sqrt{\tau_3 + \dfrac{\sigma^2}{\sum\limits_{t=0}^{m} z_{3t}^2}}}. \qquad (11.122)$$

Appendix A

Cumulative Distribution Function

The cumulative distribution function (cdf) for central t, F, or χ^2 can be viewed as a special case of non-central t, F, or χ^2 because the central t, F, or χ^2 assumes a zero non-centrality parameter. We only need to explain the cdf for the non-central t, F, or χ^2 to cover both the central and non-central cdf functions. We will first use a normal distribution to introduce the concept of the cdf, whose inverse function is a quantile. We will then express all the non-central cdf functions in a simple and unified way.

A.1 Cumulative Distribution Function and Quantile

The histogram in Figure A.1 shows the proportions of different values over the range of an arbitrary random variable X in a sample. For illustration, we can let X be a normal variable. When the sample size increases to the size of the population, the histogram on the left of Figure A.1 becomes the population distribution of X on the right. We denote any realized value of X as x. The cumulative distribution function (cdf) is the probability of obtaining any realized value smaller than or equal to an arbitrary value x, namely, $P[X \leq x]$, which is represented by the shaded area to the left of x under the distribution curve in Figure A.1. The cdf evaluates to $p = P[X \leq x]$. The inverse of the cdf function p is the quantile $x = quantile(p)$. Therefore, x is called the pth quantile of X. The illustration assumes a

347

normal variable X, although the concept of cdf and quantile applies to any other random variable, say, t, F, or χ^2.

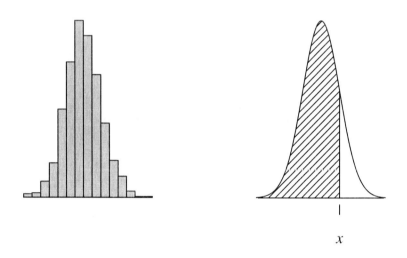

Figure A.1: Histogram and probability distribution

A.2   Non-central Cumulative Distribution Function

The current algorithms for computing the non-central cdfs involve different series of expansion and recurrence. These complicated algorithms can be greatly simplified. The three non-central cdfs can all be expressed as the integral of the normal cdf and the chi square density function. This can be implemented with the help of an integration routine readily available nowadays. This unified way of computing cdf is easy to explain, owing to its regularity.

   The non-central t distribution can be illustrated in a one sample t test. Suppose $Y \sim N(\mu, \sigma^2)$ and $H_0 : \mu = 0$. The t test is $T = \overline{Y}/(s/\sqrt{n})$, where s is the sample standard deviation of Y and n is the sample size. The T follows a non-central t distribution under $H_a : \mu \neq 0$ with a non-centrality parameter $\lambda = \sqrt{n}\mu/\sigma$. Let T' stand for the non-central t. Its cdf is then

$P[T' \leq c]$. If T' is conceived of as comprising the normal variate and chi square, its cdf can be represented in an alternative form that is easily comprehensible. By the definition of non-central t,

$$T' = \frac{Z(\lambda)}{\sqrt{\chi_\nu^2/\nu}}, \tag{A.1}$$

where $Z(\lambda)$ is the normal variate with a mean equal λ, and ν is the number of degrees of freedom. Let x stand for the chi square χ_ν^2.

The non-central cdf conditioning on x is a normal cdf (i.e., Φ); integrating the normal cdf over x yields the non-central cdf, that is,

$$
\begin{aligned}
P[T' \leq c] &= P\left[Z(\lambda) \leq c\sqrt{x/\nu}\right] \\
&= \int_0^\infty P\left[Z(\lambda) \leq c\sqrt{x/\nu} \,|x\right] f(x)dx \\
&= \int_0^\infty \Phi\left(c\sqrt{x/\nu} - \lambda\right) f(x)dx,
\end{aligned}
\tag{A.2}
$$

where $f(x)$ is the density function of a chi square x. This formula was noted before, but its computation used recursive steps in the earlier algorithm (Johnson et al, 1995, p.514).

The non-central F can be denoted by F'. By definition,

$$F' = \frac{\chi_m^2(\lambda)/m}{\chi_k^2/k}, \tag{A.3}$$

where λ is the non-centrality parameter, and m and k are the degrees of freedom in the numerator and denominator. The non-central chi square $\chi_m^2(\lambda)$ can be divided into a non-central chi square with one degree of freedom and a central chi square with $m-1$ degrees of freedom (Johnson et al, 1995). Further, the non-central chi square with one degree of freedom is a squared normal variate,

$$\chi_m^2(\lambda) = \chi_1^2(\lambda) + \chi_{m-1}^2 = [Z(\sqrt{\lambda})]^2 + \chi_{m-1}^2. \tag{A.4}$$

Substituting Equation A.4 into the cdf for the non-central F produces

$$
\begin{aligned}
P[F' \le c] &= P[\frac{\chi^2_m(\lambda)}{m} \le c\frac{\chi^2_k}{k}] \\
&= P\left[|Z(\sqrt{\lambda})| \le \sqrt{c\frac{m}{k}\chi^2_k - \chi^2_{m-1}}\right] \\
&= \int\limits_{0<y\le\infty} \int\limits_{0\le x\le c\frac{m}{k}y} \left[\Phi(g - \sqrt{\lambda}) - \Phi(-g - \sqrt{\lambda})\right] f(x)f(y)dxdy,
\end{aligned}
$$

$$(A.5)$$

where $x = \chi^2_{m-1}$, $y = \chi^2_k$, $g = \sqrt{c\frac{m}{k}y - x}$, and $f(.)$ is the density function for two chi squares x and y.

The cdf for non-central χ^2 can be computed in a similar fashion, namely

$$
\begin{aligned}
P[\chi^2_m(\lambda) \le c] &= P[(Z(\sqrt{\lambda}))^2 + \chi^2_{m-1} \le c] \\
&= P[|Z(\sqrt{\lambda})| \le \sqrt{c - \chi^2_{m-1}}] \\
&= \int_0^c [\Phi(g - \sqrt{\lambda}) - \Phi(-g - \sqrt{\lambda})]f(x)dx, \qquad (A.6)
\end{aligned}
$$

where $x = \chi^2_{m-1}$ and $g = \sqrt{c - x}$. Chou, Arthur, Rosenstein, and Owen (1984) show a similar representation of the non-central χ^2.

In summary, one needs to build one integration routine to compute all the cdf functions for non-central t, F, and χ^2. This greatly reduces coding effort and error in computing the cumulative distribution functions (Liu, 2013a).

Appendix B

R Tutorial

R is a computer language for statistical computing and graphics similar to SAS and SPSS. The R software was first developed at Bell laboratory in the mid 1990s. It is open-source software and runs on Unix, Macintosh, and Windows operating systems. Users can download a free copy of the software from `http://www.r-project.org/`.

The R software provides a variety of statistical analysis capabilities, including univariate and multivariate procedures. It has become very popular among statisticians because it produces publication-quality graphics with great ease.

B.1 Arithmetic

To start the software, we can click the R icon on the desktop or find it under the program on the start menu. A new console window will pop up with a brief description of R and a command prompt $<$ in red. We can enter commands and hit the ENTER key to get the results in an interactive mode.

R can perform basic arithmetic operations, such as $+$, $-$, $*$, and $/$. The exponentiation uses $\hat{\ }$ for power. For example, the following R code shows simple calculation:

```
> 1+2*3
[1] 7
> 4/5+1
[1] 1.8
```

```
> (6+7)*8
[1] 104
> 9^2
[1] 81
> sqrt(81)
[1] 9
> exp(1)
[1] 2.718282
> log(100,10)
[1] 2
```

The sqrt and exp are built-in functions. Their arguments are input within a pair of parentheses. The log function takes two arguments, with the first being the input and the second being the base. The relative position determines the nature of the arguments. Or we can specify the argument explicitly (i.e., >log(100,base=10)).

We can assign a value or result to a variable name by using an = sign. For example,

```
> x=10
> x
[1] 10
> y=log(10,10)
> y
[1] 1
> z=x+y
> z
[1] 11
> z=z+1;z
[1] 12.
```

Submitting a variable name returns the stored or assigned value. Semicolons can separate multiple commands on a single line. The command z=z+1;z first adds 1 to the variable z and then prints the new assigned value.

B.2   Data

R is an object-oriented programming language. One of the common objects in data entry is a vector, which contains a list of values or strings. For instance, we can assign a list of values to a column vector

```
> x=c(1,2,3,4,5)
> x
[1] 1 2 3 4 5.
```

The function c() combines the values in its arguments into a vector. We can use function seq(1,5,by=1) to generate a sequence of numbers. The by argument in the seq function sets the increment for the sequence. The function rep can generate repeated values. For example,

```
> y=rep(1,5)
> y
[1] 1 1 1 1 1.
```

The function in R can take a vector as argument. Each value in the vector is taken as a separate input argument, and its corresponding function is stored in the result vector. For example, we can easily evaluate a quadratic function over a range of values, say, -100 to 100.

```
> x=seq(-100,100)
> y=x^2-2*x+1
> plot(x,y,type="l").
```

The result vector y contains the quadratic function evaluated at each value in the vector x. The two series of data values in x and y naturally form a function plot, as shown in Figure B.1. The two vectors x and y can be combined in a new data set called dsn1, using the function data.frame():

```
> dsn1<-data.frame(y,x)
> dsn1
       y     x
1  10201  -100
2  10000  -99
3   9801  -98
4   9604  -97
```

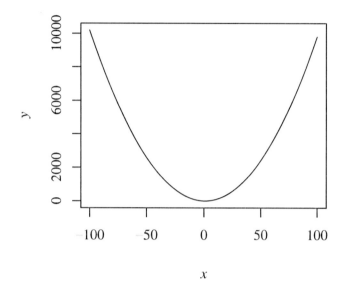

Figure B.1: Quadratic function

```
5    9409   -96
. . .
```

The operator <- assigns the name dsn1 to the new data set.

The function read.table() can read data from other sources. The following code reads the data from an external source:

```
>read.table(file="c:\\~\\table94.txt", header=TRUE).
```

B.3 Loop

Loops are often used to execute operations repeatedly over a series of data. They are useful in computer simulation, which runs the same computation again and again. The iterative process can be made easy in loops. The syntax for the loop in R is straightforward:

```
> y=c()
> for(i in 1:10){
+ y[i]=i^2
```

```
+ }
> y
 [1]   1   4   9  16  25  36  49  64  81 100
```

In this sample code a null vector y is first declared. The element in the vector can be accessed through the index i, which controls the iteration of the loop. The index goes through a sequence of 1 through 10 with an increment equal 1. During each iteration of the loop, the squared value of the ith index is assigned to the ith element of the y vector.

B.4   Statistics

R can calculates a variety of basic statistics through built-in functions. The function names are often intuitive and self-explanatory. For example, we may create a variable x on test scores:

```
> x=scan()
1: 100
2: 84
3: 95
4: 87
5: 74
6: 91
7: 99
8: 90
9: 82
10: 92
11: 91
12:
Read 11 items
> x
 [1] 100  84  95  87  74  91  99  90  82  92  91.
```

The function scan() inputs data into a vector from the console. The summary statistics are readily available:

```
> sum(x);mean(x); var(x); sd(x); summary(x)
[1] 985
```

```
[1] 89.54545
[1] 57.47273
[1] 7.581077
   Min. 1st Qu.  Median   Mean 3rd Qu.    Max.
  74.00   85.50   91.00  89.55   93.50  100.00
```

The summary function returns the five-number summary of the variable x.
The scale() function converts the variable to a standardized score z.

```
> z=scale(x)
> z
                [,1]
 [1,]   1.3790317
 [2,]  -0.7314864
 [3,]   0.7194948
 [4,]  -0.3357642
 [5,]  -2.0505602
 [6,]   0.1918653
 [7,]   1.2471243
 [8,]   0.0599579
 [9,]  -0.9953011
[10,]   0.3237727
[11,]   0.1918653
attr(,"scaled:center")
[1] 89.54545
attr(,"scaled:scale")
[1] 7.581077
```

A histogram can be produced to assess the distribution of the test scores, using hist(x) (see Figure B.2).

R provides probability functions for common distributions, such as normal (norm), t (t), F (f), and chi square (chisq). The names of the probability functions use prefixes d for density function, p for distribution function, q for quantile function, and r for the generation of random numbers. For example, dnorm is the density function for the normal distribution, and pnorm the cumulative distribution function.

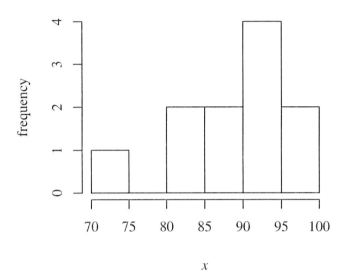

Figure B.2: Histogram

B.5   Simulation

Computer simulation often involves sampling from a population. We can manage to draw a random sample from a simulated population with a few built-in functions (i.e., `sample(,)`). In the following, we simulate the results in the central limit theorem, which describes the property of a sampling distribution. For simplicity of illustration, we start with a normal population (e.g., measurements of girls' heights). First, the probability function `rnorm(1000,60,2.5)` generates a population of 10,000 height measures with mean 60 inches and standard deviation 2.5 inches. Second, two sampling distributions are produced by setting the sample size n at 25 and 100, respectively. To simulate the sampling distribution, we draw 1000 repeated samples in the loop with the function `sample(x,n)`. The first argument of the `sample` function specifies the population to draw samples from, and the second argument sets the size of the repeated samples (n). For instance, during each iteration of the loop, a sample of 25 is produced and its calculated sample mean is stored in the ith element of the vector `xbar25`. The index i goes from 1 to 1000, that is, 1000 sample means form the sampling distribution of sample size 25. The mean and standard deviation of the sampling distribution can be computed to verify the predictions based on the central limit theorem. The two histograms in Figure B.3 portray the change in spread as the sample size increases from 25 to 100.

```
x=rnorm(10000,60,2.5)
mean(x); sd(x)

xbar25=c(); xbar100=c()
for(i in 1:1000) xbar25[i]=mean(sample(x,25))
mean(xbar25);sd(xbar25)

for(i in 1:1000) xbar100[i]=mean(sample(x,100))
mean(xbar100);sd(xbar100)

par(mfrow=c(2,1))
hist(xbar25, breaks=seq(55,65,length=50))
hist(xbar100, breaks=seq(55,65,length=50))
```

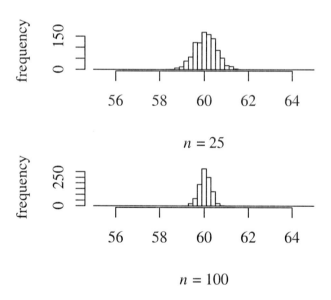

Figure B.3: Sampling distributions

B.6 Graphics

R provides low- and high-level graphic functions to draw graphs. Many types of graph can be constructed first by the high-level graphic functions and then modified by the low-level graphic functions. For example, plot() can be used to draw a scatterplot or a smooth line, which can then be customized by using a low-level function, such as par() or axis(). We will introduce a few common graphic functions here.

The graphic function plot(x,y,type=,main=,xlab=,ylab=) has a number of arguments. The x and y contain the x and y coordinates. The argument type defines how the coordinates are shown on the graph. It can take value "1" for line or "p" for point. In the former case, the points defined by the x and y coordinates are linked by line; in the latter case, the points are plotted without linking lines between them (i.e., a scatterplot). The argument main specifies the title. The arguments xlab and ylab list the labels for the x and y axes, respectively.

The graphic function curve(expr,from,to,n,add=,type=,ylab=,xlim) is versatile in plotting various function lines. Its arguments are defined as follows:

```
expr - a call or an expression written as a function of x
       or alternatively the name of a function.
from,to - the range over which the function will be plotted.
n - integer; the number of x values at which to evaluate.
add - logical; if TRUE add to already existing plot.
xlim - numeric of length 2; if specified,
it serves as default for c(from, to).
type - plot type.
```

We can use the curve() function to compare the normal distribution with the t distribution (see Figure B.4). The R code is

```
> curve(dnorm,-3,3,ylab="density",xlab=" ")
> par(col="blue",lwd=2,lty="dashed")
> curve(dt(x,5),-3,3,add=TRUE)
```

The low-level graphic function par() sets the color, line width, and line type for the superimposed t distribution. The default values will be restored on closing the graphic device.

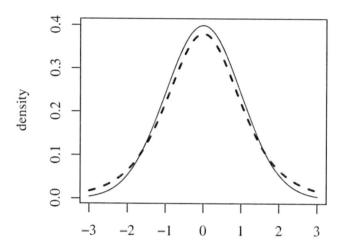

Figure B.4: Normal (solid line) and t (dashed line) distribution

B.7 Function

A function in R can be defined as follows:

```
name=function(argument1,argument2,...){
  commands
  ...
}
```

When the function is declared, the arguments can be supplied with default values (e.g., `argument1=default_value`). Otherwise, the values of the arguments can be specified as the function is called. The order of specified values needs to follow the same positions as the arguments in the definition of the function. Alternatively, the names of the arguments can be spelled out in specifying their values (i.e., `argument1=value,...`). If the names of the arguments are used, the order of the arguments does not matter.

A function in R can take an object such as a vector as its argument. For example, the following function g can take a vector and plot a histogram. The `if` function determines whether the histogram shows frequency or density on the vertical axis based on a condition. The logic expression in the condition evaluates the number of unique values contained in a variable. If the number of distinctive values is less than or equal to 10, then frequency is shown on the histogram. Otherwise, density is plotted with an imposed distribution curve.

```
g=function(var){
  if (length(unique(var)) <= 10){
      hist(var,probability=FALSE)
  }else{
      hist(var,probability=TRUE)
      lines(density(var))
  }
}
```

B.8   Statistical Analysis

B.8.1   Basic Statistics

The t test uses t.test() . The R code is:

```
#t test

y1=c(3,5,8)
y2=c(1,2,3)

#check distribution
plot(density(y1),ylim=c(0,.4))
lines(density(y2),lty=2)

t.test(y1,y2,alt="two.sided",var.equal=TRUE)
#var.equal=FALSE by default

#CI
d=y1-y2
t.test(d,conf.level=.90,alt="greater").
```

In the first procedure, a two sample independent t test is applied with the assumption of equal variances. In the second procedure, a one sample t test is calculated with a changed confidence level $1 - \alpha = .90$.

A simple ANOVA analysis can be done with aov(). The R code is:

```
#anova

t1=c(3,5,7)
t2=c(6,9,12)
t3=c(4,6,8)

dsn=stack(list(y1=t1,y2=t2,y3=t3))
names(dsn)
out=aov(values~ind,data=dsn)

summary(out).
```

The stack() function combines the list of variables and creates an indicator variable ind to differentiate the outcome measures in the three treatment conditions. The aov() routes the results to an object called out, from which we can extract the summary ANOVA table.

B.8.2   Helmert Contrast

The contrast tests in ANOVA compare treatment means. A simple comparison can be the difference between two means; a complex comparison may involve more than two means. There are many possible means comparisons. If we use orthogonal contrasts, we will have a finite number of means comparisons at a time. Orthogonal contrasts are often used because the contrast tests are independent of each other. This allows us to use the five percent significance level for each contrast test when they are planned a priori without the omnibus F test. The unadjusted significance level provides a higher statistical power than its adjusted counterpart, done posteriori.

Helmert contrasts are the most common orthogonal comparisons because they can be constructed in a predictable way. We just need to enumerate all the treatment conditions. The first Helmert contrast compares the mean of the first treatment with the average mean of the remaining treatments; the second Helmert contrast compares the mean of the second treatment with the average mean of the remaining. This goes on until the last Helmert contrast compares the mean of the last but one treatment with the mean of the last treatment. For instance, we may have three means for the three treatment conditions: $\overline{X}_1$, $\overline{X}_2$, and $\overline{X}_3$. The first Helmert contrast is

$$\beta_1 = \overline{X}_1 - \frac{\overline{X}_2 + \overline{X}_3}{2};$$

the second Helmert contrast is

$$\beta_2 = \overline{X}_2 - \overline{X}_3.$$

Using the ANOVA example from the previous section, we can calculate the two Helmert contrasts among the three means ($\overline{X}_1 = 5$, $\overline{X}_2 = 9$, and $\overline{X}_3 = 6$). The two Helmert contrasts are $5 - (9 + 6)/2 = -2.5$ for the first and 3 for the second. Had there been four treatment conditions, we would have three Helmert contrasts, that is,

$$\beta_1 = \overline{X}_1 - \frac{\overline{X}_2 + \overline{X}_3 + \overline{X}_4}{3}$$

$$\beta_2 = \overline{X}_2 - \frac{\overline{X}_3 + \overline{X}_4}{2}$$

$$\beta_3 = \overline{X}_3 - \overline{X}_4.$$

We can compute the Helmert contrasts using linear regression. The Helmert contrasts are just the regression coefficients if proper orthogonal coding is used. Referring to the same ANOVA example, we will need to create two predictors for the two Helmert contrasts in the linear regression. The values on the predictor are derived from the contrast coefficients implied in the Helmert contrast, which is a weighted sum of treatment means with the weights being the contrast coefficients:

$$c_1 \overline{X}_1 + c_2 \overline{X}_2 + c_3 \overline{X}_3.$$

The first Helmert contrast implies that the contrast coefficients are $c_1 = 1$, $c_2 = -1/2$, and $c_3 = -1/2$. The predictor x_1 for the first Helmert contrast will take 2/3 for an outcome observation y_{ij} in the first treatment, $-1/3$ for an observation in the second treatment, and $-1/3$ for the third treatment. The values on the predictor are the contrast coefficients divided by the sum of their squares, $1^2 + (-1/2)^2 + (-1/2)^2 = 3/2$. Likewise, the second Helmert contrast implies that the contrast coefficients are $c_1 = 0$, $c_2 = 1$, and $c_3 = -1$. The predictor x_2 for the second Helmert contrast will take 0 for an outcome observation y_{ij} in the first treatment, $1/2$ for an observation in the second treatment, and $-1/2$ for the third treatment. If we use x_1 and x_2 as predictors in the linear regression, their regression coefficients will be equal to the two Helmert contrasts β_1 and β_2,

$$y_{ij} = \beta_0 + \beta_1 x_1 + \beta_2 x_2 + e_{ij}.$$

We can verify this with the following R code:

```
t1=c(3,5,7)
t2=c(6,9,12)
t3=c(4,6,8)

y=c(t1,t2,t3)
h1=c(1,-1/2,-1/2)
h2=c(0,1,-1)
x1=(h1/sum(h1^2))%x%rep(1,3)
x2=(h2/sum(h2^2))%x%rep(1,3)

dsn=data.frame(y,x1,x2)
lm(y~x1+x2,data=dsn)

#output
Call:
lm(formula = y ~ x1 + x2, data = dsn)

Coefficients:
(Intercept)              x1              x2
      6.667          -2.500           3.000
```

The two regression coefficients are -2.5 and 3, and they equal the two Helmert contrasts.

Bibliography

Agresti, A. and Finlay, B. (2009). *Statistical Methods for the Social Sciences.* (4th ed.). New Jersey: Pearson Prentice Hall.

Baguley, T. (2009). Standardized or simple effect size: what should be reported? *British Journal of Psychology, 100,* 603–617.

Beal, S. L. (1989). Sample size determination for confidence intervals on the population mean and on the difference between two population means. *Biometrics, 45,* 969–977.

Bickel, P. J. and Doksum, K. A. (1977). *Mathematical Statistics: Basic Ideas and Selected Topics.* Englewood Cliffs, NJ: Prentice Hall.

Bloom, H. (1995). Minimum detectable effects: a simple way to report the statistical power of experimental designs. *Evaluation Review, 19,* 547–56.

Bollen, K. A. (1989). *Structural Equations with Latent Variables.* New York: Wiley.

Bouten, C. V., van Marken Lichtenbelt, W. D., and Westerterp, K. R. (1996). Body mass index and daily physical activity in anorexia nervosa. *Medicine and Science in Sports and Exercise, 28,* 967–973.

Browne, R. H. (1995). On the use of a pilot sample for sample size determination. *Statistics in Medicine, 14,* 1933–1940.

Carlson, D., Borman, G. D., and Robinson, M. (2011). A multi-state district-level cluster randomized trial of the impact of data-driven reform on reading and mathematics achievement. *Educational Evaluation and Policy Analysis, 33,* 378–398.

Chou, Y., Arthur, K., Rosenstein, R., and Owen, D. (1984). New representations of the noncentral chi-square density and cumulative. *Communications in Statistics - Theory and Methods, 13,* 2673–2678.

Cochran, W. (1977). *Sampling Techniques.* (3rd ed.). New York: Wiley.

Cochran, W. (1983). *Planning and Analysis of Observational Studies.* New York: John Wiley and Sons.

Cohen, J. (1969). *Statistical Power Analysis for the Behavioral Sciences.* (1st ed.). Hillsdale, NJ: Lawrence Erlbaum Associates.

Cohen, J. (1988). *Statistical Power Analysis for the Behavioral Sciences.* (2nd ed.). Hillsdale, NJ: Lawrence Erlbaum Associates.

Cumming, G. and Finch, S. (2001). A primer on the understanding, use, and calculation of confidence intervals that are based on central and noncentral distributions. *Educational and Psychological Measurement, 61,* 532–574.

Dennis, C. L., Hodnett, E., Kenton, L., Weston, J., Zupancic, J., Stewart, D. E., and Kiss, A. (2009). Effect of peer support on prevention of postnatal depression among high risk women: multisite randomised controlled trial. *British Medical Journal, 338,* 280–284.

Diggle, P. J., Heagerty, P., Liang, K. Y. and Zeger, S. L. (2002). *Analysis of Longitudinal Data.* (2nd ed.). Oxford: Oxford University Press.

Educational Testing Service (2007). *Graduate Record Examinations: Guide to the Use of Scores 2007–2008.* http://www.ets.org/Media/Tests/GRE/pdf/994994.pdf.

Englert, C. S., Raphael, T. E., Anderson, L. M., Anthony, H. M., and Steven, D. D. (1991). Making strategies and self-talk visible: writing instruction in regular and special education classrooms. *American Educational Research Journal, 28,* 337–372.

Finn, J. D. and Achilles, C. M. (1990). Answers and questions about class size: a statewide experiment. *American Educational Research Journal, 27,* 557–577.

Fuller, R. K., Mattson, M. E., Allen, J. P., Randall, C. L., Anton, R. F., and Babor, T. F. (1994). Multisite clinical trials in alcoholism treatment research: organizational, methodological and management issues. *Journal of Studies on Alcohol Suppl, 12*, 30–37.

Gatsonis, C. and Sampson, A. R. (1989). Multiple correlation: exact power and sample size calculations. *Psychological Bulletin, 106*, 516–524.

Graybill, F. (1958). Determining sample size for a specified width confidence interval. *The Annals of Mathematical Statistics, 29*, 282–287.

Grieve, A. P. (1991). Confidence intervals and sample sizes. *Biometrics, 47*, 1597–1603.

International Committee of Medical Journal Editors (1988). Uniform requirements for manuscripts submitted to biomedical journals. *Annals of Internal Medicine, 108*, 258–265.

Hancock, G. R. (2001). Effect size, power, and sample size determination for structured means modeling and MIMIC approaches to between-groups hypothesis testing of means on a single latent construct. *Psychometrika, 66*, 373–388.

Hedges, L.V. and Olkin, I. (1985). *Statistical Methods for Meta-analysis.* Orlando: Academic Press.

Hedges, L. V. and Pigott, T. D. (2001). The power of statistical tests in meta-analysis. *Psychological Methods, 6*, 203–217.

Hsu, L. (1994). Unbalanced designs to maximize statistical power in psychotherapy efficacy studies. *Psychotherapy Research, 4*, 95–106.

Jiroutek, M. R., Muller, K. E., Kupper, L. L., and Stewart, P. W. (2003). A new method for choosing sample size for confidence interval-based inferences. *Biometrics, 59*, 580–590.

Johnson, N., Kotz, S., and Balakrishnan, N. (1995). *Continuous Univariate Distributions.* (Vol. 2, 2nd ed.). New York: Wiley.

Johnson, R. A. and Wichern, D. W. (2002). *Applied Multivariate Statistical Analysis.* (5th ed.). Englewood Cliffs, NJ: Prentice-Hall.

Jöreskog, K. G. (1969). A general approach to confirmatory maximum likelihood factor analysis. *Psychometrika, 34,* 183–202.

Kaiser, H. F. and Michael, W. B. (1977). Little jiffy factor scores and domain validities. *Educational and Psychological Measurement, 37,* 363–365.

Kelley, K., Maxwell, S. E., and Rausch, J. R. (2003). Obtaining power or obtaining precision: delineating methods of sample-size planning. *Evaluation and the Health Professions, 26,* 258–287.

Kirk, R. E. (1995). *Experimental Design.* (3rd ed.). Pacific Grove, CA: Brooks/Cole.

Kraemer, H. C. and Thiemann, S. (1987). *How Many Subjects? Statistical Power Analysis in Research.* Newbury Park, CA: Sage.

Kupper, L. and Hafner, K. (1989). How appropriate are population sample size formulas? *The American Statistician, 43,* 101–105.

Land, K. C. (1973). Identification, parameter estimation, and hypothesis testing in recursive sociological models. In A. S. Goldberger and O. D. Duncan (eds.). *Structural Equation Models in the Social Sciences.* New York: Seminar.

Lehmann, E. L. (1959). *Testing Statistical Hypotheses.* New York: Wiley.

Lehmann, E. L. (1993). The Fisher, Neyman–Pearson theories of testing hypotheses: one theory or two? *Journal of American Statistical Association, 88,* 1242–1249.

Lenth, R. (2001). Some practical guidelines for effective sample size determination. *American Statistician, 55,* 187–193.

Lipsey, M. W. (1992). Juvenile delinquency treatment: a meta-analytic inquiry into the variability of effects. In T. D. Cook, H. Cooper, D. S. Cordray, H. Hartmann, L. V. Hedges, R. J. Light, T. A. Louis, and F. Mosteller (eds.). *Meta-analysis for Explanation: A Casebook* (pp. 83–127). NY: Russell Sage Foundation.

Liu, X. (2003). Statistical power and optimum sample allocation ratio for treatment and control having unequal costs per unit of randomization. *Journal of Educational and Behavioral Statistics, 28,* 231–248.

Liu, X. (2009). Sample size and the width of the confidence interval for mean difference. *British Journal of Mathematical and Statistical Psychology, 62*, 201–215.

Liu, X. (2010). A note on non-centrality parameters for contrast tests in one-way ANOVA. *Journal of Experimental Education, 78*, 53–59.

Liu, X. (2011). The effect of a covariate on standard error and confidence interval width. *Communications in Statistics: Theory and Methods, 40*, 449–456.

Liu, X. (2012). Implications of statistical power for confidence intervals. *British Journal of Mathematical and Statistical Psychology, 65*, 427–437.

Liu, X. (2013a). A unified way to represent and compute the cumulative distribution function for non-central t, F, and chi square. *Communications in Statistics: Simulation and Computation, 42*, 1433–1436.

Liu, X. (2013b). A note on statistical power in multi-site randomized trials with multiple treatments at each site. *British Journal of Mathematical and Statistical Psychology*, DOI: 10.1111/bmsp.12016.

Liu, X. (2013c). Statistical power in three-arm cluster randomized trials, *Evaluation and the Health Professions*, DOI: 10.1177/0163278713498392.

Liu, X. (in press). Orthogonal decomposition of interaction effect in analysis of variance. *Journal of Statistics and Management Systems*.

Liu, X. and Raudenbush, S. (2004). A note on the non-centrality parameter and effect size estimates for the F test in ANOVA. *Journal of Educational and Behavioral Statistics, 29*, 251–255.

MacCallum, R. C., Browne, M. W., and Sugawara, H. M. (1996). Power analysis and determination of sample size for covariance structure modeling. *Psychological Methods, 1*, 130–149.

McCambridge, J. and Strang, J. (2004). The efficacy of single-session motivational interviewing in reducing drug consumption and perceptions of drug-related risk and harm among young people: results from a multi-site cluster randomized trial. *Addiction, 99*, 39–52.

McGraw, K. O. and Wong, S. P. (1992). A common language effect size statistic. *Psychological Bulletin, 111,* 361–365.

Pan, Z. and Kupper, L. L. (1999). Sample size determination for multiple comparison studies. *Statistics in Medicine, 18,* 1475–1488.

Parker, D. R., Evangelou, E., and Eaton, C. B. (2005). Intraclass correlation coefficients for cluster randomized trials in primary care: the cholesterol education and research trial (CEART). *Contemporary Clinical Trials, 26,* 260–267.

Pearson, K. (1904). Report on certain enteric fever inoculation statistics. *British Medical Journal, 3,* 1243–1246.

Pedhazur, E. (1997). *Multiple Regression in Behavior Research* (3rd ed.). Belmont, CA: Wadsworth Publishing.

Perrin, M. A., Chen, H., Sandberg, D. E., Malaspina, D., and Brown, A. S. (2007). Growth trajectory during early life and risk of adult schizophrenia. *British Journal of Psychiatry, 191,* 512–520.

Philip, P., Sagaspe, P., Taillard, J., Valtat, C., Moore, N., Akerstedt, T., Charles, A., and Bioulac, B. (2005). Fatigue, sleepiness, and performance in simulated versus real driving conditions. *Sleep, 28,* 1511–1516.

Porter, A. C. and Raudenbush, S. W. (1987). Analysis of covariance: its model and use in psychological research. *Journal of Counseling Psychology, 34,* 383–392.

Potthoff, R. F. and Roy, S. W. (1964). A generalized multivariate analysis of variance model useful especially for growth curve problems. *Biometrika, 51,* 313–326.

Rao, C. R. (1951). An asymptotic expansion of the distribution of Wilks' criterion. *Bulletin de l'Institut International de Statistique, 33,* 177–180.

Raudenbush, S. (1997). Statistical analysis and optimal design for cluster randomized trials. *Psychological Methods, 2,* 173–185.

Raudenbush, S. and Bryk, A. (2002). *Hierarchical Linear Models: Applications and Data Analysis Methods.* (2nd ed.). Newbury Park, CA: Sage.

Raudenbush, S. W. and Liu, X. (2000). Statistical power and optimal design for multisite randomized trials. *Psychological Methods, 5*, 199–213.

Raudenbush, S. W. and Liu, X. (2001). Effects of study duration, frequency of observation, and sample size on power in studies of group differences in polynomial change. *Psychological Methods, 6*, 387–401.

Rencher, A. (1995). *Methods of Multivariate Analysis*. New York: John Wiley & Sons.

Rencher, A. C. (1998). *Multivariate Statistical Inference and Applications*. New York: Wiley.

Rothman, R., Malone, R., Bryant, B., Horlen, C., and Pignone, M. (2003). Pharmacist-led, primary care-based disease management improves hemoglobin A1c in high-risk patients with diabetes. *American Journal of Medical Quality, 18*, 51–58.

Satorra, A. and Saris, W. E. (1985). Power of the likelihood ratio test in covariance structure analysis. *Psychometrika, 50*, 83–90.

Saxena, K. M. and Alam, K. (1982). Estimation of the non-centrality parameter of a chi squared distribution. *The Annals of Statistics, 10*, 1012–1016.

Searle, S. (1982). *Matrix Algebra Useful for Statistics*. New York: John Wiley & Sons.

Sidorov, J., Gabbay, R., Harris, R., Shull, R. D., Girolami, S., Tomcavage, J., Starkey, R., and Hughes, R. (2000). Disease management for diabetes mellitus: impact on hemoglobin A1c. *American Journal of Managed Care, 6*, 1217–1226.

Singer, J. (1998). Using SAS PROC MIXED to fit multilevel models, hierarchical models, and individual growth models. *Journal of Education and Behavioral Statistics, 23*, 323–355.

Singer, J. D. and Willett, J. B. (2003). *Applied Longitudinal Data Analysis: Methods for Studying Change and Event Occurrence*. New York: Oxford University Press.

Snijders, T. and Bosker, R. (1993). Standard errors and sample sizes for two-level research. *Journal of Educational and Behavioral Statistics, 18,* 237–259.

Spearman, C. (1904) The proof and measurement of association between two things. *American Journal of Psychology, 15,* 72–101.

Specht, D. A. (1975). On the evaluation of causal models. *Social Science Research, 4,* 113–133.

Stevenson, M. D., Scope, A., Sutcliffe, P. A., Booth, A., Slade, P., Parry, G., Saxon, D., and Kalthenthaler, E. (2010). Group cognitive-behavioural therapy for postnatal depression: a systematic review of clinical and cost effectiveness and value of information analyses. *Health Technology Assessment, 14,* 1–107.

Stricker, L. J. (2002). *TOEFL Research Report: The Performance of Native Speakers of English and ESL Speakers on the Computer-Based TOEFL and GRE General Test.* ETS: Princeton.

Tarasińska, J., (2005). Confidence intervals for the power of Student *t*-test. *Statistics and Probability Letters, 73,* 125–130.

Teerenstra, S., Moerbeek, M., van Achterberg, T., Pelzer, B. J., and Borm, G. F. (2008). Sample size calculations for 3-level cluster randomized trials. *Clinical Trials, 5,* 486–495.

Wilkinson, L. (1999). Statistical methods in psychology journals: guidelines and explanations. *American Psychologist, 54,* 494–604.

Wilks, S. (1932). On the sampling distribution of the multiple correlation coefficient. *Annals of Mathematical Statistics, 3,* 196–203.

Woolhouse, R. S. (1988). *The Empiricists.* Oxford: Oxford University Press.

Index